Johannine Discipleship as a Covenant Relationship

Johannine Discipleship as a Covenant Relationship

REKHA M. CHENNATTU

Foreword by FRANCIS J. MOLONEY

ISBN 1-56563-668-6

Printed in the United States of America

First Printing — January 2006

Cover Art: Duccio di Buoninsegna (c.1260–1319). The Last Supper. Panel from the back of the Maesta altarpiece. Located in the Museo dell'Opera Metropolitana, Siena, Italy.

Photo Credit: Scala / Art Resource, NY. Used with permission.

Library of Congress Cataloging-in-Publication Data

Chennattu, Rekha M.
    Johannine discipleship as a covenant relationship /
Rekha M. Chennattu.
        p. cm.
    Includes bibliographical references and indexes.
    ISBN 1-56563-668-6 (alk. paper)
    1. Covenants—Biblical teaching. 2. Bible. N.T. John—Criticism,
interpretation, etc. I. Title.
    BS2615.6.C63C44 2006
    226.5'06—dc22

                                2005025969

To the shining memory of my Grandfather
Xavier Chennattu
who first set me to reading the Bible
and
to my parents
Mariakutty and Joseph Chennattu
in gratitude for their example of Gospel living

TABLE OF CONTENTS

FOREWORD

I was first approached by Rekha Chennattu in the Fall Semester of 1999. She had come to the Catholic University of America to work in the Johannine Literature, and her skills were immediately obvious in the Graduate Seminars required by the University's doctoral program in Biblical Studies. Once we came to discuss a dissertation topic, Chennattu expressed interest in the question of discipleship. My initial reaction was not enthusiastic, for two reasons. On the one hand, I had always felt that the powerful Christology of the Fourth Gospel left little space for a systematic development of the theme of discipleship. There was nothing in John's Gospel, it appeared to me, that matched the systematic portrayal of disciples in Synoptic Tradition, beginning with Mark's almost myopic fascination with that theme. On the other, what little had been done on disciples in the Fourth Gospel did not appear to me to be particularly significant, and some of it tended to use the text in a reflective rather than critical fashion.

The study that follows demonstrates that I was wrong. For decades scholars have suggested that there were links with Old Testament covenant themes and patterns in the Johannine Literature. For example, the work of Edward Malatesta, and the more recent suggestions of Sandra Schneiders and Yves Simoens had pointed to this literary and theological possibility. Following a suggestion that she look seriously at the relationship established between Jesus and the disciples and the disciples and God in John 13–17, Chennattu began to lay bare the presence of Covenant language and themes. This led her to look further, into all the material in the Gospel where the disciples are alone with Jesus: 1:35–51 and chapters 20–21, set firmly within the narrative and theological structure of the Gospel as a whole. Convinced that the key to understanding Johannine discipleship was the Old Testament covenant motif, she turned to a careful study of that motif, as it is found in its various forms and various places across the Old Testament. The correspondences that Chennattu had sensed in her reading of the Johannine material were further reinforced.

This study, therefore, opens a new chapter in Johannine scholarship. It provides readers with not only a new and convincing paradigm for an understanding of Johannine discipleship, but also a first-class study of Old Testament covenant theology and language. Finally, in a very important final chapter, Chennattu asks what possible *Sitz im Leben der Kirche* would have caused a turn to Old Testament covenant themes and theology to understand the role and function of the Christian disciple. While not ignoring the Hellenistic influence and the presence of the Samaritan and Greek Christians in the community, she has set the Johannine community firmly in a Jewish world. The relationship with God that had defined Israel as a people of God also defines the disciples of Jesus, according to the Gospel of John. It has been a pleasure to be closely associated with the research and writing that produced this fine study.

Francis J. Moloney, SDB
Dean of the School of Theology and Religious Studies
Katharine Drexel Professor of Religious Studies
The Catholic University of America
Washington, D.C. 20064

PREFACE

My special interest in the Johannine discipleship motif began in the spring semester of 2000 during a PhD seminar on John's Gospel with Dean Francis J. Moloney at the Catholic University of America. I explored the topic further in the published version of my seminar paper, "On Becoming Disciples (John 1:35–51): Insights from the Fourth Gospel," *Salesianum* 63 (2001): 467–98. I realized that the past thirty years of Johannine scholarship had not produced any extensive analysis of Johannine discipleship. This study sets out to fill this lacuna by pursuing a threefold objective: (1) a detailed exegetical analysis of the discipleship narratives and discourses (chs. 1, 13–17, and 20–21); (2) an investigation of the OT motifs behind the presentation of discipleship; (3) an examination of the function and relevance of the discipleship paradigm for the Johannine community.

Chapter one begins with a survey of the past three decades of scholarship on the discipleship motif in the Fourth Gospel. The survey points out that, although some research has been done on the Johannine portrayal of the disciples, the discipleship motif deserves further investigation. The study then clarifies its methodology and presuppositions and undertakes a detailed exegesis of the vocation stories in 1:35–51, suggesting that the evangelist uses the call stories to present a paradigm of discipleship as an OT covenant relationship.

Chapter two investigates the covenant metaphor in the OT and identifies the essential elements of an OT covenant relationship. It then discusses the possible OT background for the Johannine use of the covenant motifs and shows how chapters 2–12, through the ongoing revelation of Jesus' identity as the embodiment of God's loving presence and the repeated call to decision, function as a hortatory preparation for the covenant renewal and consecration of the community of the disciples in chapters 13–17. The study reveals that the structure and content of chapters 13–17 reflect a covenant renewal ceremony very similar to that of Joshua 24.

Chapter three undertakes a detailed exegetical analysis of chapters 13–17 interpreted within the literary and theological framework of a covenant renewal. The research points out that many OT covenant themes—election, intimate abiding relationship, indwelling presence of God, keeping God's commandments, and knowledge of God—run through the discourses of chapters 13–17 and provide the theological definition of what it means to be a disciple of Jesus. The chapter concludes that the evangelist programmatically organizes John 13–17 so that Jesus gradually discloses discipleship to the readers in terms of an OT covenant relationship or partnership with God, his Father, and with fellow disciples.

Chapter four explores further the discipleship-covenant motifs in chapters 20–21 to confirm the idea that the Johannine presentation of discipleship is a Christian rereading of the OT metaphor of covenant. What was programmatically promised in chapters 13–17 is now effectively actualized in chapters 20–21. The farewell discourses before the death of Jesus prepare and pray for the covenant community of the disciples; and the appearance narratives, after the glorification of Jesus, inaugurate and constitute the new covenant community.

Chapter five examines the implications of the paradigm of discipleship as a covenant relationship within the Johannine community. Here the focus of the investigation moves from the text to the *Sitz im Leben* of the community. It briefly discusses some major theological concerns of Judaism in the first century C.E., followed by an assessment of the historical context reflected in the gospel. The study then employs insights from the social sciences to understand the Johannine community and its presentation of discipleship. The analysis concludes that, amid the socio-pastoral and theological identity crises of the Johannine community, the paradigm of discipleship as an OT covenant relationship redefines the socio-religious identity of the community as the chosen people of God.

The commencement and the completion of this study owe much to the support of several people and institutions. Jnana-Deepa Vidyapeeth (the Pontifical Athenaeum, Pune, India), where I was teaching Scripture, requested that I specialize in John's Gospel. My inquiries showed that one of the best places would be the Catholic University of America. I am profoundly grateful to Lisbert D'Souza, SJ, the Vice-Chancellor, the Presidents, Anthony da Silva, SJ and Noel Sheth, SJ, and to the Faculty of Theology and the Academic Senate of JDV not only for deciding in favor of this proposal, but also for their continued encouragement, support, and friendship over the years as I pursued my doctoral studies at the Catholic University of America.

I offer heartfelt thanks to my director, Dean Francis J. Moloney, SDB, who has been a source of inspiration for this work from start to finish. I cannot thank him enough for his scholarly guidance, constructive criticism, challenging comments, and generous availability. I also owe much to my readers, Professor Timothy Friedrichsen and Professor Francis Gignac, SJ, who were very generous with their time, helpful suggestions, and encouragement. I am deeply grateful to Clare Teresa, RA, for her careful reading of my work, insightful comments, and sisterly accompaniment.

I remember with gratitude the Professors at the Jnana-Deepa Vidyapeeth, the Pontifical Biblical Institute (Rome), and the Catholic University of America, who laid the foundations of a solid grounding in the biblical languages and initiated me into the various exegetical methods. I am particularly grateful to Professor Emeritus James Swetnam, SJ, whose love and life-witness helped deepen my love for biblical research and scholarship. The participants at various workshops (in India, Rome, Paris, Jamaica, St. Cloud, Austin, Philadelphia, Tucson) on Johannine discipleship have also encouraged my interest and sharpened my mind by their questions and reflections.

I am also grateful to the staff at the Mullen Library (Catholic University of America), the Woodstock Theological Library (Georgetown University), the Library of the Pontifical Biblical Institute (Rome), and the Library of Congress for their courteous assistance and availability. I have also benefited immensely from the personal library of Dean Moloney. I am indebted to many institutions and foundations—Jnana-Deepa Vidyapeeth, the Religious of the Assumption, Missio, the Institute for Christian Oriental Research, and the Doheny Doctoral Fellowship Foundation—for their cofinancing scholarships at various stages of my research that made this PhD possible. To all of these people for their goodness and generosity I am deeply grateful.

I wish to thank the Sisters at the Centro Maria residence for their warm hospitality during my stay in Washington, D.C. I also remember with gratitude the Redemptorist community of Holy Redeemer College for accepting me as part of their eucharistic community.

I owe an immense debt of gratitude to Cristina Maria, RA, the superior general, and to the provincials, Leela Kottor, RA, Anne Françoise, RA, Jaya Mathew, RA, and Clare Teresa, RA, for their appreciation, support, and encouragement, and to all my Sisters of the Religious of the Assumption, especially the provinces of India, Italy, France, England, and the United States, for the life of a love-filled covenant community that we shared and continue to share with one another. I am also profoundly indebted to my late grandfather, my parents, sisters, brothers, and friends, whose unconditional love and encouragement revealed God's love and made God's presence an experience of my day-to-day life. Such love made the writing of this study on Johannine discipleship a grace-filled and life-giving experience.

Rekha M. Chennattu, RA

ABBREVIATIONS

AB	Anchor Bible
Abot R. Nat.	*Abot de-Rabbi Nathan*
ABR	*Australian Biblical Review*
ABRL	Anchor Bible Reference Library
ACNT	Augsburg Commentary on the New Testament
AGJU	Arbeiten zur Geschichte des antiken Judentums und des Urchristentums
AnBib	Analecta Biblica
Angelos	*Angelos*
APOT	*The Apocrypha and Pseudepigrapha of the Old Testament*
AsSeign	*Assemblées du Seigneur*
2 Bar.	*2 Baruch*
BBR	*Bulletin for Biblical Research*
BDAG	*A Greek-English Lexicon of the New Testament and Other Early Christian Literature*
BDF	*A Greek Grammar of the New Testament and Other Early Christian Literature*
BETL	Bibliotheca ephemeridum theologicarum lovaniensium
Bib	*Biblica*
BiBh	*Bible Bhashyam*
BibInt	*Biblical Interpretation*
BibIntS	Biblical Interpretation Series
BJRL	*Bulletin of the John Rylands University Library of Manchester*
BRT	Beiträge zur Religionstheologie
BTB	*Biblical Theology Bulletin*
BTS	Biblisch-Theologische Studien
BWANT	Beiträge zur Wissenschaft vom Alten und Neuen Testament

BZAW	Beihefte zur Zeitschrift für die alttestamentliche Wissenschaft
CahRB	Cahiers de la Revue biblique
Cass. Dio	*Cassius Dio*
CBET	Contribution to Biblical Exegesis and Theology
CBQ	*Catholic Biblical Quarterly*
CBQMS	Catholic Biblical Quarterly Monograph Series
CD	*Damascus Document*
CienT	*Ciencia Tomista*
Congr.	*De congressu eruditionis gratia*
CSP	Colectánea San Paciano
Demosth.	*Demosthenes*
Did.	*Didache*
Dionys. Hal.	*Dionysius of Halicarnassus*
EB	Echter Bibel
Ebib	*Etudes bibliques*
EHS	Europäische Hochschulschriften
EKKNT	*Evangelisch-katholischer Kommentar zum Neuen Testament*
Emm	*Emmanuel*
EstBib	*Estudios bíblicos*
ETL	*Ephemerides theologicae lovanienses*
EuntD	*Euntes Docete*
EV	*Esprit et vie*
EvQ	*Evangelical Quarterly*
ExpTim	*Expository Times*
FB	Forschung zur Bibel
FRLANT	Forschungen zur Religion und Literatur des Alten und Neuen Testaments
GNS	*Good News Studies*
Gos. Thom.	*The Gospel of Thomas*
GPT	Growing Points in Theology
GTS	Gettysburg Theological Studies
HBS	Herders Biblische Studien
Herm. Mand.	*Shepherd of Hermas, Mandate*
Herm. Vis.	*Shepherd of Hermas, Visions*
HeyJ	*Heythrop Journal*
HKNT	Handkommentar zum Neuen Testament
HTKNT	Herders theologischer Kommentar zum Neuen Testament
HTR	*Harvard Theological Review*

IBT	Interpreting Biblical Texts
ICC	International Critical Commentary
ILBS	The Indiana Literary Biblical Series
Int	*Interpretation*
IRM	*International Review of Mission*
IRT	Issues in Religion and Theology
ISPCK	Indian Society for Promoting Christian Knowledge
ITS	*Indian Theological Studies*
JBL	*Journal of Biblical Literature*
Jeev	*Jeevadhara*
Jo. Hom.	Chrystostom, *Joannem Homiliae*
Jos.	*De Josepho*
Jos. Asen.	*Joseph and Aseneth*
JPJRS	*Jnanadeepa: Pune Journal of Religious Studies*
JPSToC	JPS Torah Commentary
JQR	*Jewish Quarterly Review*
JR	*Journal of Religion*
JSNT	*Journal for the Study of the New Testament*
JSNTSup	Journal for the Study of the New Testament: Supplement Series
JSOTSup	Journal for the Study of the Old Testament: Supplement Series
JSP	*Journal for the Study of the Pseudepigrapha*
JSPSup	Journal for the Study of the Pseudepigrapha: Supplement Series
JTS	*Journal of Theological Studies*
LAB	*Liber Antiquitatum Biblicarum*
LAS	Libreria Ateneo Salesiano
LD	Lectio divina
Legat.	*Legatio ad Gaium*
Lev. R.	*Leviticus Rabbah*
LQHR	*London Quarterly and Holborn Review*
LTK	*Lexicon für Theologie und Kirche*
LTPM	Louvain Theological & Pastoral Monographs
Mek.	*Mekilta*
Midr. Ps.	*Midrash Psalms*
Mos. 1,2	*De vita Moysis I, II*
MT	Masoretic Text
NA	New Accents
NA[27]	*Novum Testamentum Graece*, Nestle-Aland, 27th ed.

NABPR	The National Association of Baptist Professors of Religion
NABPRSSS	NABPR Special Studies Series
Neot	*Neotestamentica*
NIB	*The New Interpreter's Bible*
NovT	*Novum Testamentum*
NovTSup	Novum Testamentum Supplements
NT	New Testament
NTL	New Testament Library
NTS	*New Testament Studies*
NTT	New Testament Theology
Num. Rab.	*Numbers Rabbah*
OT	Old Testament
ÖTK	Ökumenischer Taschenbuch-Kommentar
OTL	Old Testament Library
OTP	*Old Testament Pseudepigrapha*
OTS	Old Testament Studies
Pacifica	*Pacifica*
PassSer	The Passion Series
PG	Patrologia cursus completus, Series graeca
PHSRS	Prentice Hall Studies in Religion Series
Pss. Sol.	*Psalms of Solomon*
PT	*Poetics Today*
QE 1, 2	*Quaestiones et solutiones in Exodum I, II*
QG 1, 2, 3, 4	*Quaestiones et solutiones in Genesin I, II, III, IV*
1QS	*Serek Hayahad* or *Rule of the Community*
RB	*Revue biblique*
RechBib	Recherches bibliques
RevScRel	*Revue des sciences religieuses*
RSPT	*Revue des sciences philosophiques et théologiques*
RSR	*Recherches de science religieuse*
RTR	*Reformed Theological Review*
SA	Studia anselmiana
Sal	*Salesianum*
Sanh.	*Sanhedrin*
SANT	Studien zum Alten und Neuen Testaments
SBFA	Studium Biblicum Franciscanum Analecta
SBFLA	*Studii biblici Franciscani liber annuus*
SBLDS	Society of Biblical Literature Dissertation Series
SBS	Stuttgarter Bibelstudien

SBT	Studies in Biblical Theology
SC	Sources chrétiennes
SCJ	*Stone-Campbell Journal*
SE	*Studia evangelica*
SEDB	*SEDOS Bulletin*
SeinSend	*Sein und Sendung*
Semeia	*Semeia*
SJT	*Scottish Journal of Theology*
SNTSMS	Society for New Testament Studies Monograph Series
SNTSU	*Studien zum Neuen Testament und seiner Umwelt*
SP	Sacra pagina
Spec. 1, 2, 3, 4	*De specialibus legibus I, II, III, IV*
ST	*Studia theologica*
Str-B	*Kommentar zum Neuen Testament aus Talmud und Midrash*
StudBibT	*Studia Biblica et Theologica*
StudH	Studia Hellenistica
SVTQ	*St. Vladimir's Theological Quarterly*
T. Ab.	*Testament of Abraham*
Tanh.	*Tanhuma*
TD	Theologischen Dissertationen
TDNT	*Theological Dictionary of the New Testament*
TDOT	*Theological Dictionary of the Old Testament*
TS	*Theological Studies*
TTE	*The Theological Educator*
TU	Texte und Untersuchungen
TW	Theologie und Wirklichkeit
TynBul	*Tyndale Bulletin*
TZ	*Theologische Zeitschrift*
UBSGNT[4]	*The Greek New Testament,* United Bible Societies, 4th ed.
UBT	Understanding Biblical Themes
VEWS	Vidyajyoti Education and Welfare Society
VJTR	*Vidyajyoti: Journal of Theological Reflection*
VT	*Vetus Testamentum*
WaySup	*The Way Supplement*
WBC	Word Biblical Commentary
WMANT	Wissenschaftliche Monographien zum Alten und Neuen Testament
WUNT	Wissenschaftliche Untersuchungen zum Neuen Testament

WW	*Word & World*
Yal. Sh.	*Yalqut Shimoni*
ZAW	*Zeitschrift für die alttestamentliche Wissenschaft*
ZM	*Zeitschrift für Mission*
ZNW	*Zeitschrift für die neutestamentliche Wissenschaft und die Kunde der älteren Kirche*
ZSNT	Zacchaeus Studies: New Testament
ZTK	*Zeitschrift für die Theologie und Kirche*

ONE

AN INTRODUCTION TO THE
DISCIPLESHIP MOTIF

JOHANNINE DISCIPLESHIP IN RECENT SCHOLARSHIP

Biblical scholars have devoted little attention to the study of the discipleship motif throughout the whole of the New Testament.[1] The stark portrayal of the disciples' failure in the Gospel of Mark, however, captured the attention of Markan scholars in the 1970s and 1980s, and since then the role and the function of the disciples in the Markan narrative have become a subject of lively debate.[2] R. Alan Culpepper aptly observed in 1983 that

---

[1] In the last century, the important studies on discipleship in general include J. Wach, *Meister und Jünger* (Leipzig: Pfeiffer, 1924); E. Schweizer, *Lordship and Discipleship* (Naperville, Ill.: Alec Allenson, 1960); A. Schulz, *Nachfolgen und Nachahmen: Studien über das Verhältnis der neutestamentlichen Jüngerschaft zur urchristlichen Vorbildethik* (München: Kösel, 1962); H. D. Betz, *Nachfolge und Nachahmung Jesu Christi im Neuen Testament* (Tübingen: Mohr/Siebeck, 1967); K. H. Rengstorf, "μαθητής," *TDNT* 4.415–61; M. Hengel, *The Charismatic Leader and His Followers* (trans. J. Grieg; New York: Crossroad, 1981); F. F. Segovia, ed., *Discipleship in the New Testament* (Philadelphia: Fortress, 1985); R. N. Longenecker, ed., *Patterns of Discipleship in the New Testament* (Grand Rapids, Mich./Cambridge, UK: Eerdmans, 1996).

[2] Significant treatments are those of T. J. Weeden Jr., *Mark—Traditions in Conflict* (Philadelphia: Fortress, 1971); J. Donaldson, "'Called to Follow,' A Twofold Experience of Discipleship in Mark," *BTB* 5 (1975): 67–77; W. Kelber, "The Hour of the Son of Man and the Temptation of the Disciples (Mark 14:32–42)," in *The Passion in Mark* (ed. W. Kelber; Philadelphia: Fortress, 1976), 41–60; E. Best, "Discipleship in Mark: Mark 8.22–10.52," *SJT* 23 (1970): 323–37; Best, "The Role of the Disciples in Mark," *NTS* 23 (1976–1977): 377–401; Best, *Following Jesus: Discipleship in the Gospel of Mark* (JSNTSup 4; Sheffield: University of Sheffield, 1981); R. C. Tannehill, "The Disciples in Mark: The Function of a Narrative Role," in *The Interpretation of Mark* (ed. W. Telford; IRT 7; Philadelphia:

"the role of the disciples in John has escaped the intense interest that has recently been turned on their role in Mark."[3] Two years later, Fernando Segovia also commented that in Johannine scholarship "the question of discipleship per se has been largely by-passed."[4] This oversight or inattention is more intriguing when one realizes that the term μαθητής occurs more often (seventy-eight times) in John than in any synoptic Gospel.[5] Even though Raymond E. Brown acknowledged that "discipleship is the primary category in John," he did not investigate the theme further in his commentary and other writings on John.[6] This is not to ignore the fact that there have been a significant number of studies on the Johannine community and the Beloved Disciple,[7] Johannine ecclesiology,[8] and Johannine mission[9] that deal with the discipleship theme occasionally and indirectly.

Fortress/London: SPCK, 1985), 134–57; D. M. Sweetland, *Our Journey with Jesus: Discipleship According to Mark* (*GNS* 22; Wilmington: Michael Glazier, 1987); E. S. Malbon, "Texts and Contexts: Interpreting the Disciples in Mark," in *In the Company of Jesus: Characters in Mark's Gospel* (Louisville: Westminster John Knox, 2000), 100–130.

[3] R. A. Culpepper, *Anatomy of the Fourth Gospel: A Study in Literary Design* (Philadelphia: Fortress, 1983), 115.

[4] F. F. Segovia, " 'Peace I Leave with You; My Peace I Give to You': Discipleship in the Fourth Gospel," in *Discipleship in the New Testament* (ed. F. F. Segovia; Philadelphia: Fortress, 1985), 77.

[5] The term μαθητής appears seventy-three times in Matthew, forty-six times in Mark, and thirty-seven times in Luke.

[6] Among these writings, see the most important work on the Johannine community, R. E. Brown, *The Community of the Beloved Disciple: The Life, Loves, Hates of an Individual Church in New Testament Times* (New York: Paulist, 1979). The above quotation is from p. 84. Brown, however, demonstrates how the Beloved Disciple functions in the formation of the Johannine community (ibid., 31).

[7] See, for example, P. de Arenillas, "El discípulo amado, modelo perfecto del discípulo de Jesús según el IV Evangelio," *CienT* 83 (1962): 3–68, cited by R. Moreno, "El discípulo de Jesucristo, según el evangelio de S. Juan," *EstBib* 30 (1971): 269; Brown, *Community;* K. Quast, *Peter and the Beloved Disciple: Figures for a Community in Crisis* (JSNTSup 32; Sheffield: Sheffield Academic Press, 1989); J. H. Charlesworth, *The Beloved Disciple: Whose Witness Validates the Gospel of John?* (Valley Forge, Penn.: Trinity Press International, 1995); R. A. Culpepper, *John, Son of Zebedee: The Life of a Legend* (Columbia: University of South Carolina Press, 1994).

[8] For studies on Johannine ecclesiology, see E. Schweizer, "Der Kirchenbegriff im Evangelium und den Briefen des Johannes," *SE* 1 (ed. K. Aland et al.; TU 73; Berlin: Akademie Verlag, 1959), 363–81; R. Schnackenburg, *The Church in the New Testament* (New York: Herder & Herder, 1966), 103–17; K. Grayston, "Jesus and the Church in St. John's Gospel," *LQHR* 36 (1967): 106–15; H. van den Bussche, "L'Église dans le quatrième Évangile," in *Aux Origines de l'Église* (ed. Jean

As the survey below will show, an interest in the discipleship motif of the Fourth Gospel began among scholars in the 1970s. Therefore, to start there for a survey of the state of research on Johannine discipleship seems appropriate. The following survey presents chronologically the major contributions to the Johannine discipleship motif over the past three decades. Each presentation is followed by a brief critique.

THE PERIOD FROM 1970 TO 1979

The most significant studies during this period are those of Ramón Moreno (1971), Rudolf Schnackenburg (1975), and Marinus de Jonge (1977).

Ramón Moreno[10]

Ramón Moreno focuses on the meaning of the term μαθητής and "the theological-trinitarian presentation of the concept of disciple" in the Fourth Gospel.[11] In the first part of his study, Moreno, examining the occurrences of the term μαθητής, affirms that a universal meaning that transcends the

---

Giblet, Paulus Andriessen, et al.; RechBib 7; Paris: Desclée, de Brouwer, 1964), 65–85, or the English translation, *The Birth of the Church* (trans. Charles Underhill Quinn; New York: Alba House, 1968), 83–109; S. Pancaro, " 'People of God' in St. John's Gospel," *NTS* 16 (1969–1970): 114–29; K. Haacker, "Jesus und die Kirche nach Johannes," *TZ* 29 (1973): 179–201; J. F. O'Grady, "Individualism and Johannine Ecclesiology," *BTB* 5 (1975): 227–61; and J. P. Miranda, *Der Vater der mich gesandt hat. Religionsgeschichtliche Untersuchungen zu den johanneischen Sendungsformeln: Zugleich ein Beitrag zur johanneischen Christologie und Ekklesiologie* (2d rev. ed.; EHS 23/7; Frankfurt am Main: Peter Lang, 1976).

[9] Among the more significant monographs on mission in general or the mission of the disciples in the Fourth Gospel in the past decades are J. P. Miranda, *Die Sendung Jesu im vierten Evangelium: Religions- und theologiegeschichtliche Untersuchungen zu den Sendungsformeln* (SBS 87; Stuttgart: Katholisches Bibelwerk, 1977); A. C. Winn, *A Sense of Mission: Guidance from the Gospel of John* (Philadelphia: Westminster, 1981); R. Prescott-Ezickson, *The Sending Motif in the Gospel of John: Implications for Theology of Mission* (Ph.D. diss., Southern Baptist Theological Seminary, 1986); T. Okure, *The Johannine Approach to Mission: A Contextual Study of John 4:1–42* (WUNT 2/31; Tübingen: J.C.B. Mohr [Paul Siebeck], 1988); and a recent treatment of this theme, A. J. Köstenberger, *The Mission of Jesus and the Disciples According to the Fourth Gospel: With Implications for the Fourth Gospel's Purpose and the Mission of the Contemporary Church* (Grand Rapids, Mich./Cambridge, UK: Eerdmans, 1998).

[10] Moreno, "El discípulo de Jesucristo," 269–311.

[11] "Proyección teológico-trinitaria del concepto de discípulo" (ibid., 270).

characters of the story is implied when the Johannine Jesus speaks about disciples.[12] The author then proceeds with an investigation of 8:31, 13:35, and 15:1–12 as the key texts for the evangelist's understanding of discipleship. The essential characteristics of discipleship are faith and love: belief in the divinity of Jesus and his words and reciprocal love for one another. In his conclusion, Moreno underscores the claims of A. Schulz that the Johannine discipleship has a salvific orientation characterized by the communion of life founded on faith in the messiahship and the divine sonship of Jesus.[13] One receives this call to discipleship as "a saving grace" which consists in a life of faith expressed in mutual love.[14]

In the second part of his essay, Moreno investigates, on a more theological level, the relationship between the disciples of Jesus and the three Persons of the Trinity. The Father is both the fountain and the origin of the revelation of Jesus as well as the cause and origin of the faith of the disciples. He is also the ultimate end of the disciples' relationship with Jesus.[15] The relationship between the Son and the disciples is stressed in the metaphor of the Good Shepherd and sheep, and other titles (e.g., ἴδιοι [13:1], τεκνία [13:33], φίλοι [15:15], ἀδελφοί [20:17], etc.) used by the Johannine Jesus to address his disciples.[16] The Spirit is both the defending advocate and counselor of the disciples, who teaches them the meaning of the words and works of Jesus.[17] Moreno concludes his study by contending that the very act of the revelation of Jesus "proceeds from the Father, realizes itself in the Son, and completes itself in the Spirit forming the disciples for the glory of the Son and the Father."[18]

Moreno's overriding concern for bringing out the theological meaning of the term μαθητής forces him to present an ideal view of the disciples. The second part of his essay is conditioned by his Trinitarian spirituality

---

[12] "Cuando Jesús pronuncia en sus palabra 'discípulo' lo hace en el Evangelio de Juan con un sentido universal, que parece transcender a los presentes" (ibid., 276).

[13] "Der 'Schüler' des geschichtlichen Jesus für den Autor des vierten Evangeliums nicht mehr eine Berufsvorstellung, sondern bereits eine Heilsbestimmung ist. Sein wesentliches Merkmal ist die im Glauben an Jesu Messianität und Gottessohnschaft begründete Lebensgemeinschaft" (A. Schulz, *Nachfolgen und Nachahmen*, 143). See also Moreno, "El discípulo de Jesucristo," 279.

[14] Ibid., 279, 288.

[15] Ibid., 289–93.

[16] Ibid., 293–304.

[17] Ibid., 305–10.

[18] "En el mismo acto de la revelación, la actuación conjunta de las tres Personas de la Trinidad: procede del Padre, se realiza por el Hijo, se completa en el Espiritu, formando los discípulos para gloria del Hijo y del Padre" (ibid., 311).

since he seems preoccupied with a concern to show how Johannine discipleship echoes and reveals the activity of the Trinity.[19] This is unsatisfactory in a strictly "biblical" study of Johannine discipleship. He seems to have applied a later Trinitarian dogma of the church into an interpretation of the Johannine texts.

Rudolf Schnackenburg[20]

In his commentary on John's Gospel, Rudolf Schnackenburg includes an excursus entitled "Disciples, Community and Church in the Gospel of John."[21] In his attempt to examine the evangelist's understanding of the church, Schnackenburg investigates "the circle of the disciples and the concept of discipleship in the Gospel of John."[22] After a brief survey of the presence of the disciples in the Johannine story, he claims that the Johannine portrayal of the disciples evinces its theological significance in Jesus' work and activities in the world. In the Gospel of John, the disciples represent (a) "those who are made believers by Jesus through his word and signs," (b) "the later community in contrast to the unbelieving Jews," and (c) "the later believers."[23] Schnackenburg stresses the "ecclesial significance" given to the disciples in the Johannine narrative. His brief study, while focusing largely on the disciples and whom they represent, fails to deal extensively with the discipleship theme throughout the gospel.

Marinus de Jonge[24]

In his valuable study of John's Gospel, Marinus de Jonge describes the gospel as "the Book of the Disciples."[25] He claims that "the Fourth Gospel is primarily if not exclusively a book of the (Johannine) church" based on

---

[19] See also the comments in J. S. Siker-Gieseler, "Disciples and Discipleship in the Fourth Gospel: A Canonical Approach," *StudBibT* 10 (1980): 206.

[20] R. Schnackenburg, "Exkurs 17: Jünger, Gemeinde, Kirche im Johannesevangelium," in *Das Johannesevangelium* (3 vols.; HTKNT 4; Freiburg: Herder Verlag, 1967–1975), 3.231–45. I will be referring to the translation in *The Gospel According to St. John* (trans. C. Hastings; 3 vols.; London: Burns & Oates/New York: Herder & Herder, 1968–1982), 3.203–17.

[21] Ibid., 203–17.

[22] Ibid., 205–9.

[23] Ibid., 206–7.

[24] M. de Jonge, *Jesus: Stranger from Heaven and Son of God: Jesus Christ and the Christians in Johannine Perspective* (ed. and trans. J. E. Steely; Missoula: Scholars Press, 1977), 1–27.

[25] Ibid., 1.

the comment of the narrator in 20:30–31.[26] He then examines the role of the disciples in the narratives of chapter 20 followed by an investigation of the discipleship materials in the gospel. He focuses on the narrator's interpretative comments on the disciples' understanding of the words and deeds of Jesus in 2:22, 12:16, 13:26, and 20:9. These texts suggest that the disciples had differing understandings of the events before and after Jesus' departure to the Father.[27] This hermeneutical perspective of the evangelist leads de Jonge to explore the role of the Spirit in the mission of the disciples as narrated in chapters 13–17 and other related passages. He concludes that "the Fourth Gospel presents itself as the result of the teaching and the recalling activity of the Spirit within the community of disciples leading to a deeper and fuller insight into all that Jesus as the Son revealed during his stay on earth."[28] The discussion is then followed by two further issues: the true nature of discipleship and the divine initiative in the process of the discipleship journey.[29] True disciples of Jesus, asserts de Jonge, are those who "listen, see, believe, overcome offense, remain with Jesus and follow him."[30] This positive response of the disciples is an aftermath of the divine initiative.

De Jonge's study focuses primarily on how the disciples in the story function as models for the Johannine community and for the future disciples of Jesus.[31] His presentation does not explore the teaching of Jesus on discipleship in chapters 13–17 and the possible OT background for the Johannine presentation of discipleship.

THE PERIOD FROM 1980 TO 1989

The important studies during this period are those of Matthew Vellanickal (1980), Jeffrey S. Siker-Gieseler (1980), R. Alan Culpepper (1983), and Fernando F. Segovia (1985).

---

[26] Ibid., 2.

[27] Ibid., 3–7. C. H. Talbert also divides the discipleship theme in the Fourth Gospel into two: discipleship before Easter (John 1:19–2:11) and discipleship after Easter (John 12; 13–17; 20–21). See his commentary, *Reading John: A Literary and Theological Commentary on the Fourth Gospel and the Johannine Epistles* (London: SPCK, 1992), 86–87.

[28] De Jonge, *Jesus: Stranger from Heaven,* 12.

[29] Ibid., 13–20.

[30] Ibid., 14.

[31] See also the comments in Siker-Gieseler, "Disciples and Discipleship," 206.

Matthew Vellanickal[32]

Through an analysis of 1:35–42, Matthew Vellanickal investigates the "essential notes of the call to discipleship" and brings to light important aspects in the process of becoming disciples: election and call, human testimony, hearing, following, seeking, finding, coming and seeing, remaining with Jesus, and missionary sharing.[33] The Fourth Evangelist uses the call narrative "to summarize discipleship in its process of development."[34] The conditions of discipleship are the following: "remaining in the word" (8:31–32), "hating one's life" (12:25), and "serving Jesus" (12:26).[35] He also observes that the mutual love shared among the disciples in the community is "the keynote of discipleship."[36] The disciples of Jesus thus form a new world within the world, whose mission is "no longer a 'fishing of men,' but a testimony to the unique experience of Jesus."[37]

Vellanickal limits his study, while taking into consideration some sporadic statements about discipleship throughout the gospel, to the call story in 1:35–42. His claim that the vocation stories in John 1 summarize the whole process of discipleship can hardly be sustained. I will suggest below that the call stories uncover only the initial stage of the discipleship journey of the first disciples.[38]

Jeffrey S. Siker-Gieseler[39]

Jeffrey S. Siker-Gieseler takes a canonical approach in his analysis and proposes that the discipleship motif "has received a twofold nuance in the final form of the Gospel." He makes the distinction between disciples and discipleship. The term "disciples" refers to the "familiar disciples" such as the Twelve (6:70) "who historically accompanied Jesus." The evangelist develops the discipleship theme by individual characters like the Samaritan Woman (4:1–42), the Capernaum official (4:43–54), etc., who are created

---

[32] M. Vellanickal, "Discipleship According to the Gospel of John," *Jeev* 10 (1980): 131–47.

[33] Ibid., 134–40.

[34] Ibid., 141. R. E. Brown is also of the same opinion when he asserts that "John has used the occasion of the call of the disciples to summarize discipleship in its whole development" (*The Gospel According to John* [2 vols.; AB 29, 29A; New York: Doubleday, 1966–1970], 1.78).

[35] Vellanickal, "Discipleship," 141–45.

[36] Ibid., 145–46.

[37] Ibid., 147.

[38] See also R. Chennattu, "On Becoming Disciples (John 1:35–51): Insights from the Fourth Gospel," *Sal* 63 (2001): 467–98.

[39] Siker-Gieseler, "Disciples and Discipleship," 199–227.

by the evangelist as models of discipleship. These two models of disciple-ship "blend together in the author's portrayal of the Beloved Disciple."[40]

The characterization of the disciples is examined on the basis of both "what the disciples say and do" as well as "what is said and done to the dis-ciples."[41] Siker-Gieseler first focuses on the sayings of the disciples articu-lated in their requests for information (e.g., 1:38; 13:25) or clarification (e.g., 13:6; 16:17), their misunderstandings (e.g., 4:33; 6:7–9), and objec-tions (e.g., 13:14; 20:25). Among the deeds of the disciples discussed are the following (1:37), seeing (1:39), believing (2:11), knowing (10:4), re-membering (2:17), hearing (1:37), and keeping (17:6).[42] The author then proceeds with "what is said and done to the disciples." He concentrates on the way Jesus addresses the disciples (e.g., the Twelve [6:67, 70, 71], my brothers [20:17], friends [15:15], little children [13:33], children [21:5]), and the way Jesus teaches the disciples (e.g., exhortations [13:12–17], com-mands [1:43; 6:10, 12], explanations [9:3], and promises [14:15; 15:26, etc.]).[43] Siker-Gieseler maintains that "the disciples' relationship to Jesus is similar to Jesus' relationship to the Father."[44] The teachings of Jesus ad-dressed to the disciples "are intended to sustain them in their faith and chal-lenge them to a faith which is ever-deepening. Likewise, the disciples are recipients of actions which nurture and support them as they witness to the world that God has sent his Son."[45]

In the second part of his study, Siker-Gieseler examines individual char-acters—the Samaritan woman (4:7–30), the Capernaum official (4:46–54), the man born blind (9:1–41), and Martha (11:1–44)—arriving at the con-clusion that these individuals, while sharing much in common with the disciples, "portray a more positive model for future generations of believ-ers."[46] According to Siker-Gieseler, the Beloved Disciple functions in the Johannine narrative "as discipleship among the disciples. He personifies the discipleship seen in chapters 1–12 and manifests it among the disciples in chapters 13–21."[47]

While Siker-Gieseler's research contains many significant insights into Johannine discipleship, the distinction and the comparison between the

---

[40] Ibid., 199.
[41] Ibid., 207–15.
[42] Ibid., 208–10.
[43] Ibid., 210–15.
[44] Ibid., 211.
[45] Ibid., 215.
[46] Ibid., 221.
[47] Ibid., 222.

"disciples," viz., the pre-resurrection responses given by the named disciples, and "discipleship," viz., the post-resurrection responses displayed by the unnamed disciples, are more misleading than clarifying.[48] It is important to trace the development of the discipleship theme throughout the gospel narratives as they presently stand.

R. Alan Culpepper[49]

In his groundbreaking work that applies the insights of literary criticism to the Gospel of John, R. Alan Culpepper dedicates ten pages to the Johannine characterization of the disciples. The disciples are models or representative figures for the readers, and they are "surrogates for the church" in most of the narrative, especially in the farewell discourse.[50] The individual disciples have different representative roles in the narrative. For example, while the Beloved Disciple is presented as "the paradigm of discipleship" or "the epitome of the ideal disciple,"[51] both Thomas and Mary Magdalene stand in for all those who "embrace the earthly Jesus but have yet to recognize the risen Christ,"[52] and "Judas is the representative defector."[53] Although disciples in the Fourth Gospel sometimes display a lack of faith, unlike the disciples of Mark's Gospel, "their lack of understanding

---

[48] Among others who make the distinction between the responses of the disciples before and after the resurrection of Jesus, see Talbert, *Reading John*, 86–87; de Jonge, *Jesus: Stranger from Heaven*, 7; Segovia, "'Peace I Leave with You,'" 82. See also the discussion in Köstenberger, *Mission of Jesus*, 150.

[49] Culpepper, *Anatomy*, 115–25.

[50] Ibid., 115.

[51] Ibid., 121, 123. See also Siker-Gieseler, "Disciples and Discipleship," 222. R. Bultmann contends that the Beloved Disciple is an ideal representative figure of a Gentile community; see his commentary, *The Gospel of John* (trans. G. R. Beasley-Murray; Oxford: Basil Blackwell, 1971), 483–85. In a discussion about the representative roles played by both Peter and the Beloved Disciple, Brown comments that "the Beloved Disciple was no less a real human being than was Simon Peter, but the Fourth Gospel uses each of them in a paradigmatic capacity" (Brown, *Community*, 83). This complex issue is beyond the scope of the present work. For fuller discussions, see above, nn. 7–9.

[52] Culpepper, *Anatomy*, 124.

[53] Ibid., 125. For those who share the same view about the individual characters in the Fourth Gospel as "representative figures," see R. F. Collins, "Discipleship in John's Gospel," *Emm* 91 (1985): 248–55. This article also appeared in his book, *These Things Have Been Written: Studies on the Fourth Gospel* (LTPM 2; Louvain: Peeters, 1990), 1–45. This study will always refer to his book. Parallel studies of Johannine disciples appear in M. F. Whitters, "Discipleship in John: Four Profiles," *WW* 18 (1998): 422–27; P. Palatty, "Discipleship in the Fourth Gospel: An Acted Out Message of Disciples as Characters," *BiBh* 25 (1999): 285–306.

does not pose any threat to their discipleship."[54] The Fourth Evangelist often reminds the readers that the disciples will be able to understand fully the meaning and significance of all that has been revealed to them only after the death and resurrection of Jesus (cf. 2:22; 12:16).

Culpepper's valuable study is very brief and focuses on the characterization of the disciples and its implication for the plot of the gospel narratives. He disregards the historical context and the theological traditions that shaped these characterizations.[55] Moreover, like many other authors surveyed above, Culpepper shows no interest in the OT background to the discipleship motif in John. The present study considers this OT dimension as very significant for an integral and comprehensive understanding of Johannine discipleship.

Fernando F. Segovia[56]

In light of the Markan scholarship in the 1970s, Fernando F. Segovia examines the role or characterization of the disciples, the way in which the disciples function in the development of the Johannine narrative according to its "original sequence."[57] Note that Segovia leaves out some of the chapters in which Jesus is addressing the disciples directly (e.g., 13:1b–3, 12–20, 34–35; 15–17; 21) because he considers these sections later interpolations into the "original sequence" of the gospel.[58] He divides the "original sequence" of the gospel into four sections and shows how the characterization of the disciples takes place progressively in four stages:[59]

---

[54] Culpepper, *Anatomy,* 118.

[55] The focus of his study is "the relationships between author and text and text and reader rather than the origin of the characters or the relationship of historical persons to the author" (ibid., 105).

[56] Segovia, " 'Peace I Leave with You,' " 76–102.

[57] Ibid.

[58] In his later writings, however, Segovia manifests a fundamental shift in his thinking with regard to the tradition history of the Fourth Gospel. "I set out to define discipleship in John not according to the Gospel as it presently stands but rather, according to my view of an earlier, unrevised version of that Gospel" ("The Tradition History of the Fourth Gospel," in *Exploring the Gospel of John: In Honor of D. Moody Smith* [ed. R. A. Culpepper and C. C. Black; Louisville, Ky.: Westminster John Knox, 1996], 188 n. 10). For further indications of Segovia's change of method, see *The Farewell of the Word: The Johannine Call to Abide* (Minneapolis: Fortress, 1991); "The Journey(s) of the Word: A Reading of the Plot of the Fourth Gospel" and "The Final Farewell of Jesus: A Reading of John 20:30–21:25," in *The Fourth Gospel from a Literary Perspective,* ed. R. A. Culpepper and F. F. Segovia, *Semeia* 53 (1991): 23–54 and 167–90, respectively.

[59] Segovia, " 'Peace I Leave with You,' " 79–80.

Stage 1: The gathering of the elect and the initial incomprehension of "the world" (John 1–3)

Stage 2: The elect on "the way" and the growing rejection of "the world" (John 4–12)

Stage 3: The farewell to the elect and the exclusion of "the world" (John 13–14)

Stage 4: The vindication of the elect and the judgment of "the world" (John 18–20)

Segovia begins his analysis with an investigation of the characterization of the disciples as developed in these four stages and then reflects on the possible historical context of the community that necessitated such a portrayal of the disciples. The following three conclusions summarize the outcome of his study: (1) "The narrative presents and develops a thorough and systematic contrast between the disciples as believers and all those who reject Jesus' claims."[60] (2) The narrative demonstrates that "belief itself is presented as requiring and undergoing a process of gradual understanding and perception."[61] This process consists of the disciples' incomprehension counterbalanced by Jesus' further teaching or action. The study also underlines the fact that the disciples' understanding of Jesus remains incomplete until after the death and resurrection of Jesus (2:22; 12:16).[62] (3) The disciples' characterization in the narrative underscores the commonly accepted *Sitz im Leben* of the Johannine community, viz., a Christian community "engaged in a process of self-definition and self-assertion over against a much larger Jewish 'world.'"[63]

Segovia's study is exemplary in its balanced handling of both the "world in the text" as well as the "world behind the text."[64] It appears unduly reductionistic, however, to limit the Johannine discipleship to a few selected chapters that he considers part of the "original sequence" of the gospel and to exclude very important chapters like 15–17 from the analysis.

---

[60] Ibid., 90.

[61] Ibid., 92; see also Vellanickal, "Discipleship," 132.

[62] Segovia, "'Peace I Leave with You,'" 82. For this view, see also Vellanickal, "Discipleship," 140; de Jonge, *Jesus: Stranger from Heaven,* 7; Köstenberger, *Mission of Jesus,* 150.

[63] Segovia, "'Peace I Leave with You,'" 91.

[64] For a detailed study of these three worlds, see S. M. Schneiders, *The Revelatory Text: Interpreting the New Testament as Sacred Scripture* (2d ed.; Collegeville, Minn.: Liturgical Press, 1999), 97–179.

THE PERIOD FROM 1990 TO 2000

Since 1990, six studies deserving special attention are those of Raymond F. Collins (1990), J. A. du Rand (1991), W. Hulitt Gloer (1993), Dirk G. van der Merve (1997), David R. Beck (1997), and Andreas J. Köstenberger (1998).

Raymond F. Collins[65]

In his study of "Discipleship in John's Gospel," Raymond F. Collins considers the first call story, the encounter between Jesus and the first two disciples in 1:35–39, the key text to the evangelist's perspective on what it means to be a disciple of Jesus. Collins, having looked at the story on two levels, both as a narrative tale and as a symbolic tale, investigates briefly the symbolic significance of the verbs—follow, see, seek, and stay—in the light of their occurrences elsewhere in the gospel. He maintains that the "disciple is one to whom testimony about Jesus has been made, and so he enters into dialogue with Jesus. He addresses Jesus (Rabbi) with a faith that is as yet superficial but which will grow to greater fullness by interacting with Jesus. He finally appreciates where Jesus abides and comes to abide with him."[66] This way of perceiving discipleship, claims Collins, is the evangelist's understanding of the nature of discipleship. Collins limits his investigation to just five verses (1:35–39) in the gospel. One needs to investigate further other important discipleship texts to have a comprehensive understanding of the discipleship motif in John.

J. A. du Rand[67]

Du Rand explores μαθητής and related terms in the gospel such as ἀδελφός (20:17), υἱός (12:36), and φίλος (15:13) and concludes that friendship is the distinctive mark of Johannine discipleship. Du Rand underscores that the farewell discourses (chs. 13–17) are "narrative commentary on discipleship against the background of Jesus' death and resurrection, with an emphasis on the unity motif."[68] He then investigates the first farewell discourse of Jesus in 13:31–14:31 and identifies believing, knowing, and loving as the distinctive characteristics of Johannine

---

[65] Collins, *These Things Have Been Written,* 46–55.
[66] Ibid., 54.
[67] J. A. du Rand, "Perspectives on Johannine Discipleship According to the Farewell Discourse," *Neot* 25 (1991): 311–25.
[68] Ibid., 321.

discipleship. Du Rand asserts that the evangelist presents Jesus as the model for discipleship.[69] He finally highlights the eschatological dimension of discipleship since the disciples' witness of fraternal love makes present the eschatological salvation. In sum, discipleship is understood as the appropriation of realized eschatological salvation. While his conclusions are valuable, du Rand has not done a detailed analysis of the first farewell discourse; rather, he focuses on just three verbs: believing, knowing, and loving. Moreover, the study is limited to the first discourse. Therefore, an investigation of the discipleship motif in all the discourses in chapters 13–17 needs to be further explored.

W. Hulitt Gloer[70]

In his article, W. Hulitt Gloer examines "the principal episodes in which the disciples appear in an effort to understand how the evangelist challenges them to come to a deeper understanding of discipleship."[71] In exploring the characterization of the disciples as a group, Gloer focuses on the call narratives (1:35–51) and the account of the first sign at Cana (2:1–11). This is followed by an investigation of all the references to the disciples in the gospel (e.g., 2:23; 4:27; 4:31–38; 6:22–24).[72] He then looks at the individual disciples of Jesus identified with names like Andrew, Philip, Nathanael, Thomas, Peter, and the Beloved Disciple. This analysis is followed by other characters who provide models for authentic discipleship like John the Baptist, Nicodemus, the Samaritan woman, the official (βασιλικός), the man born blind, Martha, and Mary of Magdala.[73] According to Gloer, genuine disciples are those who hear and receive the word of Jesus, obey the commands of Jesus, make progress in their understanding of Jesus, and bear witness to Jesus.[74]

Gloer's essay is an excellent survey of the relevant literature with a few added reflections rather than an in-depth study of the discipleship motif that contributes new insights, either thematically or methodologically, to the ongoing discussion of the subject.

---

[69] Ibid., 322.

[70] W. Hulitt Gloer, " 'Come and See': Disciples and Discipleship in the Fourth Gospel," in *Perspectives on John: Methods and Interpretation in the Fourth Gospel* (ed. R. B. Sloan and M. C. Parsons; NABPRSSS 11; Lewiston/Queenston/Lampeter: The Edwin Mellen Press, 1993), 269–301.

[71] Ibid., 278.

[72] Ibid., 276–90.

[73] Ibid., 291–301.

[74] Ibid., 301.

Dirk G. van der Merve[75]

Van der Merve describes Johannine discipleship in terms of a personal relationship between Jesus and his disciples. On the basis of 17:18 and 20:21, he argues that Johannine discipleship is parallel to the Father-Son relationship, and is thus closely associated with the continuation and extension of the mission of Jesus. The mission of Jesus, therefore, constitutes the theological setting and framework for the understanding of Johannine discipleship.[76] The author begins his study with an investigation of the mission of Jesus in the gospel from the perspective of "the *descent-ascent* schema and the *agency* motif."[77] The descent-ascent schema represents Jesus' journey between the "world above" and the "world below." Van der Merve contends that the descent-ascent schema underscores Jesus' permanent relationship with God. He connects this schema with discipleship by stating that "the divine mission of Jesus started with the descent of the Son, while Jesus' ascent puts his disciples in a position to continue with this divine mission."[78] Jesus, the agent of God, appoints his disciples as his agents (17:18). Van der Merve claims that "with the appointment of the disciples as his agents, the pattern of the relationship between Jesus and the Father has been duplicated in/transferred to the relationship between Jesus and his disciples."[79] Van der Merve makes a valuable contribution to our understanding of Johannine discipleship by defining it in terms of a relationship with Jesus. He does not explore, however, what this relationship between Jesus and his disciples consists of, nor does he investigate its possible background or its implications for understanding the identity of the Johannine community.

David R. Beck[80]

David R. Beck contends that anonymity enhances the readers' potential for identifying with and participating in the discipleship paradigm portrayed by the anonymous characters in a narrative. This is possible be-

---

[75] D. G. van der Merve, "Towards a Theological Understanding of Johannine Discipleship," *Neot* 31 (1997): 339–59.

[76] Ibid., 340.

[77] Ibid., 340–56.

[78] Ibid., 346.

[79] Ibid., 355. For the understanding that the Johannine discipleship is an abiding relationship between Jesus and the disciples, see also C. L. Winbery, "Abiding in Christ: The Concept of Discipleship in John," *TTE* 38 (1988): 104–20.

[80] D. R. Beck, *The Discipleship Paradigm: Readers and Anonymous Characters in the Fourth Gospel* (BibIntS 27; Leiden/New York: Brill, 1997).

cause in the use of an anonymous character, there exists no "nomination barrier that distinguishes the character from other characters and from the reader."[81] He focuses on the anonymity of the Beloved Disciple who is the paradigm for true discipleship in John's Gospel, and examines how his anonymity invites readers to identify with and participate in that discipleship paradigm. He claims that "the Fourth Gospel uses anonymous characters to involve readers in its narrative world and to shape their responses."[82] According to Beck, even though John the Baptist is portrayed positively in the narrative, he is not presented as a model for readers. This claim is substantiated by the negative self-identification of John the Baptist in 1:19–28 and "his failure to recognize Jesus without special revelation" (cf. 1:33–34).[83]

After a detailed narrative reading focused on the characterization of both named and anonymous characters in the gospel, Beck arrives at the conclusion that the positive portrayal of Jesus' mother (ch. 2), the Samaritan woman (ch. 4), the official (ch. 4), the lame man (ch. 5), the man born blind (ch. 9), and the woman caught in adultery (7:53–8:11), combined with their anonymity and indeterminacies, facilitates the readers' identification with them.[84] He asserts that "the significant anonymous characters are offered as models because their faith response is appropriate and repeatable. Their positive portrayal encourages empathy and invites reader identification with them."[85] The discipleship paradigm attains its climax in the characterization of the Beloved Disciple. The identity of the Beloved Disciple has greater indeterminacy since nothing of his familial or social relationships, place of origin, occupation, etc., are revealed in the Johannine story. This greater anonymity enhances "readers' ability to fill the identity gaps in his characterization with their own identity, entering and accepting the paradigm of discipleship presented by him."[86]

Beck's study is not an investigation of the discipleship theme per se, even though the title of the book is *The Discipleship Paradigm*. The study is an investigation of the anonymous characters in the Fourth Gospel and

---

[81] Ibid., 1. See also his article, "The Narrative Function of Anonymity in Fourth Gospel Characterization," *Semeia* 63 (1993): 143–58.

[82] Beck, *Discipleship Paradigm*, 12.

[83] Ibid., 40–43. For John the Baptist as a true model for discipleship or as an example of authentic belief like the mother of Jesus, see the discussion in F. J. Moloney, *Belief in the Word: Reading John 1–4* (Minneapolis: Fortress, 1993), 121–29.

[84] Beck, *Discipleship Paradigm*, 51–107.

[85] Ibid., 134.

[86] Ibid., 136.

how their anonymity entices readers to participate in, and facilitates their identifying with, the discipleship paradigm portrayed by these anonymous characters. The important contribution of his work is the effect on readers of names and namelessness of the characters in a narrative. But the overriding interest in the anonymity and its effects on readers persuades Beck, on the one hand, to belittle the significant role played by some of the named characters like John the Baptist or Mary of Magdala as discipleship models for readers, and on the other hand, to overemphasize the anonymous character like the woman in a textually doubtful story (7:53–8:11) as a paradigm for discipleship.[87]

Andreas J. Köstenberger[88]

Perhaps the most extensive study so far, although it is not explicitly and entirely on discipleship, is that of Andreas J. Köstenberger, *The Mission of Jesus and the Disciples According to the Fourth Gospel.*[89] The primary concern of Köstenberger is to investigate the mission of Jesus and then infer the mission of the disciples from that. The disciples are called only for "extending the mission of Jesus" in terms of "harvesting," "fruit-bearing," and "witnessing."[90]

Köstenberger argues that John's Gospel is a theological interpretation of the life and mission of Jesus, and the evangelist tries to keep the balance between history and theology. He examines the evangelist's characterization of the disciples, the Twelve, Peter and the Beloved Disciple, and the corporate images like "sheep/flock" (chs. 10 and 21) and "branches" (ch. 15), and arrives at the conclusion that the evangelist is concerned "with both the disciples' historical role and their representative function for later believers."[91] The gap between the "original followers" and the later believers is bridged by the work of the Spirit. He agrees with the suggestion of W. John Pryor that "the fourth evangelist conceived of the disciples as the representatives of the messianic community in relation to the Old Testament Israel."[92] One realizes, however, it is not the disciples but

---

[87] On John 7:53–8:11, see C. K. Barrett, *The Gospel According to St. John: An Introduction with Commentary and Notes on the Greek Text* (2d ed.; Philadelphia: Westminster, 1978), 589–92.

[88] Köstenberger, *Mission of Jesus,* 141–98.

[89] Ibid., 141–98.

[90] Ibid., 141.

[91] Ibid., 168. See also the whole section in pp. 142–69.

[92] Ibid., 168. See J. W. Pryor, *John, Evangelist of the Covenant People: The Narrative and Themes of the Fourth Gospel* (Downers Grove, Ill.: InterVarsity Press, 1992).

Jesus who acts as a substitute for the people of Israel (cf. 15:1). According to Johannine eschatology, the disciples are called to participate in and be part of the messianic community inaugurated by Jesus (cf. 4:38). Köstenberger thus considers that "the priority of salvation history over literary strategy" portrayed in the evangelist's characterization of the disciples is the most significant result of his analysis.[93]

The next issue addressed is "the task of the disciples." Köstenberger focuses mainly on the motifs of "signs" and "works."[94] It is followed by a systematic investigation of "the charge of the disciples" in which he explores the "modes of movement in the disciples' mission" like "coming," "following," and "being sent."[95] He contends that coming to Jesus in the Fourth Gospel may or may not lead the character to believe in and follow Jesus.[96] After exploring all the occurrences of the term "follow" in the gospel, Köstenberger affirms that "not only is there a movement from literal to figurative following from 1:37–43 to 8:12, there is also a widening of the term from Jesus' historical disciples to the following of every believer."[97] Following Jesus entails "'death' to one's self-interest" (12:26; cf. also 21:15–23) and "following him [Jesus] in his death, i.e., *after* Jesus' glorification."[98] Discipleship implies "a lifestyle of self-sacrifice, albeit not of atoning value, and service (cf. 13:1–15; 15:13)."[99] Köstenberger emphasizes that "Jesus is both the *perfect* revelation and the *ultimate* sacrifice—the disciples are to witness to Jesus' person and work through their words, works, and lives (cf. 14:12; 15:26–27; 16:8–11; 17:18)."[100] Lastly, Köstenberger elaborates on the "being sent" aspect of the disciples' mission. The disciples are sent to "harvest" (4:38), and they are commissioned "to go and bear fruit" (15:16). They are sent into the world as Jesus was sent into the world (17:18).

Köstenberger's study is primarily interested in the mission of Jesus and, derivatively, that of the disciples. His overemphasis on "salvation history over against the literary strategy" in the gospel leads him to take an approach that is more theological (i.e., soteriological and eschatological) than exegetical.

---

[93] Köstenberger, *Mission of Jesus,* 168.

[94] Ibid., 169–76. For a detailed study of the view that the mission of Jesus as the "agent" of the Father is to do the "works" of God, and the disciples are appointed by Jesus as his "agents," see van der Merve, "Johannine Discipleship," 339–59.

[95] Köstenberger, *Mission of Jesus,* 176–97.

[96] Ibid., 177.

[97] Ibid., 178.

[98] Ibid., 178–79.

[99] Ibid., 179.

[100] Ibid., 196.

SUMMARY AND CONCLUSIONS

These contributions furnish us with a wealth of insights. They have asked the following important questions: (1) What is the true nature of, or what are the essential characteristics of, Johannine discipleship? (Moreno, de Jonge, Vellanickal, Collins, du Rand, Gloer, van der Merve, Köstenberger); (2) How are the disciples presented? (Siker-Gieseler, Culpepper, Segovia, Beck); (3) Whom do they represent? (Schnackenburg, Siker-Gieseler, Culpepper, Collins, Beck); (4) What is their function in the Johannine narrative? (de Jonge, Culpepper, Segovia, Köstenberger).

These studies underscore a number of essential aspects of Johannine discipleship such as the central role of faith in Jesus, reciprocal love, and the evolving or dynamic character of the process of becoming disciples. There is also a consensus among them with regard to the different roles or functions, both as historic persons and as representative figures, ascribed to the disciples in the Johannine narrative. The Johannine disciples, in general, represent the disciples of the historical Jesus, the believing Johannine community, and later believers including contemporary readers. The Johannine characterization of the disciples is intended to sustain and promote the faith of all believers (cf. 20:30–31). Many theological motifs permeate the narratives on discipleship. Therefore, the disciples in the Johannine narrative cannot be understood as historical persons whom the reader can recapture from the text.[101] The literary and theological function of the disciples in

---

[101] How twenty-first century readers can be in touch with the disciples of the historical Jesus from John's Gospel is a disputed issue. Scholars propose different criteria for reaching a decision about what material comes from the historical context of Jesus. The function of these criteria is to pass from the merely possible to the really probable. J. P. Meier spells out five primary criteria and four secondary criteria. The primary criteria, according to Meier, are those of embarrassment, discontinuity, multiple attestations, coherence, and the criterion of rejection and execution. The secondary criteria are traces of Aramaic influence, Palestinian environment, vividness of narration, and the criterion of the tendencies of the developing synoptic tradition. No single criterion, taken by itself, establishes the historicity of a particular word or event. But the convergence of a number of criteria can suggest whether the story is basically historical or not. See *A Marginal Jew: Rethinking the Historical Jesus. Vol. 1: The Roots of the Problem and the Person* (ABRL; New York: Doubleday, 1991), 167–95. For a recent assessment of the contemporary discussion, see M. A. Powell, *Jesus as a Figure in History: How Modern Historians View the Man from Galilee* (Louisville, Ky.: Westminster John Knox, 1998). On the historicity of Johannine miracle stories in chapters 5, 9, 21, 2 and 6, see J. P. Meier, *A Marginal Jew: Rethinking the Historical Jesus. Vol. 2: Mentor, Message and Miracles*

the narratives looks back to the Johannine community for whom the gospel was originally written.[102] Johannine Christians, the "intended readers," preserved and handed down the gospel to the "real readers," the contemporary believers.[103] Two thousand years of Christian reading of John's Gospel only unveils its capacity to speak to the faith experience of its contemporary believers.

Most of the works cited above are not extensive studies of the subject. The focus upon discipleship tends to be somewhat piecemeal. Among the limitations of the studies surveyed is the selection of the texts made for the investigation. Most importantly, in their unraveling of the evangelist's understanding of discipleship, not one of these studies has undertaken a detailed analysis of chapters 13–17 and 20–21, where the Johannine Jesus' teaching is directed at discipleship and addressed to the disciples. Moreover, although Köstenberger has made some sporadic statements about the disciples and the Johannine community as an eschatological covenant people, a thorough investigation of possible OT motifs behind the Johannine presentation of discipleship is lacking.

As W. D. Davies has aptly observed, the Fourth Evangelist "did not encounter Jesus and his movement with a *tabula rasa* but with a mind enriched by the wealth of the Jewish tradition."[104] Old Testament traditions seem to be the principal background for Johannine thought, although the Fourth Evangelist uses OT citations less frequently than the Synoptic Gospels.[105] The gospel makes explicit references to Abraham (8:31–59) and allusions

---

(ABRL; New York: Doubleday, 1994), 680–81, 694–98, 896–904, 934–50, and 950–56, respectively. On Jesus in relation to his disciples, see Meier, *A Marginal Jew: Rethinking the Historical Jesus. Vol. 3: Companions and Competitors* (ABRL; New York: Doubleday, 2001), 40–124. For a general discussion of the topic, see also F. J. Moloney, "The Fourth Gospel and the Jesus of History," *NTS* 46 (2000): 42–58.

[102] The question of how the Johannine presentation of the discipleship motif reflects the *Sitz im Leben* of Johannine community will be investigated in chapter 5 of this book.

[103] For a brief introduction to "intended" and "real" readers, see Moloney, *Belief in the Word*, 9–21.

[104] W. D. Davies, "Reflections on Aspects of the Jewish Background of the Gospel of John," in *Exploring the Gospel of John,* 46.

[105] For the Jewishness of the Gospel of John, see Brown, *John,* 1.lix–lxi; C. K. Barrett, *The Gospel of John and Judaism* (London: SPCK, 1975); O. Cullmann, *The Johannine Circle: Its Place in Judaism, among the Disciples of Jesus and in Early Christianity: A Study in the Origin of the Gospel of John* (London: SCM Press, 1976); M. de Jonge, "Jewish Expectations about the 'Messiah' according to the Fourth Gospel," *NTS* 19 (1973): 246–70. On the use of the OT in John, see E. D. Freed, *Old Testament Quotations in the Gospel of John* (NovTSup 11; Leiden: E. J. Brill, 1965);

to the traditions relating to Jacob's ladder (1:51) and to Jacob's well
(4:5–6).[106] The Exodus tradition of the OT is a very dominant motif in
John.[107] There are many references to the events of the Exodus in the Gospel—the tabernacle in 1:14, the bronze serpent in 3:14, manna in 6:31–58,
and water from the rock in 7:38. Moses typology in the Fourth Gospel (cf.
1:17; 5:46; 6:32, etc.) has been pointed out by many authors.[108] The farewell discourses in John are compared to the farewell speeches of Moses in
the Book of Deuteronomy.[109] It has been recognized that the OT theology
implicit in the presentation of the Deuteronomic Moses has influenced the
Johannine presentation of Jesus as the new lawgiver in his farewell discourses. The prophets Isaiah and Zechariah offer background for certain
features in Johannine theology. For example, "the last part of Zechariah
seems to lie behind John's reflections on the feast of Tabernacles and the

---

G. Reim, *Studien zum alttestamentlichen Hintergrund des Johannesevangeliums* (SNTSMS
22; Cambridge: Cambridge University Press, 1974); Reim, "Jesus as God in the
Fourth Gospel: The Old Testament Background," *NTS* 30 (1984): 158–60; J. W.
Pryor, "Jesus and Israel in the Fourth Gospel—John 1:11," *NovT* 32 (1990):
201–18; B. G. Schuchard, *Scripture within Scripture: The Interrelationship of Form and
Function in the Explicit Old Testament Citations in the Gospel of John* (SBLDS 133; Atlanta: Scholars Press, 1992); M. J. J. Menken, *Old Testament Quotations in the Fourth
Gospel: Studies in Textual Form* (CBET 15; Kampen: Kok Pharos, 1996); A. Obermann, *Die christologische Erfüllung der Schrift im Johannesevangelium: Eine Untersuchung zur johanneischen Hermeneutik anhand der Schriftzitate* (WUNT 2/83;
Tübingen: J. B. C. Mohr, 1996). For the points of contact between John's Gospel
and the Palestinian Targum traditions, see M. McNamara, *Palestinian Judaism and
the New Testament* (GNS 4; Wilmington: Michael Glazier, 1983), 234–41.

[106] See J. H. Neyrey, "The Jacob Allusions in John 1:51," *CBQ* 44 (1982):
586–89.

[107] For example, H. Mowvley, "John 1:14–18 in the Light of Exodus 33:7–
34:35," *ExpTim* 95 (1984): 135–37. J. J. Enz ("The Book of Exodus as a Literary
Type for the Gospel of John," *JBL* 76 [1957]: 208–15) argues for a parallelism of
both content and order between Exodus and John. For a critique of the efforts to
discover an Exodus literary pattern in John, see R. H. Smith, "Exodus Typology in
the Fourth Gospel," *JBL* 81 (1962): 329–42. Smith, however, attempts to find
typology for John in Exod 2:23–12:51.

[108] For a detailed study of the Moses traditions in John's Gospel, see T. F.
Glasson, *Moses in the Fourth Gospel* (SBT 40; London: SCM, 1963); W. A. Meeks,
The Prophet-King: Moses Traditions and the Johannine Christology (NovTSup 14;
Leiden: Brill, 1967); M.-É. Boismard, *Moïse ou Jésus: Essai de christologie Johannique*
(BETL 84; Leuven: University Press, 1988). This is now available in English: *Moses
or Jesus: An Essay in Johannine Christology* (trans. B. T. Viviano; Minneapolis:
Fortress, 1993).

[109] A. Lacomara, "Deuteronomy and the Farewell Discourse (John 13:31–
16:33)," *CBQ* 36 (1974): 65–84.

sayings on the living water (vii 37–38)."[110] Both Wisdom literature and Psalms are also important for an integral interpretation of John's Gospel. In chapter 2, after Jesus' cleansing of the Jerusalem Temple, the disciples' reference to the OT in verse 17 reminds the readers of Ps 69:9a.[111] It was even suggested that a messianic interpretation of Psalm 45 is behind the Johannine presentation of Jesus as God (cf. 1:1, 18; 20:28).[112] This brief glimpse is enough to show the importance of OT traditions and motifs for a comprehensive understanding of Johannine thought.

A fundamental shift began in biblical criticism from historical criticism to literary criticism in the late 1970s.[113] Literary criticism has now been further enhanced by the emergence of cultural studies.[114] The methodology followed here tries to draw from, and thus integrate, various methods used in contemporary biblical exegesis. This study presupposes that (1) OT traditions and motifs have played a significant role in the formation of Johannine thought and theology. (2) The evangelist's presentation of the discipleship motif reflects the historical–theological context of the Johannine community. (3) As Köstenberger aptly observes, "what is *primarily* true for Jesus' original followers, extends *derivatively* also to later believers."[115] (4) John's Gospel as a literary work has the power and "semantic autonomy" to communicate meaning independent of its author and the community.[116] (5) A contemporary reading of the

---

[110] Brown, *John,* 1.lx.

[111] See the discussion in Schuchard, *Scripture within Scripture,* 17–32.

[112] See the discussion in Reim, "Jesus as God," 158–60.

[113] For an overview of this paradigm shift and the nature of these new paradigms, see F. F. Segovia, "'And They Began to Speak in Other Tongues': Competing Paradigms in Contemporary Biblical Criticism," in *Reading from This Place: Social Location and Biblical Interpretation in the United States* (ed. F. F. Segovia and M. A. Tolbert; 2 vols.; Minneapolis: Fortress, 1995), 1.1–31. See also the discussion of the fundamental transition in the study of John's Gospel in U. Schnelle, "Recent Views of John's Gospel," *WW* 21 (2001): 352–59. Schnelle maintains that "the meaning of a Johannine passage is not determined by a possible prehistory or subsequent reworking; rather, the key to understanding particular texts lies in the intratextual world of the entire Fourth Gospel" (ibid., 353).

[114] F. F. Segovia, "Cultural Studies and Contemporary Biblical Criticism: Ideological Criticism as Mode of Discourse," in *Reading from This Place,* 2.1–17. For an application of this methodology, see R. Chennattu, "The Good Shepherd (Jn 10): A Political Perspective," *JPJRS* 1 (1998): 93–105.

[115] Köstenberger, *Mission of Jesus,* 152.

[116] P. Ricoeur, *Interpretation Theory: Discourse and the Surplus of Meaning* (Fort Worth: Texas Christian University Press, 1976), 29–32.

Johannine texts is shaped by our sociopolitical realities and cultural-ideological contexts.[117]

The study pursues a threefold objective:

1. A detailed exegetical analysis of the discipleship narratives and discourses (chs. 1, 13–17, and 20–21)

2. An investigation of the OT motifs behind the presentation of discipleship

3. An examination of the function and relevance of the discipleship paradigm for the Johannine community

DISCIPLESHIP MOTIF IN THE CALL STORIES OF JOHN 1:35–51

Jesus is the protagonist and most other characters are either intermediate characters or ficelles in the Fourth Gospel.[118] Jesus, the divine λόγος, is the reliable and authoritative character in the story and reveals the perspective of the implied author.[119] The other authoritative voice in the text is that of the "narrator" or the evangelist. The views of the evangelist can be identified with those of the "implied author" or the narrator in John's Gospel.[120] The evangelist's understanding of discipleship merges with that of

---

[117] For a presentation of the various cultural interpretative methods, see The Pontifical Biblical Commission, *The Interpretation of the Bible in the Church* (Vatican: Libreria Editrice Vaticana, 1993), 34–84. For an Asian biblical hermeneutics, see R. S. Sugirtharajah, *Asian Biblical Hermeneutics and Postcolonialism: Contesting the Interpretations* (Sheffield: Sheffield Academic Press, 1999); H. C. P. Kim, "Interpretative Modes of Yin-Yang Dynamics as an Asian Hermeneutics," *BibInt* 9 (2001): 287–308. For an Indian perspective, see George Soares-Prabhu, "Interpreting the Bible in India Today," *WaySup* 72 (1991): 70–80; R. Chennattu, "The *Svadharma* of Jesus: An Indian Reading of John 5:1–18," in *Seeking New Horizons: Festschrift in Honour of M. Amaladoss, S.J.* (ed. L. Fernando; Delhi: VEWS & ISPCK, 2002), 317–35.

[118] See Culpepper, *Anatomy,* 103–4. Ficelles are "characters whose main reason for existence is to give the reader in dramatic form the kind of help he needs if he is to grasp the story" (W. C. Booth, *The Rhetoric of Fiction* [2d ed.; Chicago: University of Chicago Press, 1983], 102). See also the discussion in R. Scholes and R. Kellogg, *The Nature of Narrative* (New York/London: Oxford University Press, 1966), 204.

[119] Jesus, who is presented as the divine λόγος, has a significant role to play in the pre-historical past, the historical past, the narrative present, the historical future, and the eschatological future. For the characterization of the Johannine Jesus, see Culpepper, *Anatomy,* 106–15.

[120] See Moloney, *Belief in the Word,* 7–9. M. Sternberg maintains that the above-mentioned perception is true for all biblical narrative (*The Poetics of Biblical*

Jesus.[121] There are only three occasions in the entire gospel when narratives or discourses are entirely dedicated to the discipleship motif: the call stories in 1:35–51, Jesus' farewell narrative and discourses in chapters 13–17, and the appearances of the risen Jesus in chapters 20–21. In 1:35–51, the evangelist narrates the first encounter between Jesus and his disciples. In chapters 13–17, with the exception of some important questions and comments from the disciples, *only* the voice of Jesus is heard. In chapters 20–21, the evangelist narrates the final encounter between Jesus and the disciples. Therefore, even though this study will present an overview of the discipleship motif throughout the gospel, it will limit its exegetical focus to these three sections of the gospel.

The study begins by exploring the beginnings of the disciples' journey with Jesus, the vocation stories, "the Evangelist's interlude on the nature of discipleship."[122] Narrative criticism devotes special attention to the beginnings and the temporal flow of narratives.[123] Beginnings of gospel narratives are not "cryptic summaries," but in general, they furnish a great deal of information for readers by introducing issues, presenting problems, and/ or raising questions that will be dealt with, and resolved, as the narrative unfolds.[124] Moreover, a narrative beginning, through its "primacy effect," constitutes a hermeneutical frame that will influence and shape the interpretation of the rest of the story.[125] As the opening of a story has a unique

---

Narrative: Ideological Literature and the Drama of Reading [ILBS; Bloomington: Indiana University Press, 1985], 58–83). For a detailed discussion on the relationship between the author, implied author, and narrator in the Gospel of John, see Culpepper, *Anatomy,* 15–49. See also Booth, *Rhetoric of Fiction,* 67–77; S. Chatman, *Story and Discourse: Narrative Structure in Fiction and Film* (Ithaca/London: Cornell University Press, 1978), 146–51.

[121] See the discussion about the Markan Jesus in Tannehill, "The Disciples in Mark," 138.

[122] Collins, *These Things Have Been Written,* 54.

[123] For a detailed discussion, see G. Genette, *Narrative Discourse: An Essay in Method* (Ithaca, N.Y.: Cornell University Press, 1980), 33–85; M. C. Parsons, "Reading a Beginning/Beginning a Reading: Tracing Literary Theory on Narrative Openings," *Semeia* 52 (1990): 11–31. See also the comments of F. J. Moloney, *Beginning the Good News: A Narrative Approach* (Homebush: St. Paul Publications, 1992), 15 and 161–66.

[124] See R. C. Tannehill, "Beginning to Study 'How Gospels Begin,'" *Semeia* 52 (1990): 187–88; Moloney, *Beginning the Good News,* 42–159.

[125] M. Perry defines "primacy effect" as the tendency of what comes first in the story to control readers' understanding of what follows and "recency effect" as the tendency of the most recently read to influence readers' understanding ("Literary Dynamics: How the Order of a Text Creates Its Meaning," *PT* 1 [1979]: 35–64,

role to play, the vocation stories are of great importance in understanding the discipleship motif. As we shall see, the narratives of the first disciples' vocation signal two beginnings: the Johannine Jesus' active ministry and the disciples' journey with Jesus. An exegetical analysis of the vocation stories in 1:35–51 will suggest that the Johannine text itself calls for a new paradigm in understanding Johannine discipleship.

AN EXEGESIS OF JOHN 1:35–51

The Literary Context and Function of John 1:35–51

John 1:35–51 is preceded by the witness of John the Baptist. The link between verses 19–34, the witness of John the Baptist, and verses 35–51, the disciples' following Jesus, is made by the indication of the "day" in verses 29 and 35, by the presence of John the Baptist in verse 35, and by the repetition of the testimony of John the Baptist to "the Lamb of God" in verse 29 and verse 36.[126] Here the disciples of John the Baptist become the followers of Jesus. The disciples of John the Baptist followed Jesus as a result of John's testimony. "John, who has been center stage on Days One and Two, now passes offstage and is replaced by Jesus, who attracts disciples to himself (cf. 1:6–8)."[127] In fact, the ministry of John the Baptist in verses 19–51 fulfills what was said about him in the Prologue (1:7). In verse 7, the narrator makes two statements about the role and mission of John the Baptist: (1) the purpose of his coming, to bear witness to the φῶς (v. 7a); (2) the purpose or goal of his testimony, that all might believe in Jesus through his witness (v. 7b). These two statements come true successively in the narrative section, verses 19–51. The narrator deliberately indicates four days behind this unit (cf. verses 29, 35, 43).[128] The first two days present the witness of John the Baptist (1:19–34), and the third and fourth days tell of the first disciples who followed Jesus as a result of the testimony of John the Baptist (1:35–51).

The call stories in 1:35–51 are followed by the miracle story at Cana in 2:1–11. The deliberate indication "on the third day" in 2:1 and the revelation of the δόξα in 2:11 remind the reader of the traditions concerning the

---

311–61). See also Parsons, "Reading a Beginning," 18–21; Tannehill, "Beginning to Study," 185–88.

[126] See the discussion in Schnackenburg, *John*, 1.308.

[127] Talbert, *Reading John*, 82.

[128] Some scholars see five days behind the narratives in vv. 19–51. They adopt the textual variant in v. 41 as πρωΐ ("early in the morning") which is found in the Old Latin and Old Syriac manuscripts (e.g., Talbert, *Reading John*, 80–86).

Jewish feast of Pentecost, commemorating the gift of the Torah, which takes place "on the third day" and manifests the revelation of "God's glory" on Mount Sinai (Exod 19:9–17).[129] The revelation of δόξα and the subsequent faith of the disciples indicate the partial fulfillment of Jesus' promise that the disciples will have a still greater revelation (v. 51). The literary structure of 1:35–51 can be seen in the following scheme.

1:19–34	1:35–51	2:1–11
• Witness of *John the Baptist*	• *John the Baptist,* disciples and Jesus	• Revelation of the *glory* (δόξα)
	• The *disciples* begin a journey with Jesus	• Faith of the *disciples*
	• The *promise* of Jesus	• Partial fulfillment of the *promise* of Jesus

In the light of the foregoing, it appears that the unit on discipleship, 1:35–51, functions as a bridge-building scene in at least two ways: (1) This pericope concludes the ministry of John the Baptist and sets in motion the life and mission of Jesus. John the Baptist takes the initiative to bring people to Jesus. As a result of his testimony, two of his disciples follow Jesus. By the coming of Nathanael, the "true Israelite,"[130] to faith in Jesus, the purpose for which John the Baptist had come is fulfilled (cf. 1:7, 31). (2) Readers are prepared for the revelation of δόξα in chapter 2 by the use of "days" (1:35, 43), the promise made in verse 51, and the indication of "on the third day" in 2:1. The fulfillment of the promise in 1:51 occurs as Jesus reveals his δόξα in 2:11, which is further elaborated in and through the life, words, and actions of Jesus in chapters 2–21.

A Narrative Reading of John 1:35–51

The narrative significance of the call of the disciples for the unfolding story is suggested by its "location," "narrative time," and "narration

---

[129] For the symbolism of days as a preparation for the revelation of glory at Cana, see Moloney, *Belief in the Word,* 53–76. For those who see seven days of a new creation in the narrative 1:19–2:11, see T. Barosse, "The Seven Days of the New Creation in St. John's Gospel," *CBQ* 23 (1959): 507–16.

[130] As we shall see, Nathanael, in spite of his initial resistance, is willing "to come and see" Jesus. Because of his willingness to come to the light, Jesus hails him as one truly representative of Israel, unlike "the Jews" in chs. 5–10.

time."[131] It is placed at the very beginning of the ministry of Jesus. In fact, the first active appearance of the Johannine Jesus occurs in this pericope. The "narrative time," the story time behind the call stories, and the "narration time," the amount of time allotted to narrate the call stories, are almost equal to those of the ministry of John the Baptist. The narrator allots two days each (narrative time) for John's ministry and for the call stories. John's ministry, the preparation for the appearance of Jesus, is narrated in two hundred and ninety-seven words (narration time) (vv. 19–36), and for the call stories, the author devotes three hundred and six words (vv. 35–51). The importance of the stories of the Johannine disciples is also implied by the fact that they are introduced on the third day, when we take the indications of the days at their face value (see vv. 29, 35, 43).[132] It is again "on the third day" (τῇ ἡμέρᾳ τῇ τρίτῃ [2:1]) that we have another significant moment of the Johannine story, the first sign (σημεῖον) of Jesus and the revelation of his δόξα in 2:1–11. From the narrative point of view, this pericope of the call of the disciples has a significant role to play. The call stories of the disciples who followed Jesus, initiated by John the Baptist, take place on the third day (vv. 35–42) while the call stories initiated by Jesus himself occur on the fourth day (vv. 43–51).[133]

There are indeed two stories on the third day: the call story of Andrew and his companion in verses 35–39 and that of Simon Peter in verses 40–42. Similarly, there are two stories on the fourth day: the call of Philip in verses 43–46 and that of Nathanael in verses 45–50. The capping of the narrative is found in verse 51, where Jesus makes a promise to all the disciples.

---

[131] For the distinction between the "narrative time" ("erzählte Zeit") and the "narration time" ("Erzählzeit"), see J. L. Ska, *"Our Fathers Have Told Us": Introduction to the Analysis of Hebrew Narratives* (Rome: Pontificio Istituto Biblico, 1990), 7–8; and for a detailed explanation of "narrative time" with a specific reference to the Gospel of John, see Culpepper, *Anatomy,* 53–75. See also the basic study of Genette, *Narrative Discourse,* 33–85.

[132] The first day is dedicated to revealing the identity of John the Baptist (vv. 19–28). Then the testimony of John the Baptist follows with an indication of another day in v. 29. Thus, it is narrated on the second day (vv. 29–34). The expression "the next day" in v. 35 indicates the beginning of a new day, i.e., the third day. This implies that the first call story is narrated on the third day. The narrator, however, does not explicitly indicate "on the third day" for the first call story as he does in John 2:1.

[133] For a discussion on the source behind this narrative section, see Barrett, *John,* 179–87. For its historical tradition, see C. H. Dodd, *Historical Tradition in the Fourth Gospel* (Cambridge: Cambridge University Press, 1963), 302–12.

The Third Day: verses 35–42

The first two verses, 35–36, furnish the setting for the encounter between the disciples of John the Baptist and Jesus. The narrator relates how two disciples of the Baptist "follow" Jesus and become his disciples. At this moment, the readers are informed neither of the names nor of the occupations of these disciples. Verse 40 indicates that one of the two disciples who followed Jesus is Andrew. Who is the other unnamed disciple? Scholars differ in their identification of the unnamed disciple. Some exegetes consider Philip this unnamed disciple.[134] As Raymond E. Brown has aptly pointed out, it is difficult to accept this suggestion because the narrator seems to introduce Philip for the first time in verse 43.[135] Some think that the unnamed disciple is the Beloved Disciple, the disciple whom Jesus loved.[136] This seems reasonable, but we do not have enough evidence from the text to establish the point. Moreover, knowing the identity of the unnamed disciple is not significant for the present discussion.[137]

The information, however, that the first disciples of the Johannine Jesus came from the school of John the Baptist is intriguing. Why did the author give us this detail? John the Baptist is the *first* and the *only* human person other than Jesus mentioned in the Prologue (1:1–18). He is presented as the

---

[134] M.-É. Boismard, after a lengthy discussion, concludes that the unnamed disciple in the call stories can be Philip. He says, "plutôt que Jean l'apôtre, ce pourrait être Philippe, le même qui interviendra à partir du v. 43" (*Du baptême à Cana (Jean 1:19–2:11)* [LD 18; Paris: Cerf, 1956], 72). J. Colson is also of the same opinion, viz., "le compagnon d'André, dans cette page de la vocation des premiers disciples, pourrait donc bien être l'apôtre Philippe" (*L'Énigme du disciple que Jésus aimait* [Paris: Beauchesne, 1969], 14); see also Schnackenburg, *John,* 1.310.

[135] Brown, *John,* 1.74.

[136] For a discussion on the identity of the unnamed disciple as the Beloved Disciple, see Charlesworth, *Beloved Disciple,* 326–30; see also Brown, *John,* 1.73–74. According to Charlesworth, the Beloved Disciple is Thomas; while for Brown, he is John, not necessarily one of the twelve disciples. Some oppose this view of identifying the unnamed disciple of ch. 1 with the Beloved Disciple. For example, Schnackenburg is of the opinion that the identification of the unnamed disciple with the Beloved Disciple is "fragwürdig" ("Der Jünger, den Jesus liebte," *EKKNT* 2.97–117, esp. 100). F. Neirynck also argues that John 1 does not make any reference to the Beloved Disciple; see his discussion in "The Anonymous Disciple in John 1," *ETL* 66 (1990): 5–37, esp. 27, 36. This article appears also in *Evangelica: Collected Essays by Frans Neirynck* (ed. F. van Segbroeck; Leuven: University Press, 1991), 617–50.

[137] T. Lorenzen writes: "Der andere, anonym gebliebene Jünger bleibt sachlich und theologisch uninteressant" (*Der Lieblingsjünger im Johannesevangelium: Eine redaktionsgeschichtliche Studie* [SBS 55; Stuttgart: KBW Verlag, 1971], 45).

one who is sent from God (ἀπεσταλμένος παρὰ θεοῦ). His mission is to bear witness to Jesus, the Son of God. It would seem natural, then, that the disciples of John the Baptist be the first recipients of this message. The disciples of John the Baptist respond to the call of John, the messenger of God (1:6–8), and thus receive the revelation of God through John's testimony (1:31). But they receive their call to discipleship (call to follow Jesus) as a gift from heaven, directly from God (3:27; 6:44–45; 15:16). They form the beginning of the community of the disciples of Jesus (1:35–36).

John the Baptist, the only character who has the ability to identify Jesus (1:6–8), introduces Jesus to his disciples, when he makes his first appearance in the story. The Baptist repeats the revelatory formula: Ἴδε ὁ ἀμνὸς τοῦ θεοῦ, "Behold, the Lamb of God" (v. 36).[138] What is the function of this proclamation in verse 36? Many scholars are of the opinion that it does not have a revelatory function here as it does in verse 29. Raymond E. Brown says, "Its purpose is to initiate a chain reaction which will bring John the Baptist's disciples to Jesus and make them Jesus' own disciples."[139] Charles K. Barrett is of the same opinion, that it "is repeated in order to furnish a motif for the action of the two disciples."[140] However, this formula may well have a revelatory function.[141] The purpose of the testimony of John the Baptist was to reveal the identity of Jesus to the people in general (v. 7), or to Israel in particular (v. 31), so that all might believe in Jesus through his testimony (v. 7). But when we look at the narrative in verses 29–34, it is a monologue, and there is no indication of the presence of the disciples to receive the revelation. Thus, the testimony in verses 29–34 would fulfill only partially what has been said about John the Baptist in the Prologue. From the narrative point of view, it is indeed necessary that John repeat his testimony in the presence of the disciples in order to fulfill his mission.

The revelatory nature of this testimony is further confirmed by the prompt response of his disciples (v. 37). It is reported that by "hearing" (ἤκουσαν) this testimony, the disciples "followed" (ἠκολούθησαν) Jesus. The Fourth Gospel makes a close link between "hearing" and "believing." Craig Koester has shown that genuine faith is engendered through "hearing."[142] Against this background, let us now look at the meaning of the

---

[138] On revelatory formulae in the Gospel of John, see M. de Goedt, "Un schème de révélation dans le Quatrième Évangile," NTS 8 (1961–1962): 142–50.

[139] Brown, John, 1.76.

[140] Barrett, John, 180.

[141] For those who argue for the revelatory nature of this formula in v. 36, see de Goedt, "Un schème de révélation," 143–44.

[142] C. R. Koester, "Hearing, Seeing, and Believing in the Gospel of John," Bib 70 (1989): 327–48, esp. 347.

verb ἀκολουθέω in this verse. In John, ἀκολουθέω is used both literally (meaning "to walk behind someone" or "walk in the same direction") and metaphorically (as an expression of one's commitment to Jesus).[143] Rudolf Schnackenburg claims that even though ἀκολουθέω is often used meta-phorically in John "for the dedication of faith," it is understood literally in verse 37. He, however, recognizes the "following" of the disciples here as "the first step to faith."[144] It seems that both meanings are implied. The faith response as a consequence of "hearing" needs to be understood as a genuine expression of faith. In other words, the disciples of John, after "hearing" the testimony of John, have decided to begin a journey with Jesus. They are now open to enter into the process of becoming disciples of Jesus. This response on the part of the disciples signals the completion of John the Baptist's mission (1:7).

The response of Jesus to the disciples who followed him is described in detail. Jesus stopped his journey, turned (στραφείς) and gazed upon (θεασάμενος) the disciples, and asked (λέγει) them τί ζητεῖτε, "What do you seek?" Jesus thus opens a conversation with the disciples. The first words of Jesus, τί ζητεῖτε, can have two meanings: (1) the surface meaning: What do you want? (2) the deeper meaning: What are you searching/longing for? It is necessary to listen to the Fourth Evangelist with both ears: one for the literal and the other for the symbolic sense. Raymond E. Brown takes the question on the theological level as he states: "This question touches on the basic need of man that causes him to turn to God."[145] Both the literary context of the call stories and the responses of the disciples in the narrative point to the deeper meaning of Jesus' query. The variant reading τίνα ζητεῖτε confirms this claim, as it suggests that this text was understood in antiquity in terms of a theology of discipleship.[146]

Even though John the Baptist referred to Jesus as the Lamb of God (v. 36), the disciples address him as ῥαββί, which literally means "my great one." The narrator, however, translates it as "teacher." Raymond Brown points out that "John's translation as 'teacher' is not literal but is true to usage."[147] But this deliberate translation is not meant merely for

---

[143] For the literal use of the verb in John, see 11:31; and for the metaphorical use, see 1:44; 8:12; 10:4, 27; 12:26; 21:19, 20, 22.

[144] Schnackenburg, *John*, 1.308.

[145] Brown, *John*, 1.78.

[146] The variant reading τίνα ζητεῖτε, "For whom are you looking?" seems to be an attempt by the scribes to harmonize this text with John 20:15, the encounter between Jesus and Mary of Magdala. In the words of Brown, it "reflects an under-standing of the scene as giving a theology of discipleship." See *John*, 1.74.

[147] Brown, *John*, 1.74.

the non-Jewish reader in the Diaspora,[148] it also "makes clear to the implied reader that these disciples are approaching Jesus as a teacher, and no
more."[149] This is further underscored by the query of the disciples: ποῦ
μένεις, "Where do you stay" or "abide?" Since rabbis are not wanderers,
Francis J. Moloney is of the opinion that "it is the logical question that
follows on the recognition of a newly found teacher."[150] The query
"probably indicates a desire to hear Jesus expounding the Scriptures."[151]
But the verb μένω is used not only in the literal sense of "staying" (2:12)
but also in the theological sense of "abiding" or "indwelling" (15:5).[152]
The word μένω is an important theological term for discipleship in the
Fourth Gospel.[153] John the Baptist, in his vision, saw the Spirit "abiding"
(μένον) upon Jesus (1:32–33). Dorothy Lee observes that the abiding
place of Jesus "is linked both to the Spirit who 'stays' (abides) on him and
to the disciples with whom he will abide for ever through the Spirit-
Paraclete (see 14:17)."[154] Klaus Scholtissek paraphrases the disciples'
query ποῦ μένεις (v. 38b) in the following ways: "In which area of influence ['field of force'] do you live? Who or what determines your being
[nature] most deeply? Who or what enables your abiding presence?"[155]
He interprets the query in theological terms. Those who wish to *abide in*

---

[148] It is suggested that this translation is meant for the Jews in the Diaspora or
for the Gentiles who did not know Aramaic (B. Lindars, *The Gospel of John* [Lon-
don: Oliphants, 1972], 113).

[149] Moloney, *Belief in the Word,* 68. However, one notices that the customary
address of Jesus by the disciples in the Fourth Gospel is "Rabbi" or "Teacher"
until ch. 11. For a study which claims that the Fourth Gospel shows that Jesus was
perceived by his contemporaries primarily as a Jewish religious teacher, see A. J.
Köstenberger, "Jesus as Rabbi in the Fourth Gospel," *BBR* 8 (1998): 97–128.
Köstenberger, however, agrees that the Fourth Evangelist portrays the exalted
Jesus in the farewell discourses as transcending the identity of rabbi (ibid., 108).

[150] Moloney, *Belief in the Word,* 68.

[151] Schnackenburg, *John,* 1.308.

[152] On these two meanings, see J. Heise, *Bleiben: Menein in den Johanneischen
Schriften* (Tübingen: J. C. B. Mohr [Paul Siebeck], 1967), 47–103.

[153] See D. A. Lee, "Abiding in the Fourth Gospel: A Case-study in Feminist
Biblical Theology," *Pacifica* 10 (1997): 123–36. She considers discipleship in John
"primarily in terms of witnessing and abiding" (ibid., 127). For a recent study on
the theological meaning and the significance of μένω in John, see K. Scholtissek, *In
Ihm Sein und Bleiben: Die Sprache der Immanenz in den johanneischen Schriften* (HBS
21; Freiburg: Herder, 1999).

[154] Lee, "Abiding," 127.

[155] "In welchem Kraftfeld lebst du? Wer oder was bestimmt dein Wesen
zutiefst? Wer oder was ermöglicht dein Bleiben?" (Scholtissek, *In Ihm Sein,* 240).
For the metaphorical meaning, see also Bultmann, *John,* 100.

God are constantly seeking to transcend temporality or death, striving to find something that is everlasting.[156] The literary and theological context of the story suggests that the query of the disciples ποῦ μένεις epitomizes the human drive for God or being in communion with God.

The response of Jesus in verse 39 contains both an invitation: "Come" (ἔρχεσθε) and a promise: "You shall see" (ὄψεσθε).[157] The aspect of promise in the response of Jesus is neglected by most of the exegetes.[158] Jesus' promise (ὄψεσθε) in verse 39 is analogous in nature to the promise made by Jesus to Nathanael (ὄψῃ) in verse 50 and then to all the disciples (ὄψεσθε) in verse 51. This is further established by the fact that the evangelist always takes care to distinguish the invitations of Jesus from those of the disciples. The invitations to the disciples are always in the imperative form: ἴδετε (see the invitation to Philip in 1:46 [ἴδε] and the Samaritan woman in 4:29 [ἴδετε]). The response of Jesus in 1:39, both the invitation and the promise in the future form, is a challenge to the disciples. The theme of "coming" to Jesus (3:21; 5:40; 6:35, 37, 45, etc.) and "seeing" Jesus (6:40) are used in the Gospel to describe faith. Jesus promises eternal life to those who come to Jesus (5:40) and to those who believe in him (6:40, 47; 20:31). Therefore, the invitation "to come" to Jesus is an invitation "to believe" in Jesus. As with the verb "to come" (ἔρχομαι), so also with the verb "to see" (ὁράω) the evangelist is putting both meanings in play. At a deeper level, "seeing Jesus" provides an insight into the identity of Jesus (1:41), and eternal life is promised to those who "see" Jesus (6:40). Hence the response of Jesus to the disciples in verse 39 is an invitation to enter into *a personal relationship with Jesus* and to be open to the ongoing revelation of God in Jesus.

The narrator informs the reader that the disciples not only went and saw the place where Jesus was staying but also stayed/abided (ἔμειναν) with him.[159] Abiding as an aspect of discipleship is developed much later in the

---

[156] Brown, *John*, 1.79.

[157] Most commentators translate the response of Jesus as if reading ἔρχεσθε καὶ ἴδετε ("come and see"), even though both *UBSGNT*[4] and *NA*[27] have preferred the reading ἔρχεσθε καὶ ὄψεσθε. I opt for the future tense ὄψεσθε, attested by 𝔓[5vid. 66. 75] B C* L W[s] Ψ[c] 083 *f*[1] 33 *pc*. The variant reading ἴδετε is also attested by the early manuscripts (א A C³ Θ 063 *f*[13] 𝔐 *latt*). The Latin *venite et videte* seems to have influenced many commentators. However, the reading ἴδετε seems to be an attempt by the scribes to harmonize this text with v. 46 where we have ἴδε.

[158] Schnackenburg translates it in the future tense. Even though he admits, "it sounds almost like a promise," he does not pursue the "promise" aspect of the response of Jesus (*John*, 1.309).

[159] The indication of the time in v. 39, ὥρα ἦν ὡς δεκάτη, is to be taken at its face value: "the tenth hour" means four in the afternoon. The customary usage in

gospel. Discipleship in terms of an abiding relationship is explicitly expressed in 15:1–17. The use of μένω, however, at the very beginning of the journey to discipleship suggests that something *more* is implied than just seeing the place where Jesus was staying. It implies that the disciples are on their way to seeing the ongoing revelation in Jesus, which later enables them to abide (μένω) in Jesus. As yet, this is only a hint. It will develop as the narrative unfolds.

What did the disciples "see"? The object of their "seeing" is not the place of Jesus' home, but it is the revelation of Jesus. This is evinced from the immediate response of Andrew, one of the disciples who stayed/abided (ἔμειναν) with Jesus.[160] In fact, the first thing (πρῶτον)[161] that Andrew does

---

the gospels is to reckon the hours from daylight at six in the morning. For those who hold this way of reckoning hours in John, see Barrett, *John,* 181; Brown, *John,* 1.75; Moloney, *Belief in the Word,* 68; Lindars, *John,* 114. Some others, however, hold that the event took place at ten a.m., reckoning the hours from midnight; see N. Walker, "The Reckoning of Hours in the Fourth Gospel," *NovT* 4 (1960): 69–73. Schnackenburg (*John,* 1.309) comments that it suggests a long conversation between Jesus and the disciples, and it serves also to explain why the disciples *remained* with Jesus as Jesus had not asked them to "come and remain/abide" with him. But I think the indication of the time refers to the hour of "fulfillment," as the beginning of the disciples' faith journey with Jesus could symbolize the beginning of the "Christian era." For a study of the significance of the number ten in Judaism, see F. Hauck, "δέκα," *TDNT* 2.36–37.

[160] Andrew is introduced as Simon Peter's brother. It is taken for granted that the reader knows who Peter is.

[161] There are four variant readings: (1) πρῶτον: 𝔓[66.75] ℵ[2] A B Θ Ψ 083 0233[vid] *f*[1.13] 892 1243 *l*253 *l*672 *l*673 *l*1016 *l*1074 *l*1627 it[a.aur.c.f.ff2.l.q] vg syr[p.h.] cop[sa.bo] arm geo Epiph. In this best attested reading we have an adverbial accusative modifying the verb, i.e., "the first thing Andrew did." This reading would imply that Andrew found his brother before he did anything else. (2) πρῶτος: ℵ* L W[s] Δ 0141 28 157 180 565 579 597 700 1006 1010 1071 1241 1292 1342 1505 *Byz Lect* syr[pal] Cyril. In this reading, we have a masculine nominative adjective modifying Andrew. This would imply that Andrew was the first to find his brother, Simon Peter. (3) πρωΐ: it[b, e, rl vid] sy[s]. This is an easy reading. It may be a scribal attempt to clarify the obscure πρῶτον. Another day is introduced in this reading: "early the next morning." (4) The word is omitted altogether: 1424 vg[ms] syr[c] Augustine. This study adopts πρῶτον, the best-attested reading. The adverbial use of πρῶτον is common in John (see 2:10; 7:51; 10:40; 12:16; 15:18; 18:13; 19:39). The reading πρῶτον is the *lectio difficilior,* "because nothing is said of any further action on the part of Andrew" (see Schnackenburg, *John,* 1.311). According to Metzger and the UBSGNT[4], "the reading πρωΐ ('in the morning'), implied by the word *mane* in two or three Old Latin manuscripts, avoids the ambiguities of πρῶτος/πρῶτον and carries on the narrative from ver. 39" (B. M. Metzger, *A Textual Commentary on the Greek New Testament* [2d ed.; Stuttgart: Biblia-Druck, 1994], 172).

after this experience with Jesus is to find Simon Peter and bear witness to Jesus: "We have found the Messiah" (v. 41). What this testimony entails is not described in the text. It presupposes knowledge of Jesus. As a result of the testimony of Andrew, Simon comes to Jesus. The response of Jesus to Simon is twofold: (1) an affirmation, σὺ εἶ Σίμων ὁ υἱὸς Ἰωάννου, "You are Simon the son of John,"[162] and (2) a promise, σὺ κληθήσῃ Κηφᾶς, "You shall be called Kephas." Promises are always forward looking. The use of the future tense here in verse 42 is significant as it brings out the forward-moving nature of the journey that Simon Peter undertakes. He is told of the new name, Κηφᾶς (Rock), which he will have in the future.[163] Note that this new name is given to Simon as a gift. We are not yet told of Simon's reactions. What matters at this moment of the narrative is the promise of Jesus. Jesus' promise to Simon is different from those he makes in verses 39, 50, and 51. While the promise to Simon refers to his future mission, the other promises refer to the ongoing revelation of God in Jesus, which the disciples will gradually see as they journey with Jesus. The disciples' journey of faith begins with their encounter and dialogue with Jesus, and it continues when they go and stay/abide (μένω) with him. Andrew's confession of faith in Jesus as the Messiah (v. 41) displays the partial fulfillment of Jesus' promise in verse 39.

The Fourth Day: verses 43–51

John the Baptist, having completed his mission (v. 36), disappears from the scene. A new beginning within the call stories is indicated by the introduction of a new day (τῇ ἐπαύριον) in the narrative (v. 43). Verses 43–44 furnish the setting for the story that moves now to the following of

---

[162] There are three variant readings: (1) υἱὸς Ἰωάννου, (2) υἱὸς Ἰωνᾶ, (3) υἱὸς Ἰωάννα. Some consider Ἰωνᾶ as a variant spelling of Ἰωάννου (see Barrett, *John*, 182). Metzger and a majority of his committee "regarded Ἰωνᾶ (read by A B³ Δ *f*¹ *f*¹³ and most of the later Greek witnesses) as a scribal assimilation to Bar-Jona of Matt 16.17. The reading Ἰωάν(ν)α reflects further scribal confusion with the name of a woman mentioned only by Luke (cf. Luke 8.3; 24.10)" (Metzger, *Textual Commentary*, 172).

[163] The change of Simon's name to Peter in the Gospel of John takes place in the beginning of the ministry of Jesus. The Johannine version of the story seems to be the earliest form of the tradition. John's use of the Aramaic form of the name supports the antiquity of the Johannine version of the tradition. In the Gospel of Matthew, this event takes place more than halfway through the ministry of Jesus in 16:16–18. "On this point Matthew's account is more polished than John's, for Matthew explains the relation of the new name ('rock') to Peter's role as the foundation stone of the Church. John stresses only that the name came from Jesus' insight into Simon ('Jesus looked at him')" (Brown, *John*, 1.80).

Philip[164] and then of Nathanael,[165] the third and the fourth disciples to be called respectively in the Fourth Gospel. In the Greek text of verse 43, there is some ambiguity with regard to the subject of the verbs: ἠθέλησεν ἐξελθεῖν and εὑρίσκει. Who decides to go to Galilee, and who finds Philip? Since Simon Peter was the last mentioned in the narrative in verse 42, grammatically he would be the best choice for the subject of the verbs in verse 43.[166] Why the author tells us that Peter wanted to go to Galilee remains obscure. But the information that Jesus wanted to go to Galilee fits in well with the following narrative, 2:1–11, where Jesus is at Cana in Galilee. Hence, "in the present sequence *Jesus* is probably meant to be the subject."[167] If so, then it is Jesus who takes the initiative in summoning Philip to discipleship. Whether the call of Philip takes place before the journey (in the Jordan valley) or after the journey (near the Sea of Galilee) is another disputed question. This issue does not seem to be important for the present discussion. "The indication in ii 1, however, is that the journey took place after the call of Philip and Nathanael."[168]

John's Gospel locates the hometown of Peter and Andrew at Bethsaida. This information does not agree with the Markan tradition. According to the Gospel of Mark, the city of Andrew and Peter is Capernaum (Mark 1:21, 29). How does one explain this discrepancy? Why did the author bring the name of the place, Bethsaida, into the narrative? The Hebrew name Βηθσαϊδά literally means "place of provisioning." M.-E. Boismard suggests that Bethsaida has been introduced into John's narrative to make a symbolic reference to the theme of Matt 4:19 ("Follow me and I will make

---

[164] Even though Philip is one of the twelve, he does not play any role in the synoptic narrative. In John's Gospel he appears again in 6:5–7; 12:21–22; and 14:8–9.

[165] Nathanael does not appear in any list of the twelve and is not found in the synoptic Gospels. The name Ναθαναήλ is Hebrew, and it literally means "gift of God." Many scholars identify the Nathanael of John as the Bartholomew of Matthew, Mark, and Luke. But there is no reliable evidence for this conjecture. It has sometimes been suggested that the Nathanael of John is a symbolic name rather than the name of a historical person. There is no evidence, however, to substantiate the position that Nathanael was purely a symbolic figure. According to John 21:2 Nathanael came from Cana in Galilee. For the reasons given by those who consider him as a symbolic figure, see Barrett, *John*, 183–84. Brown suggests that "it is better to accept the early patristic traditions that he [Nathanael] was not one of the Twelve" (*John*, 1.82).

[166] For those who read πρῶτος instead of πρῶτον in v. 41, Andrew may have been the subject.

[167] The emphasis is mine. See Brown, *John*, 1.81.

[168] Ibid., 86.

you fishers of men").[169] One cannot be sure whether or not the author is making a deliberate reference to Matt 4:19, yet the etymology of the word Bethsaida, "the place of provisioning," in the context of the call to discipleship is intriguing. Does it reveal the occupation of Philip as a fisherman? Or does it refer to the "fishing" mission of the disciples (cf. Mark 1:16–20)? Such assertions, though reasonable, remain highly hypothetical. They go beyond the evidence of the text. All we can affirm is that the reader is informed that the first disciples of Jesus—Andrew, Peter, and Philip—came from the same town, Bethsaida.[170]

The invitation of Jesus, ἀκολούθει μοι, "follow me," in verse 43, makes Jesus' meeting with Philip in John's Gospel very similar to that in the call stories of the Synoptic Gospels (Mark 2:14; Matt 9:9; and Luke 5:27). The Johannine usage in its present context, however, is different.[171] Like the story of Peter (vv. 40–42), the call of Philip is not narrated in detail (vv. 43–44). All that is said about Philip is that Jesus both found him and asked him to follow. One has to infer the meaning of the command of Jesus from the response of Philip in verse 45: "We have found him of whom Moses in the Law and also the Prophets wrote, Jesus, son of Joseph, from Nazareth." The response of Philip is analogous both in its nature and function to that of Andrew in verse 41. It seems reasonable therefore to understand that the invitation of Jesus in verse 43 is analogous in function to his invitation to the first disciples in verse 39, "Come and you shall see."

Philip, like Andrew, gives testimony to Jesus: "We have found him of whom Moses in the Law and the Prophets wrote" (v. 45). "The expression 'we have found him' echoes Andrew's statement (v. 41), indicating that Philip too was speaking of the Messiah."[172] The phrase "Moses in the law

---

[169] Boismard, *Du baptême,* 90. Brown, on the basis of a distinction between the prepositions ἐκ and ἀπό, suggests that Philip was from Bethsaida in the sense that he had been born there, while his actual home was at Capernaum (*John,* 1.82). Barrett thinks that "there is here no difference in meaning between the prepositions" (*John,* 183).

[170] Some consider vv. 43–44 as a later interpolation in order to harmonize John with the Synoptic Gospels. Whatever may be the history of the traditions behind it, we interpret the text as it stands today. For a recent study that demonstrates the conceptual unity of this pericope (vv. 43–51) as it stands today, see S. Schreiber, "Die Jüngerberufungsszene Joh 1:43–51 als literarische Einheit," *SNTSU* 23 (1998): 5–28.

[171] See Schnackenburg, *John,* 1.313.

[172] C. R. Koester, "Messianic Exegesis and the Call of Nathanael (John 1:45–51)," *JSNT* 39 (1990): 26; see also N. A. Dahl, *Jesus in the Memory of the Early Church* (Minneapolis: Augsburg, 1976), 112. For a different interpretation, see Moloney, *Belief in the Word,* 70.

and the prophets" embraces the whole Scripture of the OT.[173] After comparing the expression, ὃν ἔγραψεν Μωϋσῆς ἐν τῷ νόμῳ, "of whom Moses wrote in the Law," in 1:45 with 5:39, 46, Severino Pancaro claims that "in view of the strict correspondence between these three texts, it is evident that the presentation of Jesus by Philip as the one about whom Moses wrote means that they have found (εὑρήκαμεν) the one announced by the Scriptures, the Messiah (cf. 1:41)."[174] Jesus is also presented as the son of Joseph (υἱὸς τοῦ Ἰωσήφ),[175] from Nazareth (ἀπὸ Ναζαρέτ).[176] This is the first time in the narrative that the Johannine Jesus is identified in terms of his human origins.

The prompt response of Nathanael is not very appreciative (v. 46). It was suggested that the saying, ἐκ Ναζαρὲτ δύναταί τι ἀγαθὸν εἶναι, "Can anything good come out of Nazareth?" indicates an existing rivalry between two neighboring towns since Nathanael comes from Cana (21:2).[177] Some others are of the opinion that it may be a "local proverb reflecting jealousy between Cana and Nazareth."[178] None of these claims can be proved from the evidence of the text. It is striking that Nathanael does not focus on the issue of Jesus' parentage (son of Joseph) here.[179] In the light of the confession of Philip (v. 45), his objection probably arose from the fact that the Scriptures said nothing about the Messiah's coming from Nazareth.[180] The response of Nathanael in verse 46, whatever may be its origin

---

[173] Luke 16:29, 31; 24:27; Acts 26:22; 28:23, etc.

[174] S. Pancaro, *The Law in the Fourth Gospel: The Torah and the Gospel, Moses and Jesus, Judaism and Christianity According to John* (NovTSup 42; Leiden: Brill, 1975), 289.

[175] Note that the same title is attributed to Jesus in 6:42 by the disbelieving Jews in order to discredit the claim of Jesus that he has come down from heaven.

[176] Though various strands of NT tradition speak of Nazareth as the hometown of Jesus, Nazareth is not recorded as the birthplace of the expected Messiah in the OT or in the Talmud; see the discussion in G. Dalman, *Sacred Sites and Ways: Studies in the Topography of the Gospel* (trans. P. P. Levertoff; London: SPCK, 1935), 57–78.

[177] Barrett, *John*, 184.

[178] Brown, *John*, 1.83. See also K. Dewey, "*Paroimiai* in the Gospel of John," *Semeia* 17 (1980): 90–91; P. D. Duke, *Irony in the Fourth Gospel* (Atlanta: John Knox, 1985), 54–55.

[179] M. M. Thompson connects 1:46 with the reference to Jesus' parents in John 6:42 and asserts that the response of Nathanael, Can anything good come out of Nazareth? "manifests misgivings about the inauspicious origins of the putative Messiah" (*The Humanity of Jesus in the Fourth Gospel* [Philadelphia: Fortress, 1988], 16). See also Schnackenburg, *John*, 1.315.

[180] Similar objections are made by the "Jews" in 7:41–42, 52. For those who connect 1:46 with 7:41–42, 52, see Barrett, *John*, 154; and Pancaro, *Law*, 289.

and background, expresses some initial hesitance. Philip, however, invites Nathanael to "come and see" (ἔρχου καὶ ἴδε) Jesus; and Nathanael, in spite of his initial resistance, goes and sees Jesus. Nathanael, like the first disciples, begins to make a journey of faith.

The dialogue between Jesus and Nathanael seems to be symbolic. Jesus takes the initiative and greets Nathanael as ἀληθῶς Ἰσραηλίτης ἐν ᾧ δόλος οὐκ ἔστιν, "a true Israelite in whom there is no guile." The adverb ἀληθῶς here serves as the equivalent of the adjective ἀληθής or ἀληθινός.[181] Nathanael, therefore, represents someone "worthy of the name of Israel"[182] or a "worthy representative of the people of God."[183] "Here is a man worthy to recognize all that has been promised in the Scriptures (see v. 45)."[184] Nathanael is also qualified as someone ἐν ᾧ δόλος οὐκ ἔστιν, "in whom there is no guile." Many commentators have seen in this phrase an allusion to Jacob, the patriarch of Israel (Gen 27:35). This interpretation does not seem to respect the Johannine presentation of Jacob elsewhere in the Gospel.[185] Some others see here an allusion to the Suffering Servant theme, "in whose mouth was found no guile" (Isa 53:9). In this understanding, "guile" would mean "religious infidelity to Yahweh."[186] The Johannine Jesus, whether or not verse 47 alludes to the "Suffering Servant" theme, affirms Nathanael as a God-fearing man, someone faithful to God. This seems to fit in well with the story of Nathanael, as he is open to receive the revelation of God from Jesus, the one about whom Moses and the prophets wrote.[187]

---

[181] For the adjectival use of ἀληθῶς in the sense of ἀληθής or ἀληθινός in the Gospel of John, see 4:42; 6:14; 7:40. For the use of adverbs as adjectives, see BDF §434.

[182] Bultmann, *John,* 73 n. 6. Boismard comments that Nathanael "est resté fidèle à Yahvé. C'est en ce sens qu'il mérite le nom d'Israël" (*Du baptême,* 97). See also, for those who consider Nathanael's role as a representative figure of Israel, Culpepper, *Anatomy,* 123; de Goedt, "Un schème de révélation," 142–50; Meeks, *Prophet-King,* 82; R. T. Fortna, *The Fourth Gospel: From Narrative Source to Present Gospel* (Philadelphia: Fortress, 1988), 44.

[183] Brown, *John,* 1.83.

[184] Moloney, *Belief in the Word,* 71.

[185] The biblical tradition in general does not consider Jacob a "deceiver" but a great patriarch of Israel. The same view, Jacob as a great patriarch, is found elsewhere in the Gospel when the Samaritan woman challenges Jesus by asking, "Are you greater than our ancestor Jacob?" (4:12; see also 4:5). Schnackenburg (*John,* 1.316) also maintains that the evangelist is not placing Nathanael in contrast to Jacob, the "deceiver" (Gen 27:35).

[186] See the discussion in Boismard, *Du baptême,* 96–97.

[187] Some see Nathanael as "a member of God's Chosen People by spiritual birth rather than by heredity (cf. Rom 9:6–8)" (W. R. Telford, *The Barren Temple and the*

Nathanael seems to be agreeing with Jesus that he is indeed a "true Israelite" and asks Jesus, πόθεν με γινώσκεις; "Whence/how did you get to know me?" (v. 48a). The response of Jesus, πρὸ τοῦ σε Φίλιππον φωνῆσαι ὄντα ὑπὸ τὴν συκῆν εἶδόν σε, "before Philip called you I saw you under the fig tree," has been interpreted in many different ways.[188] Some claim that Jesus' seeing Nathanael "under the fig tree" (ὑπὸ τὴν συκῆν) has no particular theological significance in the story. If we accept this view, then Nathanael's leap from unbelief to faith is inexplicable. One needs to ask the question: What did Jesus reveal when he claimed that he had seen Nathanael under the fig tree?[189] The expression ὑπὸ τὴν συκῆν is often interpreted symbolically. One of the most common views has been "the suggestion that 'under the fig tree' was a traditional site for the study of the Torah."[190] It might reveal that Nathanael belonged to a group of people who were well acquainted with Scripture and who awaited the coming of the Messiah.[191] This assumption fits in well with the confession made by Philip to Nathanael, "We have found him of whom Moses in the Law and the Prophets wrote" (v. 45). The query of Nathanael, "How did you get to know me?" suggests that the response of Jesus is to be interpreted in terms of Jesus' knowledge. The evangelist stresses Jesus' ability to know things beyond the normal human range. Jesus' response thus reveals his supernatural knowledge, and it evokes Nathanael's response,[192] the confession of faith in Jesus as the Messiah (v. 49).[193] The manifestation of Jesus' supernatural

---

Withered Tree [JSNTSup 1; Sheffield: JSOT Press, 1980], 219); see also the discussion in E. Hirsch, *Das vierte Evangelium* (Tübingen: J. C. B. Mohr, 1936), 116–17.

[188] For its messianic background, see Koester, "Messianic Exegesis," 23–34; for its eschatological significance, see J. D. M. Derrett, "Figtrees in the New Testament," *HeyJ* 14 (1973): 249–65.

[189] See the discussion in Telford, *Barren Temple,* 218–24.

[190] Ibid., 221. See also Str-B, 2.371. Against this view, Derrett claims that "one can hardly say that to be under the fig-tree is to be a Torah-student, for at that rate sleepy Arab camel-drivers would be Torah-students" ("Figtrees in the New Testament," 262). This throwaway remark does not take the passage seriously enough. One needs to interpret the text within its literary context. To be under the fig tree is also understood as a sign of peace and prosperity (1 Kgs 5:5; Mic 4:4; Zech 3:10). See the discussions in Barrett, *John,* 154 and Brown, *John,* 1.83.

[191] Schnackenburg, *John,* 1.315.

[192] For a discussion on this view, see C. F. D. Moule, "A Note on 'under the Fig Tree' in John 1.48, 50," *JTS* 5 (1954): 210–11. U. C. von Wahlde holds that this supernatural knowledge functions here as a "sign," just as it does in the story of the Samaritans in John 4 (*The Earliest Version of John's Gospel: Recovering the Gospel of Signs* [Wilmington, Del.: Michael Glazier, 1989], 71 n. 17).

[193] The titles—Son of God and King of Israel—essentially acknowledge Jesus as the Messiah; see the discussion in Bultmann, *John,* 104 n. 7.

knowledge evokes a similar response elsewhere in the Gospel. Jesus' supernatural knowledge about the Samaritan woman's personal life enables her
to recognize Jesus as the messianic prophet (4:16–20).[194] In sum, the short
dialogue between Jesus and Nathanael reveals both the identity of Jesus as
the Messiah and reaffirms the identity of Nathanael as a "true Israelite"
who is open to the revelation in Jesus.

Like Andrew in verse 41, Nathanael makes his confession of faith in
verse 49. Even though he gives more theologically significant titles to Jesus,
viz., Son of God (ὁ υἱὸς τοῦ θεοῦ) and king of Israel (βασιλεὺς . . . τοῦ
Ἰσραήλ), he continues to address Jesus as Rabbi.[195] The title Son of God is
a widely used Jewish expression to talk about the Messiah.[196] In the OT, the
anointed king was said to be God's son (see Pss 2:7; 89:20–27; 2 Sam
7:13–14). Both titles, Son of God and king of Israel, imply the identity of
Jesus as the Messiah according to the Jewish expectation.[197] In the Gospel
of John, the title Son of God expresses Jesus' unique intimacy with God
(see 1:14, 18; 3:16, 18).[198] This intimate relationship between the Father and
the Son is expressed in terms of love and mission.[199] But what is the significance of this title in 1:49? Does this title have the full Johannine christological meaning? Scholars differ in their views on this question. Some claim
that it has the full christological meaning.[200] From the narrative point of view,
Nathanael meets Jesus for the first time; hence, it seems natural to understand Nathanael's confession of faith within his Jewish religious background

---

[194] For other examples, see 6:70; 9:3; 11:4, 11; 13:10–11, 38.

[195] According to Brown (*John,* 1.83), "this is an element of historical reminis-
cence within the theological theme of increased insight."

[196] See the discussion in B. Byrne, *'Sons of God'— 'Seed of Abraham': A Study of
the Idea of the Sonship of God of All Christians in Paul Against the Jewish Background*
(Rome: Biblical Institute Press, 1979), 9–78; and J. J. Collins, *The Scepter and the
Star: The Messiahs of the Dead Sea Scrolls and Other Ancient Literature* (New York,
etc.: Doubleday, 1995), 154–72. For a different view, see J. A. Fitzmyer, "4Q246:
The 'Son of God' Document from Qumran," *Bib* 74 (1993): 153–74. Fitzmyer as-
serts that "per se, the titles ['Son of God' and 'Son of the Most High'] do not con-
note 'messiah' in the Old Testament" (ibid., 171). For the divine sonship of
Christians in the Johannine writings, see M. Vellanickal, *The Divine Sonship of
Christians in the Johannine Writings* (Rome: Biblical Institute Press, 1977).

[197] Barrett, *John,* 155. For these titles together, see Ps 2:6–7.

[198] For a detailed study of this title in the Gospel of John, see D. M. Smith, *The
Theology of the Gospel of John* (NTT; Cambridge: Cambridge University Press,
1995), 127–31.

[199] The Father loves the Son (e.g., 3:35 and 5:20); and the Son continues the
"works" (ἔργα) of the Father (e.g., 4:34; 5:17; 17:4).

[200] See Barrett, *John,* 154–55; Schnackenburg, *John,* 1.317–19; and Pancaro,
Law, 288–304.

and conditioned by his religious beliefs and traditions. "Nathanael has confessed his faith *only* in terms of Jewish messianic expectation."[201]

The faith generated by the miraculous power (here the supernatural
knowledge) of Jesus is not enough according to the Johannine Jesus (see
2:23–24). The confession made by Nathanael, evoked by the wonder of his
having been seen under the fig tree, is not sufficient. "Nathanael is chided
for the limitations of his faith, expressed through the confession of Jesus as
rabbi, Son of God and king of Israel (v. 49)."[202] The response of Jesus in
verse 50a, ὅτι εἶπόν σοι ὅτι εἶδόν σε ὑποκάτω τῆς συκῆς, πιστεύεις, "because I said to you, I saw you under the fig tree, you believe," whether the
expression is a question or an affirmation, is not to be taken as skeptical.[203]
The promise of Jesus, μείζω τούτων ὄψῃ, "You will see greater things"
(v. 50), confirms that Jesus recognizes and appreciates his initial faith. The
use of the singular σοι in verse 50 and the use of the plural ὑμῖν in verse 51
are very significant. Jesus makes a promise to Nathanael in particular in
verse 50 and to the disciples in general in verse 51.[204] By using ὑμῖν in
v. 51, "the narrator has Jesus reach out of the immediate situation of the
'you' of Nathanael to the various disciples who came to him with their
limited expressions of faith, and to the reader."[205] Hence, the promise made
by Jesus in verse 51 is not only to the characters (disciples) in the story but
also to the readers.[206] What did Jesus promise? "You will see heaven
opened and the angels of God ascending and descending upon the Son of
Man" (v. 51). What does this mean?

The opening of heaven symbolizes God's communication with humanity.[207] It is commonly agreed that John 1:51 alludes to the story of Jacob in

---

[201] Moloney, *Belief in the Word,* 72.

[202] Ibid., 73.

[203] For such "rebukes" in the Gospel, see 4:48. See also the discussion in
Schnackenburg, *John,* 1.319 and Moloney, *Belief in the Word,* 72–73.

[204] Verse 51 is often identified as an independent logion; see F. J. Moloney, *The
Johannine Son of Man* (2d ed.; Rome: LAS, 1978), 24–25; Brown, *John,* 1.88–89;
R. T. Fortna, *The Gospel of Signs: A Reconstruction of the Narrative Source Underlying
the Fourth Gospel* (Cambridge: Cambridge University Press, 1970), 179–89;
Neyrey, "Jacob Allusions," 586–89. However, it is fully integrated into its present
context. See the detailed discussion in P. Palatty, "The Meaning and Setting of the
Son of Man Logion in John 1:51," *ITS* 36 (1999): 21–36.

[205] Moloney, *Belief in the Word,* 74.

[206] According to Moloney, "the narrator has used the present tense of the verb
(καὶ λέγει αὐτῷ) to report direct speech of Jesus that reaches outside story time
into the plotted time of a promised future sight of the Son of Man" (*Belief in the
Word,* 76).

[207] Cf. Ps 78:23; Acts 10:11; Rev 4:1–3.

Gen 28:12.[208] In the Johannine scene, the focus is on a vision of a heavenly figure, as the angels ascend and descend not upon the ladder, but upon the Son of Man.[209] The title of the Son of Man (ὁ υἱὸς τοῦ ἀνθρώπου) in John is different from the Jewish and early Christian apocalyptic use of the figure of Son of Man. It designates the earthly life of Jesus, in which he shares continual communication with the Father in heaven.[210] Based on the traditions about Genesis 28:12 (the targums and midrashim), it has been suggested that Jesus manifests himself in 1:51 as the *shekinah* (dwelling) of God, the *merkabah* (chariot; cf. Ezek 1:4–25), the rock,[211] Bethel,[212] "the gate of heaven,"[213] or the glory of God.[214] Jesus is depicted as the mediator who brings communion between heaven and earth. In other words, Jesus is presented as the "locus of divine glory, the point of contact between heaven and earth."[215] The Johannine Jesus promises to his disciples that they will see God made manifest in Jesus, and they witness an ongoing revelation of God's presence in the life and mission of Jesus (chs. 2–21).

OLD TESTAMENT COVENANT MOTIFS IN JOHN 1:35–51

The central characteristics of Johannine discipleship traced in the narrative of John 1:35–51 reflect essential elements of the OT covenant relationship.

---

[208] For a detailed analysis on the Jacob allusions in John 1:51, see Neyrey, "Jacob Allusions," 586–605; see also C. F. Burney, *The Aramaic Origin of the Fourth Gospel* (Oxford: Clarendon Press, 1922), 115–16; H. Odeberg, *The Fourth Gospel Interpreted in Its Relation to Contemporaneous Religious Currents in Palestine and the Hellenistic-Oriental World* (Uppsala: Almqvist, 1929), 33–36; and Barrett, *John*, 155–56.

[209] D. Burkett claims that there is no unified pre-Christian Son of Man title and its titular use is multivalent in the NT and thus "the distinctive associations of the different categories of sayings must come from the context, not from the title itself" (*The Son of Man Debate: A History and Evaluation* [Cambridge: Cambridge University Press, 1999], 122).

[210] For this understanding, see Bultmann, *John*, 107; Moloney, *Son of Man*, 23–41; and C. C. Rowland, "John 1:51: Jewish Apocalyptic and Targumic Tradition," *NTS* 30 (1984): 498–507. For an interpretation of the "Son of Man" in John 1:51 as explaining the origin of Jesus, see C. Ham, "The Title 'Son of Man' in the Gospel of John," *SCJ* 1 (1998): 67–84.

[211] Brown, *John*, 1.90–91.

[212] See Schnackenburg, *John*, 1.320; O. Cullmann, "Die Berufung des Nathanael," *Angelos* 3 (1928): 2–5.

[213] Moloney, *Belief in the Word*, 74–75.

[214] Bultmann, *John*, 106.

[215] Brown, *John*, 1.91. There has been extensive discussion about the meaning and significance of 1:51. For a survey, see Moloney, *Son of Man*, 23–41; Neyrey, "Jacob Allusions," 589–605; and Palatty, "Meaning and Setting," 21–36.

Yahweh's choice and Israel's decision constituted the covenant relationship between Yahweh and Israel. This relationship is not a static "status" but a vocation that calls for ongoing choices and decisions on the part of Israel for Yahweh.[216] Similarly, the call stories in John 1 highlight discipleship as a journey made with Jesus that demands decisions on the part of the disciples in favor of the ongoing revelation of God in Jesus. The evangelist presents discipleship as a process of becoming, a process of growth.[217] This gradual evolving of the disciples' faith appears elsewhere in the gospel (6:66–71; 14:9). Discipleship implies knowledge of God, and it calls for a commitment. Like the election of Israel, discipleship is received as a gift from God. The similarities between Israel's vocation and that of the Johannine disciples are so striking that they deserve further investigation. In the table below, the OT covenant motifs found in the call stories are given in bold print.

The Old Testament Covenant Motifs in the Call Stories of John 1:35–51

	Third day: Story 1 (vv. 35–39)	Third day: Story 2 (vv. 40–42)	Fourth day: Story 3 (vv. 43–46)	Fourth day: Story 4 (vv. 45–50)
Characters	JB, disciples and Jesus (vv. 35–36)	Andrew and Simon Peter (vv. 40–41)	Philip from Bethsaida (v. 44)	Nathanael (v. 45)
Encounter	Two disciples follow Jesus (v. 37)	Jesus looks at Simon (v. 42)	Jesus finds Philip (v. 43)	Nathanael comes to Jesus (v. 47)
Dialogue	Dialogue (vv. 38–39) ποῦ μένεις;	———	———	Dialogue (vv. 47–50)
Invitation	Ἔρχεσθε καὶ ὄψεσθε [Jesus] (v. 39)	———	Ἀκολούθει μοι [Jesus] (v. 43)	Ἔρχου καὶ ἴδε [Philip] (v. 46)

[216] E. W. Nicholson, *God and His People: Covenant and Theology in the Old Testament* (Oxford: Clarendon Press, 1986), 147–48.

[217] The presentation of discipleship as a journey, a dynamic process, is not something peculiar to John. For the same notion in the Gospel of Mark, see Best, *Following Jesus.* See also Sweetland, *Our Journey with Jesus,* 13–35, and Donaldson, " 'Called to Follow,' " 67–77, esp. 69. But John has a different understanding of this dynamism. It is apparent in the unique way he narrates the "vocation stories" (compare Mark 1:16–20 with John 1:35–51). See also Chennattu, "On Becoming Disciples," 465–96.

Response	The disciples went and **abided** (μένω) with Jesus (v. 39)	———	———	———
Confession of faith in word	Εὑρήκαμεν τὸν Μεσσίαν **(v. 41)**	———	Ὃν ἔγραψεν Μωϋσῆς ἐν τῷ νόμῳ καὶ οἱ προφῆται εὑρήκαμεν (v. 45)	σὺ εἶ ὁ υἱὸς τοῦ θεοῦ, σὺ βασιλεὺς εἶ τοῦ Ἰσραήλ (v. 49)
Confession of faith in action	Andrew brings Peter to Jesus (v. 42)	———	Philip brings Nathanael (v. 46)	———
Identity of the disciple	———	**Renaming:** Simon–Kephas (v. 42)	———	**Reaffirming:** Nathanael—A true Israelite (v. 47)
Jesus' promise to the individuals	ὄψεσθε (v. 39)	σὺ κληθήσῃ Κηφᾶς (v. 42)	———	μείζω τούτων ὄψῃ (v. 50)

The promise of Jesus to all the disciples   ὄψεσθε τὸν οὐρανὸν ἀνεῳγότα καὶ τοὺς ἀγγέλους τοῦ θεοῦ ἀναβαίνοντας καὶ καταβαίνοντας ἐπὶ τὸν υἱὸν τοῦ ἀνθρώπου, "You shall see heaven opened, and the angels of God ascending and descending upon the Son of man" (v. 51): **the divine presence in Jesus.**

The Abiding Motif (μένω)

Johannine discipleship begins with an encounter with Jesus. As we have seen, the invitation to "come" and the promise "you shall see" are essential aspects in the process of becoming disciples. The disciples are also called to enter into a personal relationship with Jesus. It is their abiding (μένω) with Jesus that, according to Johannine theology, gives them a deeper insight into the identity of Jesus as the Messiah.[218] The verb μένω is very significant in the covenantal language of the OT (LXX). Edward Malatesta, after a detailed study of the use of the verb μένω in the LXX, contends that "the combination of μένειν and its cognates with the Covenant, the commandments, and with Yahweh Himself connotes *a relationship of fidelity to and communion with Yahweh,* and that such expressions prepare for the Johannine use of the verb."[219] The covenant relationship

---

[218] Brown, *John,* 1.79.

[219] E. Malatesta, *Interiority and Covenant: A Study of εἶναι ἐν and μένειν ἐν in the First Letter of Saint John* (AnBib 69; Rome: Biblical Institute Press, 1978), 60. The italics are mine.

between Yahweh and Israel demands that the latter abide in obedience to the Law (LXX Deut 27:26) or abide in Yahweh (LXX Isa 30:18). The Johannine story relates that the first two disciples ask Jesus where he abides (v. 38); the disciples then abide with Jesus. The confession of faith in verse 41 ("we have found the Messiah") suggests the symbolic meaning of their query in verse 38 ("where do you abide?"), since the object of their seeing is not Jesus' home or village but the revelation of Jesus' identity as the Messiah. What is the theological significance of this enquiry? Jesus is not a stranger, as he has been introduced to the disciples as the Lamb of God.[220] The disciples of John the Baptist, after hearing the testimony of their master, decide to begin a journey with Jesus, but they are not blind followers of Jesus. They want to know where Jesus abides.[221] Those who abide in (οἱ ἐμμένοντες ἐν) Yahweh and in the Torah are considered to be the blessed (μακάριοι, LXX Isa 30:18). To abide in Yahweh entails a relationship of deep communion and constant communication with Yahweh. The witness of John the Baptist suggests that Jesus abides in God and in communion with God; and throughout the gospel, Jesus reveals his intimate relationship with the Father to the disciples. At the outset of the call stories, by inviting the disciples to abide in Jesus and in his words (cf. 4:40; 6:27; 6:56; 8:31–32) and making it an integral part of the process of becoming a disciple of Jesus (1:35–51; 4:4–42), the Fourth Evangelist presents discipleship in terms of an everlasting and abiding covenant relationship with God.

Knowledge of Jesus as the Messiah

The disciples display a progressing understanding of Jesus as they attribute different messianic titles to him.

Rabbi (vv. 38, 49)

The disciples address Jesus as rabbi, a significant teacher. The title occurs in verse 38 and in verse 49. Does it imply that there is no difference in their perception of the identity of Jesus from verse 38 to verse 49? The evangelist has the disciples address Jesus as rabbi (ῥαββί) in the Book of Signs[222] and as

---

[220] According to the synoptic call stories, there is nobody to introduce Jesus to the disciples (e.g., Mark 1:16–20).

[221] X. Léon-Dufour, *Lecture de l'Évangile selon Jean* (4 vols.; Paris: Seuil, 1988–1996), 1.189.

[222] See 1:38, 49; 3:2, 26; 4:31; 6:25; 9:2; 11:8. No one addresses Jesus as rabbi after ch. 11, except on one occasion when Mary calls the risen Jesus as Ῥαββουνι (20:16).

Lord (κύριε) in the Book of Glory.[223] The author is not just recounting what happened in the history; this choice is deliberate on the evangelist's part to bring out the progressive nature of discipleship.[224] Addressing Jesus as rabbi in verses 38 and 49 indicates that the call stories are only the beginning of disciples' journey with Jesus.

Messiah (vv. 41, 45, 49)

There is a gradual progression in the way Andrew recognizes Jesus the rabbi (v. 38) as the messiah (v. 41). His understanding of messiahship is not clear at the present moment of the narrative. Similarly, Philip's presentation of Jesus as the one "of whom Moses in the law and the prophets wrote" (v. 45) probably indicates that Jesus is recognized as the fulfillment of the whole OT.[225] John 5:39 says that the Scriptures testify on behalf of Jesus, in 5:46 that Moses wrote about him, and in 6:45 that Jesus is the fulfillment of what is written in the prophets. The one described in the Mosaic law could well refer to the Prophet like Moses of Deut 18:15–18. Thus, Jesus is identified as the Prophet like Moses.[226] In fact, the one described by the prophets is difficult to identify. It could be Elijah (cf. Mal 4:5). If we take these three titles—Messiah, Prophet like Moses, Elijah—attributed to Jesus by the first disciples, we see that the disciples of John the Baptist are identifying Jesus under the same three titles that the Baptist had rejected for himself in verses 19–28.[227] As already mentioned, the titles Son of God and King of Israel (v. 49) identify Jesus as the Messiah according to Jewish expectations. The disciples do not go beyond the Jewish understanding of the Messiah. Their faith has not yet grasped the reality of the Johannine Jesus.[228] However, the disciples progress in their understanding of Jesus.

The knowledge of God, a recurring theme in the prophets (Jer 1:5; Hos 2:20; 4:1, 6; 5:4), is always implied in Israel's covenant relationship with Yahweh (cf. Exod 29:45–46; Jer 9:24; Isa 11:2). It implies a profound comprehension of the right relationship with Yahweh as their God. Lack of this knowledge is understood as a failure to live up to the covenant relationship. The prophet Isaiah, in his oracles against the people of Judah, points out

---

[223] Only on two occasions is Jesus addressed by the disciples as Lord before ch. 11 (6:68; 9:38). Out of a total of thirty-nine, thirty-five occurrences of κύριος are in chs. 11–14 and 20–21.

[224] Brown, *John*, 1.75.

[225] For the synoptic comparison, see Brown, *John*, 1.86.

[226] Ibid.

[227] This observation is made by Brown, who thinks, "perhaps this is too neat"; see *John*, 1.86. See also Mark 6:14–16; 8:27–30.

[228] For this argument, see Moloney, *Belief in the Word*, 53–76.

their lack of knowledge as a moral failure (Isa 1:3). Other examples include Jer 4:22; 5:4; 22:15–16; Hos 4:6. The Fourth Evangelist makes the clear distinction between the "unbelieving world," which does not know the λόγος (1:10), the Father (8:55), and the Spirit (14:17), on the one hand, and the disciples, who know Jesus—the Messiah (1:42) and the Holy One of God (6:69), the Father (14:7), and the Spirit (14:17) on the other. As the OT covenant relationship presupposes a mutual knowledge between Yahweh and the people of Israel (Exod 29:45–46; Jer 9:24; Isa 11:2), the Johannine Jesus also makes similar claims about his disciples: "I know my own and my own know me" (10:14). In the call stories, Andrew, Philip, and Nathanael show a progression in their perception of Jesus' identity. This progressive theological understanding of Jesus is indicated by the different christological titles in John 1. The first disciples give witness to their knowledge of Jesus and proclaim their faith in him, but the full implications of their proclamation are realized only later as they continue their journey with Jesus.

Disciples Are Called to Witness

The effect of staying (μένω) with Jesus results in action, viz., witnessing (*words*) and bringing other people to Jesus (*actions*). Andrew confesses his faith in Jesus, "We have found the Messiah," and brings Simon to Jesus. Similarly, Philip brings Nathanael to Jesus after giving testimony to Jesus, "We have found him of whom Moses in the Law and also the Prophets wrote, Jesus, son of Joseph, from Nazareth." The same pattern is found in the story of the Samaritan woman in John 4.[229] Once she accepts the revelation of Jesus, the Samaritan takes the initiative in the mission of proclaiming and bringing others to Jesus. She, like Philip, fulfills the Johannine characteristics of a disciple by giving testimony to the people in the city and inviting them to "come and see" Jesus. She becomes a model of discipleship in sharp contrast to Nicodemus, who is startled by Jesus' revelation and disappears into the shadows.[230] For the Johannine Jesus, it is extremely

---

[229] John 4 has a structure almost identical to John 1:35–51. The Samaritan woman also makes a faith journey like the first disciples in John 1. Her call story, which takes place outside Judaism, is of importance for the Johannine community as they consisted of both Jewish and Gentile Christians. It is beyond the scope of this book to pursue this suggestion further. It has been discussed at length in the studies of Cullmann, *Johannine Circle;* Brown, *Community.*

[230] M. Pazdan considers the Samaritan woman a model of "mature discipleship" while Nicodemus represents "initial discipleship" ("Nicodemus and the Samaritan Woman: Contrasting Models of Discipleship," *BTB* 17 [1987]: 145–48).

important that the disciples act like "apostles" and give testimony to him.[231] Similarly, "giving testimony" in terms of handing down traditions for future generations is another important element in the covenant relationship with Yahweh. Moses entrusts the Law to the Levitical priests who carried the ark of the covenant and commands them to read it publicly to the whole people of Israel on the Feast of Tabernacles (Deut 31:9–13, 24–27). The Israelites were supposed to pass on what they had seen, heard, and experienced, viz., God's intervention in their history, to future generations (Deut 6:20–25; 11:1–9).[232] By underscoring the importance of testimony, the evangelist highlights yet another element of a covenant-type relationship between Jesus and his first disciples. This aspect of the covenant relationship is developed more forcefully in the farewell discourses (15:27; 17:20–21), where Jesus insists that the disciples should bear witness to him.

Name-giving/Renaming Aspect of the Stories

Two of the call stories have an element of either renaming (1:42), in the case of Simon, or affirming (1:47), in the case of Nathanael. Jesus looks at Simon and calls him Κηφᾶς and Jesus affirms Nathanael as a "true Israelite, in whom there is no guile." Receiving new names is very common in the biblical traditions. The new names of the individuals express their new personality, status, and role. Examples include Abram's becoming Abraham (Gen 17:5), Jacob's becoming Israel (Gen 32:28), and Simon's becoming Peter (John 1:42; Matt 16:18). In each of these cases, the reception of the new name underlines the "election motif" in the OT and has a direct relation to the role the person so designated will play in salvation history.

Name-giving in the OT is also linked to the covenant motif. Abram's name, for example, is changed to Abraham, and Sarai becomes Sarah, after the institution of the covenant with God (Gen 17:1–22). The theme of election is closely associated with an element of possession in the covenant

---

See also R. C. White, "The Nicodemites and the Cost of Discipleship," *RTR* 56 (1997): 14–27; D. A. Lee, *The Symbolic Narratives of the Fourth Gospel* (Sheffield: JSOT Press, 1994), 65–66. On the Samaritan woman as a model and challenge for the twenty-first century disciples, see R. Chennattu, "Women in the Mission of the Church: An Interpretation of John 4," *VJTR* 65 (2001): 760–73. For a detailed study of John 4, see Okure, *Johannine Approach to Mission*.

[231] Even though the noun ἀπόστολος does not appear in John's Gospel (except in 13:16, where ἀπόστολος does not refer to the disciples), the disciples are sent out by Jesus (17:18) and they act like apostles (1:42, 46; 4:29, etc.).

[232] See the discussion in Lacomara, "Deuteronomy and the Farewell Discourse," 81–82.

relationship. The theme of Yahweh's closeness and mutual possession is expressed well in Deut 7:6: "For you are a people holy to Yahweh your God; Yahweh your God has chosen you, to be God's treasured possession (סְגֻלָּה), out of all peoples that are upon the face of the earth." The expression "Yahweh your God" as indicating mutual possession is a recurring theme in the Book of Deuteronomy.[233] The Johannine Jesus makes similar claims about his disciples (10:14), and Jesus refers to the disciples as "his own" (τοὺς ἰδίους) which implies their mutual belonging (13:1).

Discipleship is Based on Promises

The Johannine call stories contain many promises. The first story begins with an invitation and a promise from Jesus, "Come and you shall see" (1:39). The second story concludes with another promise, this time from Jesus to Simon, "You shall be called Kephas" (1:42). Jesus then makes a promise to Nathanael, "You shall see greater things than these" (1:50). The capping of the narrative is accomplished by the final promise of Jesus to all the disciples, "You will see heaven opened and the angels of God ascending and descending upon the Son of Man" (1:51). Jesus promises that the disciples shall see (ὄψεσθε) the manifestation of God in and through the mission of Jesus. The verb ὁράω has a rich theological meaning in John, and can refer to an insight stemming from an experience of Jesus. This promise of Jesus (v. 51) seems to imply a deepening experience as the disciples receive an ever-greater revelation of God in Jesus. Both the act of promising and the content of Jesus' promise in 1:51 remind the readers of OT covenant promises. Yahweh had made many promises to Israel. Yahweh promises to dwell among the people of Israel and asks them to make a tabernacle for him (Exod 25:8). God will be in their midst and dwells among them (Exod 29:45–46; cf. also Num 14:14; Deut 12:11). The indwelling presence of Yahweh with the people of Israel symbolized by the tabernacle is a sign of their covenant status, and the tabernacle reminds the people constantly of their covenant with Yahweh.[234] It is against this background that we interpret the promise of Jesus in 1:51, that he will make the divine presence of Yahweh visible. The use of the future tense, "You shall see" (ὄψεσθε), brings a dimension of "not yet" into the faith experience of the disciples. This faith is not merely

---

[233] The expression "Yahweh your God" appears more than three hundred times in Deuteronomy; see S. R. Driver, *Deuteronomy* (3d ed.; ICC; Edinburgh: T&T Clark, 1902), lxxix.

[234] See Pryor, *John*, 158. For a detailed study, see R. E. Clements, *God and Temple: The Idea of the Divine Presence in Ancient Israel* (Oxford/Philadelphia: Fortress, 1965).

the outcome of something that the disciples have found (vv. 41, 45), but it is a gift (3:27; 6:44–45; 15:16). Like the election of the people of Israel, the call to discipleship is a gift from God.

CONCLUSION

The first episode of the public ministry of Jesus (1:35–51) is dedicated to an account of the call of disciples. This "beginning" suggests that the evangelist sets an agenda for the presentation of discipleship in the gospel as a whole. The discipleship motif is developed gradually and progressively as the Johannine story unfolds. The call stories uncover the initial stage of the journey of the first disciples, and in doing so, the evangelist employs elements of the OT covenant relationship.[235] On the basis of this study of 1:35–51, we can reasonably conclude that, from the beginning of the Johannine story, the presentation of discipleship is associated with the covenant relationship as it is presented in the OT. Our initial investigation suggests that the evangelist uses the occasion of the call stories to present a paradigm of discipleship as a covenant relationship. If such is the case, this paradigm should appear elsewhere in the gospel, especially in the farewell discourses, the only place where Jesus' teaching is directed entirely to the disciples before his death (chs. 13–17), and in the final encounter between Jesus and the disciples after his resurrection (chs. 20–21).

---

[235] See Chennattu, "On Becoming Disciples," 489–96.

TWO

THE OLD TESTAMENT COVENANT
MOTIF AND JOHN 13–17

COVENANT IN THE OLD TESTAMENT

The covenant metaphor (בְּרִית) is the principal image used in the OT to define the distinctive relationship between Yahweh and the people of Israel.[1] "Covenant" is a rendering for בְּרִית. Scholars recognize the close link between Akkadian *biritu* ("bond" or "binding") and בְּרִית.[2] If this is true, then בְּרִית ("bond," "fetter") describes a binding relationship between the partners. The same idea of "binding," "putting together" is suggested by συνθήκη.[3] But διαθήκη, "will" or "testament," the word commonly used in the NT, underscores the obligatory aspect of a covenant.[4] The biblical

---

[1] See the discussion in D. J. McCarthy, *Old Testament Covenant: A Survey of Current Opinions* (GPT; Oxford: Basil Blackwell, 1972), 1–9; D. N. Freedman, "Divine Commitment and Human Obligation," *Int* 18 (1964): 419; Nicholson, *God and His People,* viii; S. L. McKenzie, *Covenant* (UBT; St. Louis, Mo.: Chalice Press, 2000), 4–9. See also W. Eichrodt, *Theologie des Alten Testaments* (3 vols; Leipzig: J. G. Hinrichs, 1933–1939). All the references in this study are to the English translation, *Theology of the Old Testament* (vol. 1; trans. J. A. Baker; OTL; Philadelphia: Westminster Press, 1961). Eichrodt did not differentiate among the Abrahamic, Mosaic, and Davidic covenants in his treatment of the theme. See also the pioneering works of G. E. Mendenhall, *Law and Covenant in Israel and the Ancient Near East* (Pittsburgh: The Biblical Colloquium, 1955); K. Baltzer, *Das Bundesformular* (Neukirchen: Neukirchener Verlag, 1960), or the English translation, *The Covenant Formulary in Old Testament, Jewish, and Early Christian Writings* (trans. D. E. Green; Philadelphia: Fortress, 1971).

[2] For the OT term בְּרִית, see the discussion in G. Quell, "διαθήκη," *TDNT* 2.106–24.

[3] For example, Philo uses συνθήκη instead of διαθήκη for treaty and covenant, see *Congr.* 78; *Legat.* 37; QG 2.676.

[4] For the different usages of διαθήκη, see also the discussion in J. Behm, "διαθήκη," *TDNT* 2.124–34.

metaphor of covenant בְּרִית/διαθήκη signifies and implies a binding relationship based on commitment.

COVENANT: ITS ORIGIN AND HISTORICAL DEVELOPMENT

The origin and historical development of the covenant idea in ancient Israel are disputed questions. Even a review of the various opinions would go beyond the scope of this study. The "biblical chronology" of the OT narratives suggests that Yahweh made a covenant with Noah that applies to all future generations (Gen 6:18; 9:9–10), later with Abraham (Gen 15:18; 17:7), and then with Israel through Moses (Exod 24; Deut 5:3; 29:1). In the history of Israel, as presented in the OT, there are also many references to renewals of the covenant with God (Exod 34; Josh 24; Jer 31; Ezek 16).

It seems possible that, long before there was a nation of Israel, the idea of covenant developed as an extension of family relationships in the manner of the covenant treaties practiced in the Ancient Near East.[5] But the use of covenant imagery to describe the relationship between God and Israel was introduced, elaborated, and made a central theological motif of the OT by the author(s) of Deuteronomy and the Deuteronomistic history in the late seventh or early sixth century.[6] From the perspective of the JEDP traditions,[7] most of the references to a covenant between God and Israel are found in the priestly tradition and the sections assigned to the Deuteronomistic Historian. The three references to the covenant in the Pentateuch outside the priestly and Deuteronomistic traditions, viz., Gen 15, Exod 19–24 and Exod 34, are relatively late texts, and are dependent on Deuteronomy for their covenant setting.[8] Both the Priestly tradition and

---

[5] See the discussion in F. M. Cross, *From Epic to Canon: History and Literature in Ancient Israel* (Baltimore/London: Johns Hopkins University Press, 1998), 3–21. See also McKenzie, *Covenant,* 11–24.

[6] McKenzie, *Covenant,* 16–24. See also the discussion in Nicholson, *God and His People,* 191–217. M. Noth coined the term Deuteronomistic History, which embraces the Book of Deuteronomy plus Joshua, Judges, 1 and 2 Samuel, and 1 and 2 Kings (*Überlieferungsgeschichtliche Studien* [Halle: Max Niemeyer, 1943]). Noth's book is now available in English: *The Deuteronomistic History* [2d ed.; JSOTSup 15; Sheffield: Sheffield Academic Press, 1991]).

[7] The Yahwist tradition (J) goes back to tenth to ninth century B.C.E.; the Elohist tradition (E) is dated ninth to eighth century B.C.E.; the tradition of the Deuteronomistic Historian (D) is dated seventh or early sixth century B.C.E.; and the Priestly tradition (P) is dated sixth to fifth century B.C.E.; see McKenzie, *Covenant,* 16–17.

[8] For those who argue that Gen 15 reflects a knowledge of the Pentateuch and who date the chapter during or after the exilic period at the end of sixth century

the Deuteronomistic Historian seem to have been situated in the period of the Babylonian exile (ca. 586–539 B.C.E.) after the destruction of both Israel (722/21 B.C.E.) and Judah (586 B.C.E.) as independent nations.[9] That the notion of "the covenant as a full-blown theological concept was a late arrival in Israel is substantially vindicated."[10] Theologically, what seems to be behind the covenant metaphor is "the distinctiveness of Israel's faith."[11] The use of covenant imagery to describe the relationship between God and Israel becomes current in the history of Israel during the exilic period, when its people had no identity as a nation. Thus, according to Ernest W. Nicholson, "'covenant' is the central expression of the distinctive faith of Israel as 'the people of Yahweh,' children of God by adoption and free decision rather than by nature or necessity."[12] Through Israel's covenant with God, she is bound in relationship to a God who makes an unshared, exclusive, and absolute claim upon her loyalty in worship and social life as God's own people.

MEANING, NATURE, AND THE TYPES OF COVENANTS IN THE OLD TESTAMENT

Scholars agree that the idea of covenant in the OT is not univocal. It is almost impossible to catalogue all the interpretations of the various covenants under one description or definition. There appear to be three kinds of covenants in the Bible: (1) covenants between God and humans (e.g., Gen 6:18; 9:9–10; 15:18; 17:7); (2) covenants between humans (e.g., Gen 14:13; 21:27; 26:26–31; 31:44–50); (3) covenants made by humans or Yahweh with things or animals.[13] As Dennis J. McCarthy aptly observed, "a

---

or later, see J. Van Seters, *Abraham in History and Tradition* (New Haven/London: Yale University Press, 1975), 249–78; J. Ha, *Genesis 15: A Theological Compendium of Pentateuchal History* (BZAW 181; Berlin/New York: Walter de Gruyter, 1989). For the late dating of the covenant references in Exod 19–24 and Exod 34, see L. Perlitt, *Bundestheologie im Alten Testament* (WMANT 36; Neukirchen: Neukirchener Verlag, 1969), 167–232; McKenzie, *Covenant,* 16–22.

[9] McKenzie, *Covenant,* 17.
[10] Nicholson, *God and His People,* 188.
[11] Ibid., 191–217.
[12] Ibid., viii.
[13] Job makes a covenant with the stones (Job 5:23), with his eyes (31:1), with Leviathan (40:28); the leaders of Jerusalem make a covenant with death (Isa 28:15, 18); Yahweh makes a covenant with day and night (Jer 33:20, 25), with the beasts (Ezek 34:25; Hos 2:20).

true appreciation of covenant in all its richness must recognize the variety within the covenant traditions themselves."[14]

This study of the OT covenant motif focuses on the covenant between humans and between God and humans. Narratives concerning covenants among human partners include covenants between leaders of two ethnic groups—Abraham and Abimelech (Gen 21:25–32)—and between king and people—David and the elders of Israel (1 Chr 11:3). Covenant is also made in the context of friendship and love. Jonathan made a covenant with David by stripping himself of his robe and giving it to David as a sign of his love (1 Sam 18:1–5; 23:18).

The covenant between God and the people of Israel can be looked at from two perspectives: (1) the unconditional covenants—the covenant between God and Israel centered on God's promises; (2) the conditional covenants—the covenant between God and Israel focused on human obligations. David Noel Freedman referred to them as "covenant of divine commitment" and "covenant of human obligation," respectively.[15] The cardinal example for the first type of covenant can be found in God's covenant with Abraham in Gen 15:18–21 and 17:7–8. Other examples include God's covenant with Noah and his descendants (Gen 9:9–11), with the high priest Phinehas and his descendants (Num 25:10–13), and with the house of David (2 Sam 7:1–17; 1 Chr 17; Ps 89; Jer 33:21). Freedman observes that, in each of these examples, the covenant of divine commitment is preceded by an act of faith expressing the mutual trust of the covenant partners: Abraham believes in the word of God; Noah builds the ark; Phinehas slays the sinners; David expresses his earnest desire to build a house for God.[16] Once God makes the covenant, however, the divine commitment is unilateral and unconditional, and the humans are then the beneficiaries of God's unconditional promises.

The principal example for the second type of covenant is God's covenant with the people of Israel mediated by Moses at Mount Sinai/Horeb (Exod 19–24). Other examples belonging to this group are the many covenant renewals related in the Pentateuch and the historical books: the renewal of the covenant in the plain of Moab (Deut 28:69) and at Shechem (Josh 24:25) as well as in the days of Jehoiada (2 Kgs 11:17; 2 Chr 29:10), Josiah (2 Kgs 23:3), and Ezra (Ezra 10:3). Even though the covenant mediated by Moses at Sinai seems to be based on the divine promises to the

---

[14] McCarthy, *Old Testament Covenant,* 89.
[15] For a detailed discussion, see Freedman, "Divine Commitment," 419–31.
[16] Ibid., 422.

Fathers, the emphasis is on human obligations in maintaining the covenant relationship with God.

The two types of covenant between God and Israel, however, are not incompatible with each other. Although they differ as to which aspect is emphasized, all covenants between God and Israel include both divine promises as well as human responses. As we mentioned above, in unconditional covenants human responses precede the covenant making. In conditional covenants human commitment to observe the covenant law is an imperative for the preservation and continuity of the covenant. These two types of covenant, therefore, capture well the two-sided nature of a covenant relationship: Yahweh's election of, and commitment to, Israel, and Israel's obligation to be obedient to Yahweh's commandments. The covenant between God and Israel is then bilateral in nature (cf. Exod 24:3–8; Deut 26:17–19; Jer 31:31–34; 32:36–41).[17]

COVENANT FORMS IN ISRAELITE TRADITIONS

A large variety of forms was known and practiced in ancient Israel to create and to express covenants with Yahweh as well as with human partners.[18] Let us focus our attention on the most important covenant, namely, the Sinai covenant narrated in Exod 19:1–24:11, the first account of covenant making between Yahweh and the people of Israel at Sinai, and the narration of its renewal in the Book of Deuteronomy. The Sinai covenant is generally recognized as the covenant par excellence, fundamental to any investigation of the covenant motif in the OT.[19] Dennis J. McCarthy describes the Sinai covenant as "the oldest and certainly the most massive and important expression of the covenant concept which has come down to us."[20] The Book of Deuteronomy is "pre-dominantly a covenant document" and the center from which the OT covenant motif emanates.[21]

Whether or not the OT covenant reflects a vassal-treaty form has been a subject of lively debate. The elements of the Hittite vassal-treaty that George E. Mendenhall used for his pioneering study to compare the OT

---

[17] See the discussion in Nicholson, *God and His People,* 210–15.

[18] J. Pedersen, *Israel: Its Life and Culture I–II* (4 vols.; London: Oxford University Press, 1964), 1.263–310.

[19] D. J. McCarthy, *Treaty and Covenant* (AnBib 21A; Rome: Biblical Institute Press, 1978), 243–76.

[20] Ibid., 277.

[21] McCarthy, *Old Testament Covenant,* 22.

covenants can be summarized in the following way: (1) the preamble that introduces the sovereign and identifies the author of the covenant; (2) the historical prologue that describes previous relations between the contracting parties; (3) the stipulations that outline the nature of the community formed by the covenant; (4) the provision of a document of the treaty that is meant to be deposited in the temple for periodic public readings; (5) the list of gods who witness the treaty; (6) the curse and blessing formulae, i.e., curses corresponding to infidelity and blessings to fidelity to the covenant norms.[22] It has been widely accepted that the Decalogue, through the sequence, preamble, historical prologue, and law, follows a treaty form.[23] What we have in Exodus is a theophany followed by the commands of Yahweh, the Decalogue. By itself the Decalogue consists of the declaration, "I am Yahweh, who brought you out of Egypt, out of the house of bondage," and the series of ten direct commands. "The form of the Sinai story in Ex 19–24 as it stands today in the MT does not bear out the contention that the story reflects an organization according to the covenant form. It reveals an idea of covenant which is somewhat different from that exemplified in the treaty."[24] Dennis J. McCarthy argues therefore that the Decalogue, lacking the essential curse and blessing formula of the treaty, does not reflect the treaty genre.[25]

The Mosaic covenant motif found in Deuteronomy seems to have been influenced by the suzerainty-treaty form of the second and first millennia. The covenant in Deuteronomy has the following sequence: (1) historical and parenetic introduction (4:44–11:32); (2) laws or stipulations (12:1– 26:15); (3) conclusion: oath, rite, blessing, and curses (26:16–19; 28:1–68). This seems to reflect a structure similar to a treaty.[26] "Even though both the ancient Near East treaty form and the OT covenant form imply 'a binding agreement between two or more parties', the OT covenant form is not a treaty form according to the contract form of the ANE [Ancient Near East]."[27] The suzerain vassal-treaty model is inadequate for the biblical covenant metaphor, as it fails to explain God's concern for human welfare and

---

[22] Mendenhall, *Law and Covenant*, 31–34.

[23] For those who accept the basic identification, see Mendenhall, *Law and Covenant*, 24–50; Freedman, "Divine Commitment," 419–31; A. Kapelrud, "Some Recent Points of View on the Time and Origin of the Decalogue," *ST* 18 (1964): 81–90.

[24] McCarthy, *Treaty and Covenant*, 256.

[25] Ibid., 245–56. See also McCarthy, *Old Testament Covenant*, 15–19.

[26] McCarthy, *Treaty and Covenant*, 157–87.

[27] McCarthy, *Old Testament Covenant*, 33–34.

justice found at the heart of the OT covenant stipulations.[28] In the Book of Deuteronomy, "a covenantal formulation becomes a speech, a farewell address or, better, a testamentary discourse, for in it the ideal leader is represented as leaving the people its heritage, a defined and committed relation to its God."[29] The OT covenant is not a treaty in terms of a binding contract but a biblical metaphor that expresses a kinship relationship, God's unique relationship with Israel and Israel's to God. The essence of the covenant relationship with God is therefore friendship and fidelity. This is manifested in covenant making ceremonies and covenant renewal rituals. For example, the ceremonial form of the covenant in Josh 24 can be outlined as follows:[30] the people gathered in the presence of God at Shechem (24:1); prophetic proclamation of God's election and guidance of the people (24:2–13); [31] a call to obedience and a call to decision (24:14–15); a warning of the consequences of the decision (24:16–20); the people's response of total allegiance to Yahweh (24:21–24); a ceremony sealing the covenant (24:25–28).

The challenge to accept Yahweh and abandon other gods formed a climactic moment in ceremonies of covenant renewal in the OT (e.g., Josh 24:14–15). Joshua, after narrating to the people what Yahweh had done for their ancestors (24:2–13), challenges the people to choose (בַּחֲרוּ) between Yahweh and other gods (24:14–15). The people are called to enter into a proper relationship with Yahweh that includes an attitude of reverence and awe, and total (תָּמִים) service to Yahweh in response to the mighty works that Yahweh has performed on their behalf. Five imperatives in these two verses: fear (יְראוּ) Yahweh, serve (עִבְדוּ) Yahweh (bis), put aside (הָסִירוּ) other gods, choose (בַּחֲרוּ) Yahweh, emphasize that the people are called to decision.[32] All the OT covenant stipulations have the same function: a call to a decision accepting an exclusive relationship with Yahweh (cf. Exod 23:20–33; Deut 26:16–27:26).

---

[28] J. H. Tigay, *Deuteronomy:* דברים (JPSToC; Philadelphia/Jerusalem: Jewish Publication Society, 1996), xiv–xv.

[29] McCarthy, *Treaty and Covenant,* 187.

[30] I basically follow with some variations the structure proposed by T. C. Butler (*Joshua* [WBC 7; Waco, Texas: Word, 1983], 266).

[31] Joshua addresses the entire assembly by proclaiming, "Thus says the Lord." This introduction seems to echo the prophetic messenger speeches; see the discussion in J. Hayes, *Old Testament Form Criticism* (San Antonio: Trinity University Press, 1974), 149–55.

[32] For the dialogical structure and the literary unity of Josh 24:1–25, see C. H. Giblin, "Structural Patterns in Joshua 24:1–25," *CBQ* 26 (1964): 50–69. See also the discussion in R. G. Boling and G. E. Wright, *Joshua: A New Translation with Notes and Commentary* (AB 6; Garden City, N.Y.: Doubleday, 1982), 527–45.

Public consent is an integral element of the OT covenant renewal ceremonies. Before the covenant making in Exod 24, the people of Israel repeatedly confessed their acceptance of Yahweh. The confessions of the Israelites display a gradual progression as they repeat their promise: "all the words that the Lord has spoken we will do" (24:3); "all that the Lord has spoken we will do, and we will be obedient" (24:7). Similarly, before the renewal of the covenant at Shechem, the people repeatedly confessed their loyalty to Yahweh: "we will serve the Lord" (Josh 24:21); "the Lord our God we will serve, and him we will obey" (Josh 24:24). These declarations of commitment to Yahweh are followed by the covenant making ritual both in Exod 24:8 and in Josh 24:25–28.

COVENANT MAKING RITUALS IN ISRAELITE TRADITIONS

A covenant between humans can be ratified by a handshake or a kiss in ancient Israel. One gives one's hand to the king in order to confirm that one enters into a covenant (2 Kgs 10:15). When Zedekiah made his covenant with Nebuchadnezzar, it was confirmed by handshakes (Ezek 17:18; see also Ezra 10:19). The covenant between Samuel and Saul was confirmed when Samuel kissed Saul after having anointed him (1 Sam 10:1).[33]

In the covenant between God and humans, some kind of liturgical ceremony or ritual brings the covenant relationship into effect, whether it be a sacrifice involving a blood rite or a covenant meal, or a theophany. These rituals are meant to establish or renew a certain union and communion between God and Israel. They are therefore known as "communion sacrifices" (זְבָחִים שְׁלָמִים, Exod 24:5).[34] The blood rite or the sharing of blood symbolizes

---

[33] Pedersen, *Israel*, 1.304–8.

[34] See the discussion in McCarthy, *Treaty and Covenant*, 243–76, 294–98. In the communion sacrifice (זֶבַח שְׁלָמִים), the victim is offered or sacrificed and shared among God, the priest, and the offerer or worshiper. It functions as a tribute to God to establish or to renew the relationship with God (cf. Lev 3:1–17). Therefore, שְׁלָמִים or זֶבַח שְׁלָמִים is sometimes known as "covenant sacrifice" or "covenant meal" (see Exod 24:5; Deut 12:7, 18; 1 Sam 9:11–14, 22–24). For the origin and the meaning of the communion sacrifice (זֶבַח שְׁלָמִים), see R. de Vaux, *Studies in Old Testament Sacrifice* (Cardiff: University of Wales Press, 1964), 37–51. See also the discussion in N. H. Snaith, "Sacrifices in the Old Testament," *VT* 7 (1957): 308–17. For the practice of "blood covenants" between individuals, and between worshipers and their gods in the religions of the Semites, see W. R. Smith, *The Religion of the Semites: The Fundamental Institutions* (New York: Schocken Books: 1972), 312–26.

the sharing of the same life. A new relationship is constituted between God and the people as though they were related by blood.[35] An important covenant is frequently inaugurated by a common meal. The tradition of a covenant meal implies "admission into the family circle of another."[36] Food moreover gives life and strengthens the person. The people became covenant partners with God through a meal taken by their representatives before God (Exod 24:1, 9–11). The OT elsewhere attests that eating a common meal can validate a covenant when it is made between humans. For example, when Abimelech and the captain of his army sought Isaac and asked him to make a covenant with them, Isaac prepared a meal for them (Gen 26:26–30), or when Jacob made a covenant with Laban, Jacob offered a large common sacrificial meal (Gen 31:43–50). A particularly intimate covenant is therefore called a "covenant of salt" (Num 18:19; 2 Chr 13:5). It is understood that the ratification of a covenant by such means was based upon the assumption that a special bond of friendship and mutual acceptance is created among those who share a common meal.[37] In a theophany, "the symbolic presence of the recognized sovereign means *ipso facto* union."[38] Hence, it seems reasonable that the laws in the covenant "are not the terms of a treaty but the conditions covering continued union in the family."[39] In short, blood sacrifice, covenant meal, and theophany were elements associated with covenant making rituals. A ritual or ceremony is an integral element in establishing and sealing the covenant with God.

ELEMENTS OF AN OLD TESTAMENT COVENANT RELATIONSHIP

This study has been so far concerned with the historical aspects and literary forms of covenant in the OT. The following section will treat what is implicit in any OT covenant relationship. The term בְּרִית occurs more than three hundred times in the MT, but there are also references to covenant relationship where this technical term is not used.[40] Covenant was part and parcel of

---

[35] For the use of blood as a means to establish covenantal "brotherhood" between communities or individuals, see Nicholson, *God and His People,* 166 n. 14.

[36] McCarthy, *Treaty and Covenant,* 295.

[37] Nicholson, *God and His People,* 121–33.

[38] McCarthy, *Treaty and Covenant,* 295.

[39] Ibid., 295.

[40] For example, Deut 26:16–19 does not use the term "covenant" but articulates what a covenant relationship consists of by affirming the obligations and consequences of the covenant relationship between Yahweh and Israel and by alluding to Exod 19:5–6. See the discussion in Tigay, *Deuteronomy,* xiv n. 14.

life for the people of Israel; it was "a bond of troth and life-fellowship to all the effects for which kinsmen are permanently bound together."[41] J. Pedersen, in his fundamental work on the life and culture of the people of Israel, underscores that "one is born of a covenant and into a covenant, and wherever one moves in life, one makes a covenant or acts on the basis of the already existing covenant."[42] The OT covenant relationship between Yahweh and the Israelites shall be examined in terms of the following motifs: election, Yahweh's presence and mutual belonging, knowledge of God, witness, peace, promises, and the loving and keeping of the commandments.

Election Motif: A Call to Be God's סְגֻלָּה

God's covenant with Israel originates with the Exodus generation and is inaugurated and confirmed on Mount Sinai. Moses renews the same covenant with the next generation on the plain of Moab at the entrance to the promised land (Deut 28:69). Joshua also renews a covenant binding Israel to exclusive allegiance to Yahweh (Josh 24). At a later time, Josiah established a covenant before Yahweh, to walk after Yahweh and to keep his commandments as expressed in his testimonies and his statutes (2 Kgs 23:1–3).[43] These covenants into which the people enter in Deut 28:69; Josh 24; 2 Kgs 23:1–3 are not new covenants but renewals of the covenant of their ancestors described in Deuteronomy, which itself is a renewal of the first covenant made at Sinai/Horeb. These renewals imply that covenant relationship is not an unchanging status, but a process: a call/vocation summons the hearers over and over again to decide in favor of Yahweh.[44]

The doctrine of election is defined and developed in the Book of Deuteronomy.[45] One of the key texts, Deut 7:6, emphasizes three aspects of an election theology. First, Israel is "a people holy to God" (עַם קָדוֹשׁ). The expression עַם קָדוֹשׁ is also found in the Book of Exodus, where it highlights the privileged status of Israel (Exod 19:5–6). Deuteronomy develops this concept further and makes "the status of being holy" the basis for Israel's responsibility to fulfill the commands of Yahweh (Deut 7:6–8). In the Book of Exodus, "the special status of the people serves as a reward for being loyal to the covenant (19:5a), while in Deuteronomy the election serves as a

---

[41] Smith, *Religion of the Semites,* 316.

[42] Pedersen, *Israel,* 1.308.

[43] The close link between the OT formulation of "walking after Yahweh" and the NT understanding of "following Jesus" (discipleship) is obvious.

[44] Nicholson, *God and His People,* 147–48.

[45] For the election motif in Deuteronomy, see M. Weinfeld, *Deuteronomy 1–11: A New Translation with Introduction and Commentary* (AB 5; New York: Doubleday, 1991), 60–62.

motivation for observing the laws" (14:21).[46] The *imitatio Dei* motif articulated as the keynote of the whole Holiness Code (Lev 17–26) provides the rationale for the status of Israel's being holy: "You shall be holy, for I the Lord your God am holy" (Lev 19:2). Second, Deut 7:6 underscores that God has "chosen" (בָּחַר) Israel. In Deuteronomy, the idea of election is expressed by the verb בחר ("to choose," "to elect," "to decide for"). The same motif is expressed in the holiness code by the verb בדל ("to separate," "to set apart," "to divide"). Israel is "set apart" (בדל) for a special service to God and to be God's possession (לִהְיוֹת לִי, Lev 20:26), and thus cannot be like other nations (Num 23:9; 1 Sam 8:4–22). The Israelites have been "set apart" for a special covenant relationship with Yahweh who liberated them and brought them out of Egypt (Lev 19:36). Third, Deut 7:6 links the idea of election (בחר) to the notion of סְגֻלָּה (see also 14:2; 26:18). Israel is God's סְגֻלָּה, "treasured possession or property."[47] The term סְגֻלָּה describes Israel's privileged status before God among the nations (Deut 7:6; 14:2; 26:18; Exod 19:5; Ps 135:4). Israel's status as Yahweh's סְגֻלָּה was constituted by the decisions and choices of Yahweh and Israel, defining their covenant relationship. This relationship has both indicative and imperative aspects: the indicative stands for the new status of Israel as God's סְגֻלָּה and the imperative stands for Israel's call to be God's סְגֻלָּה.[48] The covenant is an act of sealing both Yahweh's election of Israel as his סְגֻלָּה and Israel's acceptance of this unique status.

The concept of a covenant between Yahweh and Israel is based on choices: God's choice of his people Israel and their choice of God. The choice of Israel underscores their free decision to be obedient and faithful to God. Unlike the treaty, which is typically based on the sovereign's conquest of the vassal, the covenant is grounded in Yahweh's deliverance of Israel from an oppressive ruler, the Pharaoh of Egypt (Deut 7:6–8). The election of Israel is not based on the virtue or the strength of the people, but on God's love and faithfulness to the promises made to their ancestors (Deut 4:37; 7:7–8; 9:4–6; 10:15; 23:5). The Book of Deuteronomy, the preeminent biblical document of covenant and of love,[49] underlines

---

[46] Weinfeld, *Deuteronomy*, 61.

[47] For the Akkadian background of the term סְגֻלָּה, see ibid., 60, 368. סְגֻלָּה is also a treaty word; see McCarthy, *Treaty and Covenant*, 270.

[48] See the discussion in Nicholson, *God and His People*, 210.

[49] Deuteronomy is described as "the biblical document *par excellence* of covenant" (W. L. Moran, "The Ancient Near Eastern Background of the Love of God in Deuteronomy," *CBQ* 25 [1963]: 82) and "Le document biblique par excellence de l'*agapân*" (C. Spicq, *Agapè, Prolégomè à une étude de théologie néo-testamentaire* [StudH 10; Leiden: E. J. Brill, 1955], 89).

Yahweh's love for Israel that functions as "the imperative necessity of Israel's love for Yahweh in return."[50] Scholars also suggest that the Deuteronomic notion of covenant love is elaborated by the analogy of the father-son relationship between Yahweh and Israel.[51] These different analogies show that God and people are bound by a mutual love or a covenant love.

Yahweh's Presence and Mutual Belonging

If Israel is faithful to the covenant stipulations laid out in the law, then Yahweh assures his dwelling in its midst. Yahweh promises: "I will place my dwelling (נָתַתִּי מִשְׁכָּנִי) in your midst, and I shall not abhor (לֹא־תִגְעַל) you. I will walk about among you. I will be your God (הָיִיתִי לָכֶם לֵאלֹהִים) and you shall be my people (אַתֶּם תִּהְיוּ־לִי לְעָם)" (Lev 26:11–12). It seems that for the priestly tradition the main reward for the covenant relationship is Yahweh's presence with Israel and their unique binding relationship.[52] It is worth noting that the covenant formula "I will be your God and you shall be my people" (הָיִיתִי לָכֶם לֵאלֹהִים וְאַתֶּם תִּהְיוּ־לִי לְעָם) is at the center of the covenant texts of the various traditions in the OT.[53] It communicates Yahweh's relationship to Israel and Israel's to Yahweh in a powerful way. Paul Kalluveettil, after a detailed study on the covenant formulae in the OT, concludes that "the idea 'I am yours, you are mine' underlines every covenant declaration."[54] The covenant is primarily a relationship that implies a quasi-familial bond between the partners.[55] The OT covenant makes partners in a union in which they share the same life, transcending all the barriers that may separate them.

---

[50] Moran, "Love of God in Deuteronomy," 77.

[51] See D. J. McCarthy, "Notes on the Love of God in Deuteronomy and the Father-Son Relationship between Yahweh and Israel," *CBQ* 27 (1965): 144–47.

[52] McKenzie, *Covenant,* 50–51.

[53] For example, the Priestly Pentateuch (Exod 6:7; Lev 26:12); Deut 26:17–19; 29:13; 2 Sam 7:24; Jer 7:23; 11:4; 24:27; 30:22; 31:1, 33; 32:38; Ezek 11:20; 14:11; 36:28; 37:23, 27; Zech 8:8. For a detailed study of the covenant formula, see R. Rendtorff, *The Covenant Formula: An Exegetical and Theological Investigation* (trans. M. Kohl; OTS; Edinburgh: T&T Clark, 1998), 11–37.

[54] P. Kalluveettil, *Declaration and Covenant: A Comprehensive Review of Covenant Formulae from the Old Testament and the Ancient Near East* (AnBib 88; Rome: Biblical Institute Press, 1982), 212. Non-biblical declaration formulae include "we are vassals of the king," "we are brothers," "we will be friends," "we are all one," etc. A declaration formula sometimes replaces the ceremony that establishes a covenant relationship. See the discussion ibid., 93–106.

[55] Quell, "διαθήκη," 114.

Covenant and Knowledge of God

The knowledge of God is always implied in Israel's covenant relationship with Yahweh (cf. Exod 29:45–46; Jer 9:24; Isa 11:2). Since the basis of the covenant is the Exodus, Moses frequently reminds the people of this foundational experience (Deut 1:30–33; 3:21; 4:3, 9, 34; 6:22; 7:19; 9:17; 11:2–7; 29:1–2). The emphasis on the actual experience of Yahweh's interventions is common in the OT (Deut 29:1; Josh 23:3; 24:17; Judg 2:7; 1 Sam 12:16, etc.). Making a covenant with Yahweh, or accepting Yahweh as one's God presupposes knowing Yahweh (Deut 7:9; Jer 31:31–33). A passion for keeping the commandments of God is very essential for finding or possessing the gift of knowledge of God. For example,

> My child, if you accept my words
> and treasure up my commandments within you,
> making your ear attentive to wisdom
> and inclining your heart to understanding;
> if you indeed cry out for insight,
> and raise your voice for understanding;
> if you seek it like silver,
> and search for it as for hidden treasures—
> then you will understand the fear of the Lord
> and find the knowledge of God (Prov 2:1–5 NRSV).

The knowledge of God is a recurring theme in the prophets (Hos 2:20; 4:1, 6; 5:4; 6:6; Isa 1:3; Jer 4:22). Hosea speaks of the knowledge of God as follows:

(Hos 4:1b) אֵין־אֱמֶת וְאֵין־חֶסֶד וְאֵין־דַּעַת אֱלֹהִים בָּאָרֶץ:

There is no faithfulness or covenantal love, and no knowledge of God in the land (Hos 4:1b).

(Hos 6:6) כִּי חֶסֶד חָפַצְתִּי וְלֹא־זָבַח וְדַעַת אֱלֹהִים מֵעֹלוֹת:

For I desire steadfast love and not sacrifice, the knowledge of God rather than burnt offerings (Hos 6:6).

In 4:1b, lack of faithfulness (אֱמֶת) and covenantal love (חֶסֶד) matches the lack of the knowledge of God (דַּעַת אֱלֹהִים). In 6:6, the steadfast love (חֶסֶד) parallels the knowledge of God (דַּעַת אֱלֹהִים), and sacrifice (זָבַח) parallels burnt offerings (עֹלוֹת). It is obvious from these parallels that the knowledge of God refers to the experience of God's covenantal love and loyalty shared among the fellow Israelites.[56] Lack of this knowledge is understood as a

---

[56] See the detailed discussion in R. de Menezes, *Voices from Beyond: Theology of the Prophetical Books* (Mumbai: St. Pauls, 2003), 110–13.

failure to live up to the covenant relationship. For example, in Isaiah, the oracles against the people of Judah point out their lack of knowledge as a moral failure (Isa 1:3; see also Jer 4:22; 5:4; 22:15–16; Hos 4:6). The knowledge of God implies a profound experience of God's loyalty and covenantal love for Israel as God's covenant partner as a result of which one is enabled to keep the commandments and is transformed to deal with fellow Israelites as one's covenant partners.

Covenant and Witness

The teaching of the commandments to the coming generation is important in order to ensure the continuation of the covenant relationship with Yahweh. Moses commands the people of Israel: "Teach them to your children and talk about them when you are at home and when you are away, when you lie down and when you rise" (Deut 6:7). Israel is instructed to teach God's testimonies (הָעֵדֹת), statutes (הַחֻקִּים) and ordinances (הַמִּשְׁפָּטִים) to their descendants (Deut 6:20–25).[57] Moses entrusts the Law to the Levitical priests who carried the ark of the covenant and commands them to read it publicly to the whole people of Israel on the Feast of Tabernacles (Deut 31:9–13, 24–27). The Israelites were supposed to pass on for future generations what they had seen, heard, and experienced of God's intervention in their history (Deut 6:20–25; 11:1–9).[58]

While the election motif (בחר) in Deuteronomy underscores the uniqueness of Israel (Deut 7:6; 14:1, 21), the prophecy of Deutero-Isaiah presents this motif as an instrument and vehicle for bringing other peoples to true faith in Yahweh, the God of Israel (Isa 49:6–7; see also Zech 8:20–23), and for bringing justice to the nations (Isa 42:1–4). Israel shall be the witnesses of Yahweh (עֵד, Isa 43:10). "I will give you as a light to the nations that my salvation may reach to the end of the earth" (Isa 49:6). Therefore the election and covenant relationship has a special mission for the building up of a just order and bringing the light to other peoples (e.g., Isa 42:1–4; 43:10; 49:6).

Covenant and Peace

The words בְּרִית and שָׁלוֹם are "of different origin and scope, but they do not designate different kinds of relationship."[59] The root meanings of

---

[57] See also Deut 4:9; 11:19; 31:12–13.

[58] See the discussion in Lacomara, "Deuteronomy and the Farewell Discourse," 81–82.

[59] Pedersen, *Israel,* 1.285. For a detailed discussion of the relation between peace and covenant in the lives and the culture of the people of Israel, see ibid., 1.263–310.

the term שָׁלוֹם refer to "well-being," "wholeness," and "completeness." The term also has significant social dimensions as it is used to describe a close relationship between nations and peoples (Judg 4:17; 1 Kgs 5:26). It is closely associated, moreover, with law, public actions, and righteousness (Isa 48:18; 60:17; Zech 8:16). A covenant relationship, by its very nature, generates rights and duties. Just as בְּרִית refers to the relationship that enjoys privileges and duties, שָׁלוֹם refers to the state of the people who are united and live in holistic harmony. Both words are used together for emphasis or as a stronger expression for בְּרִית (Ezek 34:25; 37:26). The two are also used interchangeably (Gen 26:28, 31; Ps 55:20–21). To make a covenant with one is sometimes described as to "make peace" (הִשְׁלִים, Deut 20:12; Josh 10:1, 4; 11:19; 2 Sam 10:19; 1 Kgs 22:45). In this sense, to enter into a covenant implies to make peace.[60] Peace and covenant are very intimately connected, and peace making is intrinsic to relationships in social life.

Covenant and Promises

Yahweh makes many promises to Israel. As we have seen, God's promises are integral components of the covenant relationship. There are covenants based primarily on God's promises. God's promises, in his covenant with Noah and his descendants, stress God's definitive assurance that life will never be destroyed (Gen 9:9–11). God promises descendants, land, prosperity, security, and victory to the patriarchs (Gen 17:7–8; 22:16–18; 26:2–5). The promise of a land is a dominant motif in Deuteronomy (e.g., 1:8, 15; 6:10, 18, 23; 7:8, 13; 8:1; 9:5).[61] God promises a "perpetual priesthood" to the high priest Phinehas and his descendants (Num 25:10–13) and an everlasting dynasty to the house of David (2 Sam 7:1–17; 1 Chr 17; Ps 89; Jer 33:21). A promise that God will raise up a prophet like Moses for Israel, the covenant people, is implied in Deut 18:15–18. The promise of God's indwelling presence in the midst of the covenant community permeates the entire OT.[62] Closely linked to the promise of God's presence is the promise of God's guidance and assistance to those who are faithful to the covenant (Isa 41:10).

---

[60] See the detailed discussion, ibid., 1.285, 308–9.

[61] See the excursus on the promises in J. J. Scullion, *Genesis: A Commentary for Students, Teachers, and Preachers* (OTS 6; Collegeville, Minn.: Liturgical Press, 1992), 272–77.

[62] For example, Gen 26:3; 31:3; Exod 3:12; Lev 26:11–12; Deut 31:23; Josh 1:5; 3:7; Judg 6:16; 1 Kgs 11:38; 1 Chr 16:33; Ps 97:5; Ps 114:7; Jer 4:26; Jonah 1:3, 10; Zeph 1:7.

Loving and Keeping the Commandments

'Love' and 'hate' are generally recognized as treaty terms both in the ancient Near East treaties and in the OT covenant. The language of the OT covenant follows the custom of the treaty in its use of the words love and hate. Steven L. McKenzie comments that "the vassal who observes the stipulations of the treaty and remains loyal to his suzerain is said to 'love' him; the one who breaks the treaty 'hates' his overlord. Similarly, those who obey the laws in the covenant with Yahweh love him; those who disobey hate him."[63] There are instances in the OT where keeping the commandment of Yahweh (שֹׁמְרֵי מִצְוֺתָיו) is understood as loving Yahweh (אֹהֲבָיו) (Exod 20:6; Deut 5:10; 7:9; 10:12; 11:1, 13, 22; 13:3; 19:9; 30:16, 20) and disobeying the commandments as "hating" (שֹׂנֵא) Yahweh (Deut 7:10). Deuteronomy defines love of God in terms of loyalty (11:1, 22; 3:20), service (10:12; 11:1, 13), and obedience, i.e., keeping the commandments (10:12; 11:1, 22; 19:9). The best way of expressing our love for God and keeping his commandments is by loving fellow humans. It is in this context that we understand the command "Love your neighbor as yourself" (Lev 19:18). Sharing life with one's covenant partner is very essential to a covenant relationship. The life that the individuals hold is not private property, but something common, which has to be shared with others.[64] In brief, keeping the commandments, loving and sharing the life with others, are intrinsic to the nature of a covenant relationship.

CONCLUSION

This short survey of the complex question of the OT covenant has drawn together several features of covenant making and covenant relationship. Covenant in the OT is a metaphor borrowed from the sociopolitical realm and used by the Israelites to establish and profess a new relationship or to renew an already binding relationship. A covenant relationship as a mutual agreement between two parties is made binding by a ritual or some other symbolic action. The covenant relationship between Yahweh and Israel implies a new status for Israel as God's treasured possession (סְגֻלָּה). This involves obligations in relationship with God, humans, and the cosmos: obligations to worship only Yahweh (Deut 6:4–5), to execute justice for the orphan and the widow (Deut 10:18), to have concern for the poor and

---

[63] McKenzie, *Covenant*, 38.
[64] Pedersen, *Israel*, 1.309.

needy (Deut 15:11; 24:12–15), to be just in legal matters (Deut 16:18–20), and to have regard for nature and the environment (Deut 20:19–20).[65] The covenant relationship thus not only recalls God's promises but also demands loving and keeping the commandments of God in return for God's love. The covenant underscores God's indwelling presence in the midst of his people as well as God's liberative and redemptive actions in human history. It calls for a commitment in witnessing or making God's presence and actions known. The loving relationship of the covenant leads its partners to God and to שָׁלוֹם, the fullness of life.

COVENANT MOTIF AND JOHN 13–17

Yves Simoens's *La gloire d'aimer* is devoted entirely to the structure and the covenant genre of chapters 13–17.[66] It is the most important treatment of the subject under discussion in contemporary Johannine scholarship.[67] I shall first critique Simoens's work and then explore the possible OT background for the Johannine use of the covenant metaphor in chapters 13–17.

AN ASSESSMENT OF SIMOENS'S ANALYSIS OF JOHN 13–17

By means of structural analysis, Y. Simoens proposes a new approach to the interpretation of chapters 13–17. He suggests that a covenant genre, more than a farewell-type scene, is reflected in these chapters. By the use of repetitions and inclusions, Simoens first attempts to establish the narrative coherence and the unity of these chapters by pointing out a chiastic structure (ABCDC′B′A′) of which 15:12–17 forms the center.[68] He substantiates his claim that these chapters manifest a covenant genre rather than a

---

[65] See the detailed classification and description in E. Achtemeier, "Plumbing the Riches: Deuteronomy for the Preacher," *Int* 41 (1987): 278–80. For the three-dimensional (God-humans-cosmos) concern elsewhere in the OT, see R. Chennattu, "The Story of Cain (Genesis 4:1–16): A Cry for Divine-human-cosmic Harmony," *BiBh* 27 (2001): 255–70.

[66] Y. Simoens, *La gloire d'aimer: Structures stylistiques et interprétatives dans le Discours de la Cène (Jn 13–17)* (AnBib 90; Rome: Biblical Institute Press, 1981).

[67] Other studies on the subject include a brief article by Lacomara who investigates the influence of the Book of Deuteronomy in the setting, formation, and theology of John 13:31–16:33 ("Deuteronomy and the Farewell Discourse," 65–84); J. W. Pryor who focuses his attention on the Johannine community as an eschatological covenant people (*John*).

[68] Simoens, *La gloire d'aimer,* 52–80; see esp. the chart on p. 77.

farewell-type scene by bringing to light the close correspondence between chapters 13–17 and the essential characteristics of a covenant form.[69] Simoens finds resemblances between Deuteronomy and John 13–17: the historical prologue in Deut 1:1–4:40 and the narrative in John 13:1–38; the great commandment in Deut 4:44–11:32 and the discourses in John 14:1–31; the stipulations in Deut 12:1–26:15 and the discourses in John 15:1–16:3; the blessings and woes in Deut 26:16–30:20 and the discourse in John 16:4–33; the canticle in Deut 32–33 and the prayer in John 17. These five resemblances are also repeated in John 17: a historical prologue (vv. 1–5); the great commandment (vv. 6–11); stipulations (vv. 12–19); blessings and woes (vv. 20–23); a canticle (vv. 24–26).[70] Because of the similarity between the literary structure of Deuteronomy and John 13–17, Simoens claims that the discourses in chapters 13–17 constitute a distinctive reformulation of the OT covenant tradition and theology. The covenant in Deuteronomy provides the backdrop for the new covenant in John 13–17 in terms of the new command to love one another and in terms of the gift of the Holy Spirit.[71]

Simoens's exclusion of the farewell tradition does not seem justified. Farewell traditions and covenant making motifs are not necessarily mutually exclusive in the OT narratives. One of the features of the testament tradition or the farewell-type scene is "an affirmation and a renewal of the never-failing covenant promises of God."[72] The Book of Deuteronomy, the paramount biblical document of the covenant,[73] is presented as the farewell discourses of Moses. Similarly, the renewal of the covenant in Josh 24 is preceded by Joshua's farewell speech just before his death (ch. 23). Second, the complex structure proposed by Simoens seems inconsistent. Fernando F. Segovia rightly points out that "the relationship between the chiastic literary structure and the covenant interpretative structure lacks coherence and congruence; the seven divisions of the former do not compare well with the latter's five, and the very center of the former, 15:12–17, disappears into the

---

[69] Ibid., 200–250. For the essential elements of the covenant genre, Simoens largely depends on J. L'Hour, *La morale de l'alliance* (CahRB 5; Paris: L. Gabalda, 1966).

[70] Simoens, *La gloire d'aimer*, 203–5.

[71] "C'est donc d'abord par une ressemblance avec la structure littéraire du Deutéronome que Jn 13–17 atteste sa propre refonte de la structure d'alliance en clé de nouvelle alliance, puisqu'il s'agit ici du commandement nouveau et du don de l'Esprit" (Simoens, *La gloire d'aimer*, 204).

[72] F. J. Moloney, *Glory not Dishonor: Reading John 13–21* (Minneapolis: Fortress, 1998), 6.

[73] Moran, "Love of God in Deuteronomy," 82.

third large section of the latter."[74] His attempt to draw exact parallels in structure between the Book of Deuteronomy and John 13–17 leads Simoens to produce a complex structure that ignores the narrative flow and the other literary characteristics he has traced in the text. Third, Simoens passes too easily over the possibility of the role played by the other books of the OT in the formation and structure of John 13–17. There are elements in the Johannine narrative (e.g., the vine-branches metaphor of John 15) that have no parallels in Deuteronomy.[75] This brief critique of the groundbreaking work of Simoens opens the way to further investigation into the relationship between the OT covenant and John's Gospel.

Old Testament Background for the Johannine Covenant Motif

We have already seen that the elements of the covenant relationship identified in John 1:35–51 are not limited to the Book of Deuteronomy but echo the covenant motifs throughout the OT.[76] In the first part of this chapter on the covenant motif in the OT, we saw that the OT covenant makings do *not* follow a unified, specific format. The OT background for the Johannine presentation of chapters 13–17 cannot be limited to the covenant form and tradition found in Deuteronomy alone, as it may also embrace elements of the covenant motif across the OT and the covenant-renewal form found in Josh 24 (see also Exod 24). I do not wish to draw exact structural parallels between these OT books and John 13–17, but to stress that chapters 13–17 constitute a covenant renewal ceremony analogous in function to those found in these traditions. Although scholars regard Josh 24 as a report of the covenant renewal ceremony, no one contests that the narrative shows how to establish a covenant partnership with God and a community seeking to become God's covenant people.[77] A structure analogous to the covenant renewal ceremony in Josh 24 emerges in John 13–17:

---

[74] Segovia, *Farewell of the Word,* 40.

[75] See also the comments of Lacomara, "Deuteronomy and the Farewell Discourse," 84 n. 60.

[76] See chapter 1, the section Discipleship Motif in the Call Stories of John 1:35–51.

[77] McCarthy considers Josh 24 a "report of covenant making" (*Treaty and Covenant,* 241). J. Muilenburg argues that we have here a covenant-renewal form that is repeatedly used within Israelite traditions ("The Form and Structure of the Covenantal Formulations," *VT* 9 [1959]: 357–60, 364–65). According to T. C. Butler, Josh 24 "represents an ancient Shechemite cultic ceremony in which Israel

Joshua 24:1–28

1. Joshua and the people gathered in the presence of God at Shechem (24:1)

2. The proclamation of God's election and guidance of the people (24:2–13)

3. A call to obedience and a call to decision (24:14–15)

4. Joshua's warning of the consequences of the decision (24:16–20)

5. The people's response of total allegiance to Yahweh (24:21–24)

6. A ceremony sealing the covenant (24:25–28)

John 13:1–17:26

1. Jesus and the disciples gathered together for the farewell meal (13:1–38)

2. The promise of God's indwelling presence and guidance (14:1–31)

3. A call to abide and keep the commandments (15:1–17)

4. Jesus' warning of the consequences of discipleship (15:18–16:24)

5. The disciples' profession of faith (16:25–33)

6. A prayer consecrating the covenant community of the disciples (17:1–26)[78]

John 13–17 also differs from the pattern found in the Book of Joshua. While the covenant ceremony in Josh 24 is preceded by the farewell speech of Joshua in chapter 23, the farewell discourses of Jesus are presented as a covenant renewal ceremony in John. Moreover, there is no covenant meal in Josh 24, but John 13–17 is situated within the context of Jesus' last meal with his disciples (see 13:1–38). As we shall see, the covenant meal in Exod 24 and Jesus' meal with his disciples in John 13 seem to have much in common with respect to their function in the renewal of a covenant relationship. One needs not look for exact parallels between John's narrative and any single OT tradition, but rather identify the essential elements of the OT covenant traditions appearing in John 13–17.[79] In chapter three, I shall explore further the features that are regularly found in the various OT traditions and that can be

---

affirmed her allegiance to Yahweh as the God of Israel rather than to the other gods of her neighbors. This marks the major turning point in the identity of Israel over against her neighbors" (*Joshua*, 268).

[78] I follow the basic structure proposed by Butler with some variations (*Joshua*, 266).

[79] As Simoens claims, one cannot find in John 13–17 a structure that reflects the Hittite treaty form or that of the Book of Deuteronomy in their entirety. See also the discussion in the earlier section of this chapter, Covenant in the Old Testament.

traced in John 13–17. This cursory survey at least indicates the strong possibility that the paradigms of various types of covenants and elements of the OT covenant relationship are significant for the interpretation of discipleship in John 13–17.[80]

COVENANT MOTIF AND LITERARY FUNCTION OF JOHN 1–12

In his detailed study of John 13–17, Fernando F. Segovia asserts that the literary context and the position of the chapters do not support the idea that chapters 13–17 reflect a covenant genre.[81] I hope to demonstrate that John 13–17 reflects a covenant renewal ceremony similar to that of Josh 24:1–28.[82] John 1–12 in general, and 12:44–50 in particular, unveils a continual call to decision as found in OT covenant renewals. The disciples as "characters" in the story—addressed to the original intended readership, the Johannine community, and all subsequent readers—must make decisions for or against believing in Jesus as the revelation of God. Such a challenge, to accept Yahweh and abandon other gods, formed a climac-

---

[80] This view is further confirmed by the presence of many other Exodus motifs in the gospel. The following are only a few among the many examples of Exodus motifs across the Gospel: the tabernacle (1:14); Moses (1:17); the paschal Lamb (1:29, 36); the bronze serpent (3:14); the manna (6:31). For Exodus motifs in John's Gospel, see also Mowvley, "John 1:14–18 in the Light of Exodus 33:7–34:35," 135–37. Some argue for a parallelism of both contents and order between Exodus and John; see Enz, "The Book of Exodus as a Literary Type for the Gospel of John," 208–15. For a critique of the efforts to discover an Exodus literary pattern in John, see R. H. Smith, "Exodus Typology in the Fourth Gospel," 329–42. Smith, however, makes an attempt to find typology for John in Exod 2:23–12:51. For a detailed study of the Moses traditions in John's Gospel, see Glasson, *Moses in the Fourth Gospel;* Meeks, *The Prophet-King;* and Boismard, *Moïse ou Jésus.* This is now available in English: *Moses or Jesus: An Essay in Johannine Christology* (trans. B. T. Viviano; Minneapolis: Fortress, 1993).

[81] Segovia, *Farewell of the Word,* 40. Segovia's second objection concerns the relevance of the covenant theme for the intended audience, the Johannine community. According to Segovia, if we accept that John 13–17 reflects a covenant genre, "the speech's character as a message from an author to an audience largely disappears" (ibid.). This objection demands a rereading of the *Sitz im Leben* of the Johannine community and an assessment of the relevance of a covenant making in such a situation. I shall discuss this issue in chapter 5 of this book.

[82] As far as the Johannine community is concerned, both covenant making and covenant-renewal are implied in John 13–17. Whether the implications are "covenant-making" or "covenant-renewal" depends upon the audience. For the non-Jewish members of the community, it is the former; for the Jewish members, it is the latter.

tic moment in ceremonies of covenant renewal in the OT (e.g., Josh 24:14–15).[83] The challenge of Joshua is "a demand for discipleship, a call to hear and obey in faithfulness and loyalty the commands of God."[84] In the OT, all covenant stipulations have the same function: a call to decision and the establishment of an exclusive relationship with Yahweh (cf. Exod 23:20–33; Deut 26:16–27:26). A similar process seems to be present in chapters 1–12. Jesus reveals his identity gradually, and the various groups of characters in the story are summoned to decision.

The following section is a rapid survey of chapters 1–12, highlighting the central themes and their possible links with the covenant motif in the unfolding story of the Johannine Jesus. I focus on two aspects: God's revelation in the person of Jesus Christ and the human response to this gift of God, whether acceptance or rejection. In John's Gospel, the disciples are initiated into a process of following Jesus in 1:35–51.[85] In chapters 2–4, the disciples are given various models of discipleship as Jesus reveals the presence of God. In chapters 5–10, within the literary context of the celebrations of Jewish feasts, the disciples and characters in the story are provided with revelations of God in Jesus' words and works, and are confronted with choices for or against Jesus. Chapters 11–12 heighten the urgency of decision and set the stage for Jesus' hour.[86]

Jesus' Ministry from Cana to Cana (2:1–4:54)

After initiating the discipleship motif in 1:35–51, the evangelist further elaborates the motif in chapters 2–4.[87] This section is framed by the two Cana signs in 2:1–11 and 4:43–54: the response of the mother of Jesus, a Jewish woman (ch. 2), and that of the official (βασιλικός), a Gentile man (ch. 4).[88] These two signs give further insight into the type of faith that is

---

[83] Josh 24:14–15 underlines the fact that the people are summoned to decision for or against Yahweh by the following imperatives: fear (יְראוּ) Yahweh, serve (עִבְדוּ) Yahweh (twice), put aside (הָסִירוּ) other gods, choose (בַּחֲרוּ) Yahweh. See also the discussion in part I of this chapter.

[84] Butler, *Joshua*, 279.

[85] See the detailed study in chapter 1.

[86] I follow the structure proposed by R. E. Brown (*John*, 1.cxxxviii–cxli) and F. J. Moloney (*The Gospel of John* [SP 4; Collegeville, Minn.: Liturgical Press, 1998], 23–24).

[87] For a detailed discussion of the journey of faith in John 2–4, see Moloney, *Belief in the Word*, 93–199. See also Brown, *John*, 1.95–198.

[88] The question whether the βασιλικός is a Jew or a Gentile is a disputed issue among scholars. For evidence to claim that the βασιλικός is a Gentile, see A. H. Mead, "The *basilikos* in John 4:46–53," *JSNT* 23 (1985): 69–72; Brown, *John*, 1.190. The term βασιλικός can refer to someone from royal blood, to a servant to a royal household, to a soldier either of Herodians or emperors, or to a royal scribe;

expected of a disciple.[89] Both the mother of Jesus and the official trust completely in the power of the word of Jesus ("Whatever he tells you, do" [2:5]; "The man believed the word that Jesus spoke to him and went his way" [4:50]). In 2:1–11, Jesus' first sign (σημεῖον) is presented as the revelation of the divine presence (δόξα) that initiates the faith of the disciples (ἐπίστευσαν εἰς αὐτόν; 2:11). The expression ἐπίστευσαν εἰς αὐτόν (using εἰς with the accusative) implies a dynamic interpersonal relationship between Jesus and the disciples.[90] In parallel fashion, the βασιλικός and his family come to believe in Jesus as a consequence of the σημεῖον performed by Jesus (4:43–54).

The first σημεῖον of Jesus is followed by stories that open the way to a journey of faith within Judaism (2:12–3:36). The Jews in the temple reject Jesus' self-revelation as the new temple (2:20), and they display no faith in Jesus (2:13–22).[91] This total rejection of Jesus' revelation is followed by an example of partial faith (3:1–21). Nicodemus is a type or a representative figure of Jews who believed in Jesus on the basis of the signs that he performed.[92] For the Johannine Jesus, such a faith is inadequate since it falls short of an unconditional trust in the words of Jesus.[93] Although Nicodemus begins the dialogue with Jesus by affirming the identity and origin of Jesus, "We know that you are a teacher come from God" (3:2), he is faced with Jesus' challenge to be born ἄνωθεν (again/from above)[94] or to be born of water and spirit (γεννηθῇ ἐξ ὕδατος καὶ πνεύματος) in order to enter into the kingdom of God (3:3–5). Nicodemus misunderstands Jesus'

---

see the detailed discussion of U. Wegner, *Der Hauptmann von Kafarnaum (Mt 7,28a; 8,5–10 par Lk 7,1–10): Ein Beitrag zur Q-Forschung* (WUNT 2/14; Tübingen: J. C. B. Mohr [Paul Siebeck], 1985), 57–60.

[89] Discipleship in John is a possibility for all who are open to the revelation of God in and through Jesus.

[90] The significance of the construction ἐπίστευσαν εἰς αὐτόν is highlighted by its repeated use, thirty-six times, in John's Gospel. For the above-mentioned meaning of πιστεύω εἰς and a discussion of the different uses of the verb, "to believe," "to believe in," and "to believe that" in John's Gospel, see S. Schneiders, *Written That You May Believe: Encountering Jesus in the Fourth Gospel* (New York: Crossroad, 1999), 87–90.

[91] See Moloney, *Belief in the Word,* 104.

[92] For a discussion of the representative figures in John's Gospel and Nicodemus as a type, see the discussion in Collins, *These Things Have Been Written,* 1–45.

[93] Moloney, *Belief in the Word,* 106–21; W. Bauer, *Das Johannesevangelium erklärt* (HKNT 6; Tübingen: J. C. B. Mohr [Paul Siebeck], 1933), 61.

[94] ἄνωθεν can mean both "again/anew" (the temporal dimension) and "from above" (the spiritual dimension); see BDAG, 92. Both these meanings seem to have implied in John 3:3. See also the discussion in Moloney, *Belief in the Word,* 109–12.

words and is confused as he says hesitatingly: "How can these things be?" (3:9).[95] This example of partial faith in Jesus is followed by a model of the authentic faith displayed from within Judaism in the confession of John the Baptist (3:25–30). John the Baptist rejoices at the voice of Jesus, the bridegroom, and declares that he must decrease while Jesus must increase (3:29–30).

The narrative now moves into the world outside Judaism. The story of John 4 recounts a journey of faith among the Samaritans (4:1–42).[96] The journey that the woman makes from unbelief to belief in Jesus reflects the characteristics of a committed believer. At the beginning, she encounters Jesus with puzzlement because of her ignorance. But as the dialogue progresses, she is willing to participate more actively even by challenging Jesus' claims (vv. 12, 15, 19–20). Her gradual recognition of Jesus' identity is manifested in her progressive insights: "Are you greater than our father Jacob?" (4:12a); "I perceive that you are a prophet" (4:19b); "Could this man possibly be the Messiah?" (4:29b). She fulfills the standard characteristics of an apostle by giving testimony to the people in the city and inviting them to δεῦτε ἴδετε, "come, see," Jesus (4:29a).[97] The transforming effect of her apostleship and Jesus' stay with the Samaritans is marked by the wholehearted response of the people from Sychar: "We know that this man is truly the savior of the world" (4:42).

By means of this carefully constructed narrative, the author instructs readers that discipleship, a journey of faith, is universally possible for both

---

[95] This is only the beginning of Nicodemus's journey with Jesus. He returns to the narrative in 7:50–52 and 19:39–42. In both of these occurrences, the narrator reminds the readers that he is the same Nicodemus who had come to Jesus before. Nicodemus appeals to the Pharisees to deal with Jesus according to the Law of Moses. He challenges their action by asking, "Does our law judge a person without giving him a hearing and learning what he does?" (7:51). Here Nicodemus "is doing the truth" according to the Law of Moses (cf. 3:21). He later associates himself publicly with Jesus and accompanies and helps Joseph of Arimathea to provide a royal burial for Jesus (19:39–42) and thus reveals his acceptance of Jesus as the fulfillment of the OT expectations. For Nicodemus as the type of the true Israelite, see the discussion in J. N. Suggit, "Nicodemus—the True Jew," in *The Relationship between the Old and the New Testament* [*Neot* 14 (1981)] (Bloemfontein, South Africa: New Testament Society of South Africa, 1981), 90–110. Suggit's claim that 19:39–42 has eucharistic overtones seems to be too farfetched a conclusion (ibid.). For a survey of the differing opinions on Nicodemus's response in John 19:39–42, see Moloney, *Glory not Dishonor*, 149–50 n. 80.

[96] For a detailed study, see Chennattu, "Women in the Mission of the Church," 760–73.

[97] Cf. John 1:35–51.

Jews and Gentiles, for both women and men. True faith is displayed as a complete and unconditional trust in Jesus, the saving revelation of God, and as a deep commitment to God's design manifested in and through the person of Jesus and his mission. As the verb πιστεύω εἰς insinuates, faith in Jesus' word leads to a personal knowledge about the identity of Jesus and initiates a personal relationship with him.[98]

Jesus and the Principal Jewish Feasts (5:1–10:42)

In chapters 5–10, the evangelist embarks on the relationship between Jesus and Jewish feasts offering choices to the disciples (and subsequently, readers) either to believe in Jesus or to take sides with the Jewish characters in the story. In this section of the gospel, the conflict between Jesus and "the Jews" intensifies and hardens. The identity of Jesus is revealed in his relationship to Yahweh, who is celebrated in and through the Jewish feasts. The author takes the four major feasts of the Jews: Sabbath (5:1–47), Passover (6:1–71), Tabernacles (7:1–10:21), and Dedication (10:22–42) and, by situating the ministry of Jesus within the setting of these feasts, develops a unique Christology. The Johannine Jesus is the incarnation or personification of the presence of Yahweh once celebrated in the Jewish feasts.[99] While Jesus unravels his true identity to the disciples progressively, conflict and rejection develop.

Within the literary context of the feast of Sabbath, Jesus reveals his oneness with the Father that enables him to continue the works of God on a Sabbath day (5:1–18). This claim of Jesus is a blasphemy for the Jews. A deathly conflict ensues and the Jews "sought all the more to kill him" (5:18a).[100] Jesus brings the witness of John the Baptist (5:33–35), Jesus' own work or the works of the Sent One of the Father (5:36), and the Father himself (5:37–40) into a "two-party juridical controversy."[101] The whole

---

[98] I used the expression "as the verb πιστεύω εἰς insinuates" to indicate that sometimes πιστεύω εἰς can also refer to a superficial faith (see, for example, 2:23–25). One needs to look at each context where the expression appears; see also the discussion in Schneiders, Written That You May Believe, 87–90.

[99] See for this interpretation Gale A. Yee, Jewish Feasts and the Gospel of John (ZSNT; Wilmington, Del.: Michael Glazier, 1989), 31–92; F. J. Moloney, Signs and Shadows: Reading John 5–12 (Minneapolis: Fortress, 1996), 1–153.

[100] According to the legal norms of Lev 24:10–16 and Num 15:30–31, Jesus' claim deserves execution. See also the discussion in A. E. Harvey, Jesus on Trial: A Study in the Fourth Gospel (London: SPCK, 1976), 67–81.

[101] For the Sabbath conflict in John 5 as a juridical controversy, see M. Asiedu-Peprah, Johannine Sabbath Conflicts As Juridical Controversy (WUNT II/132; Tübingen: J. C. B. Mohr [Paul Siebeck], 2001), 52–116. Asiedu-Peprah argues that the

debate is colored by "a rhetoric of persuasion" which is aimed at Jesus' accusers, viz., "the Jews" in the story.[102] Jesus tries to convince them and bring them to believe in his Christological claims. But the Jews in the story cannot believe in Jesus and the Father as they seek honor from one another (5:23, 44) and are unable to accept Jesus' offer of eternal life (5:24). Jesus and "the Jews" leave the juridical process with neither side having convinced the other of the truth.[103]

The narratives in chapter 6 reveal that "what was done in the Jewish celebration of the Passover was but a sign and shadow of the perfection of the gift of God in the person Jesus Christ, the true bread from heaven, the bringer of eternal life to all who would believe in him."[104] Jesus challenges all the characters in the story and his disciples to be open to the ongoing revelation of God in Jesus and to enter into a relationship with him. The different responses, both negative and positive, given by the disciples in 6:60–71 bear this point out.[105] Many of the disciples find Jesus' teaching very hard: σκληρός ἐστιν ὁ λόγος οὗτος· τίς δύναται αὐτοῦ ἀκούειν; "This is a hard saying; who can listen to it?" (6:60), and they respond to Jesus with outright rejection and completely abandon him (6:66). In this context Jesus asks the remaining disciples: "Do you also wish to go away?" (6:67), and Simon Peter makes a public confession for the first time in the story, "Lord, to whom can we go? You have the words of eternal life. We have come to believe and know that you are the Holy One of God" (6:68–69). The fact that some disciples, along with the crowd, decide to defect from the group implicitly alludes to the struggle and the division in the Johannine community.

Against the background of the celebrations of the Feast of Tabernacles, Jesus' messianic status and origin have been explicitly raised, questioned, and challenged (7:25–31, 40–44). Jesus' identity is revealed in terms of the

---

primary objective of a juridical controversy for each of the two debaters is to "*convince* the other party of the truthfulness of their position or claims" (ibid., 16).

[102] Asiedu-Peprah, *Johannine Sabbath Conflicts*, 83, 115, 184–211. For the "rhetoric of persuasion" in the OT juridical controversy, see P. Bovati, *Re-establishing Justice: Legal Terms, Concepts and Procedures in the Hebrew Bible* (JSOTSup 105; Sheffield: Sheffield Academic Press, 1994), 112–14.

[103] Asiedu-Peprah comments: "There is no reaction from the accusers to the response of the accused. Since there is no indication of withdrawal of initial accusations, the juridical controversy has clearly not ended" (*Johannine Sabbath Conflicts*, 25).

[104] Moloney, *Signs and Shadows*, 64.

[105] For similar challenges raised by Jesus to the various characters and groups in the Johannine narrative, see 5:44; 6:36; 8:45, 46; 9:35; 10:26.

elements central to the ceremonies of the Feast of Tabernacles: the water li-
bation ceremony, the mounting of the light, and the confession of faith in
one God.[106] Jesus proclaims himself as the source of the living water
(7:37–38), the light of world (8:12; 9:5), and the messianic Good Shepherd
(10:14). The proclamations of Jesus lead to a division (σχίσμα) among the
crowd (7:40–44) and among the authorities (7:45–52). Understanding
κρίσις in chapter 7 as implying three meanings, separation, decision, and
judgment, Beasley-Murray comments that "the two themes [Jesus as the
fulfillment of the Feast of Tabernacles and the κρίσις] are bound together,
for it is precisely because Jesus proclaims that Israel's faith, embodied in its
festivals, finds its fulfillment in him [Jesus] that the nation is compelled
to make a *decision* relating to him, and in so doing they *divide* according as
they *judge*."[107]

In the discourses that follow, Jesus declares that true disciples will have
to abide (μένειν) in his word (λόγος) (8:31; see also 1 John 2:14), they
"will know the truth" (8:32a) and they will be free (8:32b). The word
μένειν is charged with many symbolic meanings. Abiding in Jesus' word
would imply that the whole life of disciples is permeated by the presence
of Jesus and guided by Jesus' life-giving words or commandments.[108]
Since Jesus came into the world as light, abiding in Jesus is interpreted
elsewhere as dwelling not in darkness (σκοτία) but in light (φῶς, 12:46).
After giving the great commandment that expresses Israel's exclusive loyalty to Yahweh (see the emphasis יְהוָה אֶחָד; Deut 6:4–5),[109] Moses constantly exhorts them to keep these words in their hearts (Deut 6:6;
11:18a). He calls on Israel to make decisions in choosing between life and
death (Deut 30:15–20).[110] Similarly, the Johannine disciples have to
choose between light and darkness, slavery and freedom, sight and blindness, and life and death.

---

[106] For an extended discussion of these chapters within the literary context of
the feast of Tabernacles, see Moloney, *Signs and Shadows,* 117–42. See also R.
Chennattu, "Good Shepherd," 94–96.

[107] G. R. Beasley-Murray, *John* (2d ed.; WBC 36; Nashville: Thomas Nelson,
1999), 121. Stress in original.

[108] See the discussion in chapter 1; see also Lee, "Abiding," 126–36. For a recent study on the theological meaning and the significance of μένω in John's Gospel, see K. Scholtissek, *In Ihm Sein.*

[109] אֶחָד refers to both exclusiveness and uniqueness; see the discussion in
Weinfeld, *Deuteronomy,* 349–51.

[110] On this theme, see M. J. O'Connell, "The Concept of Commandment in
the Old Testament," *TS* 21 (1960): 351–403, esp. 352; Brown, *John,* 1.490–93;
Schnackenburg, *John,* 2.424–25.

John 9:1–10:21 recounts the second juridical controversy regarding the Sab3bath activities of Jesus that leads to a σχίσμα among the characters in the story.[111] The origin of Jesus is the issue at stake: Can he be from God? Jesus' work on the Sabbath is used as the measuring scale in discerning his identity. The Pharisees express two opposing views, both founded on the Jewish religious traditions (9:16).[112] For some of the Pharisees, Jesus' work on the Sabbath constitutes violation of the Mosaic law, and therefore they argue that Jesus is a sinner (9:16a). Others are convinced that Jesus' signs (σημεῖα) bear witness to him as coming from God. One who can perform such signs must be from God (9:16b). As the narrator informs the reader, some like the parents of the young man are afraid of professing their faith in Jesus lest they be expelled from the synagogue (9:22). This σχίσμα among the characters in the story is an implicit appeal, summoning the disciples and readers to make their own decision.[113] This is evinced by the fact that when Jesus heard that they had expelled (ἐξέβαλον) the young man born blind whom he had healed, he asks the young man: σὺ πιστεύεις εἰς τὸν υἱὸν τοῦ ἀνθρώπου; "Do you believe in the Son of Man?" (9:35), and the young man professes his faith in Jesus by declaring: πιστεύω, κύριε, "Lord, I believe" (9:38). Jesus elsewhere affirms that only those who belong to his fold will be enabled to believe in Jesus and the ongoing revelation of God in him (cf. 10:26). At the heart of Johannine Christology, we have the Son who has come from the Father, sent by the Father, who makes the Father known and returns to the Father.[114] In response to the request to be told plainly if he is the Messiah (εἰ σὺ εἶ ὁ Χριστός, εἰπὲ ἡμῖν παρρησίᾳ, "If you are the Christ, tell us plainly," 10:24), Jesus points to his own works as his witnesses (10:25) and refers to his oneness with the Father (10:30, 38). In spite of these revelations, the Jewish characters in the story have decided against Jesus, since they consider Jesus a blasphemer (cf. 10:36).

---

[111] John 5:1–47 is considered as the first juridical controversy. For an interpretation of John 9:1–10:21 as the second juridical controversy, see Asiedu-Peprah, *Johannine Sabbath Conflicts,* 117–83.

[112] See J. Calloud and F. Genuyt, *L'Évangile de Jean (II): Lecture sémiotique des chapitres 7 à 12* (Lyon: Centre Thomas More, 1987), 62.

[113] See also the study of J. A. du Rand, "A Syntactical and Narratological Reading of John 10 in Coherence with Chapter 9," in *The Shepherd Discourse of John 10 and Its Context* (ed. J. Beutler and R. T. Fortna; SNTSMS 67; Cambridge: Cambridge University Press, 1991), 99.

[114] For a detailed study of the central structure of Johannine Christology, see W. R. G. Loader, "The Central Structure of Johannine Theology," *NTS* 30 (1984): 188–216.

Jesus and the Preparation for the Hour (11:1–12:43)

In chapters 11–12, the Johannine Jesus turns toward the cross and declares that his "hour" has come. The disciples are with Jesus as he raises Lazarus from the dead and reveals his identity as "the resurrection and the life" (11:25). Jesus challenges Martha by asking explicitly, πιστεύεις; "Do you believe?" (11:26). Martha makes her profession of faith by proclaiming, "Yes, Lord, I believe that you are the Messiah, the Son of God, the one coming into the world" (11:27). The sign and its aftermath furnish the opportunity for the Jewish authorities to make the final decision that Jesus must die (11:45–57). The persistent unbelief of the crowd who followed Jesus is summarized in 12:37: "even though [Jesus] had performed so many signs in their presence, they did not believe in him."[115] The narrator also reports that many (πολλοί) from the authorities (ἐκ τῶν ἀρχόντων) believed in Jesus, but they were afraid of confessing Jesus as the Messiah lest they be expelled from the synagogue (12:42; see also 9:22, 34, 35; 16:2). The narratives of chapters 11–12 show that all—Mary, Martha, the disciples, and the Jews—fail to respond positively and fully to the dramatic acting out of the summons to transcend death and believe in Jesus as "the resurrection and the life" (11:25).[116]

Summary of Jesus' Public Ministry (12:44–50)

After an evaluation of why the Jews are unable to believe in Jesus (12:37–43), we have "a summary of Jesus' revelatory discourse" in 12:44–50.[117] This concluding discourse of the public ministry of Jesus has been referred to as "the kerygma of Jesus."[118] William Loader claims that in these verses the central structure of Johannine Christology is well established and is "determinative."[119] Jesus begins with the affirmation of his

---

[115]John 12:37 can be compared with the comment of Yahweh to Moses: "How long will they [the people of Israel] refuse to believe in me, in spite of all the signs that I have done in their midst?" (Num 14:11). Brown (*John,* 1.485) sees an echo of Deut 29:2–4 in John 12:37.

[116]See F. J. Moloney, "Can Everyone be Wrong? A Reading of John 11.1–12.8," *NTS* 49 (2003): 505–27.

[117]Schnackenburg, *John,* 3.1.

[118]C. H. Dodd, *The Interpretation of the Fourth Gospel* (Cambridge: Cambridge University Press, 1953), 382.

[119]Loader, "Johannine Theology," 195. According to Loader, the central structure of Johannine Christology consists of the terminology Son-Father and the facts that the Son comes from and returns to the Father, the Son is sent by the Father, the Father has given all things into the hands of the Son, and the Son makes the Father known (ibid., 188–99).

close relationship to the Father (vv. 44–45).[120] He then reveals the purpose of his incarnation and mission and declares that those who receive him will not "remain in darkness" but will walk in light (v. 46); he also announces that those who reject him will be judged by his word (vv. 47–48). Jesus concludes his discourse by pointing to the Father as the authority behind Jesus' promises and threats (vv. 49–50). Johannine scholars have long recognized similarities between John 12:49–50 and various passages in Deuteronomy.[121] Similarities include (1) God is the source of the words (v. 49); (2) God's word or commandment is the eternal life (v. 50). God promises that the words of God will be put into the mouth of the prophet-like-Moses (Deut 18:18–19). It is God's commandments that set the pattern of life for the people of Israel as the people of God (cf. Deut 8:3). God's commandment means "the very life" of Israel (הוּא חַיֵּיכֶם; Deut 32:45–47). Raymond E. Brown comments on John 12:50: "It is the word of God spoken through Jesus that now sums up the covenant obligations of the believer."[122] The Johannine Jesus affirms that he has not spoken on his own authority but only what the Father has inspired or commanded him to communicate (12:49), and his commandment is eternal life (ζωὴ αἰώνιος, 12:50).

This rapid overview of chapters 1–12 in general and 12:44–50 in particular shows that the characters in the story and the readers of the story are summoned to make a choice for or against Jesus. Despite some division (6:60–71) and inability to believe (11:1–44), the disciples and other characters in the story are called to decision. Jesus repeatedly calls the disciples to believe as the narrative unfolds:

"How can you believe when you accept glory from one another and do not seek the glory that comes from the one who alone is God?" (5:44)

"But I said to you that you have seen me and yet do not believe." (6:36)

"But among you there are some who do not believe." For Jesus knew from the first who were the ones that did not believe, and who was the one that would betray him. (6:64)

So Jesus asked the twelve, "Do you also wish to go away?" (6:67)

---

[120] Even though Jesus affirmed his origin from God (e.g., 6:45–46; 7:17; 8:40, 42), the Pharisees accuse and condemn Jesus saying that he is not from God (9:16).

[121] See the discussion in Beasley-Murray, *John*, 218; Brown, *John*, 1.491–93; Schnackenburg, *John*, 2.424–25.

[122] Brown, *John*, 1.493.

"But because I tell the truth, you do not believe me." (8:45)

"Which of you convicts me of sin? If I tell the truth, why do you not believe me?" (8:46)

Jesus heard that they had driven him out, and when he found him, he said, "Do you believe in the Son of Man?" (9:35)

"You do not believe, because you do not belong to my sheep." (10:26)

Then Jesus told them plainly, "Lazarus is dead. For your sake I am glad I was not there, so that you may believe." (11:14–15)

"I am the resurrection and the life. Whoever believes in me, though he/she die, will live, and whoever lives and believes in me will never die. Do you believe this?" (11:25–26)

"I knew that you always hear me, but I have said this for the sake of the crowd standing here, so that they may believe that you sent me." (11:42)

The disciples have professed their faith in Jesus (e.g., 6:68–69; 9:38; 11:27), but "the Jews" in the story have decided against Jesus (11:45–53). Jesus summarizes his promises and threats for those who believe in him and those who reject him in 12:44–50. It is against this larger (chs. 1–12) as well as more immediate (12:44–50) literary context and background that one needs to interpret chapters 13–17. The call to decision presented and the decisions taken for or against Jesus in the Johannine narrative of chapters 1–12 provide the background leading both the disciples in the story and the readers into the covenant making/renewal found in chapters 13–17.[123] It is helpful to remember that, in John's Gospel, one cannot separate narratives from discourses, as they are intimately connected and interpret each other. Chapters 1–12 serve as a "hortatory preparation" for the disciples as "characters" in the story, for the originally intended readership, the Johannine community, and all subsequent readers to participate in the covenant making or covenant renewal in chapters 13–17.[124] The covenant renewal motif in John 13–17, therefore, is well integrated into the literary context and essential to the unfolding story of the Johannine Jesus.

---

[123] As R. A. Culpepper maintains, "much of what Jesus says, particularly in the farewell discourse, is intended for the disciples, or the church, in the story world's future" (*Anatomy*, 107).

[124] Josh 23 is considered as a "hortatory preparation" for the covenant renewal in Josh 24. See the discussion in Boling and Wright, *Joshua*, 519–26.

The Covenant Motif and the Structure of John 13–17

Johannine scholars have long recognized the structural and compositional difficulties of chapters 13–17 in terms of repetitions, discrepancies in narrative sequence, and content. They have proposed various approaches—the historicizing, transpositional, redactional, symbolic, unfinished, compositional, and integrative—to account for these difficulties.[125] Although difficulties remain, there is increasing consensus among scholars today that "John 13–17 is a coherent and self-contained narrative section."[126] While we acknowledge the possible prehistory and the redactional work involved in the formation of chapters 13–17, this study interprets chapters 13–17 in their present state.[127] There are differing opinions regarding the overall structure of chapters 13–17.[128] The basic structure adopted in this analysis can be summarized in the following way:[129]

---

[125] For a presentation of the compositional difficulties and traditional and contemporary resolutions, see Segovia, *Farewell of the Word,* 20–47; Brown, *John,* 2.581–604; A. Dettwiler, *Die Gegenwart des Erhöhten: Eine exegetische Studie zu den johanneischen Abschiedsreden (Joh 13,31–16,33) unter besonderer Berücksichtigung ihres Relecture-Charakters* (FRLANT 169; Göttingen: Vandenhoeck & Ruprecht, 1995), 14–33.

[126] Segovia, *Farewell of the Word,* 2–58; the quotation is from p. 20. G. R. O'Day suggests that the metaphor of "the hour" frames chs. 13–17 and keeps them together as a single unit "within the consummation of the 'hour'" ("'I Have Overcome the World' (John 16:33): Narrative Time in John 13–17," *Semeia* 53 [1991]: 158). For more recent studies, see Moloney, *Glory not Dishonor,* 1–7; Beasley-Murray, *John,* 222–23.

[127] See the recent study by Schnelle ("Recent Views of John's Gospel," 352–59) who argues systematically that the key to understanding particular texts in John's Gospel lies neither in their prehistories nor in the postulated redactional work but "in the intratextual world of the entire Fourth Gospel." See also the discussion in Moloney, *John,* 13. However, for a discussion of the historical questions raised by the pericope, see Barrett, *John,* 435–37.

[128] See the discussion in Beasley-Murray, *John,* 223–24; Simoens, *La gloire d'aimer,* 52–80; Brown, *John,* 2.545–47; Segovia, *Farewell of the Word,* 20–25; Moloney, *Glory not Dishonor,* 2–4.

[129] The structure and content of John 13–17 are analogous in function to the covenant renewal ceremony found in Josh 24. It was pointed out that in Josh 24, as noted above, we have "a liturgical [covenant renewal] ceremony that must have been repeated in the Israelite ritual center of Shechem" (E. S. Cetina, "Joshua," in *The International Bible Commentary* [ed. W. R. Farmer et al.; Collegeville, Minn.: Liturgical Press, 1998], 545).

1. Jesus and the disciples gathered together for the farewell meal (13:1–38)

2. The promise of God's indwelling presence and guidance (14:1–31)

3. A call to abide and keep the commandments (15:1–17)

4. Jesus' warning of the consequences of discipleship (15:18–16:24)

5. The disciples' profession of faith (16:25–33)

6. A prayer consecrating the covenant community of the disciples (17:1–26)

Jesus and the Disciples Gathered together for the Farewell Meal (13:1–38)

Some exegetes consider 13:1–30 as the setting that furnishes a farewell context and 13:31–38 as part of the first discourse in John 14.[130] Others consider 13:31–38 as a bridge-building scene which concludes 13:1–30 and introduces the discourse in John 14.[131] Yet others regard 13:1–38 as a literary unit that serves as an introduction to the themes of the subsequent discourses in 14–17.[132]

The present study regards 13:1–38 as a thematically and structurally unified pericope that functions not merely as an introduction, but as a significant element of the covenant metaphor about to be unraveled throughout chapters 13–17. John 13 opens with a solemn introduction that is recognized as "the most significant transition in the Gospel, introducing not only the scene of the footwashing but the entire second half of the Gospel."[133] Verse 2 introduces for the first time the prophecy of Judas's betrayal and verses 36–38 consist in Jesus' prophecy of Peter's denial. Peter's denial reminds the reader of his earlier resistance to Jesus' offer to wash his feet (13:6–9). Both themes of betrayal in the case of Judas (vv. 2, 10–11, 18,

---

[130] Segovia, *Farewell of the Word,* 21–24. The first discourse consists of 13:31–14:31; see the discussion in Segovia, "The Structure, *Tendenz,* and *Sitz im Leben* of John 13:31–14:31," *JBL* 104 (1985): 471–93; D. B. Woll, "The Departure of 'The Way': The First Farewell Discourse in the Gospel of John," *JBL* 99 (1980): 225–39; J. A. du Rand, "A Story and A Community: Reading the First Farewell Discourse (John 13:31–14:31) from Narratological and Sociological Perspectives," *Neot* 26 (1992): 31–45; D. F. Tolmie, *Jesus' Farewell to the Disciples: John 13:1–17:26 in Narratological Perspective* (BibIntS 12; Leiden/New York/Köln: E. J. Brill, 1995), 29–30, 101.

[131] G. Mlakuzhyil, *The Christological Literary Structure of the Fourth Gospel* (AnBib 117; Rome: Biblical Institute Press, 1987), 221–23.

[132] H. A. Lombard and W. H. Oliver, "A Working Supper in Jerusalem: John 13:1–38 Introduces Jesus' Farewell Discourses," *Neot* 25 (1991): 357–78.

[133] R. A. Culpepper, "The Johannine *Hypodeigma:* A Reading of John 13," *Semeia* 53 (1991): 135; see also Moloney, *Glory not Dishonor,* 7; Schnackenburg, *John,* 3.15.

26–27, 30) and initial resistance (vv. 6–9) or denial (vv. 36–38) in the case of Peter hold this unit together. As Francis J. Moloney aptly observed, "the theme of the failure of both Judas and Peter plays no further role in the discourse proper."[134] It seems therefore more reasonable to consider verses 31–38 as part of John 13 rather than considering them part of the first discourse of John 14.[135] The whole section is situated deliberately within the literary context of a meal that is interpreted in the Synoptics as a covenant meal (cf. Matt 26:26–29; Mark 14:22–25; Luke 22:17–20). A covenant relationship is implied by both the covenant command and the covenant sign: love for one another (13:34–35). The disciples and the subsequent readers are provided with three possible ways of responding to a covenant relationship that is expressed by the expression οἱ ἴδιοι (13:1): total rejection (Judas, 13:30), temporary denial (Peter, 13:36–38), and total faithfulness (the Beloved Disciple, 13:23).

The Promise of God's Indwelling Presence and Guidance (14:1–31)

John 14:1 signals the opening of a new section both linguistically and thematically.[136] The scene moves from the dialogue between Jesus and Peter (13:36–38) to the dialogue between Jesus and the disciples, marked by the use of the imperative in the second person plural: πιστεύετε (v. 1c). The dominant themes that permeate John 14 are Jesus' promises, words of encouragement, and assurance that he will not leave the disciples alone in the world when he returns to the Father (14:1–31). An inclusion can be seen between the words of Jesus in verse 1a and verse 27b: μὴ ταρασσέσθω ὑμῶν ἡ καρδία, "Do not let your hearts be troubled."[137] There is also a

---

[134] Moloney, *Glory not Dishonor*, 8.

[135] For a detailed discussion of the thematic unity of John 13:1–38, see Moloney, *Glory not Dishonor*, 1–28; Moloney, "The Structure and Message of John 13:1–38," *ABR* 34 (1986): 1–16. Culpepper ("The Johannine *Hypodeigma*," 133–52) defends the unity of John 13:1–38 on narratological grounds. The unity of the pericope is also defended on formal structural grounds by means of chiasm and inclusio; see the analysis of Simoens, *La gloire d'aimer*, 81–104; F. Manns, *L'Évangile de Jean à la lumière du Judaïsme* (*SBFLA;* Jerusalem: Franciscan Printing Press, 1991), 321–37; Manns, "Le lavement des pieds: Essai sur la structure et la signification de Jean 13," *RevScRel* 55 (1981): 149–69. See also K. T. Kleinknecht, "Johannes 13, die Synoptiker und die 'Methode' der johanneischen Evangelienüberlieferung," *ZTK* 82 (1985): 361–88; A. Niccaci, "L'unità letteraria di Gv 13, 1–38," *EuntD* 29 (1976): 291–323.

[136] See the discussion in Moloney, *Glory not Dishonor*, 29.

[137] For those who accept this repetition verbatim as an inclusion, see J. Schneider, "Die Abschiedsreden Jesu: Ein Beitrag zur Frage der Komposition von Johannes 13:31–17:26," in *Gott und die Götter: Festgabe für E. Fascher zum 60.*

thematic inclusion: Jesus' departure (v. 1 and v. 28), call to belief (v. 1 and v. 29), and encouragement (vv. 1–3 and vv. 27b–29, 31), that holds this section together as a single unit.[138]

There are more disagreements than agreements among scholars regarding the internal structure of John 14. Scholars' divisions of the chapter vary from two major units to nine.[139] What is important for the present discussion, however, is its internal unity and dynamism centered on Jesus' covenant promises. Jesus commands the disciples, as they believe in God, to believe (πιστεύετε εἰς) also in him (v. 1; see also v. 11), and makes a plethora of promises to the disciples (vv. 12–27). Jesus promises that he will enable the disciples to do greater works than his (vv. 12–14), that he will send the Paraclete (vv. 15–17), that he will return (vv. 18–21), that the Father and Jesus will come to make their dwelling among the disciples (vv. 22–24), that the Paraclete will teach them and remind them of everything that Jesus had taught them (vv. 25–26), and that they will receive the gift of peace (v. 27). Both the act of promising and the content of the promises, viz., the indwelling presence of Jesus/God through the Paraclete and his ongoing guidance, and the gift of peace, evoke covenant overtones.

A Call to Abide and Keep the Commandments (15:1–17)

Scholars maintain differing views regarding the macrostructure of chapters 15–16.[140] The present study takes 15:1–17 as a self-contained section of the discourse united by the overarching theme of covenant relationship and its obligations. John 15:1–17 deals with both the metaphor[141] of vine and branches that describes in a symbolic way the covenant relationship between God/Jesus and his disciples, and the command to abide in Jesus and

---

Geburtstag (ed. H. Bardtke; Berlin: Evangelische Verlagsanstalt, 1958), 106; Bultmann, *John,* 599.

[138] See also the detailed discussion in Moloney, *Glory not Dishonor,* 29–54.

[139] For a detailed survey of the various opinions, see Segovia, *Farewell of the Word,* 64–65, nn. 6–13. See also A. Niccaci, "Esame letterario di Gv 14," *EuntD* 31 (1978): 209–14.

[140] For example, D. A. Carson considers 15:1–16 as a literary unit (*The Gospel According to John* [Grand Rapids, Mich.: Eerdmans, 1991], 510–24); Segovia argues 15:1–17 as the second unit of the discourse (*Farewell of the Word,* 125–67). For 15:1–16:3 as the second discourse, see Simoens, *La gloire d'aimer,* 152–58; Moloney, *Glory not Dishonor,* 55–76. Tolmie maintains 15:1–16:33 as the second phase of the farewell discourse (*Jesus' Farewell,* 30–31).

[141] The proper classification of the figurative language used in John 15:1–8 is a debated issue. See the discussion in Segovia, *Farewell of the Word,* 132–33; Moloney, *Glory not Dishonor,* 55 n. 1.

to love one another. Both the metaphor and the command describe the status and obligations of the covenant partners.

As we shall see in the next chapter, both the metaphor of the vine and the branches, and commands to abide in (μένω ἐν) and to love (ἀγαπάω), describe the covenant relationship between Jesus and his disciples and elaborate further the covenant motif toward the sealing of the covenant by a prayer in John 17.[142] The disciples are called to abide in Jesus (vv. 4–7), to abide in Jesus' love (vv. 9–11), and to love one another as Jesus loved them (vv. 12–17). The exhortation to keep God's commandments is often part of the speeches before the making or renewal of the covenant in the OT tradition (Deut 30:16; Exod 34:11; Josh 24:14–15).[143]

Jesus' Warning of the Consequences of Discipleship (15:18–16:24)

John 15:18 introduces a new section by changing the focus from "the internal affairs of the community" to "the external affairs of the community in the world."[144] The theme of "the disciples vs. the world" is introduced and the cost of discipleship is developed in 15:18–16:24. Jesus first warns the disciples of the suffering and persecution that they will encounter in their lives from the κόσμος (15:18–25)[145] and from the Jewish authorities (16:2–3). Jesus also announces the rewards they will receive from Jesus and God if they believe in Jesus and remain faithful by keeping the commandments (15:26–27; 16:4–24). The disciples' faith in Jesus leads them to be hated to the extent that they will be expelled from the synagogue (16:2). These negative consequences of discipleship are followed by

---

[142] E. Malatesta has convincingly argued that in 1 John μένειν ἐν is closely associated with covenant theology and tradition (*Interiority and Covenant,* esp. 60. J. W. Pryor has shown that the same use of μένειν ἐν is applicable in John 15 ("Covenant and Community in John's Gospel," *RTR* 47 [1988]: 49–50). See also the recent study on the theological meaning and the significance of μένειν in John by Scholtissek, *In Ihm Sein.*

[143] Brown argues for an implicit reference to a covenant theme in the new commandments of John 13:34; 15:12, 17 (*John,* 2.557). For the intrinsic relationship between the commandments and the covenant theme, see the discussion in part I. For the echoes of the OT covenant commandments (of Deuteronomy) in John's Gospel, see O'Connell, "Concept of Commandment," 351–403.

[144] Segovia, *Farewell of the Word,* 125–27.

[145] The world (ὁ κόσμος) here refers to all those who do not believe in Jesus as the revelation of God. For the different uses and meanings of ὁ κόσμος in John's Gospel, see Brown, *John,* 1.508–9; Moloney, *Belief in the Word,* 37. For its use in the Johannine corpus, see N. H. Cassem, "A Grammatical and Contextual Inventory of the Use of Cosmos in the Johannine Corpus with Some Implications for a Johannine Cosmic Theology," *NTS* (1972–1973): 81–91.

the rewards that they will receive for their commitment to discipleship: they will receive the gift of the Paraclete (vv. 4–15), their sorrow will turn into joy (vv. 20–22), their supplications will be granted and their joy will be full (vv. 23–24).

The Disciples' Profession of Faith (16:25–33)

This unit begins with the announcement of Jesus' hour as a moment of revelation (vv. 25–27). Jesus reveals his identity in terms of his origin (v. 28a) and destination (v. 28b). This climactic moment in the narrative urges the disciples and the subsequent readers to decide definitively either for or against Jesus. The disciples make a solemn profession of their faith in Jesus in 16:29–30, before the covenant prayer in John 17. It is the first time in the narrative that the disciples as a group acknowledge that Jesus now speaks plainly and knows everything. They also arrive at the conclusion that Jesus has come from God: ἴδε νῦν ἐν παρρησίᾳ λαλεῖς καὶ παροιμίαν οὐδεμίαν λέγεις. νῦν οἴδαμεν ὅτι οἶδας πάντα καὶ οὐ χρείαν ἔχεις ἵνα τίς σε ἐρωτᾷ· ἐν τούτῳ πιστεύομεν ὅτι ἀπὸ θεοῦ ἐξῆλθες, "Look! Now you are speaking plainly, not in any figure! Now we know that you know all things, and need none to question you; by this we believe that you came from God (16:29–30).[146] The emphasis on *now* (νῦν), *we* know (οἴδαμεν) and *we* believe (πιστεύομεν) points to an oath that generally precedes covenant renewals. This public acknowledgment is an integral element of the covenant renewal ceremonies found elsewhere in the OT (e.g., Exod 24:3, 7; Josh 24:21, 24). In Exod 24:8 and Josh 24:25–28, this declaration of commitment to Yahweh is followed by a covenant making ritual.[147] In John's Gospel, this public profession of faith is followed by the prayer of intercession (ch. 17), the sealing of the renewal of a covenant.

A Prayer Consecrating the Covenant Community of the Disciples (17:1–26)

John 17:1 signals the beginning of a new unit by the voice of the narrator in 17:1a, ταῦτα ἐλάλησεν Ἰησοῦς, "[when] Jesus had spoken these words." Here the literary form changes from discourse to prayer as Jesus

---

[146] This is the first time in the narrative that the disciples as a group make the profession of faith in Jesus' origin from God and his extraordinary knowledge. This profession is a climactic statement of Johannine faith; see Dettwiler, *Die Gegenwart des Erhöhten,* 258–59, 262–63. Some suggest that this profession, although correct, is still not a complete understanding of Jesus. It does not acknowledge Jesus' departure; see Moloney, *Glory not Dishonor,* 97. See also Duke, *Irony in the Fourth Gospel,* 57–59.

[147] See the detailed discussion in part I.

raises his eyes to heaven, "a formal pose for prayer."[148] Jesus changes his gaze from the disciples to heaven and addresses and prays to the Father. There is almost universal acceptance among scholars that 17:1–26 is a self-contained unit.[149]

Are the disciples present during Jesus' prayer? Some claim that in 17:1 "the disciples disappear from the purview of the narrative."[150] Although not explicitly mentioned, 17:1 implies the presence of the disciples with Jesus as he prays to the Father on their behalf. The narrator makes the link between John 17 and the previous section where Jesus was alone with the disciples by deliberately adding, ταῦτα ἐλάλησεν Ἰησοῦς, "[when] Jesus had spoken these words" (17:1a). Again after the prayer in John 17, the narrator uses a similar phrase, ταῦτα εἰπὼν Ἰησοῦς, "[when] Jesus had spoken these words" (18:1a), that is, the covenant prayer in John 17, and informs the reader that "Jesus set out with his disciples across the Kidron valley" (18:1b), which clearly indicates that the disciples were present. As such, the presence of the disciples with Jesus during the prayer supports the contention that there is a covenant making/renewal process going on in chapters 13–17.[151] As we shall see later in chapter three, John 17 is the prayer that seals the covenant making/renewal and concludes the discipleship discourses before the death and resurrection of Jesus.

CONCLUSION

The covenant motif in the OT has many forms. The evangelist rereads and interprets the OT covenant motif springing from different OT traditions, and uses them to redefine and establish the identity of his community as the children of God (1:12) or the treasured people of God (cf. John 13:1; Deut 26:16–19).

---

[148] Moloney, *Glory not Dishonor,* 102.

[149] See the major commentaries, Brown, *John,* 2.739–804; Moloney, *John,* 458–81; Beasley-Murray, *John,* 291–307; Carson, *John,* 550–71; J. Becker, *Das Evangelium des Johannes* (2 vols.; ÖTK 4/1–2; Gütersloh: Gerd Mohn; Würzburg: Echter, 1979–1981), 2.506–28; Léon-Dufour, *Lecture de l'Évangile selon Jean,* 3.273–318.

[150] See O'Day, " 'I Have Overcome the World' (John 16:33)," 163.

[151] For a survey of the *Traditionsgeschichte* of John 17, see H. Ritt, *Das Gebet zum Vater: Zur Interpretation von Joh 17* (FB 36; Würzburg: Echter Verlag, 1979), 59–91. For the liturgical background of John 17, see the discussions in Brown, *John,* 2.744–48; W. O. Walker, "The Lord's Prayer in Matthew and John," *NTS* 28 (1982): 237–56.

The covenant motif of chapters 13–17 is well integrated into the literary context of chapters 1–12. The disciples are initiated into a covenant relationship in 1:35–51. The narrative section of 2–12 calls the disciples to decision and thus functions as a hortatory preparation for the covenant renewal in 13–17. The whole process culminates in Jesus' prayer that seals the new covenant instituted by Jesus, surpassing the covenant under Moses as well as all former covenant traditions. This rapid overview demonstrates how narratives and discourses in chapters 2–17 are intimately connected by the covenant motifs that run across the gospel.

Having situated chapters 13–17 within the broad OT theme of the covenant motif and the narrower world of its Johannine literary context, we can now turn to a more thorough analysis of these chapters in an attempt to bring to light that the Johannine presentation of discipleship is a Christian rereading of the OT metaphor of covenant.

THREE

DISCIPLESHIP AND COVENANT IN
JOHN 13–17

This chapter will attempt to show that the structure and the content of John 13–17 reflect an OT covenant renewal form or genre. The evangelist programmatically organizes these chapters and gradually discloses a discipleship paradigm that manifests elements that parallel an OT covenant relationship. The following reading of chapters 13–17 is selective, focusing on the covenant and discipleship motifs.

JESUS AND THE DISCIPLES GATHERED TOGETHER FOR THE FAREWELL MEAL (13:1–38)

In 13:1–38, the evangelist introduces important covenant motifs that will provide the key to interpret the discipleship discourses in chapters 13–17. The meal setting, the footwashing, the question of sharing an inheritance with Jesus, the command to love one another, the presentation of the various responses to Jesus' call to a relationship based on a new commandment are reminiscent of OT covenant themes and introduce the paradigm of a new covenant relationship with the disciples.

A COVENANT MEAL WITH HIS OWN (13:1–3)

The solemn introduction in verses 1–3 furnishes the literary and theological setting within which one should read and interpret chapters 13–17.[1]

---

[1] W. K. Grossouw suggests that 13:1–3 functions as a "minor prologue" to the whole second part of the gospel ("A Note on John XIII 1–3," *NovT* 8 [1966]: 124–31). R. E. Brown makes a distinction between v. 1 and vv. 2–3, and argues

Verse 1 informs the reader that the event takes place before the feast of Passover. It announces Jesus' absolute knowledge of the hour (ὥρα) and his love for his own (οἱ ἴδιοι), those belonging to Jesus.[2] The entire section, chapters 13–17, insists on the recurring themes of both Jesus' knowledge of the hour and his love for his own (οἱ ἴδιοι). The expression οἱ ἴδιοι reminds the reader of the former οἱ ἴδιοι (Israel) who rejected the revelation of God in Jesus (1:11).[3] The "his own" (οἱ ἴδιοι) whom the narrator addresses in chapter 13 are the disciples whom Jesus knows, has chosen (13:18), and sends out with a mission (13:20). The expression οἱ ἴδιοι is best understood in the light of the Good Shepherd discourse. They are those who follow Jesus, who know and listen to the voice of Jesus (10:4, 27), those for whom Jesus cares (10:12), and whom Jesus knows (10:27). This relationship between Jesus and his disciples is suggestive of the OT covenant relationship between Yahweh and Israel. From the very first verse of the account of Jesus' final gathering with his own (οἱ ἴδιοι), the evangelist makes clear that the relationship between Jesus and his disciples with whom he shares his last meal is analogous to that of Yahweh and Israel, the chosen people (סְגֻלָּה) of God in the OT.

After this general introduction, the narrator moves to the specific setting for the footwashing in verses 2–3. These verses provide important details necessary for the correct interpretation of the actions and words of Jesus that will follow. Verse 2 tells the reader that the event takes place during a solemn meal (δεῖπνον, v. 2a) and makes an allusion to Satan's role in Judas's betrayal. This implies the rejection of Judas's status as a disciple and friend of Jesus (v. 2b). As Rudolf Schnackenburg observes, the allusion to the work of the devil at the beginning of the meal draws attention to an "incomprehensible breach of trust on the part of a participant at the meal."[4] Verse 3 underscores again Jesus' knowledge of his God-given authority, of his origin and destiny (see also v. 1).

Although one cannot interpret Jesus' last meal with his disciples as ipso facto indicative of a covenant meal, verses 2–3 need to be interpreted within the framework of the relationship that is emphasized by Jesus when he refers to the disciples as his own (οἱ ἴδιοι, v. 1). The evangelist portrays

---

that v. 1 introduces the entire Book of Glory (John 13–21) and vv. 2–3 prepare for ch. 13 (*John*, 2.563–64).

[2] For the significance of Jesus' absolute knowledge in John 13, see Moloney, *Glory not Dishonor*, 7–11; Culpepper, "The Johannine *Hypodeigma*," 134–37; R. H. Lightfoot, *St. John's Gospel* (ed. C. F. Evans; Oxford: Oxford University Press, 1956), 263–64.

[3] See the study of Pryor, "Jesus and Israel," 201–18.

[4] Schnackenburg, *John*, 3.16.

Jesus' last meal with his disciples as an intimate experience shared by Jesus and his disciples, with no other persons present. It was customary in the OT world to conclude the covenant ceremony by a communal meal (Gen 26:26–30; 31:43–54; Exod 24:5–11; Deut 27:6–7).[5] On such occasions, the meal shared together by the covenant partners creates and signifies a special bond of friendship, trust, mutual knowledge, and acceptance that binds together their mutual covenant commitments. As the OT covenant meals seal both Yahweh's election of Israel as his סְגֻלָּה and Israel's acceptance of this unique status, the final meal of Jesus with his own looks forward to the new covenant relationship of the disciples as God's chosen community.

FOOTWASHING AND COVENANT RELATIONSHIP (13:4–20)

The footwashing is a symbolic action.[6] Commentators differ in their responses to the question of what this act symbolizes. It has been traditionally accepted that it symbolizes in a dramatic way the humble service of Jesus, which the disciples are to imitate.[7] The narrator portrays Jesus' action by vividly describing his moves step by step: Jesus gets up from the table, takes off his outer garment, ties a towel around himself, pours water into a basin, washes the feet of his disciples, and wipes them with the towel (vv. 4–5).[8] According to Jewish traditions, actions such as taking off the outer garment and tying a towel around oneself would evoke the image of a slave. For example, a late midrash on Gen 21:14 recounts that when Abraham sent away Hagar, he put bread and a skin of water on her shoulder along with the child, and girded a shawl around her loins in order to let the people know that she

---

[5] See the discussion above, chapter 2, the section, Covenant in the Old Testament. See also the discussion in W. Johnstone, *Exodus* (Sheffield: Sheffield Academic Press, 1990), 50–53.

[6] Barrett, *John*, 436.

[7] Barrett regards John 13 as "a Johannine construction based on the synoptic tradition that Jesus was in the midst of his disciples as ὁ διακονῶν (Luke 22:27)" (*John*, 436). See also M. Sabbe, "Footwashing in John 13 and Its Relations to the Synoptic Gospels," *ETL* 58 (1982): 279–308. Against this view, see C. Niemand, *Die Fusswaschungserzählung des Johannesevangeliums: Untersuchung zu ihrer Enstehung und Überlieferung in Urchristentum* (SA 114; Rome: Pontificio Ateneo S. Anselmo, 1993), 65–71. For a survey of different views, see Brown, *John*, 2.558–59.

[8] The evangelist highlights the importance of the footwashing by the long narration time allocated for the action. On "narration time" ("Erzählzeit"), see Ska, *"Our Fathers Have Told Us,"* 7–8. See also the basic study of Genette, *Narrative Discourse*, 33–85.

was a slave (*Yal. Sh.* 1 § 95).[9] According to the *Mekilta*'s interpretation of Exod 21:1–3, washing the feet was such demeaning work that a Hebrew slave "must not wash the feet" (לא ירחוץ לו רגליו) of his master; it was reserved for Gentile slaves (*Mek.* 58).[10] Jesus' gestures and actions are thus portrayed as very similar to those of Gentile slaves and yet interpreted traditionally as the most noble and greatest example of humble service.

But something more than an example of humble self-sacrificing service is implied in Jesus' footwashing. One cannot ignore the point of view of the evangelist in interpreting the footwashing event. We must interpret Jesus washing the feet of his disciples against the background of verses 1–3. The literary setting suggests that the footwashing in itself should be viewed as both Jesus' perfect love and his love to the end (εἰς τέλος, 13:1c). Here the expression εἰς τέλος underscores both its quantitative or chronological meaning (to the end of Jesus' life) and the qualitative or christological meaning (to the perfection of Jesus' love).[11] J. Michl considers the footwashing as the representative act of love symbolizing the whole ministry of Jesus.[12] In Johannine Christology, it is important to understand the footwashing as an act of intimate love and communion.[13] This view is further confirmed by Jewish traditions of the first century as attested in *Joseph and Aseneth*.[14] B. Schwank refers to the story of Aseneth, in which she washes the feet of her husband-to-be, Joseph, with much devotion and love (*Jos. Asen.* 20:1–5), and he proposes that the footwashing of Jesus could be a symbolic act of love that promotes and fosters communion and thus has

---

[9] *Yalqut Shimoni* (Vilna edition of 1898). This large midrashic compilation of various interpretations of texts from more than fifty works covers the whole Hebrew Bible. No critical edition of the collection exists; see E. Schürer, *The History of the Jewish People in the Age of Jesus Christ (175 B.C.–A.D. 135)* (3 vols.; ed. G. Vermes and F. Millar; Edinburgh: T&T Clark, 1973–1987), 1.99.

[10] *Mekilta de-Rabbi Ishmael: A Critical Edition of the Basis of the Manuscripts and Early Editions with an English Translation* (3 vols.; trans. J. Z. Lauterbach; Philadelphia: Jewish Publication Society, 1935), 3.5. *Mekilta de-Rabbi Ishmael* is a Tannaitic midrashim on Exod 12–23; see Schürer, *History of the Jewish People*, 1.90. It is assumed that these two rabbinic texts reflect the first century Jewish customs.

[11] Moloney writes, "The marriage of both meanings produces one of the major themes for the rest of the story: Jesus' death makes known his love for his own and thus makes God known (see 3:16–17)" (*Glory not Dishonor*, 12). See also Lindars, *John*, 448.

[12] J. Michl, "Der Sinn der Fusswaschung," *Bib* 40 (1959): 697–708, esp. 701.

[13] See the discussion in Beasley-Murray, *John*, 239–40.

[14] A Jewish work composed in between 100 B.C.E. and 200 C.E.; see C. Burchard, "Joseph and Aseneth: A New Translation and Introduction," *OTP* 2.177–247.

significant ecclesiological implications.[15] On the basis of the story of Aseneth, Raymond E. Brown also sees the possibility of interpreting the footwashing "as a traditional act of love."[16] This interpretation fits in well with the Johannine theology of Jesus' death on the cross as the supreme act of redemptive love (cf. 10:11; 15:13).

There is consensus among scholars that the meal and the footwashing in chapter 13 are analogous in function to the synoptic narratives of the Last Supper and the eucharistic institution (Mark 14:17–26; Luke 22:14–23; Matt 26:20–30).[17] Sandra M. Schneiders points out that "both the action over the bread and wine and the foot washing serve as prophetic gestures revealing the true significance of the death of Jesus within the theological perspectives of the respective evangelists."[18] The use of τίθημι in 13:4 suggests a thematic link between the footwashing and the death of Jesus, since the same verb τίθημι is used for the Good Shepherd "laying down" his life for the sheep (10:11, 15, 17, 18). Similarly, the verb λαμβάνω is used to describe both Jesus' taking up of his outer garments after the footwashing (13:12) as well as the Good Shepherd's taking up of his life again (10:17, 18).[19] If this is so, then the footwashing foreshadows and symbolizes the redemptive death of Jesus and is not merely an "example" or a "representation" (ὑπόδειγμα) of humble service.[20] The Fourth Evangelist will not

---

[15] B. Schwank, "Exemplum dedi vobis: Die Fusswaschung (13, 1–17)," *SeinSend* 28 (1963): 4–17, cited by Brown, *John,* 2.558, 564–65.

[16] Brown, *John,* 2.564.

[17] For the sacramental and baptismal significance of the footwashing, see F. J. Moloney, "A Sacramental Reading of John 13:1–38," *CBQ* 53 (1991): 237–56; Moloney, *Glory not Dishonor,* 14–15; Brown, *John,* 2.558–59; S. M. Schneiders, "The Foot Washing (John 13:1–20): An Experiment in Hermeneutics," *CBQ* 43 (1981): 81–82; P. Grelot, "L'interprétation pénitentielle du lavement des pieds," in *L'homme devant Dieu: Mélanges H. de Lubac* (2 vols.; Paris: Aubier, 1963), 1.75–91; M. C. de Boer, *Johannine Perspectives on the Death of Jesus* (CBET 17; Kampen: Kok Pharos, 1996), 283–92. Against this view, see J. C. Thomas, *Footwashing in John 13 and the Johannine Community* (JSNTSup 61; Sheffield: JSOT Press, 1991), 19–25; Niemand, *Fusswaschungserzählung,* 252–56.

[18] Schneiders, "The Foot Washing," 81 n. 22. Schneiders underlines the revelatory character of the event by designating the footwashing as a "prophetic action." Prophetic action refers to "an action which is presented as divinely inspired, revelatory in content, proleptic in structure, symbolic in form, and pedagogical in intent" (ibid., n. 21).

[19] See J. D. G. Dunn, "The Washing of Disciples' Feet in John 13:1–20," *ZNW* 61 (1970): 248; C. R. Koester, *Symbolism in the Fourth Gospel: Meaning, Mystery, Community* (Minneapolis: Fortress, 1995), 10–11; Culpepper, "The Johannine Hypodeigma," 137; Moloney, *Glory not Dishonor,* 14.

[20] Beasley-Murray, *John,* 235.

portray Jesus' death as a moment of suffering and humiliation but as "the hour of his passing over to the Father and the moment of a consummate act of loving self-gift."[21] Jesus' death is the crowning moment of his whole earthly existence, the moment of glorification that makes known the redemptive power of God's love, revealing Jesus' love for his own (3:16–17; 10:11, 14–15), God's new chosen community.

The dialogue between Jesus and Peter is another important narrative moment that helps the readers to determine the symbolic meaning and significance of the footwashing (vv. 6–10).[22] The dialogue points out "what Jesus has done in the footwashing is essential if the disciples are to gain a heritage with him (v. 8) and apparently this action cleanses them of sin (10)."[23] What follows will explore the significance of sharing a heritage (μέρος) with Jesus. The aspects of cleansing and sharing a μέρος with Jesus as a result of Jesus' footwashing take us further into OT covenant motifs.

Jesus' footwashing enables the disciples to have a share (ἔχειν μέρος) with Jesus. The response of Jesus to Peter, ἐὰν μὴ νίψω σε, οὐκ ἔχεις μέρος μετ' ἐμοῦ, "If I do not wash you, you have no part in me" (v. 8b), suggests that it is not a question of Peter's allowing himself to be washed by Jesus but "a salvific action of Jesus is involved."[24] What is the significance of having a μέρος with Jesus within the literary and theological context of Jesus' footwashing? The OT attests the practice of footwashing as a gesture of hospitality (Gen 18:4; 19:2; 24:32; 43:24; Judg 19:21; 1 Sam 25:41).[25] In the Jewish tradition, footwashing is also regarded as a preparation for meeting God. Yahweh said to Moses that Aaron and his sons should wash their hands and their feet so that they would not die (Exod 30:17–21, esp. v. 21).[26] In the OT, "washing" is also associated with the new life and the covenant relationship that one shares with God. According to the promise

---

[21] Moloney, *Glory not Dishonor*, 13.

[22] Schnackenburg comments that "since the evangelist concentrates all his attention on the following conversation between Jesus and Peter, any attempts to provide a further interpretation are out of the question here" (*John*, 3.18). See also Brown, *John*, 2.565; Schneiders, "The Foot Washing," 82–83.

[23] Brown, *John*, 2.558.

[24] Ibid., 2.565.

[25] See also other Jewish documents, *T. Ab.* 7.44; *Jos. Asen.* 7.1; 13.12; 20.1–5. See also the detailed study of A. J. Hultgren, "The Johannine Footwashing (13:1–11) as Symbol of Eschatological Hospitality," *NTS* 28 (1982): 539–46, esp. 541–42.

[26] See also Philo, *QG* 4.5; 4.60; *QE* 1.2; *Mos.* 2.138; *Spec.* 1.206–207. For other Jewish documentation in support of this view, see H. Weiss, "Foot Washing in the Johannine Community," *NovT* 21 (1979): 298–325, esp. 302–5.

of the new covenant in Ezekiel, it is the washing of the people in clean
water, the outpouring of the spirit, and the observances of the law that will
usher in the new age (Ezek 36:25–28).[27] This washing and cleansing on the
part of Yahweh seems to be a necessary condition for the people to return
to their land, their heritage (חֵלֶק), and to re-establish their covenant relationship (וִהְיִיתֶם לִי לְעָם וְאָנֹכִי אֶהְיֶה לָכֶם לֵאלֹהִים, Ezek 36:28). God cleanses them
and gives them a new heart that enables them to be faithful to their
covenant relationship.

The LXX uses μέρος/μερίς to render the Hebrew חֵלֶק (e.g., Num 18:20).
The term חֵלֶק refers to the God-given portion or share of the land to each
tribe of Israel in the promised land (Deut 12:12; 14:27).[28] In the OT, חֵלֶק is
the inheritance in the promised land that is intimately connected to and
dependent on the covenant relationship. For example,

וַיֹּאמֶר יְהוָה אֶל־אַהֲרֹן בְּאַרְצָם לֹא תִנְחָל וַחֵלֶק לֹא־יִהְיֶה לְךָ בְּתוֹכָם

(Num 18:20 MT)   אֲנִי חֶלְקְךָ וְנַחֲלָתְךָ בְּתוֹךְ בְּנֵי יִשְׂרָאֵל:

Καὶ ἐλάλησεν Κύριος πρὸς Ααρων· ἐν τῇ γῇ αὐτῶν οὐ κληρονομήσεις,
καὶ μερὶς οὐκ ἔσται σοι ἐν αὐτοῖς, ὅτι ἐγὼ μερίς σου καὶ κληρονομία
σου ἐν μέσῳ τῶν υἱῶν Ισραηλ (Num 18:20 LXX).

Then the LORD said to Aaron: "You shall have no allotment in their
land, nor shall you have any <u>share</u> among them; I am your <u>share</u> and
your possession among the Israelites" (Num 18:20).

In the first part of the verse, μερίς/חֵלֶק refers to the God-given portion
of the land, but in the second part, God becomes the μερίς/חֵלֶק for Aaron
and his family members. To have a μερίς/חֵלֶק with God implies accepting
God as their possession or inheritance (κληρονομία/נַחֲלָה). This status can
prevail only when Aaron and his clan remain faithful to the covenant relationship with Yahweh: וִהְיִיתֶם לִי לְעָם וְאָנֹכִי אֶהְיֶה לָכֶם לֵאלֹהִים, "You shall be my
people and I shall be your God (Ezek 36:28)."

The primary meaning of ἔχειν μέρος is "to have a share with," or "be
a partner with."[29] The expression thus alludes to a fellowship or partnership with Jesus (μετ' ἐμοῦ, 13:8): the relationship of the disciples as Jesus'

---

[27] See the discussion in M. Greenberg, *Ezekiel 21–37: A New Translation with
Introduction and Commentary* (AB 22A; New York: Doubleday, 1997), 726–40.
[28] See the discussion in P. Dreyfus, "Le thème de l'héritage dans l'Ancien Testament," *RSPT* 42 (1958): 3–49.
[29] BDAG, 633–34 s.v. "μέρος."

own (cf. οἱ ἴδιοι, 13:1; 15:16) and sharing the eternal heritage or reward with Jesus.[30] The presence of the disciples with Jesus after his return to the Father is a recurring theme in chapters 13–17 and is developed further in 14:3 and 17:24. George R. Beasley-Murray interprets μέρος with Jesus as κοινωνία with him in the life after death.[31] But the use of the present tense, ἔχεις μέρος μετ' ἐμοῦ (v. 8b), suggests that μέρος with Jesus is not only a future communion but a present reality. In other words, sharing a μέρος with Jesus has both "already" and "not yet" dimensions. This understanding is further underscored by Jesus' command that the disciples wash one another's feet (13:14–15). As a present reality, sharing a μέρος with Jesus, the κοινωνία or the intimate relationship with Jesus, initiates and deepens the κοινωνία or the fellowship among the disciples. Rudolf Bultmann claims that "13:1–20 describes the founding of the community and the law of its being."[32] To have μέρος with Jesus implies "to be part of the self-giving love that will bring Jesus' life to an end (cf. v. 1), symbolically anticipated by the footwashing (v. 8)."[33] In the light of the above discussion, it seems that sharing a μέρος with Jesus is best paraphrased as entering into a covenant relationship with Jesus characterized by mutual belonging, intimacy, and commitment. The covenant overtones are further accentuated by the covenant command of Jesus (13:31–35).

A NEW COVENANT COMMANDMENT (13:31–35)

The Johannine Jesus claims that he is giving a new commandment (ἐντολὴν καινήν) by exhorting his disciples to love one another (ἀγαπᾶτε ἀλλήλους, 13:34). One needs to look into both the act of giving a commandment and the newness of this commandment. The very idea of giving a commandment (ἐντολή) carries covenant overtones. The Ten Commandments are given to the people within the context of establishing a covenant between Yahweh and Israel (Exod 34:10–28; Deut 4:13, etc.). These commandments and other stipulations are existential imperatives for Israel to continue to be God's chosen people or סְגֻלָּה (e.g., Exod 24:3–8; Josh 24:1–28). The Johannine Jesus gives his disciples a new love com-

---

[30] For the eschatological use of μέρος, see Rev 20:6; 21:8; 22:19. See also the discussion in Brown, *John*, 2.565–66.

[31] Beasley-Murray, *John*, 237.

[32] Bultmann, *John*, 479.

[33] Moloney, *John*, 375.

mandment: "Love one another as I have loved you" (13:34).[34] The novelty of this love commandment has been a subject of much scholarly discussion (cf. "You shall love your neighbor as yourself," Lev 19:18; "You shall love the alien [גֵּר] as yourself," Lev 19:34).[35] Raymond E. Brown suggests that the newness consists in the context of the new covenant that reflects the fulfillment of Jeremiah's prophecy in Jesus and his disciples: "Behold, the days are coming when I will make a covenant with the house of Israel and the house of Judah" (31:31–34).[36] To claim that the love command is new just because it is presented within the context of a new covenant seems insufficient. The question still remains unanswered: what is new about this love command even in the context of the new covenant?[37] The newness of the Johannine love command consists in (1) the aspect of its reciprocity—love one another, both giving/sharing and receiving love; (2) the fact that God is its source and Jesus is its model—love one another as I have loved you (cf. "as the Father has loved me, so I have loved you," 15:9).[38] The first aspect, "love one another," underlines the mutuality of a relationship; it is not only loving the other but also being loved by the other. The second aspect, "as I have loved you," highlights the quality of Christian love and relationship among the disciples. Referring to the use of καθώς in 13:15, 34; 15:9–10, 12; 17:11, 21, Rudolf Bultmann argues that the adverb καθώς in the gospel has both a sense of comparison and a causative or explanatory sense.[39] The disciples' love is thus both modeled after Jesus' love and grounded in Jesus' love for them. Wiard Popkes's study points out that the adverb "καθώς establishes a correlation containing elements of participation and of analogy or correspondence."[40] Jesus' love has been both to perfection and to the end (εἰς τέλος, 13:1c) and shared generously to the

---

[34] Cf. the synoptic version in Mark 12:28–31//Matt 22:34–40//Luke 10:25–28. The synoptic Jesus combines both Deut 6:5 and Lev 19:18.

[35] The love commandment is important in the rabbinic writings of Judaism. For example, Hillel says: "Be of the disciples of Aaron, loving peace and pursuing peace, loving mankind and drawing them to the Torah" (*Pirqe Abot* 1.12; *Abot R. Nat.* 12).

[36] Brown, *John,* 2.614.

[37] B. Schwank is of the opinion that there is nothing new in this commandment ("Der Weg zum Vater [13, 31–14, 11]," *SeinSend* 28 [1963]: 100–114), cited by Brown, *John,* 2.613–14.

[38] For the opinion that the love command of the Fourth Gospel is a gift, see Brown, *John,* 2.612.

[39] Bultmann, *John,* 382 n. 2. See also the detailed discussion in O. de Dinechin, "καθώς similitude dans l'Évangile selon saint Jean," *RSR* 58 (1970): 195–236.

[40] W. Popkes, "Zum Verständnis der Mission bei Johannes," *ZM* 4 (1978): 66; cited by Köstenberger, *Mission of Jesus,* 189 n. 175.

extent of laying down his life for his friends (cf. 15:13). The disciples are invited to participate in Jesus' love for them. The newness of the love command springs from the redemptive love of Jesus that holds the disciples
in the eschatological realm. Both of these dimensions of the Johannine
command, viz., the reciprocal love of the disciples and the redemptive love
of Jesus/God as its source, illustrate its newness. The new covenant command of Jesus insinuates that the disciples should possess the redemptive
love of Jesus/God as well as exchange the love of Jesus/God among them
by loving and being loved by the other. What the Johannine Jesus demands
from the disciples—loving and thus sharing the life of Jesus/God (cf. 20:22)
with one another (i.e., with one's covenant partner or the community
members)—is intrinsic to the nature of an OT covenant relationship.[41]
There is no better metaphor than the OT covenant relationship to describe
this love and communion that should exist among the disciples, between
the disciples and Jesus, and between Jesus and the Father. This covenant
relationship shared among the disciples becomes the sign of their true
identity in the world and enables the world to encounter Jesus after his
death and resurrection (13:31–35).

Different Responses to the Covenant Relationship

In the preparatory exhortation (chs. 2–12), the Johannine Jesus calls the
disciples to decision for or against Jesus, the true light. John 13 offers three
possible responses to this call to a covenant relationship: total rejection (Judas),
partial failure (Peter), and complete faithfulness (the Beloved Disciple).[42]

Judas (13:2, 11, 18–31)

From the very beginning of the narrative in chapter 13, the evangelist
gives much attention to the response of Judas (vv. 2, 11, 18, 21–30, 31). Although Jesus knew the decision of Judas in favor of the darkness or devil
(vv. 11, 18), Jesus offers the gift of μέρος to him by washing his feet (implied in the narrative) and giving him the piece of bread (ψωμίον) (v. 26).[43]

---

[41] See above chapter 2, pp. 58–66, esp. p. 65.

[42] I focus on these three characters whose importance is highlighted in the narrative by "focalization." On this narrative technique, see S. Rimmon-Kenan, *Narrative Fiction: Contemporary Poetics* (NA; London: Methuen, 1983), 71–85.

[43] The Greek noun ψωμίον means a little bit, morsel, or crumb of food (see
BDAG, 1100 s.v. "ψωμίον"). In v. 26, ψωμίον could refer to a piece of bread, or
herbs, or meat. Some exegetes argue that ψωμίον refers to meat (M.-J. Lagrange,

But the narrator informs the reader that, after the reception of the ψωμίον, Satan (Σατανᾶς) entered into Judas (v. 27a).[44] It was argued that Jesus' remark, "What you are about to do, do quickly" (v. 27b), is meant to call Judas to a decision for or against Jesus. As L. Newbigin comments, "The final gesture of affection precipitates the final surrender of Judas to the power of darkness."[45] Once the decision is made, Judas goes out and the narrator reminds the readers that "it was night" (ἦν δὲ νύξ, v. 30c). Toward the end of Jesus' ministry, Jesus speaks about the night that is fast approaching, "night is coming" (ἔρχεται νύξ, 9:4), and warns his disciples, saying, "If anyone walks at night (νύξ), he/she stumbles, because the light (φῶς) is not in him/her" (11:10). Judas seems to be among those who "have loved darkness (σκοτία) rather than light (φῶς) because their deeds were evil" (3:19).[46] The role of Judas in the story thus epitomizes the acceptance of darkness (σκοτία) and the total rejection of light (φῶς) and the covenant relationship or the fellowship (μέρος) offered to a disciple.

Peter (13:6–9, 36–38)

The narrator has given Peter a prominent role in the story by twice focusing on the dialogue between Jesus and Peter (vv. 6–9 and vv. 36–38). In the former, Peter fails to understand the significance of the footwashing and objects. In the latter, Jesus predicts Peter's different responses and his

---

Évangile selon saint Jean [EB; Paris: Gabalda, 1936], 362), or to bitter herbs (R. Kysar, *John* [ACNT; Minneapolis: Augsburg, 1986], 214). For those who consider it a piece of bread, supported by John 13:18 ("He who eats my bread lifted up his heel against me"), see Brown, *John*, 2.575; Moloney, *Glory not Dishonor*, 22; Beasley-Murray, *John*, 238.

[44] The purpose of Jesus' action of giving the morsel to Judas has been a much-discussed issue. For example, A. Schlatter reads it as a sign of severing the fellowship with Judas (*Das Evangelium nach Johannes* [Stuttgart: Calwer, 1928], 286); W. Wrede considers it "a kind of satanic sacrament, which Judas takes to himself" (*Vorträge und Studien* [Tübingen: J. B. C. Mohr (Paul Siebeck), 1907], 136). Brown interprets Judas's acceptance of the piece of bread without changing his plans as an indication that "he has chosen for Satan rather than for Jesus" (*John*, 2.578); Schnackenburg views it as a way of expelling Judas from the upper room (*John*, 3.30–31). For a detailed discussion, see Beasley-Murray, *John*, 237–40. In the Christian tradition, ψωμίον was commonly used to refer to the eucharistic host. Moloney is therefore of the opinion that the text has eucharistic overtones and is a concrete example of what it means for Jesus to love εἰς τέλος (*Glory not Dishonor*, 20–23).

[45] L. Newbigin, *The Light Has Come: An Exposition of the Fourth Gospel* (Grand Rapids: Eerdmans, 1982), 173.

[46] Brown, *John*, 2.578–79.

final destiny. On both occasions, Peter has been picked out "as the one to represent the disciples' lack of understanding."[47] The first two statements of Peter, "Lord, do you wash my feet?" and "You shall never wash my feet," reveal his complete ignorance of what it means to be washed by Jesus (vv. 6, 8a). Once Jesus explains the significance of his action, Peter is over-zealous in his third statement, "Lord, [wash] not only my feet, but also my hands and my head" (v. 9). Jesus' response to Peter demonstrates again that Peter cannot understand what is going on between Jesus and his disciples (v. 10).

Jesus' absolute knowledge of his destiny and Jesus' insistence that the disciples have this knowledge are concerns of the discourses and dialogues of chapter 13. Peter's query in verse 36, "Lord, where are you going?" indicates that he has not fully understood Jesus' discourses with the disciples. Peter still fails to comprehend fully the destiny and mission of Jesus. Jesus' response predicts two things about Peter's future responses: (1) Peter will follow Jesus later; (2) Peter will shortly deny Jesus three times. Parallel to these predictions, Peter expresses his desire by promising that he will follow Jesus and lay down his life for Jesus (v. 37). As Edwyn C. Hoskyns comments, Peter's response has "a double significance: its eventual truth as well as its present falsehood (cf. xi. 50)."[48] The section that follows and the early traditions show that, although Peter denied Jesus at first, later he laid down his life for Jesus (cf. 12:26; 21:18–19). Although Peter does not understand many things, he never stops his journey with Jesus. Peter's responses epitomize the faith journey of the disciples and their ongoing struggle to be faithful to their call and mission in continuing God's work and in revealing God's unconditional love to the world.

The Beloved Disciple (13:21–30)

The Beloved Disciple emerges in the gospel as the one sharing an intimate relationship with Jesus—the one who reclines on the bosom of Jesus (13:23), receives Jesus' mother at the cross (19:27), arrives first at the empty tomb (20:4), believes first in the resurrection (20:8), recognizes first the risen Lord (21:7).[49] The narrator makes an explicit reference to the Beloved Dis-

---

[47] Culpepper, "The Johannine *Hypodeigma*," 139.

[48] E. C. Hoskyns, *The Fourth Gospel* (ed. F. N. Davey; London: Faber & Faber, 1947), 452.

[49] It is accepted that the anonymous "another disciple" (18:15) and "other disciple" (18:16; 20:2, 3, 4, 8) are designations for the Beloved Disciple. For a detailed discussion of the identity and function of the Beloved Disciple, see Culpepper, *John,* 56–88. See also Charlesworth, *Beloved Disciple.*

ciple (ὃν ἠγάπα ὁ Ἰησοῦς) for the first time in 13:23. What is said about the Beloved Disciple here is very significant. He is reported as reclining on the bosom of Jesus (ἐν τῷ κόλπῳ τοῦ Ἰησοῦ) and is thus portrayed as the disciple closest to Jesus (v. 23a). This is confirmed by the comment of the narrator at the end of the sentence, ὃν ἠγάπα ὁ Ἰησοῦς (v. 23b).[50] This scene reminds the reader of the prologue where Jesus is said to have been at the Father's side (εἰς τὸν κόλπον τοῦ πατρός, 1:18) and the intimate relationship that exists between the Father and Jesus (14:10–11). The relationship between Jesus and the Beloved Disciple represents the covenant relationship and communion that is expected from the disciples and the subsequent readers of the gospel (15:4–10), those who are summoned to be like the Beloved Disciple (20:3–10) by believing without seeing Jesus (20:29).

THE PROMISE OF GOD'S INDWELLING PRESENCE AND GUIDANCE (14:1–31)

The OT covenant promises are bilateral in nature: God's commitment to Israel and Israel's obligation to be obedient to Yahweh.[51] The covenant promises presuppose Israel's knowledge of Yahweh as their God. This is evident because God reminds Israel repeatedly that being obedient to Yahweh or keeping the commands of Yahweh implies a deep knowledge of Yahweh as their God who brought them out of the land of Egypt (e.g., Exod 29:45–46; Deut 7:9; Jer 31:31–33).[52] The OT covenant includes various promises such as descendants (e.g., Gen 15:5; Exod 32:13), land (e.g., Gen 15:18; 17:8; Exod 32:13), and victory (e.g., Deut 20:4; 1 Sam 14:23). One of the covenant promises of God is to dwell among the people so that the people would know Yahweh as their God (Exod 29:45–46; Lev 26:11–12). The promise of God's indwelling presence is made right after ratifying the covenant with Israel at Mt. Sinai (Exod 24), when God commands Moses to instruct the people to build a sanctuary (מִקְדָּשׁ) for God

---

[50] The position of ὃν ἠγάπα ὁ Ἰησοῦς at the end of the sentence signals the emphasis given it. See BDF, § 473. Some consider ὃν ἠγάπα ὁ Ἰησοῦς as a later scribal interpolation because of its position at the end. For a discussion in favor of its presence in the original text, see Schnackenburg, *John,* 3.29.

[51] See above chapter 2, part I. See also the discussion in Freedman, "Divine Commitment," 419–31; Nicholson, *God and His People,* 210–15.

[52] On Israel's covenant faithfulness and Sabbath commandments (Exod 31:12–17), see B. Childs, *The Book of Exodus: A Critical Theological Commentary* (OTL; Philadelphia: Westminster, 1974), 541–42.

to dwell in their midst (cf. וְשָׁכַנְתִּי בְּתוֹכָם, Exod 25:8).[53] However, Israel's apostasy compels and persuades God to withdraw from the sanctuary (Exod 33:7–11).[54] God's presence in the sanctuary or tabernacle therefore signals both God's faithfulness to the covenant relationship (e.g., Lev 26:11; Ezek 37:27) and Israel's obedience to the commandments of God (Exod 31:12–17). Against this background the promises attributed to Jesus in chapter 14 will be explored.

The major concern of the evangelist in chapter 14 is to encourage and console the disciples who are troubled by his departure to the Father ("Do not let your hearts be troubled," 14:1a, 27d).[55] Jesus reassures the disciples, who are bewildered and struggling to comprehend the departure and destiny of Jesus, by making many promises of his ongoing presence with them (e.g., vv. 3, 7, 16–17, 18, 20, 21, 23, 26, 28), and commanding them to believe in him (14:1), to love him and the Father, and to keep his commandments (e.g., vv. 15, 21, 23). The promises and commandments of Jesus to the disciples before his departure provide important insights into Johannine discipleship.

THE INDWELLING PRESENCE OF GOD/JESUS/THE PARACLETE

Jesus speaks of various types of indwelling presence: the indwelling that involves Jesus and the Father (e.g., 10, 11); Jesus and the disciples (e.g., vv. 3, 18, 28); the Paraclete and the disciples (e.g., v. 17); the Father, Jesus, and the disciples (e.g., v. 23).[56] By means of the metaphor "indwelling," chapter 14 underscores the descending movement of the transcendent God to the human realm in general and to the believing community in particular (cf. 1:14, 51).[57] Jesus promises his everlasting communion to the disciples who remain faithful to the covenant relationship.

---

[53] The sanctuary is later referred to as both a dwelling or tabernacle (מִשְׁכָּן) and the "tent of meeting" (אהל מועד). For a detailed study of the dwelling presence of God in the OT, see C. R. Koester, *The Dwelling of God: The Tabernacle in the Old Testament, Intertestamental Jewish Literature, and the New Testament* (CBQMS 22; Washington, D.C.: Catholic Biblical Association of America, 1989), 6–22.

[54] R. W. L. Moberly, *At the Mountain of God: Story and Theology in Exodus 32–34* (JSOTSup 22; Sheffield: JSOT, 1983), 63–65; Childs, *Exodus,* 592–93.

[55] See Brown, *John,* 2.624–57; Segovia, *Farewell of the Word,* 80–121; Moloney, *Glory not Dishonor,* 29–54.

[56] See also the discussion in Brown, *John,* 2.602–3.

[57] See the comment of A. Dettwiler that there is a "grosse Bewegung von der Transzendenz zur Immanenz Gottes" (*Die Gegenwart des Erhöhten,* 202). See also M. L. Coloe, *God Dwells with Us: Temple Symbolism in the Fourth Gospel* (Collegeville, Minn.: Liturgical Press, 2001), 163.

I Will Come to You (vv. 2–3, 18, 28)

Verses 2–3 bristle with many exegetical and theological difficulties as the evangelist tries to combine both future and realized eschatology.[58] Jesus informs his disciples that he is going to the Father's οἰκία to prepare a dwelling or home (μονή) for the believing disciples, and promises that he will come again (πάλιν ἔρχομαι) to take the disciples with him to the Father's οἰκία. The exegesis of the verses in favor of one or other eschatology depends on the interpretations of μοναί and ἡ οἰκία τοῦ πατρός μου (v. 2) and the promise of Jesus, πάλιν ἔρχομαι καὶ παραλήμψομαι ὑμᾶς πρὸς ἐμαυτόν, ἵνα ὅπου εἰμὶ ἐγὼ καὶ ὑμεῖς ἦτε, "I will come again and will take you to myself, so that where I am you may be also" (v. 3).[59] The term μονή occurs only twice in the gospel (14:2, 23); it refers to a dwelling where God is present in 14:2 and to God's permanent abiding presence among believers in 14:23.[60] The metaphor ἡ οἰκία τοῦ πατρός μου is open to various interpretations. The noun ἡ οἰκία can refer either to a house as a building (Matt 2:11; 5:15; 7:24–27; 10:12a) or to a family or household (John 4:53; Matt 10:12b; 12:25; Mark 6:4), and figuratively, it can mean either the human body as the house of the soul (2 Cor 5:1a) or heaven as God's dwelling place (cf. 2 Cor 5:1b).[61] It can be a designation of the OT בֵּית יהוה, the Jerusalem temple (cf. οἶκος, 2:16–17).[62] Since the Jerusalem temple is replaced by the body of Jesus and ἡ οἰκία τοῦ πατρός μου is the goal of Jesus' final departure from the disciples, it could also be a reference to the heavenly temple.[63] In the Fourth Gospel, all the occurrences of the term οἶκος refer to a building (2:16, 17; 11:20), but the term οἰκία is used both for the building (11:31; 12:3) and for the household or family (4:53; 8:35). The use of οἰκία instead of οἶκος in 14:2 suggests the meaning of a "household" or "family."[64] It

---

[58] For examples of both future and realized eschatology in the gospel, see John 5:25–29; 6:35–40, 44–48.

[59] See the detailed study of J. McCaffrey, *The House with Many Rooms: The Temple Theme of Jn 14,2–3* (AnBib 114; Roma: Editrice Pontificio Istituto Biblico, 1988), 29–220; Coloe, *God Dwells with Us*, 160–78.

[60] See F. Hauck, "μοναί," *TDNT* 4.579–81. See also BDAG, 658 s.v. "μοναί."

[61] O. Michel, "οἰκία," *TDNT* 5.131–34; BDAG, 695 s.v. "οἰκία." See also O. Michel, "οἶκος," *TDNT* 5.119–31; BDAG, 698–99 s.v. "οἶκος."

[62] For the importance of John 2:16–17 for the interpretation of John 14:2–3, see also O. Schaefer, "Der Sinn der Rede Jesu von den vielen Wohnungen in seines Vaters Hause und von den Weg zu ihm (Joh 14,2–3)," *ZNW* 32 (1933): 212; Brown, *John*, 2.627.

[63] McCaffrey, *House with Many Rooms*, 31.

[64] R. H. Gundry comments that "The Father's house is no longer heaven, but God's household or family" ("'In my Father's House are Many Μοναί' [John 14,2]," *ZNW* 58 [1967]: 70).

seems therefore reasonable to think that οἰκία in 14:2 can be a reference to the family of God (cf. 1:12).[65] Scholars interpret the "return of Jesus" in verse 3 in terms of both a realized eschatology and an end-time eschatology.[66] Francis J. Moloney claims that "He [Jesus] is going away, and he will return at some future time, but there is also the promise of an ongoing presence of Jesus."[67] Jesus is promising that he will be in communion with the disciples, and they will share the same abiding place (ὅπου εἰμὶ ἐγὼ καὶ ὑμεῖς ἦτε) after his death. This promise is repeatedly made (ἔρχομαι πρὸς ὑμᾶς, vv. 3, 18, 28) to comfort and console the bewildered disciples.

I Will Give You Another Paraclete to Be with You Forever (vv. 16–17)

The first Paraclete (παράκλητος) saying of Jesus appears in verses 16–17.[68] The verbal adjective παράκλητος originally meant in the passive sense, "one who is called to someone's aid," and later acquired a more active meaning such as "one who appears in another's behalf," or "mediator," or "intercessor," or "helper."[69] Jesus promises that he will request the Father to send another Paraclete to be with the disciples forever (v. 16). The expression ἄλλον παράκλητον, "another Paraclete" implies the role of

---

[65] For similar views, see D. E. Aune, *The Cultic Setting of Realized Eschatology in Early Christianity* (NovTSup 28; Leiden: E. J. Brill, 1972), 130; Coloe, *God Dwells with Us,* 160–64.

[66] For a realized eschatology, see B. Witherington III, *John's Wisdom: A Commentary on the Fourth Gospel* (Louisville: Westminster John Knox, 1995), 249. M. C. de Boer argues that the return of Jesus in v. 3 alludes to the coming of the Paraclete (*Johannine Perspectives,* 130–32). For a future eschatology in v. 3, see Gundry, "'In my Father's House,'" 71–72; J. Beutler, *Habt keine Angst: Die erste johanneische Abschiedsrede (Joh 14)* (SBS 116; Stuttgart: Verlag Katholisches Bibelwerk, 1984), 37–41. For a survey of the debate, see J. Neugebauer, *Die eschatologischen Aussagen in den johanneischen Abschiedsreden* (BWANT 140; Stuttgart: Kohlhammer, 1995), 14–34; Moloney, *Glory not Dishonor,* 32–36 nn. 14–15.

[67] Moloney, *Glory not Dishonor,* 34–35.

[68] See also 14:26; 15:26; 16:7–11, 12–15.

[69] See BDAG, 766 s.v. "παράκλητος." In secular Greek παράκλητος refers to a "legal advisor" in a court. But in the pre-and post-Christian literature, it is used with a more general meaning such as a helper, mediator, or intercessor (e.g., *Demosth.* 19.1; *Dionys. Hal.* 11.37.1; *Cass. Dio* 46.20.1). For the use of παράκλητος as an intercessor, see also the writings of Philo (*Jos.* 239; *Mos.* 2.134; *Spec.* 1.237). For a summary of its historico-religious background and its different usages outside as well as in the NT, see the discussion in J. Behm, "παράκλητος," *TDNT* 5.800–814. For a survey of the contemporary discussion of the use of παράκλητος in the Fourth Gospel, see Moloney, *Glory not Dishonor,* 40–41 n. 35.

Jesus as the first Paraclete (cf. 1 John 2:1).[70] Jesus will depart from the disciples, but the other Paraclete will be with them forever (εἰς τὸν αἰῶνα). Jesus describes παράκλητος further as τὸ πνεῦμα τῆς ἀληθείας, "the Spirit of truth." The Johannine Paraclete is the Spirit of truth, the Spirit that reveals truth or bears witness to the truth that is Jesus (cf. 14:6). What is being promised to the disciples is "the ongoing presence of the revelation of God in the world."[71] This ongoing revelation of God's active presence is actualized by the Spirit of truth abiding with the disciples (cf. παρ' ὑμῖν) and being in them (cf. ἐν ὑμῖν) permanently after the departure of Jesus (v. 17). By the use of two distinct prepositional phrases, παρ' ὑμῖν and ἐν ὑμῖν, the evangelist combines and maintains two traditions together, namely, the presence of the Spirit-Paraclete in the midst of the disciples as a community (cf. Matt 18:20), and its presence within the individual disciples (cf. 1 Cor 6:19; 2 Cor 6:16).[72] The permanent and active presence of God will be manifested both in the believing community (παρ' ὑμῖν) as well as in the individual believers as an indwelling presence (ἐν ὑμῖν). As we shall see later, both the communitarian and the personal aspects of the indwelling presence of the Spirit-Paraclete are significant in appreciating the uniqueness of the Johannine understanding of discipleship.

My Father and I Will Make Our Dwelling/Home with You (v. 23)

Jesus announces repeatedly the promise of his indwelling presence with the disciples through various images and metaphors. One can perceive a progression in these promises: (1) Jesus is coming to the disciples (e.g., ἔρχομαι πρὸς ὑμᾶς, vv. 18, 28; see also πάλιν ἔρχομαι in v. 3), and they will share the same abiding place (v. 3); (2) Jesus is promising that the Paraclete, the Spirit of truth, will be permanently with the disciples and in the disciples (vv. 16–17); (3) Jesus and the Father, who share an intimate communion and oneness (v. 10–11), will make their "dwelling" (μονή) with the disciples (v. 23). The μονή of the Father and Jesus with the disciples reaffirms the personal experience of the disciples who are faithful and obedient to the commandments of Jesus.[73] A reading of end-time eschatology in verse 23 does not take seriously the subject of the verb ποιησόμεθα; it is not the disciples, but the Father and Jesus who will make their μονή

---

[70] For this view, see R. E. Brown, "The Paraclete in the Fourth Gospel," *NTS* 13 (1966–1967): 113–32; Segovia, *Farewell of the Word,* 95.

[71] Moloney, *Glory not Dishonor,* 41.

[72] For similar interpretations of these prepositions, see Schnackenburg, *John,* 3.76; Beasley-Murray, *John,* 257–58.

[73] For a similar interpretation of v. 23, see Barrett, *John,* 466.

with the disciples who are bewildered by the departure of Jesus. What Jesus promises and brings to light repeatedly in chapter 14 is the active, dynamic, and abiding presence of Jesus and the Father through the dwelling of the Spirit-Paraclete *with* and *in* the disciples (vv. 2–3, 16–17, 18, 23, 28) who are faithful to the covenant commandments of Jesus (vv. 15, 21, 23a). These promises echo the ardent desire of Yahweh to dwell (שׁכן) in the midst of the people of Israel that reminds them of their covenant obligations (e.g., Exod 29:45–46; Lev 26:11; Ezek 37:27; Zech 2:10–11).

The Knowledge of God/Jesus

The OT covenant texts place the promises of God's dwelling presence and Israel's knowledge of God as mutually inclusive pronouncements. For example, "I will dwell among the Israelites, and I will be their God. And they shall know that I am the Lord their God, who brought them out of the land of Egypt that I might dwell among them; I am the Lord their God" (Exod 29:44–45). These promises share a dialectic relationship as one leads to the other. Similarly in chapter 14, parallel to the promises of the indwelling presence of the Father, Jesus, and Spirit-Paraclete in the believing community are the assurances that the disciples will know the Father (v. 7) and the Spirit of truth (v. 17), that Jesus will manifest himself (vv. 20–21), and that the Paraclete will teach the disciples and enable them to remember everything (v. 26).

You Will Know My Father (v. 7)

As far as the textual evidence is concerned, 14:7 is open to two different interpretations. It is either a promise or a reproach. Some of the earlier text traditions read it as a real conditional clause, a positive statement and a promise: "If you have come to know me (εἰ ἐγνώκατέ με), you will know (γνώσεσθε) my Father as well."[74] Other traditions read it as a contrary-to-fact conditional clause, a negative response and a reproach: "If you had known me (εἰ ἐγνώκειτέ με), you would have known (ἐγνώκειτε ἄν or ἄν ἤδειτε) my Father as well."[75] I favor the former reading as a promise, since

---

[74] εἰ ἐγνώκατέ με is attested in 𝔓66 (ℵ D* ἐμέ) 579 *l* 524 it(a).b.c.d arm geo. γνώσεσθε is attested in 𝔓66 ℵ D W itd copsa.bo.ach2 arm geo.

[75] εἰ ἐγνώκειτέ με is attested in (A omit με) B C (D1 ἐμέ) L Δ Θ Ψ 0141 *f*1 *f*13 28 33 157 180 205 565 597 700 892 1006 1010 1241 1243 1292 1342 1424 1505 *Byz* vg *al*. ἐγνώκειτε ἄν is attested in A C3 Δ *f*13 28 157 180 205 597 700 892 1006 1010 1071 1241 1243 1292 1342 1424 1505 *Byz al*.

the change from a promise to a reproach can be explained by the lack of understanding on the part of the disciples in general, and the query of Philip and Jesus' response in verses 8–9 in particular.[76] Jesus reveals that he is departing from the disciples and going to the Father's οἰκία (v. 2), and now promises that the disciples will know the Father as they have known Jesus (v. 7). The knowledge of the Father and Jesus, the Sent One, is very important for Johannine discipleship (e.g., 4:22; 8:55 [negatively]; 10:14–15; 14:7; 14:17 [positively]) and for the new form of worship that Jesus promised to the Johannine community (cf. 4:22–24).

You Will Know the Spirit of Truth (v. 17)

Jesus guarantees the disciples that they will know the Spirit of truth, unlike the world (κόσμος), which neither sees nor knows the Spirit (v. 17). Jesus makes a sharp distinction between the unbelieving κόσμος and the disciples elsewhere in the gospel. The unbelieving κόσμος does not know the λόγος (1:10), the Father (8:55), and the Spirit (14:17). What distinguishes the disciples from the κόσμος is that they have come to know Jesus as the Holy One of God (6:69; see also 8:28 [ἐγώ εἰμι]; 10:14 [Good Shepherd]), and they will know the Father (14:7) and the Spirit-Paraclete (14:17).

You Will Know the Loving Relationship between the Father and the Son (vv. 20–21)

Jesus promises that on the day of his departure or "hour" (cf. ἐν ἐκείνῃ τῇ ἡμέρᾳ, v. 20) the disciples will know (γνώσεσθε) the intimate union and mutual oneness that he shares with the Father and with the disciples, ἐγὼ ἐν τῷ πατρί μου καὶ ὑμεῖς ἐν ἐμοὶ κἀγὼ ἐν ὑμῖν, "I am in my Father, and you in me, and I in you" (v. 20).[77] As Francis J. Moloney points out, "the oneness between the Father and the Son has been at the heart of much of Jesus' teaching and has been the basis of his authority (see, e.g.,

---

[76] It could also be an attempt to harmonize the present text with 8:19: "If you had known (εἰ ᾔδειτε) me, you would have known (ἂν ᾔδειτε) my Father as well." For those who accept it as a promise, see Barrett, *John*, 458–59; Moloney, *Glory not Dishonor*, 37; Beasley-Murray, *John*, 241, 253. For those who read it as a reproach, J. H. Bernard, *A Critical and Exegetical Commentary on the Gospel According to St. John* (2 vols.; ICC; Edinburgh: T&T Clark, 1928), 2.538–39; Brown, *John*, 2.621; Segovia, *Farewell of the Word*, 87.

[77] For the expression ἐν ἐκείνῃ τῇ ἡμέρᾳ as a reference to Jesus' "hour" or death on the cross, see E. Haenchen, *John* (trans. R. W. Funk; 2 vols.; Hermeneia; Philadelphia: Fortress, 1984), 2.126–27.

5:19–30), but the introduction of the believer into that oneness is new."[78] Verse 21 defines this mutual oneness between the Father, the Son, and the disciples in terms of a binding love relationship and commitment to the commandments, which is best paraphrased as an OT covenant relationship. Faithfulness to this covenant relationship on the part of the disciples enables each of them to receive an ongoing revelation or manifestation of Jesus, ἐμφανίσω αὐτῷ ἐμαυτόν, "I will manifest myself to him" (v. 21c). The use of ἐμφανίζω is very significant here since it is the traditional term for the theophanies of the OT (e.g., Exod 33:13, 18; Wis 1:2).[79] As Exod 33:12–23 indicates, the manifestation of Yahweh was necessary for the right knowledge of God and relationship with God. Jesus announces that he will be present to the disciples in a new way, more powerful and intimate than his presence during the earthly ministry that was conditioned by time, place, and religious traditions. What Jesus is promising here is the gift of discipleship itself as a new existence that shares a covenant relationship with the Father and Jesus, and receives the revelation of God's glory.

The Paraclete/Holy Spirit Will Make You Remember (v. 26)

The Paraclete is described as the Holy Spirit and the Sent One (πέμπω) by the Father with the mission of teaching (διδάσκω) the disciples or reminding (ὑπομιμνήσκω) the disciples of all that Jesus had taught them during his earthly ministry (v. 26).[80] Jesus' teaching elsewhere in the gospel refers to the revelatory activity of Jesus himself as the one who does the works of the Father (e.g., 7:16–17, 28; 8:28). The activity of reminding the disciples of the teaching of Jesus (πάντα ἃ εἶπον ὑμῖν [ἐγώ]) is entrusted to the Spirit (v. 26) who will be dwelling with and in the disciples forever (v. 17).[81] There are three other occasions when the evangelist uses the re-

---

[78] Moloney, *Glory not Dishonor*, 44.

[79] Barrett comments that ἐμφανίζω "is an appropriate word since it is used of theophanies" (*John*, 465). See also the discussion in Moloney, *Glory not Dishonor*, 45. In the NT, ἐμφανίζω and its cognates are used in the context of resurrection appearances (e.g., Mark 16:9; Acts 10:40).

[80] The verb διδάσκω is further specified by ὑπομιμνήσκω connected by an explicative καί. See the detailed discussion in I. de la Potterie, *La Vérité dans Saint Jean* (2 vols.; AnBib 73–74; Rome: Biblical Institute Press, 1977), 1.367–78.

[81] As U. B. Müller has observed long ago, there is no parallel in the NT for this explicit reference to the Spirit as the one who is assigned to remind the disciples of all that Jesus taught ("Die Parakletenvorstellung im Johannesevangelium," *ZTK* 71 [1974]: 46). On the "remembering" theme in the NT, see O. Michel, "μιμνήσκομαι," *TDNT* 4.675–83.

membering motif (2:17, 22; 12:16).[82] In all three occurrences the evangelist has the disciples remembering Scripture in terms of understanding Jesus' works as fulfillment of Scripture or the traditions of the covenant God. The remembering in verse 26 implies two things: the Spirit makes the teaching of Jesus (πάντα ἃ εἶπον ὑμῖν) available to the disciples, and they are called on to be obedient and faithful to the words or commandments of Jesus. The remembering motif (זכר) of recalling what Yahweh has done for Israel and what the covenant relationship with Yahweh entails with respect to the statutes and commandments permeates the whole OT.[83] The plea for both God and Israel to remember is based on God's past covenant relationship with, and commitment to, Israel. The memory was a means of encountering God and making the traditions of God's great acts in the past a present event, thus summoning Israel's fidelity to the covenant relationship.[84] The remembering motif in chapter 14 within the context of the covenant promises of Jesus strengthens the interpretation of Johannine discipleship as a covenant relationship that demands faithfulness to the traditions of Jesus and the revelation of God's work through the Spirit-Paraclete.

THE GIFT OF PEACE (V. 27)

The promise of the gift of peace (εἰρήνη) in 14:27 draws attention to the many covenant motifs that permeate chapter 14. The Greek εἰρήνη is a rendering of שָׁלוֹם. The intimate association between שָׁלוֹם and בְּרִית is evident in that they are occasionally used interchangeably in the OT (Gen 26:28, 31; Ps 55:20–21). Sometimes, both words are put together for emphasis or as a stronger expression for בְּרִית (בְּרִית שָׁלוֹם, Ezek 34:25; 37:26).

---

[82] For the "remembering motif" (ὑπομιμνήσκω) in the gospel and its function in John 14:26, see D. B. Woll, *Johannine Christianity in Conflict: Authority, Rank, and Succession in the First Farewell Discourse* (Chico, Calif.: Scholars Press, 1981), 98–105.

[83] There are more than 300 occurrence of the verb זכר and its cognates in the OT (e.g., Gen 9:15–16; Exod 13:3; Lev 26:42; Num 15:40; Deut 16:12; Josh 1:13; Judg 8:34; 2 Kgs 20:3; 2 Chr 16:12; Neh 1:8; Ps 105:5; Eccl 12:1; Isa 44:21; Jer 14:21; Ezek 16:60; Amos 1:9; Mal 4:4). For the significance of זכר in the theology and traditions of Israel, see B. S. Childs, *Memory and Tradition in Israel* (London: SCM Press, 1962). See also F. Chenderlin, *"Do This as My Memorial": The Semantic and Conceptual Background and Value of Anamnêsis in 1 Corinthians 11:24–25* (AnBib 99; Rome: Biblical Institute Press, 1982), 88–122.

[84] For the close association between memory and covenant, see Childs, *Memory*, 35, 36, 63–65, and 74.

After promising the indwelling presence and the knowledge of God, Jesus assures the disciples that he leaves his peace, שָׁלוֹם/εἰρήνη, with them (14:27). We shall see later that the gift of peace promised to the disciples is the life of Jesus (20:19–23) and thus inaugurates the new messianic era (cf. Isa 9:6–7; 52:7; 57:19; Ezek 37:26; Hag 2:9).[85] It will be discussed in detail in chapter 4 of this study.

A Call to Believe and Keep the Commandments

Other covenant motifs that can be gleaned from chapter 14 are the obligation to believe in Jesus and the command to love God and keep the commandments. Like the people of Israel, the disciples are called to manifest their fidelity to the covenant relationship by believing, i.e., keeping the commandments.

Believe in Me (vv. 1, 10–12)

This is not the first time that the disciples receive the command to "believe" (e.g., 5:44; 6:36, 64; 8:45, 46; 9:35; 10:26). Chapter 14, however, makes this command very precise and concrete with regard to its challenges and implications in the light of Jesus' departure. First, Jesus demands that the disciples should believe in Jesus and his words, as they believe in God (v. 1).[86] This command is defined and elaborated further by revealing the oneness of love that exists between the Father and the Son and their common mission or work (v. 10). Jesus is not talking about metaphysical union but the intense union of love that is shared by them (cf. 5:20; 14:20–24). The command to believe in this union of love is an invitation to participate in the life-of-love of Jesus and God by sharing a mutual relationship of knowing Jesus/God/the Paraclete and being known and loved by them (e.g., 14:7, 17). As Sandra M. Schneiders claims, "[the Johannine] faith is not a spiritual acquisition or a state of being but an activity, an ever-active relationship in the present."[87] The oneness or the relationship of love and life between the Father and the Son is to be understood in terms of their

---

[85] See the comment of Hoskyns, "The new order is simply the peace of God in the world" (*Fourth Gospel*, 461).

[86] In 14:1, I take the first πιστεύετε as an indicative and the second πιστεύετε as an imperative. Believing in God is not a problem for the listeners of Jesus, but believing in Jesus is. Some scholars, however, take both verbs as imperatives; see Moloney, *Glory not Dishonor*, 29.

[87] Schneiders, *Written That You May Believe*, 51–52.

common work or mission (vv. 11–12). Jesus is making an inseparable dialectic link that exists between believing, loving, and doing God's work.

Love God and Keep the Commandments (vv. 15, 21, 23–24)

There is a twofold command to the disciples: to love and keep the word/ words or commandment. Like the OT covenant relationship, Jesus describes discipleship in terms of a relationship characterized by mutual love, fidelity, and obedience to the covenant commandments (vv. 15, 21, 23–24).[88] Francis J. Moloney aptly observes that "the association of belief, love, and loyalty leads to a new promise: disciples who, in the presence of the Paraclete, love Jesus and keep his commandments in the in-between time, will come to know God and be loved by God and Jesus."[89] The covenant promises of Jesus are available only to those who know and love God by keeping the commandments, and who are committed to the ongoing revelation of God in the world. The disciple, lover and follower of Jesus, experiences a new depth of intimacy with God as a covenant partner and lover.

A CALL TO ABIDE AND KEEP THE COMMANDMENTS (15:1–17)

John 15:1–17 is an evocative and powerful *mashal* (מָשָׁל) about discipleship in terms of an abiding covenant relationship.[90] It is often suggested that

---

[88] For the concept of commandment and its importance for the OT covenant relationship, see M. J. O'Connell, "Concept of Commandment," 351–403.

[89] Moloney, *Glory not Dishonor,* 48.

[90] The literary genre of John 15:1–8 has been a subject of lively debate among Johannine scholars. R. E. Brown says that it is a מָשָׁל (*John,* 1.390–91; 2.668–69). As Brown acknowledges, this was first suggested by M. Hermaniuk, *La parabole évangélique* (Louvain: Louvain University Press, 1947). In the Jewish traditions מָשָׁל includes and integrates *all* types of figurative illustrations and discourses (e.g., allegory, maxim, metaphor, simile, parable, proverbs). However, Brown suggests that the מָשָׁל in John 15 emphasizes the allegorical aspects. Two other important suggestions are that John 15:1–8 reflects the literary genre of a figurative discourse (*Bildrede*) in which both allegorical and parabolic aspects are combined (R. Borig, *Der wahre Weinstock: Untersuchungen zu Jo 15, 1–10* [SANT 16; Munich: Kösel, 1967], 21–23) and a metaphorical discourse in which a metaphor is presented first and then is developed in the discourse that follows (D. Wead, *The Literary Devices in John's Gospel* [TD 4; Basel: Friedrich Reinhardt Kommissionsverlag, 1970], 74–82, 92–94). Segovia agrees with Wead with some modifications (*Farewell of the Word,* 132–35). Suggestions of Brown, Borig, Wead, and Segovia highlight one or other aspect of a מָשָׁל. The evangelist has integrated allegorical and metaphorical aspects of the מָשָׁל in John 15.

this small unit lies at the heart of the discourses in chapters 13–17.[91] This small unit consists of the metaphor of the vine and branches that defines discipleship in term of an abiding relationship with Jesus and the teaching of Jesus that underlines the mission of the disciples in terms of bearing fruit and glorifying the Father. The metaphor of the vine and branches also emphasizes the importance of loving and keeping the covenant commandments, and brings out the election motif of the discipleship paradigm. Four major components of Johannine discipleship can be identified: (1) a call to abide in Jesus and in his love; (2) a call to bear much fruit and to glorify the Father; (3) a call to keep the commandments and to love one another; and (4) a call to the status of being the chosen people of God.

THE METAPHOR OF ABIDING

The verb μένω is charged with persuasive theological significance in the gospel. The evangelist applied the verb μένω for the first time in the context of Jesus' baptism to reveal the divine origin and identity of Jesus as the one in whom the Spirit abides (1:31–34).[92] The abiding of the Spirit in Jesus is the sign of his identity as the incarnate Word of God (1:14), the one who baptizes with the Holy Spirit (1:33), the one who is constantly in communication with God and in relationship with God (1:1–2, 18).[93] The second occurrence of μένω is during the dialogue between Jesus and the disciples in 1:38: "Rabbi, where do you abide?"[94] The disciples want to know where Jesus abides. This is what Jesus reveals

---

[91] W. Brouwer considers the metaphor of the vine and branches "the climax around which the rest of the discourse turns" (*The Literary Development of John 13–17: A Chiastic Reading* [Atlanta: Society of Biblical Literature, 2000], 9–10, 11–18). See also Simoens, *La gloire d'aimer*, 130–50; Moloney, *John*, 416–18.

[92] Both the OT use of μένω (God's abiding presence) and κατασκηνόω (God's indwelling presence) are important for the understanding of Johannine use of μένω. See the discussions in F. Hauck, "μένω," *TDNT* 4.574–76; Heise, *Bleiben*, 22–28; D. Lee, *Flesh and Glory: Symbolism, Gender and Theology in the Gospel of John* (New York: Crossroad, 2002), 88–89.

[93] See the detailed discussion in D. A. Lee, "Abiding," 123–36.

[94] The dialogue between Jesus and the disciples can be interpreted either literally (Where do you stay?) or symbolically (Where do you abide?). The confession of faith in v. 41 ("We have found the Messiah") suggests the symbolic meaning of their query in v. 38 ("Where do you abide?"), since the object of their seeing is not Jesus' home or village but the revelation of Jesus' identity as the Messiah. For the symbolic reading of v. 38, see also Léon-Dufour, *Lecture de l'Évangile selon Jean*, 1.189.

to the disciples throughout the gospel, viz., the intimacy shared between Jesus and the Father (e.g., 5:19–20; 14:2, 23; 15:9–10). By inviting the disciples to abide in Jesus and in his words (cf. 4:40; 6:27, 56; 8:31–32) and making it an integral part of the process of becoming a disciple of Jesus (1:35–51; 4:4–42), the evangelist presents discipleship, from the very beginning, in terms of an everlasting covenant relationship with God. As the narrative unfolds, after revealing his identity as the bread of life (6:48), Jesus makes two claims, that those who eat this bread abide in him (6:56) and live forever (6:58).[95] Abiding in Jesus therefore enables the disciples to share the new life of God that transcends death.[96] Abiding in the word of Jesus that perfects the Mosaic law is the hallmark of Johannine discipleship: "If you abide (μείνητε) in my word, you will truly be my disciples" (8:31). Later on the evangelist describes discipleship in terms of overcoming darkness and abiding and dwelling in the true light that is Jesus (12:46).

In 15:1–17, the evangelist develops the abiding motif by the use of the metaphor of the vine and branches and teases out the intimate and binding covenant relationship between Jesus and his disciples. Jesus is presented as the true vine and the Father as the vinedresser who cares for the well-being of the vine and its branches, the disciples (vv. 1–2).[97] According to the prophetic traditions, Yahweh is the gardener and Israel is God's fruitful vine full of branches (Ezek 19:10; see also Ps 80:8–16 [LXX Ps 79:9–17]) or a choice vine (Jer 2:21) or God's vineyard (Isa 5:1–7; 27:2–6).[98] The Johannine account remains very faithful to Jewish traditions concerning Yahweh with regard to the role ascribed to the Father as the vinegrower (γεωργός),[99] but it reinterprets the identity and designation of God's vine or vineyard. Many commentators have recognized a replacement theme here,

---

[95] The symbol of bread in the OT is later reinterpreted in the prophetic tradition as the Torah (see Amos 8:11–12).

[96] For the Johannine discipleship in terms of an abiding relationship, see Winbery, "Abiding in Christ," 104–20. D. Lee compares the abiding relationship between Jesus and his disciples with that of Sophia and her followers (*Flesh and Glory*, 90–91). See also M. Scott, *Sophia and the Johannine Jesus* (JSNTSup 71; Sheffield: JSOT Press, 1992), 157–59.

[97] The presentation of Jesus as the true vine reminds the readers of the earlier descriptions of Jesus as the true light (1:9) and the one who gives the true bread from heaven (6:32).

[98] For the rabbinic use of the vine to describe Israel, see *Lev. R.* 36.2. See also Str-B, 2.563–64.

[99] The idea of God as the γεωργός of the cosmos and all that contains is also familiar to the Hellenistic readers; see Dodd, *Interpretation,* 411.

namely, Jesus the true vine replaces Israel.[100] But the text says something more than that by deliberately repeating and developing the metaphor of the vine and the branches: "I am the vine and you are the branches" (v. 5). The disciples of Jesus are presented as the branches of the true vine. While the commentators focus mainly on the revelation of Jesus' identity, the metaphor of the vine and branches serves to unravel the mystery of Johannine discipleship.[101] The organic oneness of the branches with the vine and with one another communicates so powerfully the mutual indwelling of Jesus and his disciples. Jesus together with his disciples now stands for the new Israel, the faithful and fruitful vine of God. The image of the vine and branches is essentially a symbol of the community of the disciples in covenant relationship with Jesus.[102] Jesus is described as the true vine (v. 1) and the disciples as the fruitful branches who are made clean by Jesus' word (v. 3–5).[103] Jesus' words, "You have already been made clean by the word," involve the acceptance of, and commitment to, the revelation of God in Jesus.[104] One cannot ignore the binding intimate relationship implied here and separate the fruitful branches from the true vine. Just as there can be no branches without the vine, one cannot talk about the vine and its fruitfulness without its branches. The mutual and binding covenant relationship between Jesus and the disciples is underlined. The community of the disciples designated in the metaphor as the fruitful branches (vv. 3–5) abiding in Jesus, the true vine, becomes the new vineyard of Yahweh. The

---

[100] For example, "Jesus has replaced Israel as the faithful and fruitful vine of God" (Segovia, *Farewell of the Word,* 136), or "The striking feature of the symbolism of the vine in John 15 is that it ceases to represent Israel and takes on Christological significance" (R. Alan Culpepper, *The Gospel and Letters of John* [IBT; Nashville: Abingdon, 1998], 214). See also A. Jaubert, "L'image de la vigne (Jean 15)," in *Oikonomia: Heilsgeschichte als Thema der Theologie: Oscar Cullmann zum 65. Geburtstag gewidmet* (ed. F. Christ; Hamburg: H. Reich, 1967), 93–96.

[101] C. H. Dodd argues that the LXX Ps 79:14–19 (Ps 80:13–18) makes the link between the vine and the Son of Man; both represent the people of God (*Interpretation,* 410–12).

[102] Johannine ecclesiology lies at the center of John 15:1–17, offering a parallel metaphor to the Pauline metaphor of the church as the body of Christ (1 Cor 12:12–27). See the discussion of G. R. O'Day, "John," in *The Women's Bible Commentary* (ed. Carol A. Newsom and Sharon H. Ringe; expanded ed.; London: SCM, 1998), 303.

[103] Some read the eucharistic symbol of wine here, e.g., Bernard, *John,* 2.477–78. See also the discussion in Brown, *John,* 2.672–74.

[104] See the discussion in Brown, *John,* 2.676–77; Moloney, *Glory not Dishonor,* 59–61.

Johannine community is told that they are called to remain faithful to Yahweh by believing and abiding in Jesus the true vine. Abiding is therefore an imperative for the disciples, and it is an evocative and powerful metaphor of communion shared among the disciples in the community.[105] A certain commitment and way of life—manifesting God's life-of-love and revealing God's creative presence—are expected from the disciples of Jesus (v. 8). The disciples' abiding covenant relationship with Jesus is further explored in terms of their fruitfulness or mission.

THE MISSION OF GLORIFYING THE FATHER

An abiding relationship between Jesus and his disciples entails bearing much fruit (καρπὸν πολύν, vv. 5, 8). The disciples are called to be the fruitful branches of the vine. Jesus and his committed life that springs forth from his abiding relationship with the Father is given as the model for the disciples. This short section brings together many aspects of Jesus' life: Jesus has shared the love of the Father with his disciples (vv. 9, 12); Jesus was faithful in observing the commandments of the Father (v. 10); Jesus has spoken the words of the Father and made known to the disciples all that he heard his Father speaking to him (vv. 3, 11, 15). There is no other way to prove themselves to be and to become (γενήσεσθε) disciples of Jesus except by bearing much fruit (v. 8).[106] The verb γίνομαι (γενήσεσθε) highlights the becoming aspect of the Johannine discipleship (see also 1:12). The narrator's voice in verse 8 suggests that bearing fruit is the disciples' way of glorifying the Father. The disciples must abide in Jesus in order to bear fruit (v. 5). There is an intrinsic communion with God, in which one shares the life of God, which constitutes the true nature (being) of the disciples. "Abiding is an expression of the divine life, revealed in the Johannine Jesus, who lives in profound union with the One who is the source of all being and whose nature is revealed as relational and immanent."[107] The actions

---

[105] For a detailed discussion on abiding as a symbol of community and friendship, see Lee, *Flesh and Glory*, 88–109, esp. 105–9.

[106] There are two variant readings: γένησθε (aorist subjunctive) and γενήσεσθε (future indicative). γένησθε is attested in 𝔓[66vid] B D L Θ 0250 1 565 597 it[a.aur.b.c.d.e] vg *al*, and γενήσεσθε is found in ℵ A Δ Ψ 0141 0233 *f*[13] 28 33 157 180 205 700 892[supp] 1006 1010 1071 1241 1243 1292 1342 1424 1505 *Byz al*. The future indicative is preferred since one would expect a subjunctive after a ἵνα clause and thus one can explain the correction from the future indicative to an aorist subjunctive.

[107] Lee, *Flesh and Glory*, 106.

that flow from this new life and existence as disciples of Jesus are therefore manifestations of their new existence (γεννηθῇ ἄνωθεν, 3:3, 5). As the vine and its fruits are so intimately connected (fruits reflect the quality of the vine), so also, the "being" of the disciples and their fruits or actions are inseparable. Johannine discipleship transcends the dichotomy that is traditionally attributed to one's being and one's doing, since one's deeds are manifestations of one's true being.

Johannine Christology lies at the heart of Johannine discipleship. The mission of the disciples to glorify the Father is grounded in and modeled after the ministry of Jesus. His mission of doing the works of the Father (cf. 5:17) is described elsewhere in the gospel as his way of glorifying the Father (cf. 17:4). The works of the Father include God's work of creation (Gen 1–11), liberation (the whole Exodus event), and salvation (the entire salvation history). Jesus glorifies the Father or reveals God's glory by actively participating in the creative, liberating, and salvific works of the Father, which include, for example, providing abundance of wine (2:11), doing the works of the Father (4:34), healing and giving life (cf. 5:17), revealing his (Jesus') identity as the source of the living water that is symbolic of his re-creating and transforming work (7:37–39), and loving until death (cf. 13:1; 15:13, 24). The disciples are called to the same mission, to glorify the Father, to make God's ongoing revelation present in and through their life and ministry. The foundational basis for the disciples' mission is Jesus' love for them that has its origin in the Father's love for Jesus and his obedience to the Father (15:9) and that encompasses the whole of Jesus' life until his passion, death, and resurrection (13:1).[108] Jesus' covenant relationship with God manifested in Jesus' communion with, and fidelity to, the Father becomes a model for the disciples, who continue to reveal the glory of God by keeping the commandments (15:10). The community of the disciples is reminded of their covenant commitment to Yahweh or to the Father as an indispensable condition for discipleship and their status as the true vineyard.

The Covenant Command Motif (15:9–17)

Keeping the commandments is an indispensable condition for abiding in Jesus' love (v. 10) and for being friends of Jesus (v. 14). The command to abide in Jesus' love is preceded by a conditional clause, "if you keep (τηρήσητε) my commandments (τὰς ἐντολάς μου)" (v. 10), and the call to be Jesus' friends is followed by a similar conditional clause, "if you do

---

[108] Segovia, *Farewell of the Word,* 150.

(ποιῆτε) what I command (ἐντέλλομαι) you" (v. 14). Viewed from the perspective of these conditional clauses, how do we interpret the abiding relationship and the friendship that Jesus is proposing for his disciples?[109] According to the Johannine Jesus, if the disciples want to abide in his love and if they want to remain as his friends, then they must keep the commandments. By using these conditional clauses and the command to keep the commandments, the evangelist parallels the abiding relationship and friendship between Jesus and the disciples with the OT covenant relationship between Yahweh and Israel. One needs to obey God's voice and keep God's covenant commandments in order to be God's vine (cf. Jer 2:21; 3:13) and God's treasured possession (Exod 19:5; see also Josh 7:11; 24:25). According to the Johannine Jesus, the disciples are expected to keep the commandments in order to establish and maintain their friendship with Jesus and their covenant status in the community.

The covenant renewal in Josh 24 does not emphasize the whole Mosaic law of the covenant; rather, it focuses on the central aspect of the law, viz., complete loyalty and reverence to Yahweh and total commitment to be at the service of Yahweh.[110] In a similar way, the final discipleship discourses of Jesus focus on the heart of the covenant commandments: to abide in Jesus and in his love (15:4, 9) and to love one another as Jesus has loved (15:12, 17).[111] Jesus' permanent intimacy with God transforms his disciples and empowers them with the gift of a parallel relationship with God, with one another, and with the cosmos.[112] The commandment (ἡ ἐντολή) of love here implies and includes the great concerns and obligations of a

---

[109] On the basis of v. 15, Lee suggests that "Jesus uses the language of personal friendship, overturning servile models of relationship" (*Flesh and Glory,* 103). S. van Tilborg interprets Jesus' friendship with his disciples as a way of extending the household (οἶκος) of his heavenly Father. The greater and more influential the οἶκος is, the more numerous are the friends (*Imaginative Love in John* [BibIntS 2; Leiden/New York/Köln: E. J. Brill, 1993], 148–50).

[110] As indicated earlier, the five imperatives in Josh 24:14–15 bear this point out. T. C. Butler comments: "All other stipulations are simply presupposed as common knowledge of the people" (*Joshua,* 276).

[111] Both in the book of Deuteronomy and in Joshua, renewals of covenant relationship were part of the farewell speeches of Moses and Joshua respectively. For the proposal that covenant renewal is part of the farewell genre, see W. Kurz, "Luke 22:14–38 and Greco-Roman and Biblical Farewell Addresses," *JBL* 104 (1985): 262–63; E. Cortès, *Los Discursos de Adiós de Gn 49 a Jn 13–17* (CSP 23; Barcelona: Herder, 1976), 434–43.

[112] Scott, *Sophia and Johannine Jesus,* 157; S. H. Ringe, *Wisdom's Friends: Community and Christology in the Fourth Gospel* (Louisville, Ky.: Westminster John Knox, 1999), 76.

covenant relationship that demand fidelity and integrity (e.g., Deut 6:4–5; 16:18–20; 20:19–20).

THE ELECTION MOTIF (15:16)

The metaphor of vine and branches symbolizing the community of Jesus' disciples alludes to the idea of God's chosen people.[113] Jesus' words "I chose (ἐξελεξάμην) you and appointed (ἔθηκα) you" (v. 16) underline the election motif and remind the readers of the Old Testament election of the people of Israel. The election of Israel is alluded to at various occasions in the unfolding story of Israel: in the call of Abraham (Gen 12:1–3), in Jacob's vision at Bethel (Gen 28:13–15), in God's revelation in Egypt (Exod 6:2–8; cf. Ezek 20:5), in the experience of God's presence at Sinai (Exod 19–24).

The most powerful articulation of Israel's election is found in the words of Moses to the people of Israel in Deut 7:6–11 that highlight three important aspects: (1) the status of Israel as God's treasured possession: "The Lord your God has chosen (בָּחַר) you out of all the peoples on earth to be his people, his treasured possession" (v. 6); (2) the driving force behind the election is not Israel's power or worthiness but God's love and faithfulness to the covenant promises (vv. 7–8); (3) covenant obligations articulated negatively in terms of punishments if Israel fails to respond to the covenant demands (vv. 10–11). The basic concept of election is intimately linked to the theology of the covenant relationship in terms of both divine promises and human commitments. A similar process is going on in the unfolding metaphor of the vine and branches. Jesus, the light of the world (8:12; 9:5),[114] now claims that he has chosen the disciples (15:16).[115] The disciples have received this vocation as a gift from God (see 3:16, 27). As the election motif elicits the necessity for Israel to choose God, the disciples are called to abide in Jesus' love and keep the covenant commandments. This is the choice that they must make. Just as the failure in living up to the expectations of the OT covenant led Israel to exile, the failure to abide in Jesus and bear fruit will lead the disciples to destruction and death (15:6).

---

[113] R. Schnackenburg, *The Church in the New Testament,* 109. See also Dodd, *Interpretation,* 410–12.

[114] According to the prophetic traditions, the elect one is called to be a "light to the nations" (Isa 42:1, 6; cf. also Isa 49:5–9).

[115] The disciples of Jesus as the "chosen people" of God is attested throughout the NT books (e.g., Mark 13:20; Matt 24:31; Luke 18:7; Rom 8:33; 1 Thess 1:4; Eph 1:4; 2 Tim 2:10; Titus 1:1; 2 John 1:1; Rev 17:14).

JESUS' WARNING OF THE CONSEQUENCES OF DISCIPLESHIP (15:18–16:24)

Scholars differ in their view of the internal structure of chapters 15–16.[116] The present study proposes that Jesus' warning of the consequences of discipleship holds this long section together as a single unit (15:18–16:24).[117] One can perceive a threefold structure, beginning with the reactions of the world or the unbelieving community in general and Jesus' assurance of the help from the Paraclete (15:18–27), followed by a statement regarding the purpose of Jesus' warning (16:1). The unit ends with the reactions of the Jews to the disciples, and Jesus' assurance of the Paraclete (16:2–24). Both of these sections, 15:18–27 and 16:2–24, have a threefold structure: (1) persecution (15:18–20; 16:2); (2) the reason for the persecution (15:21–25; 16:3); (3) reward in terms of the gift of the Paraclete (15:26–27; 16:4–24). In the center is the purpose of Jesus' warning: to prevent the disciples from apostasy (16:1).[118] The detailed sevenfold structure of 15:18–16:24 can be summarized as follows:

A	Persecution:	the world will hate you (15:18–20)
B	Reason:	they do not know him who sent me (15:21–25)
C	Reward:	the gift of the Paraclete (15:26–27)
D	Purpose:	to prevent the disciples from apostasy (16:1)
A'	Persecution:	they will expel you from the synagogues (16:2)
B'	Reason:	they have not known the Father nor me (16:3)
C'	Reward:	the gift of the Paraclete (16:4–24)[119]

---

[116] Some consider 15:1–16:3 the second discourse (e.g., Simoens, *La gloire d'aimer,* 152–58; Moloney, *Glory not Dishonor,* 55–76). Segovia considers John 15:18–16:4a the second discourse (*Farewell of the Word,* 169–212). Some maintain that 15:1–16:33 is the second phase of the farewell discourse (see Tolmie, *Jesus' Farewell,* 30–31; Carson, *John,* 510–50). For those who see a break at John 15:25, see Hoskyns, *Fourth Gospel,* 479–87; L. Morris, *The Gospel According to John* (NICNT; Grand Rapids, Mich.: Eerdmans, 1992), 677–82; and for those see a break at John 15:27, see Barrett, *John,* 478–83; Haenchen, *John,* 2.133–42.

[117] These warnings are part of the covenant renewal procedures (e.g., Josh 24:16–20); they have also been recognized as part of the farewell genre, see Moloney, *Glory not Dishonor,* 67 n. 35.

[118] I use the hard expression "apostasy" to continue the OT theme associated with Israel's betrayal of the covenant relationship with God.

[119] The distribution of the material here is thematic, not quantitative. Why twenty-one verses are taken up with the theme of the Paraclete in 16:4–24 is

PERSECUTION (A): THE WORLD WILL HATE YOU (15:18–20)

The disciples have to face many consequences because of their faith in Jesus. Jesus predicts that the world (ὁ κόσμος) will hate the disciples because they belong to the chosen community of God (15:18–22).[120] The negative consequence of discipleship is described first in terms of hatred (μισέω) by the world (15:18–19). The response of the world to Jesus' revelation has elsewhere been described in terms of hatred (e.g., 3:20; 7:7). The unbelief explained as their evil works (αὐτῶν πονηρὰ τὰ ἔργα, 3:19) is the basis for the hatred toward Jesus (3:19–20; 7:7). As Segovia aptly pointed out, "Hatred of Jesus implies a rejection of his mission and claims."[121] The response of the world to Jesus and his disciples is further looked at in terms of persecution (διώκω, 15:20a) and keeping or not keeping the word of Jesus (τηρέω, 15:20b). The disciples will meet with persecution, as Jesus had experienced it during his ministry.[122] Although it has sociological implications, the rationale behind the world's hatred and persecution is more theological and christological than sociological.[123] The abiding relationship of the disciples with Jesus constitutes a community of love that stands out as a contrast community over against the world, which hates Jesus and does not keep his word. Jesus prepares his disciples to meet the challenges of discipleship better and to remain as a visible communitarian sign of God's ongoing revelation in human history.

---

explained by both thematic unity and pedagogical reason. The theme of what the Paraclete accomplishes for the disciples in the world holds this long section together as a single unit. The final discipleship discourses in general and the Paraclete sayings in particular are pedagogical in intent, preparing the disciples for Jesus' departure and empowering the disciples for their ongoing work in the world. The Johannine Jesus naturally focuses less on suffering (15:18–20; 16:2) and more on the benefits of the gift of the Paraclete whose work makes God's ongoing presence visible to the disciples.

[120] The term ὁ κόσμος refers to the unbelievers who rejected the Father and Jesus. ὁ κόσμος is used in the gospel with three different meanings: (1) the universe (e.g., 11:9; 17:5, 24; 21:25); (2) humanity (e.g., 3:16; 6:14; 8:26); (3) all those who rejected the revelation of God in Jesus (e.g., 7:7; 14:17; 15:18; 12:31). For the different uses and meanings of ὁ κόσμος in John's Gospel, see Brown, *John*, 1.508–9; Moloney, *Belief in the Word*, 37.

[121] Segovia, *Farewell of the Word*, 182.

[122] For the dialectical relationship between the consequences of the mission of Jesus and that of the disciples, see B. Lindars, "The Persecution of Christians in John 15:18–16:4a," in *Suffering and Martyrdom in the New Testament: Studies Presented to G. M. Styler by the Cambridge New Testament Seminar* (ed. W. Horbury and B. McNeil; Cambridge: Cambridge University Press, 1981), 48–69, esp. 59–62.

[123] Carson, *John*, 524; Barrett, *John*, 483–84.

REASON (B): THEY DO NOT KNOW THE FATHER (15:21–25)

The references to hatred and persecution by the world are followed by the reason for the hatred and persecution described in terms of their lack of knowledge of God: οὐκ οἴδασιν τὸν πέμψαντά με, "they do not know the one who sent me"(15:21; cf. Ισραηλ δέ με οὐκ ἔγνω, "Israel does not know me," Isa 1:3). The lack of knowledge of God in the OT signals a rupture in the covenant relationship between Yahweh and Israel (Isa 1:3–4). This ignorance and the consequential unbelief are often referred to by the symbolism of darkness. The world that does not know God does not have the light of life and lives in darkness.[124] The failure of knowledge leads one to sin, and it is the rationale for the rejection and crucifixion of Jesus. As Dorothy Lee argues, "Sin and evil are bound up with a failure of recognition, an incomprehensible absence of knowledge."[125] Jesus' claim that if "the world" had known the Father, they would have recognized the presence of God in Jesus, challenges his opponents' claim to be faithful to the covenant relationship with Yahweh (cf. Exod 29:45–46; Jer 9:24; Isa 11:2).

REWARD (C): THE GIFT OF THE PARACLETE (15:26–27)

The reassuring words of Jesus consist of a threefold statement about the gift of the Paraclete and a statement about the role of the disciples as witnesses (15:26–27). Jesus promises that he will send the Paraclete to the disciples (v. 26a).[126] Jesus reveals the divine origin of the Paraclete by explicitly mentioning that he proceeds from the Father (v. 26b).[127] As the

---

[124] As Craig R. Koester has pointed out, darkness in the Fourth Gospel symbolizes (1) "the powers that oppose God"; (2) "the lethal estrangement from God"; (3) human "ignorance and unbelief" (*Symbolism,* 125–26).

[125] Lee, *Flesh and Glory,* 168.

[126] Scholars have noticed the discrepancy between John 14:16 where Jesus asks the Father to send the Paraclete and John 15:25 where Jesus sends the Paraclete to the disciples. Who is sending the Paraclete: the Father or Jesus? As Brown has pointed out, "whether or not the difference of agency in sending the Paraclete reflects different stages in the development of Johannine thought, the variation is not really significant on the theological level, for in Johannine thought the Father and Jesus are one (x 30)" (*John,* vol. 29A, 689).

[127] The idea that the Paraclete proceeds from the Father created confusion in the doctrinal debate on Trinity in the fourth century. For a discussion of this Trinitarian debate, see G. Bray, "The Filioque Clause in History and Theology," *TynBul* 34 (1983): 91–144.

origin of Jesus is intimately connected to his mission, one needs to interpret the origin of the Paraclete not in terms of metaphysics or ontological "procession" from the Father but in terms of Paraclete's mission in the world.[128] As the works of Jesus were to reveal the love and glory of the Father, the works of the Paraclete are to bear witness to Jesus in the world (v. 26c). With regard to the work of the Paraclete, there is a progression in the Paraclete sayings from 14:16–17, 26 to 15:26. In chapter 14, the work of the Paraclete was among the disciples of Jesus (14:26); but in chapter 15, the task of the Paraclete is not only among the disciples (implied) but also extended to the world (15:26).[129] Jesus also reminds the disciples, as the recipients of the Paraclete, of their work to bear witness to him (15:27). Jesus is sent by the Father to make God's presence visible; Jesus now in turn sends the Paraclete and the disciples to bear witness to his unconditional love and abundance of life in the world after his departure to the Father.

Purpose (D): To Prevent the Disciples from Apostasy (16:1)

The purpose of these warnings of Jesus is to keep the disciples away from giving up their faith (σκανδαλίζω, 16:1). The verb σκανδαλίζω is used twice in John's Gospel (6:61; 16:1), and on both these occasions it has the meaning of causing someone to sin or to give up one's faith.[130] There is also ample evidence in the gospel of hostile arguments against Jesus' messianic claims (8:31–59). The real danger that Jesus envisages is not the possibility of persecution per se but the likelihood that the disciples might give up their belief in the revelation of God in Jesus.[131] Just before the renewal of the covenant with Yahweh, a similar concern against forsaking Yahweh is expressed in the warnings of Joshua and in his commands "to put away other gods" (cf. 24:16, 23). Just as in the case of the OT covenant renewals, the real concern of Jesus' warning lies in the danger of disciples' apostasy, the denial of the revelation of God in Jesus.

---

[128] Carson, *John*, 528–29.

[129] See Segovia, *Farewell of the Word*, 200 n. 50.

[130] Schnackenburg, *John*, 3.121. For a detailed discussion of the meaning of σκανδαλίζω, see also K. Müller, *Anstoss und Gericht: Eine Studie zum Jüdischen Hintergrund des paulinischen Skandalon-Begriffs* (SANT 19; München: Kösel-Verlag, 1969), 46–67. For the use of σκανδαλίζω in the synoptic gospels, see Matt 24:25; Luke 22:31. The verb is used in later Christian writings with a specific reference to those who have stumbled from the faith or apostates; see *Did.* 16.5; *Herm. Vis.* 4.1.3; *Herm. Mand.* 8.10.

[131] Barrett, *John*, 483–84; Schnackenburg, *John*, 3.121.

PERSECUTION (A'): THEY WILL EXPEL YOU FROM THE SYNAGOGUES (16:2)

Jesus further foresees that the Jewish community ("they") will expel the disciples from the synagogues because of their faith in Jesus as the one coming from God (16:2a).[132] The fear of being put of out of the synagogue (ἀποσυνάγωγος) alluded to elsewhere in the gospel (9:22; 12:42) reflects not only the experience of the characters in the story but also the experience of disciples of the subsequent generations.[133] The expulsion from the synagogues implies a definitive breaking of the bond between the Jewish community and the disciples, and it reflects the experience of the Johannine community (9:22; 12:42; 16:2).[134] Jesus also foresees that those who put the disciples to death would think that they are offering a "spiritual service" or "worship" (λατρείαν προσφέρειν) to God (16:2b).[135] B. Lindars

---

[132] As Moloney points out, " 'the world,' which has become 'they,' must be 'the Jews' of the earlier narrative" (*Glory not Dishonor*, 68). Moloney considers the use of "they" in 15:20–25 and in 16:2 a reference to "the Jews." The present study maintains the distinction that the designation "they" in 15:20–25 is a reference to "the world," unbelieving humanity in general that includes "the Jews," but "they" in 16:2 is an exclusive reference to the Jewish community because of its explicit reference to the excommunication from the synagogues (ἀποσυνάγωγος).

[133] R. E. Brown suggests that "crypto-Christians" believed in Jesus but did not acknowledge their faith publicly as they were afraid of being expelled from the synagogues (*Community*, 71–73).

[134] Schnackenburg, *John*, 3.121; Moloney, *Glory not Dishonor*, 72. J. L. Martyn has argued that the twelfth benediction of the *Birkat ha-Mînîm* of the *Tefillah* (Eighteen Benedictions) was reformulated ("Let the Nazareans [Christians], the *mînîm* [heretics] be destroyed in a moment") to include Christians among the *mînîm* to recognize and expel the Jewish Christians from the synagogues (*History and Theology in the Fourth Gospel* [3d ed.; Louisville: Westminster John Knox, 2003], 46–66). There is very little support today to make the link between the expulsion (ἀποσυνάγωγος) in John's Gospel and the *Birkat ha-Mînîm*; see P. W. van der Horst, "The Birkat ha-minim in Recent Research," *ExpTim* 105 (1993–1994): 363–68. For a modified view that the Sages at Jamnia were aware of the messianic claims of Christians who were thus identified among the *mînîm* whom they sought to exclude from the synagogue, see W. D. Davies, "Aspects of the Jewish Background," 43–64, esp. 49–52.

[135] Paul's pre-Christian persecution of the church was understood by him as a service to God. A similar conviction among the first-century Jewish community is reflected in rabbinic writings. For example, "if a man sheds the blood of the wicked it is as though he had offered a sacrifice," *Num. Rab.* 21.3. See also *m. Sanh.* 9:6.

claims that 16:2b "comprises John's most serious warning to his readers. It is a real fear that a violent persecution is about to begin; . . . this action will be carried out with a genuinely religious motive."[136] Jesus now argues that those who persecute the disciples live under the delusion that they are offering service to God. By placing this alarming possibility before the disciples and readers, the Johannine Jesus encourages them to endure it within the framework of Jesus' own suffering and sacrifice (17:17–19). The presence of irony is very clear: on the one hand, the persecutors mistakenly think that they are offering a service to God; on the other, the martyrdom of disciples is an offering to God.

REASON (B′): THEY DO NOT KNOW THE FATHER (16:3)

The reference to the expulsion from the synagogues is followed by the reason for this exclusion: the lack of knowledge of God (οὐκ ἔγνωσαν τὸν πατέρα οὐδὲ ἐμέ, "They have known neither the Father nor me," 16:3; cf. Ισραηλ δέ με οὐκ ἔγνω, "Israel does not know me," Isa 1:3). Despite their claim to the contrary, Jesus accuses "the Jews"[137] for their lack of knowledge and communion with God: "You have never heard his voice or seen his form; . . . you do not believe him whom he has sent" (5:37–38); "You do not know him [God]" (7:28; see also 8:27, 55). Their lack of knowledge of God implies that they are in darkness or they do not share the light of life (cf. 1:4–5).[138] As D. A. Carson pointed out, "These people enjoyed far less antecedent knowledge of God than they claimed."[139] This is a serious accusation against the Jewish characters in the story, since lack of knowledge of God is interpreted by the prophetic tradition as a failure to live up to the covenant relationship (Isa 1:3–4). In contrast to the experience of the world, Jesus promises the disciples that they would know the Father (14:7) and the Spirit of truth (14:17), and the disciples in turn love Jesus and believe in the revelation of God embodied in Jesus (16:27, 30).

---

[136] Lindars, "Persecution of Christians," 65.

[137] The expression "the Jews" refers to the characters in the story who are ignorant of Jesus' identity and origin and thus reject the revelation of God in Jesus. For a detailed discussion of the use of the expression "the Jews" in John's Gospel, see F. J. Moloney, " 'The Jews' in the Fourth Gospel: Another Perspective," *Pacifica* 15 (2002): 16–36.

[138] Koester, *Symbolism*, 126.

[139] Carson, *John*, 526.

REWARD (C'): THE GIFT OF THE PARACLETE (16:4–24)

The negative consequences of discipleship are followed by the comforting promises of Jesus that he will send the Paraclete who will accompany the disciples, empower them to meet the challenges of the persecutions, and help them remain faithful to their abiding covenant relationship with God (16:4–24). In what follows, the gift of the Paraclete is seen from the perspective of what the Spirit accomplishes and what the disciples receive.

The Paraclete as the Judge of the World (16:4–11)

Jesus' discourse first introduces the inseparable bond between his departure and the arrival of the Paraclete (16:4–7), and then focuses its attention on the juridical role of the Paraclete (16:8–11). In the Psalms, Yahweh has been depicted as the judge of the world: "God has taken his place in the divine council; in the midst of the gods he holds judgment" (Ps 82:1). The Johannine Jesus argues elsewhere in the gospel that the Father has given him the authority to judge (5:22, 27). Jesus' role as judge of the world is a dominant theme in the gospel (3:19; 5:27; 8:26; 9:39), and it reaches its climax in the passion narrative when Jesus stands before Pilate (18:28–19:16). Jesus now passes this authority on to the Paraclete.

The judging activity of the Paraclete is described as ἐλέγχω (16:8). The verb ἐλέγχω has an extensive semantic range, but it can be translated as either "to bring to light" (cf. 3:20) or "to prove guilty" (cf. 8:46). Perhaps the English verb that is closest to the Greek ἐλέγχω is "to expose," since it has the same double meaning as ἐλέγχω: "to make visible" and "to hold up to reprobation."[140] The Paraclete will expose the world concerning sin, righteousness, and judgment (16:8). First, the world's sin that it does not recognize the presence of God in Jesus or does not believe (οὐ πιστεύουσιν) in Jesus as the incarnation of God will be exposed (16:9).[141] Second, the truth regarding righteousness is revealed in Jesus' departure: the death and resurrection of Jesus (16:10). Jesus' absence or departure or death is the vindication and ratification of Jesus' life by the Father. Jesus' departure and return to the Father experienced in the death of Jesus is "God's imprimatur upon

---

[140] Hoskyns, *Fourth Gospel,* 484.

[141] In John's Gospel, sin is a "theological, not a moral, category" (G. R. O'Day, "The Gospel of John," in *The New Interpreter's Bible* [ed. L. Keck; 12 vols.; Nashville: Abingdon Press, 1995], 9.772).

the righteousness manifested in the life and death of His Son."[142] Third, the judgment of "the ruler of this world" by the world is defeated by God's vindication of Jesus, which in turn exposes God's judgment on them (16:11). The world that does not recognize God's ongoing presence in Jesus' life and death is continually judged by God's work in the Paraclete. In sum, the Paraclete's role in the judgment of the world is to continue the works of the covenant God and Jesus in human history.

He Will Guide You into the Truth (16:12–15)

Jesus reassures the disciples that the Paraclete will guide (ὁδηγέω) them into the truth. The Greek verb ὁδηγέω reminds the readers of the story in the LXX of God's leading the people of Israel in the desert (Num 24:8; Deut 1:33).[143] Yahweh, the God of the covenant, is presented as the one who guides the people of Israel to the safe pastures (Exod 15:13, 17). The same notion is recognized in the language of the Psalms, where "guide me in your truth" recalls the covenant relationship and its obligations (Pss 25:5, 9; 143:10). The role ascribed to the covenant God in the OT, viz., guiding the people to the truth and life, is assumed by Jesus when he is presented as the way, the truth, and the life (14:6), and the same task is now entrusted to the Paraclete: "He will guide you into the truth" (ἀλήθεια, 16:13). The Paraclete's role as the guide is another example of how the Paraclete continues the works of the covenant God and Jesus. Truth (ἀλήθεια) is a theologically charged term in John's Gospel. The prologue first speaks of Jesus as the one filled with grace and truth (1:14) and then claims that grace and truth (ἡ χάρις καὶ ἡ ἀλήθεια) came from Jesus Christ (1:17). As Charles H. Dodd pointed out, "the combination of χάρις and ἀλήθεια is so unusual in Greek that we must suppose that the expression was derived from a Hebrew source."[144] In Jewish thinking, חֶסֶד וֶאֱמֶת (χάρις and ἀλήθεια) are attributes of God revealed in the Torah.[145] They are the qualities of Yahweh as the covenant partner with Israel abounding in steadfast love and faithfulness (Exod 34:6). In a similar way, the evangelist uses ἡ χάρις καὶ ἡ ἀλήθεια in the prologue to illustrate the new covenant relationship and life of God that have come through Jesus Christ (cf. 1:17). The evangelist an-

---

[142] Hoskyns, *Fourth Gospel,* 485.

[143] Ibid., 485–86.

[144] Dodd, *Interpretation,* 175.

[145] See *Midr. Ps.* 25.10, "All the paths of the Lord are mercy and truth [חֶסֶד וֶאֱמֶת]: By *mercy* is meant deeds of loving kindness, and by *truth* is meant the Law of the Lord. For to whom shall the paths of the Lord be given? Unto such as keep His covenant and His testimonies."

nounces that the revelation of God's grace and truth is perfected in Jesus Christ. When the author presents Jesus as the truth, he is presenting Jesus as the revelation of the life of God (5:33; 8:32).[146] Jesus' accusation that "there is no truth in him" can be paraphrased as "there is no life of God in him" (8:44). Truth in John's Gospel is often closely associated and identified with the Spirit: τὸ πνεῦμα τῆς ἀληθείας, "the Spirit of Truth" (14:17; 15:26; 16:13). Like Jesus the incarnate Word, the Paraclete will reveal the life of God (15:26). Viewed from this perspective, the task of the Paraclete in 16:13 is to guide the disciples into truth (ἀλήθεια) or to the life of God or a covenantal relationship with God.

Your Hearts Will Rejoice and Your Joy Will Be Full (16:16–24)

There exists an intrinsic relationship among the Johannine concepts of joy/rejoicing, work/mission, and persecution/suffering. Both rejoicing (χαίρω) and joy (χαρά) are presented from the point of view of the fulfillment of an appointed mission. John the Baptist proclaims that his joy is full when he has completed his mission as the revealer of the incarnate Word (3:29). Similarly, Jesus' rejoicing has been associated with the fulfillment of his mission that includes the important roles played by the chosen disciples in that mission (4:36; 11:25). Jesus' instructions about abiding and keeping the commandments signal the completion of his appointed task as the revealer of God and are meant to make the disciples' joy full (15:11). Since the departure of Jesus is part of his mission, Jesus' return to the Father will make his joy fulfilled in the disciples (17:13). The joy of the disciples is an outcome of their obedience to Jesus' commands (cf. 15:11) and their understanding of and belief in Jesus' revelation (cf. 14:28; 20:20).[147] The intrinsic relationship between joy and one's mission is reaffirmed in the context of suffering and persecution (16:20, 21, 22, 24). Sufferings are thus indispensable in the pursuit of accomplishing one's mission. The metaphor of the woman in childbirth bears this point out (16:20–21). The evangelist "uses childbirth as a powerful image of suffering and hope within the believing community."[148] Just as the mother at childbirth moves from pain to joy, so also the disciples' sorrow will be turn into joy at Jesus' departure with the gift of the Paraclete. The joy of the disciples ultimately lies in the

---

[146] For a detailed study of "Jesus and the truth" (Jésus-vérité) in John's Gospel, see de la Potterie, *La vérité dans Saint Jean*, 1.116–278.

[147] For the interrelationship between rejoicing and believing, see the detailed discussion in Segovia, *Farewell of the Word*, 110–13, 153.

[148] Lee, *Flesh and Glory*, 152.

fulfillment of their call to be the fruitful branches of the true vine, Jesus, in their obedience to the covenant commandments and fidelity to the covenant relationship.

THE DISCIPLES' PROFESSION OF FAITH (16:25–33)

The change of time from future (16:23–24) to the present hour (ὥρα) of Jesus (16:25a) indicates a new beginning. The imminence of the hour is characterized by the fact that Jesus stops speaking in symbols and figures (16:25b). This is reconfirmed by the announcement of the disciples, "now you are speaking plainly, not in any figure" (16:29). The unit begins with Jesus' announcement of the hour (ὥρα), the affirmation of disciples' belief, the affirmation of God's love for the disciples, and Jesus' self-revelation in terms of his origin and destiny (16:25–28). This is followed by the disciples' profession of faith (16:29–30) and Jesus' response (16:31–33) that reconfirms their belief and the imminent presence of the hour (ὥρα).

THE SELF-REVELATION OF JESUS (16:25–28)

Jesus begins with a proclamation regarding the coming "hour" when the ultimate revelation of God takes place on the cross (16:25). The event of the hour has the transforming power to change the relationship between the Father and the disciples (cf. 16:26–27). This new and transformed covenant relationship of love between the Father and the disciples as the abiding branches of the true vine is possible because the disciples, unlike "the Jews" in the narratives, love Jesus and believe in the divine origin of Jesus (16:27). Jesus reaffirms his origin and destiny: "I came from the Father . . . and am going to the Father" (16:28).[149] The intimacy that Jesus shares with God will also be granted to the disciples who love and believe in Jesus.

---

[149] Barrett suggests the shorter reading (attested in D W *l* 127 it^b, d, ff2 vg^ms syr^s) that omits ἐξῆλθον παρὰ τοῦ πατρός at the beginning of 16:28 (*John,* 496). The longer reading is attested in 𝔓^5, 22 ℵ A C² Θ 0141 *f*¹ *f*¹³ 28 157 180 205 565 579 597 700 892^supp 1006 1010 1071 1241 1243 1292 1342 1424 1505 *Byz*. For those who support the longer reading, see Brown, *John,* 2.724–25; Moloney, *Glory not Dishonor,* 96.

THE PROFESSION OF FAITH (16:29–33)

The basic identity of Israel resides in their single-minded commitment to Yahweh expressed in their pledge to be obedient to the covenant laws and to serve only Yahweh (Josh 24:24).[150] The public acknowledgment and profession of faith in Yahweh is an important aspect of the covenant renewal ceremonies elsewhere in the OT (e.g., Exod 24:3, 7; Josh 24:21, 24). In a similar way, the Johannine disciples express their total commitment to Jesus in 16:30. Whether the confession of faith in 16:30 is an expression of a limited Johannine faith or the manifestation of the expected faith response with its full implications is still a debated issue.[151] For the Fourth Evangelist the basic identity of the disciples does not merely depend on their profession of faith. The disciples "who move toward the light, no matter how fumbling and inept their journey, no longer belong to the darkness."[152] The true sign of discipleship resides in their abiding covenant relationship with God (15:8) and keeping the commandments or loving one another (8:34–35). This relationship and journey of faith is a dynamic and ongoing process.

From the very beginning of the Johannine story in the prologue (1:1–5, 18), the revelation of Jesus' origin from God has been a primary concern. The motif of Jesus' origin, the description of Jesus as the one who has come from God, or from above, or from the Father is frequently repeated in the gospel (e.g., 1:51; 3:13; 6:33, 38, 41, 42, 50, 51, 58; 7:28; 8:14, 42; 13:3).[153] This motif was also the key issue that emerged during the christological debate in chapters 5–10 and divided the characters in the story (e.g., 1:46; 7:25–31, 40–44; 8:42, 48–59). In the revelation that precedes the profession of the disciples' faith, Jesus' reassuring words affirm two things: (1) the disciples have loved Jesus (16:27b); (2) they have believed that he came from God (16:27c). The solemn profession of the disciples picks up Jesus' affirmation regarding their response to him: (1) they know Jesus (16:30a); (2) they believe that Jesus has come from God (30:16b).[154] The disciples

---

[150] See the comment on Josh 24:24 in Butler, *Joshua*, 276.

[151] Moloney sees their faith as "parallel to that of Nicodemus and the Samaritan Woman" (*Glory not Dishonor*, 97). For a similar opinion, see also Duke, *Irony in the Fourth Gospel*, 57–59. For those who consider it a climactic expression of faith, see Dettwiler, *Die Gegenwart des Erhöhten*, 258–59, 262–63.

[152] Lee, *Flesh and Glory*, 189.

[153] See the discussion in Loader, "Johannine Theology," 188–99.

[154] Loving Jesus/God presupposes and implies knowing Jesus/God (cf. 14:28; 17:3).

thus acknowledge Jesus' divine origin, knowledge, and authority to reveal the Father (cf. 16:25).[155] The emphatic use of "now" (νῦν) and the repeated expressions, we know (οἴδαμεν) and we believe (πιστεύομεν), point to an oath that generally precedes covenant making. Jesus' response to the disciples, ἄρτι πιστεύετε ("Do you now believe?") reveals Jesus' recognition and appreciation of the faith professed by the disciples in verse 30. This solemn profession as a group is something that they have not done before. This profession of faith on the part of the disciples and its appreciation on the part of Jesus were necessary for Jesus to make the claim that he had accomplished the work that God gave him (17:4), and that the disciples had kept God's word (17:6) and believed that Jesus has come from God and was sent by God (17:8). Just as the people of Israel professed their absolute commitment to Yahweh during the covenant-renewal ceremonies, the disciples together as one body pledge their faith in Jesus as the only true and authentic revelation, the revealer of God.

A PRAYER CONSECRATING THE COVENANT COMMUNITY OF THE DISCIPLES (17:1–26)

The evangelist has meticulously crafted and placed the prayer of Jesus at the solemn and climactic moment of the fulfillment of the hour. From the very outset of the Johannine story, everything has been moving toward Jesus' last covenant fellowship meal with his disciples (13–17).[156] This is particularly the case with Jesus' prayer in chapter 17 that deals with his own glorification (17:1–5) and that is for the disciples of all generations as a

---

[155] Brown, *John,* 2.725–26. Some scholars suggest here the reflections of the Johannine community's experience of rubbing shoulders with other religions and propose a comparison between Jesus, the true revealer, and other "revealers" from the Greek worlds; see H. N. Bream, "No Need to be Asked Questions: A Study of John 16:30," in *Search the Scriptures: New Testament Studies in Honor of Raymond T. Stamm* (ed. J. M. Myers, O. Reimherr, and H. N. Bream; GTS 3; Leiden: Brill, 1969), 49–74.

[156] For the view that the prayer of Jesus is the theological climax of the gospel, see Dodd, *Interpretation,* 420; O'Day, "Gospel of John," 787. In his controversial study, E. Käsemann rejects the passion narrative as an integral part of the gospel and goes so far as to claim that John 17 "is a summary of the Johannine discourses and in this respect is a counterpart to the prologue" (*The Testament of Jesus: A Study of the Gospel of John in the Light of Chapter 17* [trans. G. Krodel; NTL; London: SCM Press, 1968], 3). For a critique of this approach and various positions, see Thompson, *The Humanity of Jesus,* 1–6.

covenant community of God (17:6–26).[157] Jesus begins the prayer for his
glorification with the reaffirmation that he has completed his work by revealing God's name and words to the disciples (17:1–5). Jesus' prayer for
the disciples is preceded by the affirmation that the disciples have believed
in God's self-disclosure in Jesus (17:6–8). Jesus' prayer for the disciples and
future believers consists of three central requests followed by an expanded
descriptive explanation of the respective requests: (1) keep (τηρέω) the disciples in God's name (v. 11) followed by the clarification in verses 12–16;
(2) consecrate (ἁγιάζω) the disciples in the truth (v. 17) followed by the
elucidation in verses 18–19; (3) may the disciples be one (v. 21) followed
by the detailed explanation in verses 22–26.[158] In the content of Jesus'
prayer for the disciples (vv. 6–26), the readers hear echoes of themes from
the OT covenant relationship and its obligations. In the light of Jesus' discourses and dialogues with the disciples to this point in the gospel, careful
analysis suggests that Jesus' prayer in chapter 17 is the final scene in the process of consecrating the disciples as a covenant community. Brooke F.
Westcott claims that "the general scope of the prayer, which is at once a
prayer and a profession and a revelation, is the consummation of the glory
of God through Christ, the Word Incarnate."[159] Edwyn C. Hoskyns enunciates the same view: "the prayer is the solemn consecration of Himself in
the presence of His disciples as their effective sacrifice, it is His prayer for
glorification in and through His death; it is His irrevocable dedication of
His disciples to their mission in the world."[160] Agreeing with both Westcott and Hoskyns, Charles H. Dodd describes the prayer as "the crown of
the process of initiation" into a new life and light.[161] The function of Jesus'
prayer therefore seems to be analogous to that of the covenant-making

---

[157] The internal structure of John 17 has been much discussed. A threefold division is proposed by B. F. Westcott (*The Gospel According to St. John* [London:
Murray, 1908], 237–38) and is followed by many Johannine scholars with minor
or no variations: Jesus and the Father (vv. 1–5); Jesus and the immediate disciples
(vv. 6–19); Jesus and the church (vv. 20–26). For a detailed survey of the various
proposals, see Ritt, *Das Gebet zum Vater*, 92–147. See also Beasley-Murray, *John*,
295–96; Moloney, *Glory not Dishonor*, 104–17.

[158] As vv. 6–10 introduce the disciples of the story in the prayer of Jesus, v. 20
introduces the future believers or disciples in the prayer. The present study views
Jesus' prayer for the disciples of the story (vv. 6–19) and that for the future believers (vv. 20–26) together as a single unit (vv. 6–26).

[159] Westcott, *John*, 237. Accepting v. 19 as the theological center of the prayer,
Westcott describes John 17 as a "prayer of consecration" (ibid.).

[160] Hoskyns, *Fourth Gospel*, 494.

[161] Dodd, *Interpretation*, 420.

rituals in the OT stories (Exod 24:8; Josh 24:25–28), initiating the disciples
into a new form of life sharing a covenant partnership with God. The
prayer reveals Jesus' intimate relationship with God and initiates the
disciples to share the same intimacy by invoking God's assistance, and it
communicates Jesus' dream and vision for the new covenant community of
his disciples.

Keep the Disciples in Your Name (17:6–16)

Jesus has manifested (φανερόω) God's name to the disciples (v. 6) and
now prays to the Father to keep the disciples united in God's name (v. 11).
The expression "in God's name" has echoes of covenant-relationship motifs. Declaring God's name to one's kindred is understood as the vocation of
the servant of God (Ps 22:22). The covenant relationship of Israel necessitates knowing the name of God, or knowing that God's name is יהוה: "I am
surely going to teach them, this time I am going to teach them my power
and my might, and they shall know that my name is the Lord" (Jer 16:21).
Viewed from the perspective of the OT covenant theology, knowing God's
name is a sign of the eschatological realization of the covenant relationship
with Israel in the age to come: "My people will know my name" (Isa 52:6;
cf. also Exod 3:13–15). In the OT God's name is also associated with the
glory (δόξα/כָּבוֹד) of God: "I am the Lord, that is my name; my glory I give
to no other, nor my praise to idols" (Isa 42:8).[162] The glory (δόξα/כָּבוֹד) of
Yahweh refers to the manifestation of the presence of God in a manner ac-
cessible to human experience (Exod 16:10).[163] Jesus' testimony that he has
manifested God's name to the disciples and the prayer to keep them
in God's name therefore affirms God's supreme self-disclosure in Jesus
(17:6) and inaugurates the messianic era to renew the covenant relationship
between God and the new covenant community represented by the
disciples (17:11, 26).

The portrayal of the disciples as the locus of Jesus' glorification (17:10b)
implies that the identity of Jesus as the manifestation of God is made visible
in them. Jesus is thus praying that the disciples will be kept in God's name.
In other words, the mutual abiding of the disciples in God will protect
them at the time of suffering and persecution, and in turn they become the

---

[162] See the detailed discussion of the name of God in Dodd, *Interpretation,*
93–96, 349–50, 417.
[163] Von Rad, "כָּבוֹד in the OT," *TDNT* 2.238–42.

visible presence of God in the world. The community of the disciples is characterized as the locus of God's active presence in the world after Jesus' departure from the world.

CONSECRATE THE DISCIPLES IN THE TRUTH (17:17–19)

The second intercession of Jesus for the disciples in verse 17 enunciates further the vocation of the disciples, what it means to be the disciples of Jesus in the world. Jesus prays that God will consecrate or set apart (ἁγιάζω) the disciples for a sacred duty or service. In the LXX, the verb ἁγιάζω means to dedicate or "set apart" a person for a sacred duty and is thus used for the consecration of priests (e.g., Aaron and his sons, Exod 28:41), prophets (e.g., Jer 1:5; Sir 49:7), and the chosen people of God for the service of God ("You chose the ancestors and consecrated them," 2 Macc 1:25).[164] The election of Moses is described as consecration ("For his faithfulness and meekness he [God] consecrated him [Moses], choosing him out of all humankind," Sir 45:4). The election motif of a covenant relationship is thus implied in ἁγιάζω as one is chosen and set apart by God to participate actively in the history of salvation. What is significant in the consecration of the disciples in 17:17 is that the entire community of the disciples, like "the ancestors" of the OT traditions (2 Macc 1:25), not merely the leaders or the representatives, is consecrated in truth for the service of God's word (17:21). The community of the disciples, as one body, assumes the roles of priests and prophets, who are the mediators and reminders of God's covenant relationship with Israel, and forms the new covenant community. The verb ἁγιάζω occurs four times in the gospel (10:36; 17:17, 19 [twice]). Its first occurrence in 10:36 is situated within the literary context of the Feast of Dedication (Hanukkah) that remembered and celebrated the consecration of the temple of Jerusalem (10:22). Jesus thus proclaims that he is the new temple consecrated by God, making God's active presence visible (see also 1:14; 2:21).[165] This idea is further elaborated by the fact that Jesus is sent by God (10:36b). In the Semitic worldview the officially commissioned envoy represents and has the authority of the sender. One who is sent is "legally identifiable with the sender."[166] Jesus thus reveals his identity as the one consecrated and sent by God to make God manifest in human history.

---

[164] See the detailed discussion of Hoskyns, *Fourth Gospel*, 502–4.

[165] Moloney, *Signs and Shadows*, 149–50.

[166] Brown, *John*, 1.411.

The evangelist preserves the intrinsic link between consecration and sending when he uses ἁγιάζω a second time, applying it to the disciples (17:17–18). Just as (καθώς) Jesus was set apart for God's work and sent into the world (10:36), the disciples are also consecrated to become God's treasured possession and the chosen people for the mission and works ascribed in the OT to the priests and prophets (17:17) and sent into the world (17:18). The disciples share in the mission and work of Jesus that in turn mirrors the work of God.[167] The use of ἁγιάζω for the self-consecration of Jesus in verse 19 refers to the death of Jesus. In the LXX ἁγιάζω means also "to dedicate as a sacrifice" (e.g., Exod 13:2; Deut 15:19). As Raymond E. Brown comments, "John xvii 19 has Jesus consecrating himself, seemingly as a victim."[168] It is Jesus' death that ultimately seals the new covenant and consecrates the disciples, the new people of God.[169] This idea is well founded in the NT traditions: "We have been sanctified through the offering of the body of Jesus Christ once for all" (Heb 10:10).[170] However, one cannot ignore that Jesus' death, viewed from the perspective of the Johannine theology, is the manifestation of the redemptive power (cf. 3:14) and the unconditional love of God (cf. 3:16).

The Fourth Evangelist has two ways of explaining Jesus' death on the cross. First, the gospel has three "lifting up" (ὑψόω) sayings that introduce its readers to and prepares them for the Johannine theology of cross (3:14; 8:28; 12:31–33). The evangelist makes a direct allusion to Num 21 where Moses lifted up the serpent by the command of God (3:14). The evocative biblical image of being "lifted up" has a life-giving function and symbolizes God's redemptive power (Wis 16:7). The evangelist applies this image of being lifted up to the crucifixion of Jesus on the cross and interprets Jesus' death as a symbol of God's saving action (3:14; 8:28; 12:31–33). Second, the evangelist presents Jesus' death as the best disclosure of God's love (3:16). Jesus' death is also compared to the Good Shepherd laying down his life for the sheep (10:11) or to one sacrificing his life for his friends (cf. 15:13).[171] It is therefore Jesus' death, revealing God's love and redemptive

---

[167] For a detailed study of the missionary aspect of Jesus' prayer, see Manns, *L'Évangile de Jean*, 396–400. For the intimate relationship between God's work and Jesus' mission, see R. Chennattu, "The *Svadharma* of Jesus," 317–35.

[168] Brown, *John*, 2.767.

[169] This tradition goes back to Cyril of Alexandria (*In Joannis Evangelium*, xi 8; PG 74.545). See also Hoskyns, *Fourth Gospel*, 501–4; Kysar, *John*, 261.

[170] See also Matt 26:28; Mark 14:24; Luke 22:17–20; Acts 20:32; 26:18; 1 Cor 1:2; 6:11; Heb 2:11; 9:20; 10:14, 29; 1 Pet 1:2.

[171] Chennattu, "Good Shepherd," 93–105, esp. 100.

power, that consecrates and empowers the disciples to be the new covenant community. Jesus' prayer envisages that his disciples will form a "counter-community" as the visible sign of God in the world that has no knowledge of God.

May the Disciples Be One (17:20–26)

Jesus prays that the oneness shared between the Father and the Son be manifested among his disciples. The importance of oneness among the disciples is highlighted by the repeated pleas of Jesus: "That they may be one" (v. 21); "That they may be one as we are one" (v. 22); "That they become perfectly one" (v. 23). The prayer "that they may be one" is explained further as their abiding in God: "that they may be in us" (v. 21).[172] The idea of unity or יחד played a significant role in the self-description of the Qumran community.[173] John P. Maier has pointed out the covenantal overtones of the יחד motif in Qumran documents.[174] Similarly, although the covenant motif is not explicit in Jesus' prayer for the unity of the disciples, what is implied in the oneness that is expected from the disciples is the mutual abiding in God's love, the covenant relationship with God, which unites and empowers them to become the visible presence of God in the world. The oneness among the disciples is modeled on the intimate relationship of the Father and Jesus revealed in the redemptive works of God in Jesus (17:22, 26; see also 10:30).

The Johannine Jesus makes the bridge between present and eschatological time. Jesus claims that the eschatological expectations are anticipated

---

[172] For the different interpretations of what it means to be *one* in Jesus' prayer, see Brown, *John,* 2.774–79. For a detailed study of the oneness motif in John's Gospel, see M. L. Appold, *The Oneness Motif in the Fourth Gospel: Motif Analysis and Exegetical Probe into the Theology of John* (WUNT 2/1; Tübingen: J. C. B. Mohr, 1976).

[173] F. M. Cross, *The Ancient Library of Qumran* (New York: Doubleday, 1961), 209. Cross has pointed out the many similar expression in John's Gospel and 1QS (e.g., 1QS 5.2 "to be a unity" and John 17:21 "they may be one"). See also E. Koffmann, "Rechtsstellung und hierarchische Struktur des יחד von Qumran," *Bib* 42 (1961): 433–42. For a general survey on the Qumran scrolls and the Johannine Gospel and Epistles, see R. E. Brown, *New Testament Essays* (London: Chapman, 1967), 102–31.

[174] J. Maier, "Zum Begriff יחד in den Texten von Qumran," *ZAW* 72 (1960): 148–66. For the difference between the unity that was claimed by the Johannine community and that of the Qumran community, see Beasley-Murray, *John,* 302.

and presented as already taking place in the earthly life of Jesus, especially at
the moment of prayer. Jesus prays that the disciples may be given the glory
(δόξα/כָּבוֹד) of God (v. 22) and see the glory (δόξα/כָּבוֹד) of Jesus (v. 24).
Now the vision of God's glory (δόξα/כָּבוֹד) is the ultimate goal of Israel's
hope (Isa 35:2; 66:18).[175] According to the Book of Isaiah: "The glory
of the Lord shall be revealed, and all people shall see it together; for the
mouth of the Lord has spoken" (Isa 40:5). The community of the disciples
is comprised of those who believe in Jesus (3:16, 36), love one another
(13:34–35), abide in Jesus' word (8:31–32), abide in Jesus and his love
(15:4, 8–9), know Jesus' identity and divine origin (17:8), and see the vision
of God's glory (δόξα/כָּבוֹד) manifested in Jesus (17:22, 24). The purpose of
Jesus' prayer for unity among the disciples is that the world may recognize
Jesus as the Sent One and the disciples as God's beloved, reflecting the
union of love that exists between God and Jesus (17:23). Jesus' selfless love
for humanity was the sign of his messiahship and revelation of God's redemptive power in human history (10:11; 15:13). Similarly, the disciples
are to make God's presence visible by loving one another as Jesus has loved
them (13:34–35; 15:12, 17). The ultimate objective of discipleship is to
make God's love known (v. 23). The disciples' abiding covenant relationship with the Father enables them to continue the work of Jesus in making
God known to the world (17:21–26). The indwelling presence of God's
love among the disciples implied in verse 26 is an echo of the OT covenant
motifs.[176] After the covenant at Sinai, Yahweh repeatedly reminded Israel
of his presence in their midst (Exod 29:45; Num 11:20; Deut 7:21; 23:14),
and the name of God or the glory of God (δόξα/כָּבוֹד) was set upon the
Tabernacle that symbolized God's dwelling place (cf. Exod 40:34–35). The
revelation of the name of God is referred to elsewhere in the prophetic tradition as the glory of God (Isa 42:8). Jesus now prays that the disciples will
see the glory of God (17:22, 24) and that the name of God given to Jesus
will be handed over to the disciples (17:26). Jesus promises the glory of
God to the disciples and consecrates them as a covenant community of God.

The evangelist used the OT covenant traditions, and the Jesus material at
hand, in order to drive home what he wanted to say about discipleship. He
attained this purpose by the careful arrangement and modification of the
Jesus material within the theological and structural framework of OT cove-

---

[175] According to *Tanh.* במדבר 20, God promises, "In the age to come, when I
have led my dwelling place [שְׁכִינָה] to Sion, I will reveal myself in my glory [כָּבוֹד] to
all Israel, and they shall see and live for ever." See also the discussion in Kittel,
"δόξα in the LXX and Hellenistic Apocrypha," *TDNT* 2.242–55.
[176] Brown, *John*, 2.781.

nant renewals. The above reading shows that the covenant relationship motifs run through the discourses of Jesus in chapters 13–17 and define Johannine discipleship.

CONCLUSION: DISCIPLESHIP AS A COVENANT RELATIONSHIP

After the call stories of 1:35–51, the only occasion when we find Jesus and his disciples *alone* before his passion, death, and resurrection is in chapters 13–17. In this section various elements of the OT covenant relationship introduced in the call stories receive further expansion and development.

As the discussion above indicates, the ongoing revelation of Jesus' identity as the embodiment of God's loving presence and the repeated call to decision in chapters 2–12 serve as a hortatory preparation for a covenant renewal and the consecration of the community of the disciples in chapters 13–17. Chapter 13 functions as an immediate preparation for the consecration of the new covenant community. This is accomplished by the disclosure of the new identity of the disciples as οἱ ἴδιοι or God's סְגֻלָּה. Jesus' intimate love for them is revealed in the footwashing and in his offer to share the μέρος or the covenant relationship with the disciples. The disciples are called to continue Jesus' deeds (καθὼς ἐγὼ ἐποίησα, 13:15) and Jesus' love (καθὼς ἠγάπησα, 13:34) when he returns to the Father (cf. 13:1). The Johannine Jesus introduces his new covenant commandment to "love one another" and invites the disciples to establish a covenant with him and with one another (13:34–35). Through the focus upon Judas, Peter, and the Beloved Disciple, the narrator progressively prepares the characters in the story as well as the readers and invites them to enter gradually into a covenant relationship with God through Jesus and consequently with one another.

Chapter 14 is rich in close parallels between the covenant promises of Yahweh to Israel and those of Jesus to the disciples. Jesus primarily guarantees the indwelling presence and the knowledge of God, and invites the disciples who are steadfast in loving and keeping his commandments to participate in the life-of-love or the covenant relationship with Jesus and God. Just as in the OT covenant relationship, so also in John's discipleship discourses, a distinction between those who know God, the disciples, and the world that does not know God is made clear. Jesus assures the gift of the Spirit-Paraclete, which will bring to remembrance the ongoing revelation of God in the personal life as well as in the communitarian life of the believers. Jesus will depart from the disciples leaving his own peace, the life-of-love, and summoning them to a binding covenant relationship.

The Johannine paradigm of what it means to be disciples of Jesus dominates 15:1–17: to abide in Jesus' love, to glorify the Father by bearing much fruit, to keep the covenant commandments of love, and to be the chosen people of God. The commands of Jesus, to abide in his love and to keep the commandments (15:10), encompass the central obligations of an OT covenant relationship: to abide in Yahweh (LXX Isa 30:18) and to abide in obedience to the Law (LXX Deut 27:26). By using a variety of covenant motifs, the evangelist explicitly enunciates Johannine discipleship in terms of an OT covenant relationship that includes privileges as well as obligations and the disciples' status in terms of covenant partners. Just as the election theme in the OT entails Israel's privileges as well as the challenges and risks involved in living among other nations, the section that follows, 15:18–16:28, explores the consequences of discipleship.

Jesus' warnings in 15:18–16:24 are an invitation to come to grips with the historical denial or rejection of their faith commitment to the revelation of God in Jesus. Before renewing the covenant with God, Joshua reminds Israel of the temptation and the possibility for them to abandon Yahweh and serve other gods and urges them to make a definitive decision in favor of Yahweh (Josh 24:19–20). Similarly, Jesus expresses his great concern lest the disciples fall into the trap of apostasy. On the one hand, Jesus warns the disciples of the approaching persecutions from outside the community and, on the other, assures them of God's gift of the Paraclete (ὁ παράκλητος) and the fullness of joy (χαρά) in their lives. The call to discipleship implies a decision-making in response to a gracious gift of God that enables the disciples to share the life of God. It is a call to keep the commandments of God in faithfulness and loyalty as the new covenant people of God.

Toward the end of the discipleship discourses the disciples give an extended response, demonstrating they have understood the teachings of Jesus and what they entail. They accept that Jesus has come from God and knows everything. This is the climactic profession of faith in Jesus. Just as the declaration of commitment to Yahweh is usually followed by a covenant making ritual (Exod 24:8; Josh 24:25–28), the public profession of the disciples' commitment to Jesus as the authentic revelation of God is followed by the covenant prayer of Jesus to consecrate the disciples as the new covenant community (17:1–26).

The disciples' profession of faith in 16:30 ("now we know . . . and . . . believe that you came from God") signals the completion of Jesus' work and forms the foundational interpretative key to the theological and narrative significance of Jesus' prayer. The literary setting, form, and content suggest that Jesus' prayer seals the new covenant between God and the disciples, the new covenant community. The prayer looks forward to the ongoing work of both the immediate and future disciples, asking God to consecrate the community of the disciples of all generations as a covenant community, closely knit together by God's abiding presence and love, set apart for the mission of making God's active presence known and loved to a world that has not known God and is living in darkness (17:25–26). The prayer of Jesus binds the disciples to their decision to be faithful to their vocation as the new covenant community of God.

In sum, the covenant themes—election, intimate abiding relationship, indwelling presence, keeping God's commandments, and mutual knowledge—run through the discipleship discourses in 13–17 and provide the theological definition of what it means to be a disciple of Jesus. The evangelist presents the paradigm of discipleship in terms of a covenant relationship that mirrors the mutuality, reciprocity, and intimacy of the Father-Son relationship revealed to the disciples in Jesus' life, mission, and death. The disciples are called to participate in the fellowship of the Father and the Son. The revelation of God's name to the disciples molds and fashions the unique identity and distinctiveness of the new covenant community. The unity among the disciples results from the mutual indwelling presence of God in them. They now know and understand God's name, i.e., God's identity, nature, and visible presence embodied in Jesus and his works. Just as in an OT covenant relationship, Johannine discipleship demands a deep knowledge of God and is embedded in the promises and the indwelling presence of God. The promises of Jesus bring a dimension of "not yet" into the faith journey of the disciples. Like the election of Israel, the call to discipleship is a gift from God. Abiding in God's love and keeping God's commandments is the hallmark of both OT covenant relationship and Johannine discipleship. However, Johannine discipleship characterized by the universal membership—that includes Jews, Samaritans, and Gentiles or Greeks—transcends and perfects the exclusive OT covenant relationship between Yahweh and Israel. The evangelist takes the OT covenant metaphor, redefines and broadens its prospect, and applies it to the relationship between God and the new covenant community of Jesus' disciples.

FOUR

COVENANT-DISCIPLESHIP MOTIFS IN JOHN 20–21

The covenant prayer of Jesus in chapter 17 is followed by the passion narrative in chapters 18–19, which opens with Jesus' arrest at the hands of the ruling authorities of Jerusalem (18:1–12). This event leads first to a Jewish hearing (18:13–27), and then to judgment before Pilate, the Roman authority (18:28–19:16), and concludes with a description of the death and burial of Jesus (19:17–42). The discovery of the empty tomb and the appearances of the risen Jesus to the disciples constitute chapters 20–21. Although it is often suggested that 21:1–25 is a later interpolation,[1] this study considers chapter 21 an integral part of the final redactor's design of the unfolding story of Jesus.[2] It therefore suggests that the narrative of the Johannine story would be incomplete without chapter 21.

---

[1] For example, the comment of C. H. Dodd, "[John 21] has the character of a postscript, and falls outside the design of the book as a whole," summarizes the conventional position that ch. 21 is not an integral part of the original gospel (*Interpretation,* 290). D. M. Smith regards John 21 as "the key and cornerstone for any redactional theory" (*The Composition and Order of the Fourth Gospel* [New Haven: Yale University Press, 1965], 234). After a survey of various opinions on the issue, R. E. Brown concludes: "We consider it certain that ch. xxi is an addition to the Gospel, consisting of a once independent narrative of Jesus' appearance to his disciples" (*John,* 2.1078). For a survey of this position, see G. Reim, "Johannes 21: Ein Anhang?" in *Studies in New Testament Language and Text: Essays in Honor of George Dunbar Kilpatrick on the Occasion of His Sixty-Fifth Birthday* (ed. J. K. Elliott; NovTSup 44; Leiden: Brill, 1976), 330.

[2] This contention is made on three grounds: textual evidence, vocabulary and literary style, and thematic unity. First, there is no manuscript evidence of the gospel without ch. 21; all the available manuscripts including the most ancient, $\mathfrak{P}^{66}$, have ch. 21. As R. Mahoney points out, "There is no manuscript evidence whatsoever that the Gospel of John was ever circulated without chapter 21" (*Two Disciples at the Tomb: The Background and Message of John 20,1–10* [TW 6; Bern: Herbert Lang, 1974], 12). Studies of Johannine literary style indicate that ch. 21 is

The narratives of chapters 20–21 unfold the post-resurrection stories of the encounters between Jesus and the disciples. Integrated into these narratives are significant covenant-discipleship themes. While exploring the discipleship motifs in these stories, I will also discuss covenant themes as they emerge. The structure of this long narrative section rests on three major changes of locations: at the tomb, at the upper room, and by the sea of Tiberius. The threefold structure can be summarized as follows: (1) the discovery of the empty tomb and the encounter between Jesus and Mary of Magdala (20:1–18); (2) Jesus' appearances to the disciples in Jerusalem (20:19–31); (3) Jesus' final farewell appearance to the disciples in Galilee (21:1–25).[3]

RECLAIMING THE COVENANT RELATIONSHIP OF THE DISCIPLES (20:1–18)

The narratives at the tomb consist in the discovery of the empty tomb, the burial cloths and the face towel of Jesus (20:1–10), and the encounter between Jesus and Mary of Magdala (20:11–18).[4] Although two sets of characters are involved in this narrative—Mary, Peter, and the Beloved

---

homogeneous with that of the rest of the gospel; see the important study of E. Ruckstuhl on Johannine vocabulary and style, *Die literarische Einheit des Johannesevangeliums* (Freiburg: Paulus, 1951), 141–49. See also the discussion and survey of various attempts to link 21:1–25 with the rest of the gospel in Moloney, *John,* 558 and 565–66. In what follows, the present study will explore how John 21 fulfills some of the covenant promises of Jesus made in chs. 13–17 and support the view that John 21 is an integral part of the gospel as it stands today. See also Hoskyns, *Fourth Gospel,* 550; P. S. Minear, "The Original Functions of John 21," *JBL* 102 (1983): 85–98; P. F. Ellis, "The Authenticity of John 21," *SVTQ* 36 (1992): 7–15; Segovia, "Final Farewell of Jesus," 167–90; Talbert, *Reading John,* 248–64; O'Day, "Gospel of John," 854–55.

[3]The narrative in 20:1–18 comprises the discovery of the empty tomb (vv. 1–10) and the encounter between Jesus and Mary of Magdala (vv. 11–18). John 20:19–31 can be divided into three parts: (1) the first appearance to the disciples (vv. 19–23); (2) the second appearance to the disciples (vv. 24–29); (3) the summary statement of the narrator to the readers (vv. 30–31). The structure of 21:1–25 has four units: (1) the third appearance to the disciples (vv. 1–14); (2) Peter and the primacy of authority (vv. 15–19); (3) the Beloved Disciple and the primacy of love (vv. 20–23); (4) the summary statement of the narrator to the readers (vv. 24–25).

[4]John's account of the empty tomb and resurrection narratives has affinities with, yet significant differences from, the most commonly received synoptic and Pauline traditions (cf. Matt 28; Mark 16; Luke 24; 1 Cor 15:1–11). See the

Disciple on the one hand, Mary, angels, and the risen Jesus on the other—the location at the tomb and the reference to the time "on the first day of the week" hold this unit together. The narrative begins with Mary's search for Jesus (20:1–2) and concludes with Mary's announcement that she has seen the Lord (20:18).

Discovery of the Empty Tomb, the Burial Cloths, and the Face Towel (20:1–10)

Setting (vv. 1–2)

Verses 1–2 furnish the literary context for the narratives that follow in verses 3–18. On the first day of the week, Mary goes to the tomb and realizes that "the stone had been taken away (τὸν λίθον ἠρμένον) from the tomb" (20:1). The use of passive voice (ἠρμένον) makes the readers wonder who the agent might be. Since the readers were informed earlier that Jesus would be raised from the dead (2:22; 12:16), they can now suspect God's active role in the event.[5] Mary, however, misunderstands and assumes that Jesus' body has been stolen from the tomb; she leaves the tomb to report this to the disciples.[6] As a response to Mary's testimony, both Peter and the Beloved Disciple go to the tomb.[7]

One of the elements of the discipleship paradigm of 1:35–51 is resumed in 20:1–2. At the beginning of the gospel, the disciples of John the Baptist followed Jesus to learn where he abides (ποῦ μένεις, 1:38). Now, in 20:1–2, Mary of Magdala expresses that they do not know where (ποῦ) Jesus' body

---

discussion of the composition of John 20 in B. Lindars, "The Composition of John XX," *NTS* 7 (1960–1961): 142–47. Frans Neirynck regards John 20:3–10 as an expansion of Luke 24:12 and argues for John's dependence on Luke; see "Tradition and Redaction in John XX, 1–18," *SE* 7 (1982): 359–63; "John and the Synoptics: The Empty Tomb Stories," *NTS* 30 (1984): 161–87; "Note sur Jean 20:1–18," *ETL* 62 (1986): 404.

[5] Moloney, *Glory not Dishonor,* 158 n. 13.

[6] Although Mary is alone, she reports: "We do not know where they have laid him" (20:2). The use of the first person plural may be a reminiscent of an early tradition (Matt 28:1; Mark 16:1; Luke 24:1, 10). Scholars have tried to deal with this discrepancy and proposed various explanations. For a survey of different views, see Moloney, *Glory not Dishonor,* 159 nn. 17–19.

[7] The narrator identifies "the other disciple" with "the disciple whom Jesus loved" in 20:2. This would help the reader to identify "the other disciple" mentioned in 18:15–16 with the two other references to "the disciple whom Jesus loved" in 13:23–26 and 19:25–27.

is (20:2, 13, 15).[8] The query that inspires the first disciples to follow Jesus (1:38) and that motivates Peter and the Beloved Disciple to run to the tomb has to do with Jesus' whereabouts (20:2, 13, 15). The "where" (ποῦ) of Jesus is not merely geographical, but has theological meaning.[9] The prologue informs the readers that Jesus is always in communion with the Father (1:18), and this theme runs across the gospel narrative (e.g., 5:19–30; 10:30, 38). The query concerning Jesus' whereabouts reminds the readers of the indwelling communion shared between Jesus and the Father. On three occasions in his final prayer Jesus speaks of his return to oneness with the Father (17:5, 11, 13), and on a fourth occasion he prays that his followers may be there with him (17:24). Hence the final abiding place of Jesus and his disciples is with the Father who is later identified with the covenant God (cf. 20:17). The search for Jesus' abiding place on the part of the disciples is another way of presenting Johannine discipleship in terms of a covenant relationship, since the covenant partners of the OT (Israel) are expected to abide in Yahweh (cf. LXX Isa 30:18).

Two Disciples at the Tomb (vv. 3–10)

Peter and the Beloved Disciple run to the tomb (vv. 3–4). In their search for Jesus, or more accurately Jesus' body, Peter and the Beloved Disciple find the empty tomb, the burial cloths (ὀθόνια), and the face towel (σουδάριον) of Jesus. A large amount of research has been done on the symbolic meaning and implications of ὀθόνια and σουδάριον and of the significance and the narrative impact of the faith of the Beloved Disciple as expressed in the narrative.[10]

The narrator takes care to describe in detail that each disciple saw the burial cloths (ὀθόνια) and the neatly folded face towel (σουδάριον) of Jesus lying there not with the ὀθόνια, but lying apart (vv. 5–7).[11] In the expression τὰ ὀθόνια κείμενα, the present middle participle of the verb κεῖμαι

[8] See the detailed discussion of P. S. Minear, " 'We Don't Know Where . . .' John 20:2," *Int* 30 (1976): 125–39.

[9] D. Mollat, "La découverte du tombeau vide (Jn 20, 1–9)," *AsSeign* 221 (1969): 90–100.

[10] F.-M. Braun, *Le linceul de Turin et l'Évangile de S. Jean: Étude de critique d'exégèse* (Tournai/Paris: Casterman, 1939); W. E. Reiser, "The Case of the Tidy Tomb: The Place of the Napkins of John 11:44 and 20:7," *HeyJ* 14 (1973): 47–57; B. Osborne, "A Folded Napkin in an Empty Tomb: John 11:44 and 20:7 Again," *HeyJ* 14 (1973): 437–40; Brown, *John,* 2.1007–8; Moloney, *Glory not Dishonor,* 161–62; Schneiders, *Written That You May Believe,* 180–88.

[11] The reader perceives a dynamic movement in the discovery of the empty tomb by Mary in vv. 1–3, Peter in vv. 6–7, and the Beloved Disciple in vv. 5 and 8.

suggests the cloths were lying there as if they had been emptied when Jesus rose from the dead. The use of passive voice, ἐντετυλιγμένον, "[the face towel] has been rolled up" (v. 7; cf. τὸν λίθον ἠρμένον, v. 1) again suggests to the readers God's intervention and active role in the story.[12] The presence and the position of both ὀθόνια and σουδάριον indicate that the body of Jesus has not been stolen. As John Chrysostom has aptly argued: "If anyone had stolen the body, he would not have stripped it first; nor would he have taken the trouble to remove and roll up the *soudarion* and put it in a place by itself."[13] The term σουδάριον appears only twice in the gospel: 11:44 and 20:7. In both occasions, σουδάριον denotes the towel used to cover the face of a dead person. The presence of the burial cloths and a σουδάριον in the present story reminds the readers of the Lazarus story in chapter 11. When Lazarus was called out of the tomb, he came out with the σουδάριον covering his face (11:44). The presence of the σουδάριον covering his face symbolized the fact that the resuscitated Lazarus was to die again. In contrast to the resuscitated Lazarus, the risen Jesus has left these cloths in the tomb.[14] The readers, aware of the tradition that Jesus would rise from the dead and never die again (2:22; 12:16; Mark 8:31; 9:31; 10:33–34; cf. Rom 6:9), perceive Jesus' resurrection. Sandra Schneiders suggests that the evangelist uses the tradition of the empty tomb and presents the σουδάριον as a Johannine sign (σημεῖον) revealing Jesus' glorification or return to the Father.[15] The presence of many passives and symbols of the empty tomb, the empty ὀθόνια, and σουδάριον, signals that Jesus is returning to the Father, fulfilling his promises to the disciples (13:33; 14:28) and his request to the Father for himself (17:5, 11, 13).

The narrative respects both the primacy of Peter as the bearer of authority (cf. v. 5) and the primacy of the other disciple as Jesus' beloved (cf. vv. 2, 8).[16] The Beloved Disciple outruns Peter, arrives at the tomb first

---

[12] Moloney, *Glory not Dishonor,* 161.

[13] *Jo. Hom.* 85:4; PG, 59.465. See also Culpepper, *Gospel and Letters of John,* 240; Brown, *John,* 2.1007–8.

[14] Moloney, *Glory not Dishonor,* 161. See also Reiser, "The Case of the Tidy Tomb," 47–57.

[15] Schneiders, *Written That You May Believe,* 180–88. Schneiders suggests a possible link between the σουδάριον of Jesus in John 20:7 and the face veil of Moses in Exod 34:33–35 and concludes: "Like Moses, who put aside the veil when he ascended to meet God in glory, Jesus, the new Moses, has put aside the veil of his flesh as he ascends into the presence of God" (ibid., 186).

[16] On various occasions, the Fourth Gospel acknowledges Peter as the spokesperson of the disciples (e.g., 1:42; 6:66–69; 13:36–38; 18:10–11; 21:3, 10–11, 15–19). For a detailed study, see R. E. Brown, K. P. Donfried, and J. Reumann,

and sees the burial cloths lying there; but it is Peter who enters the tomb first and sees not only the burial cloths but also the face towel (vv. 4–7). Nothing is revealed in the text about Peter's response to the empty tomb and to the symbols of burial cloths and face towel. The narrator, however, informs the readers that the Beloved Disciple saw and believed (εἶδεν καὶ ἐπίστευσεν, 20:8).[17] The absence of Jesus' body and the presence in the tomb of the empty burial cloths and neatly folded face towel lead the Beloved Disciple to believe that God has entered the story and raised his Son. He believes in the living presence of Jesus. As we have seen elsewhere in the gospel, the Beloved Disciple is portrayed as an ideal covenant partner who shares an intimate relationship with Jesus and as an example for all who would become the disciples of Jesus (e.g., 13:23–25; 19:26–27, 34–35; 20:1–10; 21:7, 20–23, 24).[18] This relationship and in-depth knowledge seem to have enabled the Beloved Disciple to come to belief at the empty tomb.[19] As we shall see, a similar response on the part of the Beloved Disciple is found in chapter 21 on Jesus' third appearance to the disciples at the Sea of Tiberias. Here it is the Beloved Disciple who first recognizes the risen Jesus and announces: Ὁ κύριός ἐστιν (21:7). This spontaneous recognition of the identity of Jesus reconfirms that the Beloved Disciple had indeed believed in the resurrection of Jesus at the empty tomb (20:8). Moreover, the Beloved Disciple's faith mentioned in 20:8 is appreciated by

---

eds., *Peter in the New Testament: A Collaborative Assessment by Protestant and Roman Catholic Scholars* (Minneapolis: Augsburg/New York: Paulist, 1973), 129–47.

[17] Some exegetes refute the contention that the belief of the Beloved Disciple reported in 20:8 is authentic Johannine faith. On the basis of v. 9, "for as yet they did not know the Scripture," D. A. Lee is of the opinion that the Beloved Disciple's belief in v. 8 "has no narrative impact" ("Partnership in Easter Faith: The Role of Mary Magdalene and Thomas in John 20," *JSNT* 58 [1995]: 39–40). Some exegetes, following Augustine and other Fathers, apply the profane meaning of πιστεύω ("accept as true" or "be convinced") and argue that the Beloved Disciple's belief indicates his acceptance of the testimony of Mary of Magdala that the tomb is empty (e.g., G. C. Nicholson, *Death as Departure: The Johannine Descent-Ascent Scheme* [SBLDS 63; Chico, Calif.: Scholars Press, 1983], 69–71). This interpretation seems improbable since the verb πιστεύω has been used throughout the gospel with a theological meaning (e.g., 1:12; 2:11; 3:15), and the Beloved Disciple is portrayed as an ideal disciple.

[18] See chapter 3, pp. 100–101.

[19] Brown, presupposing the fact that the love between Jesus and the Beloved Disciple was reciprocal (cf. 13:23), comments on the response of the Beloved Disciple: "The lesson for the reader is that love for Jesus gives one the insight to detect his presence" (*John*, 2.1005).

the narrator as an expression of faith prior to knowledge of the Scripture.[20] The comment of the narrator, "as yet they did not know the Scripture" (γραφή, 20:9), is addressed to the readers who, unlike the disciples in the story, are fortunate to know the Scripture (γραφή). John's Gospel is itself Scripture (γραφή) for the Johannine community.[21] By reading John's Gospel (γραφή), the readers are called to acknowledge and believe in the active role of God in the resurrection. As Francis J. Moloney aptly argues, the Beloved Disciple comes to faith in the resurrection of Jesus in verse 8, but the readers are told that they know more than the Beloved Disciple as they have and know the γραφή.[22] Being enlightened by the gospel (cf. 2:22; 12:16; 20:9) and being guided by the Paraclete (cf. 14:26), the readers are in a better position to understand the words of Jesus regarding his death and resurrection.

THE ENCOUNTER BETWEEN JESUS AND MARY AND COVENANT MOTIFS (20:11–18)

Mary of Magdala: A Representative Figure of the New Covenant Community

Mary of Magdala plays a significant role in the Johannine resurrection narrative as the commissioned apostle to the apostles. A number of literary difficulties have been detected in the narrative that signal the presence of editorial seams: (1) Mary first appears at the tomb and then moves away from the tomb (vv. 1–2), then disappears from the scene (vv. 3–10) and is abruptly introduced again at the tomb (v. 11); (2) what Mary sees in the empty tomb is different from what the Beloved Disciple and Peter have

---

[20] On the basis of the narrator's comment in v. 9, R. E. Brown considers the faith of the Beloved Disciple in v. 8 an expression of true Johannine belief ("The Resurrection in John 20—A Series of Diverse Reactions," *Worship* 64 [1990]: 197–98).

[21] Moloney, *Glory not Dishonor*, 162–63. On the Johannine perception of its own gospel as γραφή, see Obermann, *Die christologische Erfüllung der Schrift im Johannesevangelium*, 418–22. Against this view, see J. Beutler, "The Use of 'Scripture' in the Gospel of John," in *Exploring the Gospel of John*, 147–62.

[22] According to Moloney, John 20 is directed at the readers (cf. v. 29 and vv. 30–31). True Johannine faith is expressed by the Beloved Disciple in v. 8, by Mary of Magdela in v. 18, and by Thomas in v. 28. Thomas's expression of faith leads Jesus to address the readers who have not seen and yet believed in v. 29 and to indicate to the readers that they are to have life in the name of Jesus because of the γραφή in vv. 30–31 (*Glory not Dishonor*, 162–63).

witnessed (20:3–10).[23] These narrative problems indicate that the Fourth Evangelist is concerned to use his traditions to rewrite the story of Jesus' encounter with Mary from the perspective of a promise-fulfillment schema. He attempts to demonstrate how the covenant promises of Jesus in chapters 13–17 are fulfilled in the resurrection narratives by giving narrative shape to the unique Johannine understanding of glorification that begins on the cross but achieves its completion in Jesus' return to the Father.[24]

Mary's earnest desire to discover where Jesus is, coupled with her sorrow and anguish (note that Mary's wailing, κλαίω, at the tomb is repeated four times: vv. 11 bis, 13, 15), reminds the readers of the many prophecies of Jesus: "You will look for me" (13:33b) and "you will wail (κλαίω) and mourn" (16:20a) or "you now have sorrow" (16:22a). In John's account, unlike the version in the synoptic traditions (Matt 28:5–7; Luke 24:4–6), it is Jesus who first reveals his living presence to Mary (20:14–17).[25] The encounter between the risen Jesus and Mary and the subsequent rejoicing recall the words of Jesus: "I will not leave you orphans; I am coming to you. In a little while the world will no longer see me, but you will see me; because I live, you also will live. On that day you will know that I am in my Father, and you in me, and I in you" (14:18–20); "I am going away, but I am coming to you" (14:28); "your sorrow will turn into joy" (16:20b); "I will see you again, and your hearts will rejoice" (16:22b). Mary's encounter and the following experiences fulfill what has been foretold about Jesus' return to the Father and the post-resurrection experiences of the disciples.

Some exegetes consider Mary's role in chapter 20 parallel to that of the mother of Jesus at the foot of the cross in chapter 19.[26] In 19:26–27, Jesus addresses both his mother and the Beloved Disciple, announcing: "Woman, behold (ἴδε) your son. . . . Behold (ἴδε) your mother." The double use of

---

[23] For a discussion, see Lee, *Flesh and Glory,* 220–21.

[24] I am taking the Johannine use of ἀναβαίνω ("I ascend") as a reference to Jesus' return to the Father. It has been pointed out that the evangelist uses interchangeably verbs like ἀναβαίνω (cf. 20:17), ὑπάγω (cf. 13:33), and πορεύομαι (cf. 14:2, 3; 16:28); see Bernard, *John,* 2.668–69; Moloney, *John,* 529.

[25] O'Day suggests that the angels located as sitting "one at the head and the other at the feet" (20:12; cf. Matt 28:2; Mark 16:5; Luke 24:4) has an echo of the promise of Jesus that the disciples will see "the angels descending and ascending upon the Son of Man" (1:51). She therefore concludes that "the angels are not messengers, but are evidence of the inbreaking of the promised new age in Jesus' death and resurrection" ("Gospel of John," 842). Although this reading is possible, the static imagery of the angels sitting (20:12) and the dynamic imagery of the angels ascending and descending (1:51) are significantly different.

[26] For example, see Lee, *Flesh and Glory,* 225–26.

ἴδε underlines the revelatory function of Jesus' words.[27] Raymond Brown
considers it an "act of empowerment that both reveals and makes come
about a new relationship."[28] The power of Jesus' revelatory words makes
this new relationship a present reality. The mother of Jesus becomes the
mother of the Beloved Disciple who represents the community of the disciples.[29] Through his mother, Jesus establishes new relationships between
himself and the community of the disciples, and among the disciples themselves as brothers. As we shall see, 20:17 demonstrates that Jesus reveals to
Mary of Magdala a new identity and a new relationship that are applicable
to all the disciples as she makes a journey with the risen Jesus into openness
and faith. It seems reasonable to accept that Mary is portrayed as a representative figure of the new covenant community constituted by the disciples
of Jesus. Mary's restless yearning for Jesus, fearless search, and overwhelm-
ing joy in rediscovering Jesus have been compared to Israel's longing for
Yahweh in their covenant partnership.[30] In the light of the steady and continual use of covenant background in Jesus' relationship with his disciples
across the gospel, the narrative comes to a climax. Mary represents and
recapitulates the longing and aspirations of the new covenant community
of the disciples of Jesus.

The Angelophany (vv. 11–14)

The angelophany in verses 11–14 furnishes the literary setting and the
theological framework for the interpretation of the encounter between
Mary and Jesus. Like the disciples, Mary stoops to look into the tomb
(v. 11), but instead of the burial cloths and face towel (cf. vv. 6–7), she sees
two angels in white (v. 12). As seen above, the use of several passives in
20:1–10 makes the reader wonder who the agent is! The accumulation of
these passives implies the active role of God in the story from its very beginning. Mary's vision of the angels reaffirms the divine presence and inter-

---

[27] On the revelatory function of ἴδε in the Gospel of John, see de Goedt, "Un
schème de révélation," 142–50.

[28] R. E. Brown, *The Death of the Messiah: From Gethsemane to the Grave* (2 vols.;
ABRL; New York: Doubleday, 1994), 2.1021.

[29] Coloe, *God Dwells with Us,* 187–88.

[30] Mary's restless search for, and the overpowering joy of rediscovering, Jesus is
compared with the image of the lover in Cant 3:1–4; see the study of A. Feuillet,
"La recherche du Christ dans la Nouvelle Alliance d'après la Christophanie de Jo
20,11–18," in *L'homme devant Dieu* (2 vols.; Mélanges H. de Lubac; Paris: Aubier,
1963), 1.93–112, esp. 103–7; T. Okure, "The Significance of Jesus' Commission to
Mary Magdalene," *IRM* 81 (1992): 181; Léon-Dufour, *Lecture de l'Évangile selon Jean,*
4.220. Against this view, see Minear, "'We Don't Know Where . . . ,'" 129–30.

vention in the story. The "whiteness" (λευκός) of the angels' clothing symbolizes the presence of the "heavenly world."[31] That there is something more than a general indication of a divine intervention is suggested by the description of the angels (v. 12). The position of the angels on either side of the place where the body of Jesus had once lain symbolically represents the ark of the covenant: the image of the mercy seat and the two golden cherubim on both ends of the mercy seat facing each other (Exod 37:5–9).[32] The Hebrew cherub (or cherubim) refers to supernatural creatures associated with the presence of God.[33] According to both Exod 25:22 and Num 7:89, Yahweh spoke to Moses *from between the two cherubim.* One of the roles of the cherubim, as described in the Book of Exodus and the First Book of Kings, is that of protective bearers of God's ark.[34] In God's instruction as to how to make the ark in Exod 25:18–20 and Moses' execution of it in Exod 37:7–9, the cherubs stand at either side with wings outstretched to protect the ark of the covenant. Similarly, the narrative in 1 Kgs 8:1–11, which describes the procession of the ark of the covenant to the temple, points out that the ark contains nothing but the two tablets of stone, and was placed underneath the wings of the cherubim.

> Then the priests brought the ark of the covenant of the LORD to its place, in the inner sanctuary of the house, in the most holy place, underneath the wings of the cherubim. For the cherubim spread out their wings over the place of the ark, so that the cherubim made a covering above the ark and its poles. . . . There was nothing in the ark except the two tablets of stone that Moses had placed there at Horeb, where the LORD made a covenant with the Israelites, when they came out of the land of Egypt. (1 Kgs 8:6–7, 9 NRSV)

A significant comparison can be made: just as the OT cherubim guarded the ark and the tablets symbolizing Torah or God's words, the angels at the tomb are guarding the place where Jesus' body had lain in order to make visible the living presence of Jesus, the incarnate and risen Word. Viewed

---

[31] Bernard, *John,* 2.663.

[32] The symbolism of the mercy seat in v. 12 was noticed by Lee, *Flesh and Glory,* 223. Brown also makes a passing reference to the symbolism of "the two cherubs on either side of the Ark of the Covenant in the Holy of Holies" in John 20:12 (*John,* 2.989).

[33] *The Oxford Companion to the Bible* (ed. B. M. Metzger and M. D. Coogan; New York, Oxford: Oxford University Press, 1993), 107.

[34] Other roles of the cherubim include their function as guardians of paradise (Gen 3:24; Ezek 28:14–16), as guardians of the tree of life (1 Kgs 6:29–35), and as providers of power that enables God's chariot to fly (Ezek 1 and 10). See the discussion in *The Oxford Companion to the Bible,* 107–8.

from the Johannine theological perspective, the two angels on either side of the place where Jesus' body had lain reveal the living presence of the cove-nant God in the empty tomb. The symbolism of the ark of the covenant evoked by the presence and the position of the two angels provides the theological framework for the rest of the dialogue between Jesus and Mary that reclaims and confirms disciples' covenant relationship with God.

The Dialogue between Jesus and Mary (vv. 15–16)

The episode of Mary and the risen Jesus (20:1–2, 11–18) is reminiscent of the call stories (1:35–51).[35] Covenant motifs gleaned there can also be detected in the encounter of Mary with the risen Jesus. Her vision of the angels inside the tomb and Jesus' commission to go and proclaim to the dis-ciples his return to the Father is unique to the story of Mary of Magdala.[36] In the table below, the narrative moments that 20:1–18 shares with the call stories in 1:35–51 are given in bold print:

Shared Narrative Moments of John 20:1–18 and the Call Stories of John 1:35–51

	Third day (1:35–42)	Fourth day (1:43–51)	Jesus and Mary (20:1–18)
Setting	JB, disciples, and Jesus (vv. 35–36) Andrew and Simon Peter (vv. 40–41)	Philip from Bethsaida (v. 44) Nathanael (v. 45)	Mary at the tomb (vv. 1, 11)
Dialogue	Dialogue (vv. 38–39) **τί ζητεῖτε;** **ποῦ μένεις;**	Dialogue (vv. 47–50)	Dialogue (vv. 2, 14–15) **τίνα ζητεῖς;** **ποῦ ἔθηκαν αὐτόν;** **ποῦ ἔθηκας αὐτόν;**
Invitation	**Ἔρχεσθε καὶ ὄψεσθε** [Jesus] (v. 39)	**Ἀκολούθει μοι** [Jesus] (v. 43) **Ἔρχου καὶ ἴδε** [Philip] (v. 46)	**Μαριάμ** (v. 16)
Response	The disciples went and **abided** (μένω) with Jesus (v. 39)		**Ῥαββουνι** (v. 16)

---

[35] See chapter 1, pp. 22–49.

[36] The basic structure of John 1:35–51—encounter, dialogue, recognition of the identity of Jesus, confession of faith in words and deeds—is also followed in the case of the dialogue between Jesus and the Samaritan woman in John 4:4–42; see Chennattu, "Women in the Mission of the Church," 760–73.

Knowledge of God/Jesus	Εὑρήκαμεν τὸν Μεσσίαν (v. 41)	Ὃν ἔγραψεν Μωϋσῆς ἐν τῷ νόμῳ καὶ οἱ προφῆται εὑρήκαμεν (v. 45) σὺ εἶ ὁ υἱὸς τοῦ θεοῦ σὺ βασιλεὺς εἶ τοῦ Ἰσραήλ (v. 49)	Ἑώρακα τὸν κύριον (v. 18)
Identity of the disciple/ disciples	Renaming (v. 42) σὺ κληθήσῃ Κηφᾶς	Reaffirming (v. 47) Ἴδε ἀληθῶς Ἰσραηλίτης ἐν ᾧ δόλος οὐκ ἔστιν	Reclaiming the covenant relationship (v. 17) πρὸς τοὺς ἀδελφούς μου πρὸς τὸν πατέρα μου καὶ πατέρα ὑμῶν θεόν μου καὶ θεὸν ὑμῶν
Commission and Response (found only in John 20)			Μή μου ἅπτου . . . πορεύου . . . Εἰπέ (v. 17) Mary went and told the disciples . . . (v. 18)

Reading the narrative of 20:11–18 from the point of view of covenant-discipleship motifs, one readily perceives how Mary's story reflects the many narrative moments and covenant elements that this study has identified and explored in 1:35–51, such as the moments of encounter, dialogue, renaming/affirming or calling by name, recognition/knowledge of Jesus, and the response to the call in terms of testimony or witness. In both occasions of invitation to discipleship, the encounter begins with the disciples' quest for Jesus, and is followed by a dialogue initiated by Jesus' query about what they are seeking. The first words of the risen Jesus (τίνα ζητεῖς, 20:15) to Mary who is searching for Jesus remind the readers of the first words of Jesus to the first disciples in the call stories: τί ζητεῖτε. The disciples of John the Baptist are searching for Jesus' abode or dwelling place (1:38), and Mary is searching for Jesus' body (20:15).

Just as abiding with Jesus enables the first disciples to recognize Jesus as the Messiah (1:38–41), or affirming the identity of Nathanael as the true Israelite empowers him to make the leap from unfaith to the recognition of Jesus, ῥαββί, σὺ εἶ ὁ υἱὸς τοῦ θεοῦ, σὺ βασιλεὺς εἶ τοῦ Ἰσραήλ (1:49), Jesus' calling Mary by her name enables her to identify Jesus as her master (ῥαββουνί, 20:16). Calling by name in the ancient world has the power to evoke identity and deep relationship.[37] This is reflected in the words of

---

[37] Lee, *Flesh and Glory*, 223.

Jesus that empower Mary to recognize Jesus' living presence, already symbolized, but not yet understood by Mary, by the presence of the two angels
in verse 12.[38] Jesus' personal knowledge of Mary and her knowledge of
Jesus, as expressed in her response, unravel the mystery of Jesus' identity as
the messianic Good Shepherd described in chapter 10 and fulfill what has
been said about the Good Shepherd: "I know my own and my own know
me" (10:14). See also the expressions such as "my sheep hear my voice" or
"I call them by name" (10:3–4). The encounter with the risen Jesus empowers Mary to discover her true covenant relationship with God. As indicated above, the profound and mutual knowledge of God and Israel is
presupposed in their covenant relationship in the OT.

Jesus' Commission: A Reclaiming of the Covenant Relationship (vv. 17–18)

The command of the risen Jesus to Mary consists in both a prohibition
and a commission (20:17). Jesus first commands Mary to leave him ("Do
not hold on to me") and then asks her to go to the disciples, who are referred to as his "brothers" (τοὺς ἀδελφούς μου), to announce that Jesus is
ascending to his Father and their Father and to his God and their God.
Contrary to the synoptic traditions, nothing is said in the Fourth Gospel
about Jesus' resurrection from the dead, but the risen Jesus commands Mary
to remind the disciples of his return to the Father, the covenant God.[39] The
theological concern of the hour and the necessity that Jesus return to the
Father in order that the disciples receive their new identity as the new
covenant people of God is well articulated in the covenant discourses in
chapters 13–17 (see especially 16:7; cf. 14:28; 16:28). Jesus' command in
verse 17 fulfills his claim that his return to the Father makes new life as
children of God possible for the disciples.

Jesus' prohibition "Do not hold on to me" (μή μου ἅπτου) has been
interpreted with ingenuity and imagination.[40] Jesus' words need to be in-

---

[38] Carla Ricci regards the double naming (Μαριάμ and ῥαββουνί) as a supernatural moment in the narrative awakening Mary to a deep mystical experience of
the revelation of God in the risen Jesus (Mary Magdalene and Many Others: Women
Who Followed Jesus [trans. P. Burns; Tunbridge Wells: Burns & Oates, 1994], 143).
This is possible, but the text does not describe a mystical experience here (e.g., the
mystical experience of Paul narrated in Acts 9; 22; 26).

[39] According to the Matthean tradition, the good news to be announced is that
"he (Jesus) has risen from the dead" (Matt 28:7; see also Mark 16:6–7; Luke 24:5–7).

[40] For some suggestions, see D. C. Fowler, "The Meaning of 'Touch me not' in
John 20:17," EvQ 47 (1975): 16–25; Brown, John, 2.1011–12; Westcott, John, 292–93.

terpreted in the light of the reason that Jesus himself gives that he has *not yet ascended* (20:17b) and the commission in verse 17c. Jesus promised the disciples that he would not leave them orphans and that he would come to them (14:18–20; 14:28), that they would have joy (16:20, 22) and a new relationship whereby the glorified Jesus and the Father would come and make their home with the disciples (14:21–23). Raymond E. Brown argues that "[Mary] is trying to hold on to the source of her joy, since she mistakes an appearance of the risen Jesus for his permanent presence with the disciples."[41] Jesus thus makes a distinction between the resurrection appearances and his permanent presence through the Paraclete, and he reclaims the new relationship that will be established with the disciples after his return to the Father, to the glory that was his before the world was (17:5).

Jesus wants Mary to go to his *brothers* and announce, "I am ascending to my Father and your Father, to my God and your God" (20:17c). Three aspects of this commission merit special attention: (1) the reference to the disciples as Jesus' brothers; (2) Jesus is ascending to the Father; (3) the double identification formula: "to my Father and your Father, to my God and your God." Jesus sends Mary as a representative to his disciples who are now referred to as his brothers (ἀδελφοί). The disciples have now become Jesus' ἀδελφοί who share in the covenant relationship with his Father and God. The hour of Jesus, which culminates in Jesus' return, signals the completion of Jesus' mission and creates a new family of the disciples characterized by a new relationship with God. In this new status, the disciples have become his brothers, the children of God (cf. 1:12; 11:52).[42] Although in the prologue (1:12) the evangelist promises to the believers the power (ἐξουσία) to become children of God (τέκνα θεοῦ), 20:17 is the first time in the story that characters are informed of their new status as Jesus' brothers or children of God.

Jesus commands Mary to communicate that he is ascending (ἀναβαίνω) to the Father. The use of the present tense ἀναβαίνω indicates an action in the immediate future that Jesus is about to ascend. Jesus' first prohibition, μή μου ἅπτου, οὔπω γὰρ ἀναβέβηκα, coupled with his announcement, ἀναβαίνω, suggests that the post-resurrection appearance is just a passing experience in contrast to the permanent indwelling presence of the Spirit

---

[41] Brown, *John*, 2.1012.

[42] Moloney, *Glory not Dishonor*, 167–68; Culpepper, *Gospel and Letters of John*, 241–42; D. Mollat, "La foi pascale selon le chapitre 20 de l'Évangile de Jean: Essai de théologie biblique," in *Études johanniques* (Parole de Dieu; Paris: Editions du Seuil, 1979), 173–74.

(14:16–17).[43] Jesus' return to the Father completes the hour of his glorification that began on the cross (12:23; 13:1; 17:1), making it possible for the
Paraclete to dwell among the disciples forever (cf. 7:37–39; 16:7).

Jesus' commission reveals the new status of his disciples as a result of his
glorification and the completion of his mission. This is indicated by the
double identification "to my Father and your Father, to my God and your
God" (20:17c).[44] The double identification claims that Jesus' Father has
now become the Father of the disciples and his God, the disciples' God.[45]
With the double identification of the Father and God, the Johannine Jesus
is explicitly making a link between his Father and the covenant God of the
OT.[46] The expression "my God and your God" reminds the readers of the
covenantal formula "I will be your/their God" which is repeatedly used in
the OT at the moments of covenant renewal.[47] Talking about the new covenant (διαθήκη καινή),[48] Jeremiah recalls the old covenant formula "I will
be their God and they shall be my people" and appropriates it as part of the

---

[43] The chronological order of the events in these chapters is confusing. According to Johannine theology, Jesus' glorification begins at the cross and is completed
in his return to the Father. Where do the resurrection appearances belong? No return to the Father is mentioned after Jesus' appearances to the disciples. Brown interprets it as the evangelist's tendency to ignore temporal consistencies for
theological interest (Brown, *John*, 2.1015). As Gail O'Day has put it, "The conversation between Jesus and Mary in the garden is the Fourth Evangelist's attempt to
give narrative shape to a theological reality" ("Gospel of John," 843). Like the theology of the Word (λόγος), the theology of the hour and glorification transcend
both temporal and chronological order that modern exegetes would like to have
in the Johannine narrative.

[44] In his study of John 20:17, W. Grundmann confirms that the new relationship that is implicit in Jesus' statement is in harmony with other NT texts in general
(e.g., Eph 2:18) and the Letters of John in particular (e.g., 1 John 3:1) ("Zur Rede
Jesu vom Vater im Johannesevangelium," *ZNW* 52 [1961]: 213–30).

[45] Gail O'Day asserts, "[Jesus'] ascension is the confirmation that the believing
community now knows God as Jesus knows God, that Jesus has opened up the
possibility of new and full relationship with God" ("Gospel of John," 845). However, O'Day does not identify this new relationship established by Jesus' ascension
with an OT covenant relationship.

[46] See also Feuillet, "La recherche du Christ," 101–2.

[47] Exod 29:45; Lev 26:12; Jer 7:23; 24:7; 32:38; Ezek 11:20; 14:11; 36:28;
37:23; Zech 8:8; Bar 2:35. See also 2 Cor 6:16; Heb 8:10. Brown (*John*, 2.1016) il-
lustrates a close similarity between Jesus' statement and that of Ruth when she became part of the people of God, "Your people shall be my people and your God
my God" (Ruth 1:16).

[48] The expression διαθήκη καινή appears only once in the OT (Jer 31:31 [LXX
Jer 38:31]).

new status of the people of Israel giving them hope in exile (Jer 31:33b). The newness is that the law will be written in their hearts: "I will put my law within them, and I will write it on their hearts" (Jer 31:33a). Knowledge of God has now become innate, guaranteeing the intimate reciprocal covenant relationship. Jeremiah's concern in chapters 30–31 is the restoration and return of Israel to the promised land, and he thus presents an image of God who is not only retrieving past glory but also bringing something new to the history of salvation by creating a new existence for Israel. In and through Jesus' return to the Father, a similar process of reclaiming a new covenant relationship is going on with the disciples of Jesus. The double affirmation of the new relationship established between Jesus and his disciples, and between the covenant God and the disciples (20:17), creates a new covenant family of the disciples who believe in the living presence of God in Jesus. The communion and intimate knowledge implied in the relationship between Jesus and his Father has now become true of the relationship between the covenant God and the disciples.

EMPOWERING THE NEW COVENANT COMMUNITY OF THE DISCIPLES (20:19–31)

After commissioning Mary of Magdala to announce to the disciples Jesus' return to his Father and their Father, the risen Jesus encounters the disciples twice as a group in Jerusalem (vv. 19–23 and 26–29).[49] Jesus' first appearance to the disciples (20:19–23) and his second appearance to the disciples with Thomas (20:26–29) follow a similar structure.[50] In both

---

[49] Whether by "disciples" the evangelist means the inner circle of Jesus' friends or the outer circle of the followers of Jesus is a disputed issue. For example, B. Rigaux considers the disciples a reference to the inner circle of the apostolic group who will communicate the message to the larger community (*Dio l'ha risuscitato: Esegesi e teologia biblica* [Parola di Dio 13; Rome: Edizione Paoline, 1976], 367–68). See also F. Blanquart, *Le premier jour: Étude sur Jean* (LD 146; Paris: Serf, 1992), 107–9. There is, however, simply no evidence in the gospel that this is so; see Barrett, *John,* 568; Moloney, *Glory not Dishonor,* 169.

[50] X. Léon-Dufour, *Resurrection and the Message of Easter* (London: Chapman, 1974), 188. Talbert suggested a ABA′B′ pattern for the structure of 20:18–29. He considers v. 18 both a conclusion to vv. 1–18 and an introduction to vv. 18–29. In his structure, v. 18 (A) is parallel to vv. 24–25 (A′) and the first appearance story (B) is parallel to the second story (B′) (*Reading John,* 252–53). Some scholars consider vv. 19–23 as a bridge scene between the empty tomb (20:1–18) and the second appearance story (20:24–29); see Moloney, *Glory not Dishonor,* 168–69;

cases, there is a reference to time (vv. 19a and 26a), the doors are shut
(v. 19b and 26b), and Jesus enters, stands among the disciples (v. 19c and
26c), and greets them "peace to you" (vv. 19d and 26d). In the first story,
Jesus shows his hands and side (v. 20a) and in the second, Jesus shows his
hands and invites Thomas to put his finger into his side (v. 27).[51] Both stories narrate the responses of the disciples: in the first story, the disciples re-
joiced when they saw Jesus (v. 20b) and in the second, Thomas made his
confession of faith (v. 28). Jesus' commissioning of the disciples in the
first story (20:21–23) is parallel to the blessing (of Jesus) for the disciples of
future generations in the second story (20:29). The prophetic blessing of
the risen Jesus (20:29) is followed by the narrator's voice to the readers in
verses 30–31.[52]

In 20:30–31, the evangelist refers to the signs that Jesus performed
among his disciples (ἐνώπιον τῶν μαθητῶν αὐτοῦ, v. 30a) and addresses the
readers of the gospel. Three things merit special attention: (1) the use of the
preposition ἐνώπιον,[53] (2) the detail of τῶν μαθητῶν αὐτοῦ,[54] and (3) the motifs of believing in Jesus, confessing one's faith, and receiving new life. Here
the expression ἐνώπιον τῶν μαθητῶν αὐτοῦ implicitly suggests that the
signs referred to in verse 30 are the signs performed among his disciples and
not a reference to the many signs that Jesus had performed in the midst of
the crowd of the earlier chapters (e.g., 2:23; 6:14, 26; 7:31; 11:47–48).[55]

J. P. Heil, *Blood and Water: The Death and Resurrection of Jesus in John 18–21*
(CBQMS 27; Washington, D.C.: The Catholic Biblical Association of America,
1995), 133–36.

[51] There is no mention of the fear of the disciples in the second story because
the disciples have already experienced the joy of meeting the risen Jesus in his first
appearance (20:20).

[52] Although 20:30–31 might have well been the solemn conclusion of the entire gospel at one point in the process of its composition, as it stands today, for the
final redactor, vv. 30–31 are only a conclusion to ch. 20. For an excellent survey of
the recent scholarship on the issue of 20:30–31 and the continuity and discontinuity of John 21, see Moloney, *Glory not Dishonor,* 183–85, 187–91.

[53] For this meaning of ἐνώπιον, BDAG, 342 s.v. "ἐνώπιον," which explicitly
cites John 20:30 as an example.

[54] The possessive *his* (αὐτοῦ) disciples is attested by most of the important
manuscripts for the Gospel of John ($\mathfrak{P}^{66}$ ℵ C D L W Θ Ψ 0141 f^1 f^{13} 33 *al*).

[55] Although the evangelist does not explicitly describe the events in ch. 20 as
signs, the events related in ch. 20 reveal the action and presence of God in the glorification of Jesus and can thus be described as Johannine *signs* (σημεῖα). The reference to the word *signs* (σημεῖα) with a wider meaning is not unusual in the Fourth
Gospel. For example, Jesus' actions in the cleansing of the temple in 2:12–22 are
not explicitly referred to as a *sign* (σημεῖον), but it is implied in the comment of
the narrator in 2:23 addressing the readers, "Now when he was in Jerusalem at the

Moreover, the quality of faith induced by some of those signs is significantly different from that of Thomas and of the readers implied in 20:30–31. After making an implicit reference to the signs among his disciples, the evangelist talks about Jesus' blessing for those who believe without seeing and resumes in 20:31 the main theological motifs of chapter 20, viz., believing in Jesus (20:8), confessing one's faith (20:18, 25, 28), and receiving new life (20:17–18, 20). Paul Minear is of the same opinion that verses 30–31 are a conclusion to the Thomas episode (vv. 24–29) when he argues: "Vv 30, 31 furnish an intended sequel to the Thomas episode, a sequel that effectively shifts attention to the readers of the gospel, in whose faith the evangelist was primarily concerned."[56] It does not seem unreasonable, therefore, to consider verses 30–31 an appropriate conclusion to chapter 20 in general and to the Thomas episode in particular.

This contention is further supported by the occasional interventions of the narrator to the readers. When there is an opportune moment, the evangelist addresses the readers directly either to defend the authenticity of the gospel or to encourage their faith. For example, after narrating the crucifixion in 19:34, the narrator speaks directly to the readers to reclaim the authenticity of the gospel message by taking recourse to the testimony of the Beloved Disciple who had witnessed the crucifixion, so that the Johannine community and the readers may believe (19:35). Similarly, when the risen Jesus makes the contrast between Thomas and the believing community who believed without seeing Jesus and calls them blessed (μακάριοι, 20:29), the narrator makes the point clearer to the readers that these things are written so that they may go on believing (πιστεύητε, 20:31).[57]

As far as the covenant-discipleship motifs are concerned, six narrative elements deserve special attention in these two appearance stories: Jesus'

Passover feast, many believed in his name when they saw the signs (σημεῖα) which he did." The second *sign* with an explicit reference takes place only in 4:43–54, δεύτερον σημεῖον (4:54). Raymond Brown also applies the designation "sign" to the post-resurrection appearance stories. He defines "signs" as events "capable of revealing the heavenly truth about Jesus" (*John*, 2.1058; see also p. 1081). In her study of John 20:1–10, Sandra Schneiders makes a case that the face veil is a Johannine "sign" (*Written That You May Believe,* 180–88). See also Minear, "The Original Functions of John 21," 88–90.

[56] Minear, "The Original Functions of John 21," 88; see further 87–98.

[57] In 20:31, although the textual evidence is evenly balanced (πιστεύητε is attested by 𝔓[66vid] ℵ* B Θ 0250 157 892[supp] and πιστεύσητε is attested by ℵ[2] A C D L N W Δ Ψ 0141 *f*[1] *f*[13] 33 *al*), I am reading the present subjunctive rather than the aorist subjunctive. See the discussion in Brown, *John,* 2.1056; Schnackenburg, *John,* 3.337–38; Moloney, *Glory not Dishonor,* 179–80.

greeting, the commissioning of the disciples as "apostles" (those sent), the conferral of the Holy Spirit, Jesus' commission to forgive and retain sins, confessions of faith, and Jesus' blessing for the disciples of future generations.

JESUS' GREETING: "PEACE TO YOU"

Many of the covenant promises of Jesus in 13–17 are fulfilled in the narrative of 20:19–31.[58] The encounter between the risen Jesus and the disciples fulfills Jesus' promise that he would come to the disciples (14:18), that the disciples would see him (14:19), that the disciples would rejoice (15:11; 16:20–24), and that the disciples would receive peace (14:27–28; 16:33). Verse 19a–b provides the setting for the first encounter between the disciples and Jesus in general (20:19–23) and Jesus' greeting, "Peace to you" (εἰρήνη ὑμῖν), in particular (20:19c). The narrator informs the reader that the doors of the disciples' room were shut for "fear of the Jews" (διὰ τὸν φόβον τῶν Ἰουδαίων, v. 19b).[59] Jesus' entry into the room, despite the locked doors, underscores the ability of the risen Jesus to transcend the boundaries of human limitations.[60] It also signals that the risen Jesus now shares in the glory of God that he had with God before the creation of the world (17:5). Moreover, the specific detail regarding the fear of the disciples provides the readers with the immediate context for Jesus' greeting and highlights its significance: "Peace to you" (20:19, 20).[61]

The OT traditions of Israel supply a rich background for Jesus' greetings. This is a regular greeting among Israelites when they meet or depart, bless one another, or wish "well-being" for one another (e.g., שָׁלוֹם לָכֶם/לְךָ; Gen 43:23; Judg 19:20). As we have discussed earlier, peace and the covenant

---

[58] E. C. Hoskyns claims, "The whole episode is narrated as the fulfillment of teaching previously given to the disciples. Words are now accomplished in deeds" (*Fourth Gospel,* 546). For the fulfillment aspect of this narrative, see also Culpepper, *Gospel and Letters of John,* 242–43; Talbert, *Reading John,* 253; O'Day, "Gospel of John," 848.

[59] The "fear of the Jews" reminds the readers of the reaction of the parents who refused to make the confession of faith in Jesus because they feared the Jews (ἐφοβοῦντο τοὺς Ἰουδαίους, 9:22) and may reflect the fear of persecution in the Johannine community at the time of the composition of the gospel (Culpepper, *Gospel and Letters of John,* 242).

[60] See Léon-Dufour, *Resurrection,* 183–84; Moloney, *Glory not Dishonor,* 170.

[61] The conventional greeting in NT letters is "grace and peace to you" (see Rom 1:7; Gal 1:3; 1 Cor 1:3; 2 Cor 1:2; Eph 1:2; Phil 1:2; Col 1:2; 1 Thess 1:1; 2 Thess 1:2; Phlm 1:3; Rev 1:4).

relationship are intimately related to each other.[62] Making peace was a necessary precondition for establishing a covenant relationship. Sometimes both peace and covenant are used interchangeably (Gen 26:28, 31; 1 Kgs 5:26). Ezekiel speaks of the covenant of peace (בְּרִית שָׁלוֹם, 34:25; 37:26). In the Johannine story, Jesus' bestowal of peace before commissioning the disciples as "apostles" (those sent) is significant in understanding discipleship as a covenant relationship. The gift of peace liberates the disciples from fear of the Jews and makes them an "integral community" or "harmonious community," to borrow from Johannes Pedersen.[63] Jesus' blessing of peace prepares the disciples to become covenant partners with God.

JESUS' COMMISSION: "I SEND YOU"

The gift of peace is followed by the revelation of Jesus' living presence by showing his hands and his side (v. 20a). The wounds (implied) in Jesus' hands and side establish continuity between Jesus' life before the crucifixion and after the resurrection.[64] The presence of the risen Jesus brings a radical transformation into the lives of the disciples, as the situation changes from the "fear of the Jews" to that of rejoicing and happiness reflecting the characteristics of a covenant community (v. 20b). According to the OT traditions, joy or rejoicing is understood as one of the characteristics of the messianic community that signals the inauguration of the messianic era (Isa 25:6–9; 54:1–5; 61:1–3).

The repetition of Jesus' greeting "Peace to you" just before the commissioning of the disciples confirms that the gift of peace that accompanies the disciples is both the precondition and the consequence of becoming his disciples by accepting Jesus' commission as "those sent" (v. 21a) and by receiving the gift of the Holy Spirit (v. 22). This is confirmed by the gift of the Holy Spirit (14:26) instantly followed by the gift of peace (14:27).

The apostolic mission of the disciples is modeled after Jesus' own mission that flows from the Father-Son relationship. Jesus announces, "as (καθώς) the Father has sent me, so also I (κἀγώ) send you" (20:21b). The expression "καθώς . . . κἀγώ . . ." indicates the close links between the

---

[62] See the detailed discussion in chapter 2, part I. See also Pedersen, *Israel*, 1.263–310.

[63] The fundamental meaning of שָׁלוֹם is "totality" or "wholeness." Pedersen writes "there is 'totality' in a community when there is harmony, and the blessing [of peace or שָׁלוֹם] flows freely among its members" (*Israel*, 1.264).

[64] Brown, *John*, 2.1033.

mission of Jesus and that of the disciples.[65] Both sending passages, 17:18 and 20:21, highlight that the disciples are sent as (καθώς) Jesus is sent by the Father.[66] As Rudolf Bultmann argues, the adverb καθώς in the gospel has both a sense of comparison and a causative or explanatory sense.[67] Raymond E. Brown integrates both aspects of καθώς when he affirms, "The special Johannine contribution to the theology of this mission is that the Father's sending of the Son serves both as the model [comparative sense] and the ground [causative sense] for the Son's sending of the disciples."[68] The adverb καθώς also introduces a correlation of participation and correspondence.[69] The use of καθώς in the context of the sending of the disciples indicates that the disciples are empowered to participate both in Jesus' relationship with the Father as the one sent and in his mission. Jesus is always totally engaged in the works of the Father who sent him (τὰ ἔργα τοῦ πέμψαντός με, 9:4; see also 4:34; 5:36; 17:4). The perfect tense of the verb ἀποστέλλω (ἀπέσταλκεν) in 20:21b suggests that Jesus' mission still continues and is effective in the works of the disciples.[70] This commission reminds the readers of the earlier proclamation of Jesus where the relationship between Jesus and the disciples is drawn by the use of καθώς. Just as (καθώς) the living Father sent Jesus, and he lives because of the Father, so the disciples (those who eat the bread of life) will live because of Jesus (6:57). The relationship between Jesus and his disciples as those who are sent is parallel to Jesus' relationship with the Father, his sender. The adverb καθώς is also used to express the intimate knowledge (10:14–15), love (15:9; 17:23), and communion (17:22) between Jesus and his disciples. All the disciples are called to share an intimate knowledge, abiding relationship, and communion with the Father that enables them to share in doing the works of God, as Jesus did during his ministry (5:17). The mission of Jesus is continued in the works of the disciples who share in Jesus' life and abide in his love through the gift of the Holy Spirit.

---

[65] See Barrett, *John*, 569–70; Moloney, *Glory not Dishonor*, 171; Köstenberger, *Mission of Jesus*, 186–94.

[66] Köstenberger paraphrases as "in the same way as" or "in like manner" (*Mission of Jesus*, 186).

[67] Bultmann, *John*, 382 n. 2. See also the detailed discussion in O. de Dinechin, "καθώς similitude dans l'Évangile selon saint Jean," *RSR* 58 (1970): 195–236.

[68] Brown, *John*, 2.1036.

[69] Popkes, "Zum Verständnis der Mission bei Johannes," 66; cited by Köstenberger, *Mission of Jesus*, 189 n. 175. See also the discussion in chapter 3, pp. 96–98.

[70] Westcott, *John*, 294; Beasley-Murray, *John*, 379–80. The evangelist uses both the verbs ἀποστέλλω and πέμπω interchangeably or synonymously (e.g., 3:17, 34 [ἀποστέλλω]; 14:24; 15:21 [πέμπω]). See Barrett, *John*, 569.

In John's Gospel, John the Baptist is sent by God to witness to the incarnate Word (1:6–8), and Jesus is sent by God to reveal God's active presence among human beings (5:23–24). Just as the Son is sent by the Father to do God's works and to make God's presence visible (4:34; 5:23, 24, 30, 36, etc.), the disciples are sent by the Son to continue the same mission (4:38; 17:18; 20:21). Jesus' commission of the disciples fulfills his promise, "As you [God] sent me into the world, so I have sent them [disciples] into the world" (17:18). The one who is sent represents the one who sends.[71] Jesus' life and actions made God's life and actions visible. Similarly, the disciples are now commissioned to become the representatives of the Father as Jesus sends them out (13:20; 20:21). The disciples are thus expected to be in communion with the Father (14:23–24) and to continue the creative and life-giving works of God in the world (cf. 5:17). The works of God, however, are larger than the work of Jesus, and the work of Jesus is broader than that of his disciples. One cannot equate the "works of God" with the work of Jesus as they include and at the same time transcend the work of the Son, Jesus Christ.[72] The commissioning of the disciples to be the "ones sent" is an integral part of the process of constituting a new covenant community of the disciples.

THE GIFT OF THE HOLY SPIRIT: JESUS BREATHES ON THE DISCIPLES

During his dialogue with Mary of Magdala, Jesus reclaimed for the disciples the covenant status of the disciples by using the covenant language of the OT: "My Father and your Father . . . my God and your God" (20:17). Just as the Pentateuch has Moses climb a mountain to be in the presence of, and in communication with, the covenant God and bring the covenant law down to the Israelites, John 20:17 has the risen Jesus ascend to his Father and God, and John 20:22 has the ascended Jesus bring the gift of the Holy Spirit down to the disciples. Viewed from this covenant perspective, Jesus' breathing on the disciples recalls the new life promised in Jeremiah and Ezekiel. The promise of the new covenant in Jer 31:31–34 and Ezek 36:22–38 (cf. Gen 2:7) emphasizes four aspects of the covenant renewal: (1) a new covenant life marked by the infusion of the Spirit and the

---

[71] See the detailed study of J.-A. Bühner, *Der Gesandte und sein Weg in 4. Evangelium* (WUNT 2/2; Tübingen: J. C. B. Mohr [Paul Siebeck], 1977), 118–433. A section of this work (pp. 166–80) is translated into English by John Ashton; see Bühner, "The Exegesis of the Johannine 'I-Am' Sayings," in *The Interpretation of John* (ed. J. Ashton; Edinburgh: T&T Clark, 1997), 207–18.

[72] Chennattu, "The *Svadharma* of Jesus," 325–29.

presence of the law in the heart (Jer 31:33a; Ezek 36:26); (2) a covenant relationship that manifests Yahweh as Israel's God and Israel as God's people (Jer 31:33b; Ezek 36:28); (3) the hope that Israel will know their Lord (31:34a; Ezek 36:38); and (4) the hope that the Lord will forgive the iniquity of Israel and will remember their sin no more (Jer 31:34b; Ezek 36:25). The evangelist presents all four elements in portraying the new covenant relationship of the disciples.

The bestowal of the Holy Spirit signals a new beginning of the covenant community, now sharing the life of God.[73] The comment of the narrator, "when he had said this" (20:22a), suggests that the gift of the Holy Spirit ("receive the Holy Spirit") is deliberately and inseparably linked to both Jesus' words, "I send you" (πέμπω ὑμᾶς), and Jesus' action, he "breathed (ἐνεφύσησεν) on the disciples." The verb ἐμφυσάω ("breathe on") appears only in 20:22 in the NT, but the same verb is used in the LXX to describe the action of God in Gen 2:7: God breathed (ἐνεφύσησεν) the breath of life into the nostrils of the first human being.[74] Yahweh invites Israel to enter into a process of conversion, "make (or accomplish, עשׂה) yourself a new heart and new spirit" (Ezek 18:31). Later on there is a reversal; not the people of Israel but God takes the initiative and gives a new heart and new spirit. A new heart is created by God's Spirit in the days of the new covenant with Israel (Ezek 36:22–32; Isa 44:3; Rom 8:3–6). A

---

[73] The discussion on the gift of the Spirit implied in 19:30 and the specific function of the bestowal of the Holy Spirit in 20:22 is still unresolved among exegetes. For example, some scholars disregard 19:30 and regard 20:22 as the only time that Jesus actually bestows the gift of the Spirit (e.g., G. M. Burge, *The Anointed Community: The Holy Spirit in the Johannine Tradition* [Grand Rapids: Eerdmans, 1987], 116–31, 147–49); on the other hand, de la Potterie regards 19:30 as the moment of the gift of the Spirit ("Parole et Esprit dans S. Jean," in *L'Évangile de Jean: Sources, redaction, théologie* [ed. M. de Jonge; BETL 44; Gembloux: Duculot, 1977], 195–201). J. Swetnam argues that the gift of the Spirit in 19:30 is meant to empower all the believers, while 20:22 refers to the empowerment of the inner circle of the disciples who have received the authority to forgive sins ("Bestowal of the Spirit in the Fourth Gospel," *Bib* 74 [1993]: 571–74). The present study argues that what is symbolically presented in 19:30 is actualized in the experience of the community of the disciples in 20:22. See also the discussion in Moloney, *Glory not Dishonor*, 172.

[74] Hoskyns noticed long ago the link between John 20:22 and Gen 2:7, Ezek 37:5–10, 14, and Wis 15:11 (*Fourth Gospel*, 547). See also Bultmann, *John*, 692; Brown, *John*, 2.1022–23; Culpepper, *Gospel and Letters of John*, 243; Moloney, *Glory not Dishonor*, 171 n. 60; Beasley-Murray, *John*, 380. Some Johannine scholars have thus described John 20:22 where Jesus breathes on the disciples as a "formal inauguration of a new covenant community" (Pryor, *John*, 157). S. Schneiders mentioned in passing the theme of covenant in 20:22 (*Written That You May Believe*, 187).

heart of stone will be replaced by a heart of flesh (Ezek 26:26). Yahweh promises to put his spirit into the heart of Israel, the spirit that empowers Israel to follow the statutes and observe the commandments of God (Ezek 26:27). Hosea also emphasizes the active role of God in transforming the people of Israel and bringing them back to the covenant relationship: "I will heal their disloyalty" (Hos 14:4) and "I will be like the dew to Israel" (Hos 14:5). Jesus' breathing on the disciples also evokes the description of the prophecy of Ezekiel regarding the breath of God that gives new life and brings the slain back to life (Ezek 37:5–10).

The risen Jesus assumes the role of Yahweh and breathes onto the disciples a new life that embodies the love and life of God and, at the same time, reveals the presence and the ongoing activity of God in human history. The presence of the Spirit is significant in the mission of Jesus (1:32–33; 3:34) and in that of the disciples (14:21; 20:21).[75] The Spirit supplies continuity between the work of Jesus and that of the disciples.[76] By the gift of the Spirit and through the enactment of a new creation, the disciples are empowered by and filled with the life of God that was promised in the age of the new covenant.

Mission: Forgive and Retain Sins

The OT covenant renewals and God's bestowal of new covenant life are usually accompanied by the forgiveness of sin (Jer 31:34b; Ezek 26:25; Josh 24:14–15). Ezekiel speaks of God's purification of Israel with clean water

---

[75] For the role of the Spirit in the missions of Jesus and the disciples, see F. Hahn, "Sendung des Geistes—Sendung der Jünger: Die Pneumatologische Dimension des Missionsauftrages nach dem Zeugnis des Neuen Testamentes," in *Universales Christentum angesichts einer pluralen Welt* (ed. Andreas Bsteh; BRT 1; Mödling bei Wien: St. Gabriel, 1976), 87–106. For a comparison between the mission of Jesus and that of the disciples, see M. Stibbe, " 'Return to Sender': A Structuralist Approach to John's Gospel," *BibInt* 1 (1993): 189–206. Stibbe's study, however, ignores the role of the Spirit in Jesus' mission. M. Vellanickal makes the distinction that "the work of the Spirit is entirely subordinated to the work of Christ and strictly related to the disciples' life of faith in Christ" ("Evangelization in the Johannine Writings," in *Good News and Witness* [ed. L. Legrand, J. Pathrapankal, and M. Vellanickal; Bangalore: Theological Publications in India, 1973], 136).

[76] For a detailed discussion on the Lukan tradition of Pentecost and the Johannine tradition of the gift of the Spirit, see Burge, *Anointed,* 114–49. Léon-Dufour concludes: "John sets forth an essential dimension of the Easter mystery which Luke has deliberately extended in time, thereby running the risk of separating the Spirit and Jesus" (*Resurrection,* 186). See also the discussion in Moloney, *Glory not Dishonor,* 171–73.

that marks a radical new life (26:25). After the infusion of the breath of life into the disciples, the risen Jesus commissions the disciples to forgive (ἀφίημι) and retain (κρατέω) sins (20:23). The verbs ἀφίημι and κρατέω appear together only once in John's Gospel. Charles H. Dodd suggests that 20:23 is an alternative form of the Matthean tradition of "binding" and "loosing" (Matt 18:18).[77] Unlike the Matthean version, John's Gospel has Jesus address the community of the disciples.[78] Just as the entire community of the disciples is sent by Jesus (20:21) and receives the Holy Spirit (20:22), the mission to forgive and retain sins must be interpreted in the light of Jesus' work to which all the disciples are called (20:23).

Jesus' identity and mission are very closely linked to the "removal" or the forgiveness of sin (αἴρω, 1:29) or "cleansing" from sin (καθαρός, 13:10; 15:3). The LXX uses the same verb καθαρίζω for the cleansing of Israel on the Day of Atonement (Lev 16:30). As we have seen, cleansing from sin is one of the requirements of those who have a μέρος with Jesus, i.e., a characteristic of members of the new covenant community (13:8). Hence the forgiveness of sins is an integral part of the work of Jesus and also of the Spirit-filled disciples who continue the work of Jesus in revealing the active presence of God in the world. Interpreted from the theological perspective of the evangelist, sin refers to spiritual blindness to the revelation of God in Jesus (9:35–41) and to unbelief in Jesus (16:9). Gail R. O'Day suggests that in verse 23 "Jesus commissions the community to continue the work of making God in Jesus known in the world and thereby to bring the world to the moment of decision and judgment with regard to sin (cf. 15:22–24)."[79] Whether the mission of the disciples includes forgiving and retaining sins

---

[77] For a comparison between Johannine "forgiving" and "retaining" of sins and Matthean "binding" and "loosing" (16:19; 18:18), see Dodd, *Historical Tradition,* 347–49; Brown, *John,* 2.1039–41. A. J. Emerton argues for an Aramaic saying, "close and open" (Isa 22:22), behind both Matthean use of "bind and loose" and Johannine use of "retain and forgive" ("Binding and Loosing—Forgiving and Retaining," *JTS* 13 [1962]: 325–31). For the use of John 20:23 in the history and traditions of the church, see Brown, *John,* 2.1041–45. See also G. M. Lee, "Presbyters and Apostles (John 20,23)," *ZNW* 62 (1971): 122; A. Feuillet, "La communication de l'Esprit-Saint aux Apôtres (Jn XX, 19–23) et le ministère sacerdotal de la réconciliation des hommes avec Dieu," *EV* 82 (1972): 2–7; B. de Margerie, "La mission sacerdotale de retenir les péchés en liant les pécheurs. Intérêt actuel et justification d'une exégèse tridentine (Jn 20, 23; Mt 16, 19)," *RevScRel* 58 (1984): 300–317.

[78] As Bultmann argues, "It is self-evident that it is not a special apostolic community that is imparted here [John 20:23], but that the community as such is equipped with this authority" (*John,* 693).

[79] O'Day, "Gospel of John," 847.

has been a subject of debate. Francis J. Moloney clarifies the issue by underscoring the close association between the mission of the Paraclete (16:7–11) and that of the disciples (20:23), and the specific role of the former in the mission of the latter (2:22).[80] According to Raymond E. Brown, powers given to the disciples are "partial manifestations of a much larger power, namely, the power to isolate, repel and negate evil and sin, a power given to Jesus in his mission by the Father and given in turn by Jesus through the Spirit to those whom he commissions."[81] It is this power or new life in the Spirit that enlightens and empowers the disciples to continue the mission of Jesus. The testimony of the disciples as the visible sign of God's presence will enable the world to make its decision either in favor of or against the offer to enter a covenant relationship with God. The world's decision determines its judgment regarding sins, whether they are forgiven or retained. The mission of the disciples is to continue the mission of Jesus by making God's presence visible and God's love tangible in the world and thus leading an unbelieving community to decision and judgment.

CONFESSIONS OF FAITH: "WE HAVE SEEN THE LORD" AND "MY LORD AND MY GOD"

Jesus invited the disciples to continue to journey with him and promised that the disciples would see or experience the ongoing revelation of God in Jesus (1:35–51). From the beginning of the discipleship story, the knowledge of God or a deep knowledge of the identity of Jesus acquired through a personal encounter with Jesus is presupposed in all the confessions of faith (e.g., 1:41, 45, 49; 4:29, 53). The evangelist elsewhere describes eternal life as knowing God and Jesus Christ whom God has sent (17:3).

The announcement of the disciples that "we have seen the Lord" (20:25) and the confession of Thomas, "My Lord and my God" (20:28), fulfill the hope of the knowledge of God promised in the age of the new covenant (cf. Jer 31:34). By confessing Jesus as his Lord and God, Thomas is taking up the covenant language of the OT. The combination of Lord and God (אֱלֹהִים and יַהְוֶה; κύριος and θεός) is very common in the OT (e.g., Gen 24:3, 12; Exod 3:15; 5:1; Lev 18:4; Num 22:18; Deut 26:14). The psalmist uses converse expression to address Yahweh, "My God and my Lord" (אֱלֹהַי וַאדֹנָי, ὁ θεός μου καὶ ὁ κύριός μου, Ps 35:23). In the context of the OT covenant relationship, Yahweh frequently uses the expression: "I am the

---

[80] Moloney, *Glory not Dishonor,* 173–75.
[81] Brown, *John,* 2.1044.

Lord your God" (e.g., Lev 18:4; Judg 6:10). In Josh 24, when the people declare their solemn vow to be faithful to the covenant relationship with Yahweh, they announce both at the beginning (24:17) and at the end (24:18) of their confession that the Lord is their God (יְהוָה אֱלֹהֵינוּ).

By repeating the personal pronoun in his confession, "*my* Lord and *my* God," Thomas is declaring publicly and accepting the covenant God ("*my* God and *your* God") that Jesus announced to Mary of Magdala in 20:17.[82] Raymond Brown regards Thomas's confession of faith as "the supreme Christological pronouncement of the Fourth Gospel."[83] Donald Senior describes the confession as "one of the Gospel's most profound confessions of Jesus' true identity."[84] Thomas's confession of faith in Jesus as his Lord and God epitomizes the response of the new covenant community recreated and empowered by the bestowal of the Holy Spirit that in Jesus they have experienced the fullness of God's revelation as their covenant God.

JESUS' BLESSING

As a response to Thomas's confession of faith, the risen Jesus first challenges Thomas, "Have you believed because you have seen me?" and then blesses the disciples and the readers or the second generation of the disciples (the members of the Johannine community) who believe without seeing (20:29).[85] All the disciples had to experience the presence of the

---

[82] Léon-Dufour, *Resurrection,* 189. Since the Emperor Domitian (81–96 C.E.), who arrogated the title "*Dominus et Deus noster*" to himself (Suetonius, *Domitian,* 13), reigned around the time when the Gospel of John was composed (see the discussion in chapter 5, pp. 180–82), Thomas's confession of faith ("my Lord and my God") has political significance: Thomas declares his allegiance to Jesus Christ rather than to the Roman Emperor. See also B. A. Mastin, "The Imperial Cult and the Ascription of the Title to Jesus (John 20,28)," *SE* 6 (1973): 352–65; R. J. Cassidy, *John's Gospel in New Perspective: Christology and the Realities of Roman Power* (Maryknoll, N.Y.: Orbis, 1992), 13–16, 69–88; Chennattu, "Good Shepherd," 98–100.

[83] Brown, *John,* 2.1047. G. J. Riley, somewhat speculatively, argues that the evangelist uses the Thomas story as a literary device to summon the unbelievers in the Thomas community (*Resurrection Reconsidered: Thomas and John in Controversy* [Minneapolis: Fortress, 1995], 119–24).

[84] D. Senior, *The Passion of Jesus in the Gospel of John* (PassSer 4; Collegeville, Minn.: Liturgical Press, 1991), 139. According to Bultmann, the evangelist uses Thomas's story to belittle the importance of faith based on sight (20:29a) and to appreciate the faith generated by the Word (20:29b) (*John,* 695–96).

[85] Barrett regards ὅτι ἑώρακάς με πεπίστευκας as a statement rather than a question (*John,* 573). See also Moloney, *Glory not Dishonor,* 178.

risen Lord to believe in the resurrection of Jesus; Thomas is no exception.[86] The motif of Thomas's "seeing and believing" echoes in the comment of the narrator concerning the response of the Beloved Disciple: "He saw and believed" (20:8). The Beloved Disciple sees the empty tomb and the burial cloths, but like the future believers, he did not see the risen Jesus but believed.[87] Francis J. Moloney comments, "The risen Jesus led these fragile disciples through their hesitation into authentic belief, yet the faith of those who believe without seeing matches that of the greatest disciple (v. 29. See v. 8)."[88] The evangelist uses Thomas's doubt to address later disciples who would be entering the new covenant community.

The future disciples will share in all the privileges of the founding members of the community. In his final prayer (17:20), Jesus has already made a reference to the future disciples or to those who will believe in Jesus through the testimony of his eyewitness disciples. Thomas's story furnishes an occasion for the risen Jesus to give further instructions to the disciples.[89] He proclaims that the faith of the future generations "without seeing" is as authentic as the faith of the eyewitness disciples of the gospel.[90] The structural comparison between the two appearance stories in 20:19–29 shows that Jesus' blessing for the disciples of future generations in 20:29 is in parallel to Jesus' commissioning of the disciples in 20:21–23. Jesus' prophetic blessing in 20:29 thus implies that the future disciples will share the same privileges attached to the intimate relationship with the Father and receive the same mission as those who had the grace of being eyewitnesses (Matt 13:16; 1 Pet 1:8–9).

---

[86] For a comparison between the faith journey of Thomas and that of Mary of Magdala in 20:1–18, see D. A. Lee, "Partnership in Easter Faith," 40–46. The story of doubting Thomas is not to downplay the significance of Thomas's faith response. *The Gospel of Thomas* portrays Thomas as someone who has attained the fullness of his vocation as a disciple of Jesus: "Whoever drinks from my mouth will become like me; I myself shall become that person" (*Gos. Thom.* 108).

[87] See the detailed discussion in B. Byrne, "The Faith of the Beloved Disciple and the Community in John 20," *JSNT* 23 (1985): 83–97.

[88] Moloney, *Glory not Dishonor,* 178–79. See also Riley, *Resurrection Reconsidered,* 124–26; P. J. Judge, "A Note on Jn 20,29," in *The Four Gospels 1992: Festschrift Frans Neirynck* (ed. F. van Segbroeck, C. M. Tuckett, G. van Belle, and J. Verheyden; 3 vols.; BETL 100; Leuven: Leuven University Press, 1992), 3.2183–92.

[89] Senior, *Passion of Jesus,* 138–40.

[90] The motif of blessings on those who believe without seeing is found also in the later Jewish traditions and practices. For example, according to the *Tanhuma* (ca. 250 C.E.), Rabbi Simeon ben Laqish blesses those who are faithful to the Covenant God without seeing the Sinai theophany (6:32a).

Blessings in the OT strengthen and enhance the bond of a covenant relationship. "Those who have peace with one another impart a mutual blessing, and if one gives blessing, then one creates peace and covenant."[91] After a long discussion of peace, covenant, and blessing, Johannes Pedersen concludes that blessing someone is the same as making a covenant with him/her, because the covenant among human beings consists in mutual blessing (cf. 2 Kgs 18:31; Isa 36:16).[92] The blessing of the risen Jesus thus reaffirms the knowledge of God that is available to all the disciples of future generations and more importantly empowers them to share in the mission of Jesus. It enables them to enter into a covenant relationship with God.

CONSTITUTING THE NEW COVENANT COMMUNITY (21:1–25)

Some commentators question the narrative unity of chapter 21.[93] Whatever may have been the prehistory of these different scenes, the text as it stands in the gospel is a well-unified narrative.[94] A concern for the development of the covenant-discipleship motif permeates the whole of the finished text. The evangelist narrates the final manifestation (ἐφανέρωσεν, 21:1) of the risen Jesus to his disciples in 21:1–25.[95] This manifestation of the risen Jesus in Galilee is also his final farewell to the disciples.[96] The story begins with an encounter between Jesus and the disciples as a group within

---

[91] Pedersen, *Israel,* 1.303.

[92] Ibid., 1.304.

[93] According to B. Lindars, the dialogue between Jesus and Peter (21:15–19) has "no inherent connection with the preceding story" (*John,* 632). R. E. Brown regards 21:20, which links the section on Peter's death (vv. 18–19) and that on the Beloved Disciple's destiny (vv. 21–23), an artificial suture (*John,* 2.1117–18).

[94] T. Wiarda argues against the claim that "the text is a composite of several independent pieces of tradition" and shows the narrative unity of the text ("John 21.1–23: Narrative Unity and Its Implications," *JSNT* 46 [1992]: 53–71, esp. 71).

[95] For the similarities between the first sign in 2:1–11 and that of the last in 21:1–25, see O'Day, "Gospel of John," 856–59. It was suggested that the call stories of ch. 1 are fulfilled in ch. 21. For example, J. Breck concludes that "the disciples are initially called by Jesus to 'come and see.' This invitation only achieves its purpose, however, with the apostolic commissions of ch. 21: implied in the miraculous catch of fish and made explicit in the dialogue between Jesus and Peter" ("John 21: Appendix, Epilogue OR Conclusion," *SVTQ* 36 [1992]: 49).

[96] Following the narrative conventions of ancient biographical writings, F. F. Segovia identifies a "farewell type-scene after death" in John 20:31–21:25 ("Final Farewell of Jesus," 167).

the context of a wondrous catch of fish that leads to a common meal (21:1–14). The common meal provides the literary and theological context for Jesus' commissioning of Peter as the shepherd and the Beloved Disciple as the true witness (21:15–23).[97] This final sign sets the stage for the conclusion that establishes the authority and authenticity of the testimony of the gospel (21:24–25). Chapter 21 on the one hand establishes the authority of Peter as the appointed shepherd, and on the other acknowledges the authority of the Beloved Disciple behind the Johannine tradition.[98]

A Preview of the New Covenant Community (21:1–14)

This section will focus on the three aspects of the narrative that highlight the characteristics of a covenant community: (1) Jesus' manifestation and the responses of the disciples; (2) Jesus' greeting; and (3) symbols of universality and unity: the abundance of fish and the unbroken net.

Jesus' Manifestation and the Responses of the Disciples

The comments of the narrator in verses 1–3 provide the setting for the whole narrative of chapter 21. The evangelist links the narratives in chapter 21 with those of chapter 20 by the detail μετὰ ταῦτα in verse 1a. The verb φανερόω appears twice in verse 1 and is resumed again in verse 14, and thus forms an inclusion. The manifold use of φανερόω ("manifest oneself" or "reveal" or "make known") provides the hermeneutical key for the readers to interpret the story as a theophany or manifestation of God's presence among the disciples.[99] The sign of the wondrous catch of fish (21:1–14) needs to be interpreted as a continuation of the revelatory aspect (φανερόω) of Jesus' works. The verb φανερόω is used nine times in the gospel (1:31; 2:11; 3:21; 7:4; 9:3; 17:6; 21:1 bis; 21:14) and is closely associated with the mission of those who are sent by God, John the Baptist and Jesus. The evangelist used φανερόω for the first time to summarize the ministry of

---

[97] According to the analysis of Segovia, vv. 1–14 provide the "farewell context" and vv. 15–23 comprise the "farewell conversation" ("Final Farewell of Jesus," 185–87). Edwyn C. Hoskyns argues that in John 21 "the readers are given complete confidence in the power of the Church" (*Fourth Gospel*, 550).

[98] Moloney, *Glory not Dishonor*, 187; Schneiders, *Written That You May Believe*, 202–7; Talbert, *Reading John*, 260.

[99] Schnackenburg writes, "The whole verse [v. 1] makes the effect of an announcement of a theme, and this impression is strengthened by the corresponding closing comment in v. 14" (*John*, 3.352). For the revelatory dimension of the sign in ch. 21, see S. S. Smalley, "The Sign in John XXI," *NTS* 20 (1974): 275–88.

John the Baptist in terms of revealing Jesus to Israel (1:31). The remaining eight occurrences of the verb are in the context of Jesus' mission—revealing his glory (2:11), God's work (3:21; 7:4; 9:3), God's name (17:6), himself (21:1 bis, 14).

The presence of Nathanael in the present story (21:2) and the subsequent manifestation of Jesus (21:3–14) fulfills what has been promised to Nathanael that he would "see greater things" (1:51). However, as with the empty tomb (20:8), it is the Beloved Disciple who recognizes the presence of Jesus among the disciples. The impetuous character of Peter is evident in his response of casting himself into the sea (21:7; see also Matt 14:28–32). In other words, by this narrative, the contemplative perception and receptivity of the Beloved Disciple (20:8; 21:7) and the impetuosity of Peter are reconfirmed (20:6; 21:7). God continues to manifest himself to the world, but the recognition and deep appreciation of the divine presence and action in human history is one of the challenges faced by the new covenant community.

Jesus' Greeting: "Children" (21:5)

Jesus addresses the disciples as children (παιδία, v. 5). The term "disciples" here includes only a small group of seven: Simon Peter, Thomas, Nathanael, the sons of Zebedee, and two other unnamed disciples of Jesus (v. 2).[100] It has been suggested that the number seven is symbolic and represents the whole community of disciples.[101] Jesus' greeting παιδία hints at an intimacy (21:5). Although different words are used, the same sentiments are expressed in one of the earlier greetings of Jesus, "little children" (τεκνία, 13:33), and his reference to the disciples as his own (οἱ ἴδιοι, 13:1).[102] The author of the Letters of John uses παιδία or τεκνία to refer to the whole community of disciples in general (1 John 2:1–18), in contrast to the leaders ("fathers," πατέρες; 1 John 2:13a) or the younger disciples ("young people," νεανίσκοι; 1 John 2:13b).[103] The greeting of Jesus recalls the status

---

[100] Some exegetes argue that "the sons of Zebedee" was a marginal gloss (identifying the "two others of his disciples"), which became part of the text at a later period (e.g., Lagrange, *Évangile selon saint Jean,* 523). If this is so, then the term "disciples" refers to these five disciples. For the various suggestions with regard to the identity of the unnamed disciples, see Brown, *John,* 2.1068.

[101] Talbert, *Reading John,* 259; Beasley-Murray, *John,* 399.

[102] The Johannine tendency to use different words to express the same reality is well known (cf. ἀγαπάω and φιλέω).

[103] The Letters of John use both παιδία and τεκνία interchangeably, e.g., 1 John 2:1 (τεκνία), 12 (τεκνία), 14 (παιδία), 18 (παιδία), 28 (τεκνία).

and the identity of believers as "children of God" (1:12) and furthers the covenant-discipleship motif of the gospel (13:1, 33).[104]

Symbols of Universality and Unity: The Abundance of Fish and the Unbroken Net

The wondrous catch of fish foreshadows the mission of the disciples, its wide impact and effectiveness.[105] From the beginning, the story portrays the unity of the community of disciples under the leadership of Peter. He takes the initiative to go fishing and the others follow him.[106] The unity and love portrayed in the story were also at the center of Jesus' prayer for the disciples (17:6–26). The narrator informs the readers that the disciples were fishing all night without any results, thus underlining the inability of the disciples to accomplish their work without the assistance of Jesus (15:5; Mark 14:20). Jesus changes the situation of catching no fish ("they caught nothing," v. 3) to an abundance of fish ("they were not able to haul it in because there were so many fish," v. 6). This reminds the readers of the abundance of wine in 2:1–11 and the abundance of bread in 6:1–14.[107] All three signs reveal the identity of Jesus as the source of messianic gifts and the giver of abundant life (4:13–15; 6:35; 7:37–39; 10:9–10). The risen Jesus, the giver of new life, comes to make efficient and effective the work of the disciples. The abundance motif brings home the presence of the messianic era and signals the actualization of the new messianic covenant community.

The response and the action of the disciples, namely, "dragging the net full of fish" (21:8) or "hauling the net full of large fish" (21:11) seem to be highly symbolic. One can interpret the action (εἴλκυσεν, v. 11) in two ways: at the story level, to draw the net to the seashore, or at the deeper

---

[104] In the debate between Jesus and the Jewish authorities, Jesus distinguishes between the children of the devil and the free sons [children] of God who listen to the words of God (8:31–59). See the discussion in B. Lindars, "Slave and Son in John 8,31–36," in *Essays on John* (ed. C. M. Tuckett; Leuven: Leuven University Press, 1992), 167–82.

[105] Smalley, "Sign in John XXI," 284.

[106] For the similarity between John 21:1–14 and Luke 5:1–10, see Brown, *John,* 2.1090; Culpepper, *Gospel and Letters of John,* 245–46. See also J. A. Bailey, "Miraculous Catch of Fish: Luke 5:1–11, John 21:1–14," in *The Traditions Common to the Gospels of Luke and John* (Leiden: Brill, 1963), 12–17; F. Neirynck, "John 21," *NTS* 36 (1990): 321–36. It is beyond the scope of this study to trace the *Traditionsgeschichte* of the narrative under discussion.

[107] For the theme of abundance in ch. 21, see B. R. Gaventa, "The Archive of Excess: John 21 and the Problem of Narrative Closure," in *Exploring the Gospel of John,* 240–51.

level, to share in the mission of Jesus. The verb ἕλκω ("drag" or "haul" or "draw") shows that the disciples are now actually sharing in the mission of Jesus, namely, bringing others to the revelation of God in Jesus (21:6, 8, 11).[108] The verb ἕλκω occurs in the context of the work of the Father, that no one can come to Jesus unless they are "drawn by the Father" (6:44) and that of Jesus "drawing all people to himself" (12:32). The story fulfills what Jesus has promised regarding the mission of the disciples in 14:12; 15:7–8, 16; 17:18, 20–21.

When we compare the Johannine story (21:1–13) with the Lukan story (5:1–11), from the perspective of the wondrous catch and the net, we see that the details highlighted by John contrast sharply with the Lukan account.[109] The Lukan story does not specify the number of fish the disciples caught ("a great number of fish"), but informs the reader that the nets were breaking (Luke 5:5) and the boats were sinking (Luke 5:7). On the contrary, the Johannine story is steeped in symbolism and provides the details of the number of fish caught ("one hundred and fifty-three") and the status of the net which was not torn apart (οὐκ ἐσχίσθη, 21:11).[110] From the perspective of the Johannine context, the hundred and fifty-three fish symbolize the all-embracing or the universal character of the mission making disciples of every race on the earth.[111] The unbroken net is a sign of the realization of the unity of the community for which Jesus prayed in 17:6–26. The verb used to describe the unbroken net, σχίζω (21:11), is a cognate of σχίσμα, the division that is referred to in 7:43; 9:16; 10:19. The unbroken net thus refers to the communion and harmony of the new covenant community: despite the great numbers of the disciples from every race, the dis-

---

[108] O'Day, "Gospel of John," 857–58. For this understanding of the mission of the disciples, see also 4:31–38.

[109] The Lukan story is in the context of the call of Peter, but the Johannine story is situated within the context of a post-resurrection appearance of Jesus. See the detailed study of the call stories of Peter in S. O. Abogunrin, "The Three Variant Accounts of Peter's Call: A Critical and Theological Examination of the Texts," *NTS* 31 (1985): 587–602.

[110] Luke does not develop this symbolic character of the story; see J. M. Creed, *The Gospel According to St. Luke* (London: Macmillan & Co., 1965), 66–67.

[111] Talbert, *Reading John*, 260; Brown, *John*, 2.1097. Many interpretations of the number based on Gematria have been suggested. For example, the hundred and fifty-three fish refers to "the children of God" (בני האלהים); see J. A. Romeo, "Gematria and John 21:11: The Children of God," *JBL* 97 (1978): 263–64. For a summary of the various interpretations, see the discussion in Beasley-Murray, *John*, 402–4. Hoskyns argues that "there is no symbolic significance of the number 153" but agrees to the fact that it symbolizes "a perfect and unique catch of fish" (*Fourth Gospel*, 556).

ciples are united and can work together fruitfully under the guidance of the risen Jesus. Sandra Schneiders interprets the scene as "a symbolic presentation of the life of the church in the time after the resurrection."[112] An authentic revelation of the presence of God in the risen Jesus takes place in and through the wondrous catch of fish that symbolically underscores the unity and mission of the disciples in the new covenant community.

PETER AND JESUS: A COVENANT RELATIONSHIP RECONFIRMED (21:15–23)

From the very beginning of chapter 21, the narrative places a steady focus on Peter. Peter takes the initiative to go fishing (21:3); Peter reacts promptly to the presence of Jesus in their midst (21:7); Peter responds to Jesus' confronting and challenging queries (21:15–17); Peter is informed of his martyrdom and is invited to follow Jesus (21:18–19); Peter receives a rebuke and a command to follow Jesus (21:20–22). The narrative depicts a progression in the series of events related. Jesus "confronts Peter at every stage in the narrative, upsetting his equilibrium and challenging him to make decisions and take new action."[113] Since Peter is the protagonist of the whole narrative in chapter 21, the dialogue between Jesus and Peter merits special attention.

The reappearance of Simon Peter on center stage and his subsequent commissioning as the shepherd of the community fulfills what has been promised to Simon in the call story (1:42). In the words of Smalley, "The call to discipleship in John xxi. 15–19, on the historical basis of the resurrection, matches the call in John i. 35–51, on the historical basis of incarnation."[114] Some exegetes consider 1:35–42 "a preliminary call," with the definite call to active discipleship in 21:1–19.[115] But the Fourth Evangelist does not suggest a second call in the gospel. No one contests that the main purpose of the narrative is to develop further the challenges and demands of discipleship for the leader of the disciples.

---

[112] Schneiders, *Written That You May Believe,* 207. Hoskyns interprets the scene as a fulfillment of 16:32, an example of the apostasy on the part of the disciples (*Fourth Gospel,* 552). He interprets the scene as a reflection of the division in the Johannine community.

[113] Wiarda, "John 21.1–23," 53.

[114] Smalley, "Sign in John xxi," 283.

[115] For example, see M. Franzmann and M. Klinger, "The Call Stories of John 1 and John 21," *SVTQ* 36 (1992): 7–15, esp. 11. See also the discussion in Abogunrin, "Accounts of Peter's Call," 594.

The dialogue between Jesus and Peter takes place within the context of a meal. The narrator resumes the meal motif by deliberately stating the time when the dialogue between Jesus and Peter takes place: "when they had finished breakfast" (21:15a). Jesus' meal with the disciples portrays fellowship and care for his disciples. The meal has also taken on a covenant motif and reminds the readers of the meal shared before Jesus' death and the subsequent dialogue between Jesus and Peter on sharing a μέρος with Jesus (13:1–11).[116] As we have seen, a shared meal plays a significant role in deepening a friendship bond and the commitment to one another within the context of making a covenant. The breakfast with Jesus on the seashore not only provides physical nourishment to the disciples but also deepens their binding covenant relationship with Jesus and God.

In this context of a covenant meal that symbolizes their communion and mutually binding relationship, Jesus asks Peter three times whether he loves him (ἀγαπάω in vv. 15 and 16 and φιλέω in v. 17).[117] What determines the meaning of Jesus' query, more than the variations of the use of ἀγαπάω and φιλέω, is the phrase, "more than these" (πλέον τούτων, v. 15).[118] The context and grammar allow two meanings of the clause under discussion with the query of Jesus ἀγαπᾷς με πλέον τούτων (21:15): (1) Do you love me more than these [disciples] love me?[119] or (2) Do you

---

[116] For the eucharistic symbolism in the narrative of the meal in John 21 and its similarities with the bread discourses in John 6, see Brown, *John*, 2.1098–1100.

[117] R. Bultmann suggests that there is no theological difference in meaning between ἀγαπάω and φιλέω in John's Gospel (*John*, 253 n. 2 and 711 n. 5). See also the discussion in Carson, *John*, 676–77; J. Barr, "Words for Love in Biblical Greek," in *The Glory of Christ in the New Testament: Studies in Christology in Memory of George Bradford Caird* (ed., L. D. Hurst and N. T. Wright; Oxford: Clarendon, 1987), 3–18. K. L. McKay judges otherwise and argues that the variation of forms of ἀγαπάω and φιλέω in 21:15–17 "constitute a contextual distinction" that is significant ("Style and Significance in the Language of John 21:15–17," *NovT* 27 [1985]: 319–33, esp. 333).

[118] Against this view, see Bultmann, *John*, 711 nn. 3–4. Brown follows the suggestion of Bultmann and proposes that "the implications of the clause should not be considered too seriously, for it is only an editorial attempt to bring the other disciples into the picture and thus to bind 15–17 to 1–13" (*John*, 2.1104). Brown presupposes two things: (1) the clause was not part of the original words of Jesus; (2) the purpose of the clause is to make the link between the two scenes. The first clause, "when they had finished breakfast," makes the close connection between the two scenes.

[119] For the arguments in favor of this view, see Barrett, *John*, 584; Carson, *John*, 677. The passages (13:8, 37–38; 18:10, 15–18) used by Barrett (*John*, 584) to support the claim that Peter loves Jesus in a superior way are not convincing enough

love me more than you love these others/things? The comparison seems to be between the objects of Peter's love, "me" (με) and "these" (τούτων), rather than Peter's love and other disciples' love for Jesus.[120] The second reading of the clause reminds the readers of the absolute claim that the covenant God makes in the OT when he gives the command to love: "You shall love the Lord your God with all your heart, and with all your soul, and with all your might" (Deut 6:5). Yahweh maintains covenant loyalty with those who love him wholeheartedly and keep his commandments faithfully (7:9; 10:12; 11:1; 13:3; 30:36). Within the context of the OT covenant relationship, the absolute and unconditional love for God is set over against Israel's love for everything else (Josh 22:5). The risen Jesus is asking Peter whether his love for him is absolute, definite, and conclusive. This absolute claim of the love of God is found elsewhere in the gospel (12:43; see also 1 John 2:15; Matt 6:24; Luke 16:13–14).[121] The threefold repetition of the question and the response communicates a progression in the dialogue and stresses the importance and the significance of the event: the appointment of Peter and his commitment to the new covenant community. Just as the covenant God, so also the risen Jesus demands precedence, primacy, and absolute loyalty to God from the disciples in their relationship with God.

Viewed from this perspective, the prompt response of Peter, "Yes, Lord, you know that I love you" (21:15b), seems to imply that Peter loves Jesus more than anything else. Peter's affirmative response is followed by the command to feed Jesus' lambs (21:15c). As Charles K. Barrett observes, the commission of Peter "is described in verbs, not nouns: Tend, feed, not be a pastor, hold the office of pastor."[122] The evangelist presents the shepherding ministry of Peter as a command to be obeyed.[123] Peter's confirmation of his love with Jesus' subsequent commission to feed/tend his lambs/sheep

---

to claim a greater love on the part of Peter. See the detailed discussion of Wiarda, "John 21.1–23," 61–63.

[120] R. Hanna supports this view on grammatical grounds as he holds, "If 'more than these do' would have been the desired translation, the pronoun σύ would have been included" (*A Grammatical Aid to the Greek New Testament* [Grand Rapids: Baker, 1983], 185). See also Wiarda, "John 21.1–23," 62–63. Wiarda, however, interprets τούτων as referring to the fishing activity of Peter and thus gives an exclusive meaning to τούτων, which could also refer to things, actions, and people.

[121] See also Wiarda, "John 21.1–23," 63.

[122] C. K. Barrett, *Essays on John* (London: SPCK, 1982), 165–66.

[123] G. Osborne points out the link between Peter's affirmation of love and Jesus' commission ("John 21: A Test Case for History and Redaction in the Resurrection Narratives," in *Gospel Perspectives II: Studies of History and Tradition in the Four Gospels* [ed. R. T. France and D. Wenham; Sheffield: JSOT Press, 1981], 309).

combines the covenant-discipleship motifs of loving God with obeying the commandments (14:15; 15:10). The double-Amen formula in 21:18 (ἀμὴν ἀμὴν λέγω σοι) marks the climax of the dialogue between Peter and Jesus. The destiny of Peter as a martyr signifies the deepest level of discipleship and commitment to the commandment of love (15:12–14). The command to follow Jesus in 21:19 (ἀκολούθει μοι) indicates that the radical call to following in discipleship unto death is modeled after the example of Jesus.

The shepherd-sheep symbolism brings home yet another covenant-discipleship motif. Jesus is presented as the true shepherd, who enters through the door as opposed to climbing over the wall (10:1), who gives life in abundance as opposed to destroying and killing (10:10), who lays down his life as opposed to leaving the sheep and fleeing (10:11–12), and who knows his sheep as opposed to being a stranger (10:14).[124] Jesus' call to follow him in 21:19b fulfills the promise of Jesus to Peter that later he would follow Jesus until death (13:36).[125] That Peter is called to follow Jesus in his unique role and mission is reconfirmed by the confrontation in 21:20–23.

Peter's query regarding the destiny of the Beloved Disciple is responded to by a rebuke and a command (τί πρὸς σέ; σύ μοι ἀκολούθει, 21:22). The explicit use of the pronoun σύ reaffirms the fact that Peter should focus on Jesus and follow Jesus, and not anybody else. Both Peter and the Beloved Disciple have unique roles to play, which cannot be imitated or replaced by the other. Peter is portrayed as shepherd of the community and witness by his martyrdom (21:15–19), while the Beloved Disciple is the one who abides with Jesus from the beginning till the end (21:22) and is a true witness to the works and life of Jesus (21:24).

SUMMARY AND CONCLUSIONS

As Jesus' instructions on discipleship before his death (1:35–51; 13–17), his interventions after his resurrection (20–21) reaffirm that the author of the gospel presents discipleship in terms of a covenant partnership with God. If the first farewell discourses before the death of Jesus prepare and pray for the new covenant community of the disciples, the final farewell appearances after the glorification of Jesus inaugurate and constitute the new covenant community.

---

[124] Chennattu, "Good Shepherd," 98–101.
[125] Brown, *John,* 2.616.

The promise-fulfillment motif that is essential to the covenant materials of the OT has been developed by the evangelist in the second half of the gospel. The narratives in chapters 20–21 fulfill many of the covenant promises of Jesus recounted in chapters 13–17. The discovery of the empty tomb and its aftermath fulfill Jesus' predictions that he is going to the Father (13:33; 14:28), that he has conquered the world (16:30), that the disciples would look for Jesus (13:33), and that the disciples might believe when Jesus returns to the Father (14:29). The encounter between Jesus and Mary of Magdala fulfills the promises of Jesus that he will come to the disciples and will not leave them orphans (14:18–20; 14:28) and they will have joy (16:20, 22). Jesus' commission to Mary in general, and the statement regarding his ascension in particular in 20:17, signal the completion of Jesus' mission and the establishment of a new covenant relationship between Jesus' Father or God and his disciples.

By means of the double identification formula, "to my Father and your Father, to my God and your God," Jesus explains to Mary, and to the disciples through her testimony, the theological significance of their new status as the followers of Jesus. By the use of several theological passives in the narrative, the evangelist emphasizes that God has now reclaimed his covenant relationship with the disciples of Jesus. God has thus made it possible for the disciples to share Jesus' intimate relationship with God. Mary's prompt response in 20:18 signals the acceptance and the appropriation of the new identity as the covenant community of God. The action of God in the resurrection transforms the promises of Jesus related in the earlier part of the gospel with this final definitive establishment of the covenant relationship between God and the disciples of Jesus.

Jesus' glorification and the endowment of the Spirit empower the disciples to become God's children, and Jesus' Father thus becomes the Father of the disciples (20:17). Jesus' commission in 20:21 ("as the Father has sent me, even so I send you") coupled with the visible sign of discipleship as articulated in 13:34–35 ("Love one another as I love you") enables the readers to interpret the forgiveness of sins in 20:23 as a call to bear witness to the presence of God and his unconditional love as Jesus revealed them in his life and mission. Just as Moses climbed a mountain to be in the presence of God and brought the covenantal law down to the Israelites, the risen Jesus ascended to his Father and God and brought the gift of the Holy Spirit down to the disciples. The primary purpose of the bestowal of the Holy Spirit is the empowerment of the community for a fruitful accomplishment of its mission in continuing the work of Jesus to make God's active presence known and loved. The gift of the Holy Spirit reaffirms the permanent presence of the covenant God and Lord (14:23; 16:7). The confession of the disciples in general ("We have seen the Lord," 20:25), and that of Thomas in particular ("My Lord and my God," 20:28), affirm that the disciples have now experienced the full revelation of God in Jesus ("Whoever has seen me has seen the Father," 14:9). The presence and work of the Spirit transform, recreate, and empower the disciples to continue to be the new covenant community of God.

Chapter 21 provides a narrative conclusion to the covenant-discipleship motifs. The appearance of the risen Jesus to the disciples engaged in their fishing occupation and his intervention to make their work fruitful reaffirms the need for an abiding relationship, the fact that without Jesus the disciples cannot be fruitful ("Whoever abides in me bears fruit, for apart from me you can do nothing," 15:5). The one hundred and fifty-three fish symbolize the universality and perfection of the missionary activity of the disciples in obedience to Jesus' command, and the unbroken net is a symbol of the unity and communion of the new covenant community of the disciples, despite their great number and differences. An abiding relationship with God, with the ongoing communication and communion with the life-giving revelation of God in Jesus, is the source of life for the community. Such a relationship with God deepens the faith of the disciples and molds their works in the world.

Peter's role as the shepherd of the new covenant community is portrayed as a manifestation of his absolute love for Jesus ("Do you love me more than these?") and his faithful obedience to the command of Jesus ("Feed my lambs," "Tend my sheep," and "Feed my sheep"). The dialogue between Jesus and Peter suggests that Peter's shepherd role is intimately linked to his martyrdom. Jesus is the model and source of Peter's mission as the leader of the new community; as the Good Shepherd Jesus gave his life for his flock, the leader (or shepherd) Peter will give his life. The sign of discipleship is love for one another (13:34–35; 15:12, 17). The threefold profession of love and commitment on the part of Peter therefore reinforces the idea that Peter's unconditional love for Jesus is the foundation and source of his mission as the shepherd of the new covenant community. By the commission of Peter as the shepherd, grounded in love unto death and modeled after the mission of Jesus, and the reaffirmation of the Beloved Disciple as the true witness, based on his everlasting abiding relationship with Jesus, the evangelist constitutes and establishes the parameters of the new covenant community for the disciples of the story and of future generations (21:15–23). This final chapter, moreover, resumes some of Jesus' predictions such as persecution and martyrdom (16:2–3 and 21:18–19), actualizes some of his dreams such as the disciples' sharing in his works (14:12 and 21:4–14, 15–19), and realizes some of Jesus' hopes (15:12–13; 17:17–18, 20–24, and 21:15–24) for the new covenant community.

The above interpretation suggests that in chapters 20–21, the Fourth Evangelist uses traditional resurrection materials to expound theologically what was announced and promised in the covenant discourses of Jesus in chapters 13–17. What was programmatically promised in chapters 13–17 is now effectively actualized in chapters 20–21. If there is a renewal and consecration of the community of the disciples as the new covenant community of God in chapters 13–17, then `the realization of the covenant promises and the actualization of the community of the disciples as God's children take place in chapters 20–21. Through the extended encounter between the risen Jesus and the disciples in general, and the dialogue between Jesus and Peter, the evangelist develops the covenant-discipleship motif that he began in the call stories in 1:35–51. What happens in chapters 20–21 verifies Jesus' glorification (return to God), fulfills Jesus' promise to send the Paraclete as his continuing presence in the community, reclaims the covenant relationship of the disciples with God, and constitutes the covenant community of the disciples. In sum, in the narratives of chapters 20–21, Jesus fulfills many of the covenant promises made before his death and gives further instructions to the disciples as to what it means to be a follower of Jesus in terms of their covenant relationship with God and commitment to the ongoing revelation of God in human history.

FIVE

THE COVENANT-DISCIPLESHIP MOTIF AND THE JOHANNINE COMMUNITY

The foregoing exegetical analyses of 1:35–51; 13–17; and 20–21 have shown that OT covenant motifs are of paramount significance in understanding John's Gospel in general and the Johannine discipleship motif in particular. The convergence of several covenant motifs in discipleship material across the gospel defines discipleship in terms of an OT covenant partnership with God and with one another.

Why did the evangelist present discipleship in terms of a covenant relationship? Or what function did the covenant-discipleship paradigm have for the Johannine community?[1] This final chapter must necessarily raise the question of the *Sitz im Leben der Kirche* that led a Christian community to articulate its understanding of Christian discipleship in terms that reflect the OT covenant motif. A grasp of the social and religious contexts of the community that produced the gospel will enhance our understanding of the significance of the covenant-discipleship motif. A study of the context requires a determination of the place and time of the composition of the gospel. This study presupposes the provenance of the gospel from Jesus traditions and Palestinian Judaism; but the final form of the gospel was produced by, and for, a community living outside Palestine, most probably in Ephesus or somewhere in Asia Minor.[2] This would suggest a community

---

[1] In his interpretation of John 13–17, Fernando Segovia has argued against any relevance of the covenant theme for the intended audience. If chs. 13–17 reflect a covenant genre, "the speech's character as a message from an author to an audience largely disappears" (*Farewell of the Word,* 40). This objection demands a rereading of the *Sitz im Leben* of the Johannine community and an assessment of the relevance of covenant motifs in such a situation.

[2] Both R. E. Brown (*An Introduction to the Gospel of John* [ed. F. J. Moloney; New York: Doubleday, 2003], 199–206) and J. Painter (*The Quest for the Messiah: The History, Literature and Theology of the Johannine Community* [2d ed.; Edinburgh:

living in a milieu where diaspora Jewish religious traditions and Hellenistic philosophies rubbed shoulders with each other.[3] Although the early period in the development of the Johannine community, as Moody Smith has argued, began before the Jewish War (before 66 C.E.), the final composition of the gospel probably took place during the period between 90 and 110 C.E.[4] We can infer, then, that at least some of the final editions of the gospel were written during the reigns of the Roman emperors Domitian (81–96 C.E.) and Trajan (98–117 C.E.),[5] thus suggesting some influence of Roman political power.[6] Despite differing opinions concerning the place of origin, it is widely accepted that the community was primarily composed of Jewish Christians, as well as Christians of Samaritan, or Gentile, origin.[7] The

---

T&T Clark, 1993], 66–79) argue for the growth and movement of the community beginning in Palestine and completed somewhere in the Diaspora, most probably in Ephesus. It has also been suggested that the provenance of the gospel was strictly Jewish and located in Palestine. K. Wengst suggests the region of Batanea and Gaulanitis (*Bedrängte Gemeinde und verherrlichter Christus: Ein Versuch über das Johannesevangelium* [3d ed.; BTS 5; Munchen: Kaiser Verlag, 1990], 80); see also J. Ashton, *Understanding the Fourth Gospel* (Oxford: Clarendon Press, 1993), 196–98. J. T. Sanders suggests Galilee (*Schismatics, Sectarians, Dissidents, Deviants: The First One Hundred Years of Jewish-Christian Relations* [Valley Forge, Pa.: Trinity Press International, 1993], 40), and E. W. Stegemann and W. Stegemann suggest a Jewish milieu (*The Jesus Movement: A Social History of Its First Century* [trans. O. C. Dean Jr.; Minneapolis: Fortress, 1999], 226–27).

[3] It is important to remember that during the first century C.E., the boundaries between religious traditions and philosophies were very flexible and fluid. One cannot deny some sort of osmosis or gradual, often unconscious, processes of assimilation and absorption within diaspora Judaism of Hellenism and Eastern Mediterranean cultures. See the discussion in Archibald M. Hunter, *According to John: The New Look at the Fourth Gospel* (Philadelphia: Westminster Press, 1968), 23–35. See also the study of Scholtissek, *In Ihm Sein,* 23–130.

[4] D. Moody Smith, "Johannine Christianity: Some Reflections on Its Character and Delineation," *NTS* 21 (1974–1975): 222–48, esp. 246. For a detailed discussion on the time of the composition of the gospel, see Brown, *Introduction to the Gospel,* 206–15.

[5] Cassidy, *John's Gospel in New Perspective,* 2–5.

[6] In his review of Cassidy's *John's Gospel in New Perspective,* J. E. Bruns comments: "There is simply not enough in the Fourth Gospel to suggest that the Roman Empire was *the* enemy" (*CBQ* 56 [1994]: 135, emphasis original). However, one cannot totally deny some influence of the political power of the Romans (cf. John 11:48, "If we let him go on like this, everyone will believe in him, and the Romans will come and destroy both our holy place and our nation"). See also H. C. Orchard, *Courting Betrayal: Jesus as Victim in the Gospel of John* (JSNTSup 161; Sheffield: Sheffield Academic Press, 1998), 54–56.

[7] For the Jewish background of the Gospel of John, see Davies, "Aspects of the Jewish Background," 43–64. On Samaritan influence on the Fourth Gospel, see J.

present study accepts this consensus. No one disputes that the *Sitz im Leben* of the Johannine community and its social and religious concerns need to be assessed in the wider context of the Judaism of the first century C.E. I shall therefore briefly discuss the main theological concerns of Judaism of the first century C.E. This will be followed by an assessment of the historical context reflected in the gospel. I shall then employ insights from the social sciences in my attempt to explore and interpret the Johannine community and its presentation of discipleship as a covenant relationship.

JUDAISM OF THE FIRST CENTURY C.E. AND COVENANT MOTIFS

First-century Judaism and its theological motifs are of great importance for an understanding of the Jewish background to the NT.[8] The prewar period (6–66 C.E.) is characterized by a fundamental breakdown of law and order coupled with economic instability and religious persecutions from the Roman authorities in Palestine.[9] During this period the relationship between the Jewish nation and the Romans progressively deteriorated throughout the Jewish province, leading to the war and destruction of the temple in 70 C.E. James S. McLaren proposes the events of 70 C.E. and their aftermath as the starting point of turmoil and instability in Palestine.[10] "The 'dark age' of the first century C.E. (70–100 C.E.) may be . . . the time of increased turmoil and tension in Jewish-Roman relations, in which the ideological edge to the way Jews related to the Roman overlords was defined."[11] Whether 70 C.E. is the culmination or the starting point, both

---

Bowman, "The Fourth Gospel and the Samaritans," *BJRL* 40 (1958): 298–308; E. D. Freed, "Samaritan Influence in the Gospel of John," *CBQ* 30 (1968): 580–87; M. Pamment, "Is There Convincing Evidence of Samaritan Influence on the Fourth Gospel?" *ZNW* 73 (1982): 221–30. For Christians of Gentile origin, see R. E. Brown, "Not Jewish Christianity or Gentile Christianity, but Types of Jewish/Gentile Christianity," *CBQ* 45 (1983): 74–79. See also Brown, *Introduction to the Gospel,* 115–44.

[8] McNamara, *Palestinian Judaism and New Testament,* 45–64.

[9] D. M. Rhoads, *Israel in Revolution: 6–74 C.E.: A Political History Based on the Writings of Josephus* (Philadelphia: Fortress, 1976), 47–93.

[10] J. S. McLaren questions the dependence on Josephus' interpretation of the events in the first century that considers 70 C.E. the culmination of the turmoil in Judaea (*Turbulent Times? Josephus and Scholarship on Judaea in the First Century C.E.* [JSPSup 29; Sheffield: Sheffield Academic Press, 1998]).

[11] Ibid., 294.

the turmoil and instability that led to the destruction of the temple and its aftermath created the need for the Jewish community to restore its identity and religious symbols.

From a religious perspective, Judaism of the first century C.E. is characterized by its variety. The existence of many groups—Sadducees, Pharisees, Essenes, members of the Qumran community, apocalyptic writers and their communities, and Christian communities, each with a differing theology and way of life—bears this out.[12] The Jewish War and the subsequent destruction of the Jerusalem Temple in 70 C.E. brought an end to much of the religious activities associated with the land and temple. This produced a situation of crisis in the loss of social identity, which in turn initiated a process of unification of Jewish religious beliefs and practices. The multifaceted Judaism of the prewar period eventually led to the consolidation and unification of both Pharisaic Judaism (later known as rabbinic Judaism) and Christianity. During the postwar period, so-called Pharisaic Judaism played an important role in reshaping and renewing Judaism.[13] This renewal process focused largely on the study of the Torah and its implications for daily life, resulting in the Mishnah and the Talmudim. Pharisaic Judaism was particularly committed to the Torah as the rule of life for the people of Israel.[14] As we shall see, foreign invasion and the destruction of the temple were often interpreted as a consequence of Israel's having broken the covenantal relationship with God. This interpretation necessitated a rethinking of Israel's covenantal relationship with God. Along with monotheism, the theology of covenant then became one of the important pillars of Pharisaic Judaism.[15] The urgency of the times pressed the people to return to the covenant with God. This rethinking of the covenantal relationship is

---

[12] McNamara, *Palestinian Judaism and New Testament,* 45. For a discussion of the major religious groups of first-century Judaism, see Rhoads, *Israel in Revolution,* 32–46; J. D. Newsome, *Greeks, Romans, Jews: Currents of Culture and Belief in the New Testament World* (Philadelphia: Trinity Press International, 1992), 113–27; Meier, *A Marginal Jew,* 3.289–613.

[13] See the detailed discussion of first-century Judaism in Schürer, *History of the Jewish People.* See also Stegemann and Stegemann, *Jesus Movement,* 221–23.

[14] Richard A. Horsley, *Bandits, Prophets and Messiahs: Popular Movements in the Time of Jesus* (Harrisburg: Trinity Press International, 1999), 23–29. See also J. Neusner, *From Politics to Piety: The Emergence of Pharisaic Judaism* (Englewood Cliffs, N.J.: Prentice-Hall, 1973), 45–66.

[15] J. D. G. Dunn speaks of monotheism, election, covenant, and land as "the four pillars of second temple Judaism" (*The Partings of the Ways Between Christianity and Judaism and their Significance for the Character of Christianity* [London: SCM Press/Philadelphia: Trinity Press International, 1991], 18–36).

reflected in many Jewish documents of the period.[16] What follows is a representative sample of Jewish literature from both before (e.g., the Qumran documents and Pseudo-Philo's *Liber Antiquitatum Biblicarum*) and after (e.g., *4 Ezra* and *2 Baruch*) the destruction of the temple.[17]

THE QUMRAN COMMUNITY AND ITS DOCUMENTS

There is a growing consensus among scholars today "to conceive of the theology of the [Qumran] community as part of the general doctrinal evolution of ancient Judaism."[18] As John J. Collins observes, "We should expect the scrolls to reflect some notions that were widespread in the Judaism of their day, as well as those that were peculiar to the sect itself."[19] Since some Qumran documents are roughly contemporary with some of the earliest NT texts (and with the stage of the oral traditions behind other NT texts), they throw light on some aspects of the Jewish religious traditions of the world of the apostolic communities.[20] This is particularly true of the Johannine community and its gospel. One can draw many parallels between the Gospel of John and the Qumran documents in terms of symbolic language, motifs such as creation, dualism, Spirit of Truth, and reciprocal love among the community members.[21] James H. Charlesworth argued for

---

[16] The idea of covenant is central to the theology of the Letter to the Hebrews (cf. 7:22; 8:6, 7, 8, 9, 10, 13; 9:1, 4, 15, 16, 18, 20; 10:16, 29; 12:24; 13:20); it is also important for the apostle Paul (cf. Rom 11:27; 1 Cor 11:25; 2 Cor 3:6, 14; Gal 3:17).

[17] It is beyond the scope of this study to offer a detailed analysis of late Second Temple Jewish literature and early Christian texts, which return to the theme of covenant. For an initial and important study, see Baltzer, *Covenant Formulary*, 97–175.

[18] G. Vermes, *The Complete Dead Sea Scrolls in English* (New York: Penguin Books, 1998), 67. See also S. Talmon, "The Community of the Renewed Covenant: Between Judaism and Christianity," in *The Community of the Renewed Covenant: The Notre Dame Symposium on the Dead Sea Scrolls* (ed. E. Ulrich and J. VanderKam; Notre Dame, Ind.: University of Notre Dame Press, 1993), 3–4.

[19] Collins, *Scepter and the Star*, 9.

[20] J. VanderKam and P. Flint, *The Meaning of the Dead Sea Scrolls: Their Significance for Understanding the Bible, Judaism, Jesus and Christianity* (New York: HarperCollins, 2002), 321–78. For the history and religious ideas of the community, see, among many, Vermes, *Dead Sea Scrolls*, 49–90, esp. 67–77 for the theme of covenant.

[21] For example, see James H. Charlesworth, "A Critical Comparison of the Dualism in 1QS 3:13–4:26 and the 'Dualism' Contained in the Gospel of John," in *John and Qumran* (ed. J. H. Charlesworth; London: Chapman, 1972), 76–106; Charlesworth, "The Dead Sea Scrolls and the Gospel according to John," in *Exploring the Gospel of John*, 65–97.

a direct influence of the symbolic language and theology of the Qumran documents on John's Gospel.[22] Raymond E. Brown was of the opinion that the ideas of Qumran community may have been fairly widespread in certain Jewish circles and the Johannine writings may have been indirectly influenced by this common source of Jewish heritage.[23] Discussion of this topic over the past fifty years confirms that the Fourth Evangelist was influenced at least indirectly, if not directly, by the theology and writings of the Qumran community.

The Qumran community was a group that separated itself from mainstream Judaism,[24] and the members regarded their community "as the sole legitimate representative of biblical Israel."[25] The remnant covenant theology served as the foundation of the community's basic beliefs, and they saw the realization of Jeremiah's prophecy in their lives.[26] The members also believed themselves called by God "in the wilderness to prepare the way of the Lord" (cf. Isa 40). They eventually abandoned Jerusalem

---

[22] Charlesworth, "Dead Sea Scrolls and John," 65–97. John Ashton suggests that the Fourth Evangelist had once belonged to the Essenes and argues for a more significant influence from Qumran on the Gospel of John. Ashton identifies the Essene group with the Qumran community (*Understanding the Fourth Gospel,* 235–37).

[23] See the detailed discussion in R. E. Brown, "The Qumran Scrolls and the Johannine Gospel and Epistles," in *The Scrolls and the New Testament* (ed. Krister Stendahl; New York: Crossroad, 1992), 183–207. See also Painter for the same view (*Quest for the Messiah,* 35–52). For significant points of comparison between John and Qumran documents, see also Brown, "John, Gospel and Letters of," in *Encyclopedia of the Dead Sea Scrolls* (ed. L. H. Schiffman and J. C. VanderKam; 2 vols.; New York: Oxford University Press, 2000), 1.414–17; A. R. C. Leaney, "John and Qumran," *SE* 6 (1973): 296–310.

[24] For an understanding of Qumran community as a sect, see Collins, *Scepter and the Star,* 4–7. Against this view, see Talmon, "Community of the Renewed Covenant," 8. For the purposes of this study, there is no need to identify them with Essenes or Sadducees or any other group. For the identification of the Essenes with the Qumran community, see J. A. Fitzmyer, *The Dead Sea Scrolls and Christian Origins* (Grand Rapids: Eerdmans, 2000), 249–60. For arguments in favor of Sadducean identification, see J. M. Baumgarten, "Sadducean Elements in Qumran Law," in *Community of the Renewed Covenant,* 27–36; L. H. Schiffman, "The Temple Scroll and the Nature of Its Law: The Status of the Question," in *Community of the Renewed Covenant,* 37–55.

[25] Talmon, "Community of the Renewed Covenant," 12–15; the quotation is from p. 12.

[26] For a comparison between the Qumran covenant theology and that of the NT, see R. F. Collins, "The Berith-Notion of the Cairo Damascus Covenant and Its Comparison with the New Testament," *ETL* 39 (1963): 555–94.

and withdrew into the wilderness under the leadership of their "Righteous Teacher" (מורה הצדק).

What is significant for the present discussion is that the members of the Qumran community considered themselves not only part of the ancient covenant between God and his people but more importantly the members of the new covenant. The designation of "those who entered into the new covenant" (באי בברית החדשה) is very significant (see, e.g., CD 6.19; 8.21). The members of the community thought of themselves as belonging to the "covenant for all Israel" (ברית לכל ישראל; CD 15.5) or to the "covenant of God" (ברית אל; 1QS 5.8).

The significance of covenant theology for the community is evident in the annual initiation ceremony when the community both renewed its covenantal commitments and welcomed new members (1QS 1.16–2.25). This annually repeated ceremony was modeled upon the "blessing and curse" covenant-renewal ceremonies found in Deut 27–28 and Josh 8:30–35; 23:1–16. As Shemaryahu Talmon has put it, the Qumran community "perceived the reenactment of the biblical ceremony in their induction ritual as the confirmation of their community's claim to be the only legitimate heir to biblical Israel."[27] The members insisted on both the free choice of the new members to enter into the covenant (1QS 1.5–9) and total allegiance to God by obeying all God's commandments (1QS 1.15–18). The Rule speaks repeatedly of their self-understanding as the community of the "everlasting covenant" (ברית עולמים; 1QS 3.11–12; 4.22–23; 5.5–6). The members regarded themselves as "the sons of Zadok, the priests that keep the covenant" (1QS 5.2, 9) and engaged in intense study of the Torah following a strict interpretation and application of the new covenant theology.

LIBER ANTIQUITATUM BIBLICARUM

Pseudo-Philo's *Biblical Antiquities* (*Liber Antiquitatum Biblicarum* [*L.A.B.*]) is a rewritten biblical history of Israel from Adam to David that appeared sometime around the time of Jesus.[28] One of the purposes of the rewritten

---

27 Talmon, "Community of the Renewed Covenant," 14.

28 D. J. Harrington, "Pseudo-Philo: A New Translation and Introduction," *OTP* 2.297–377. To establish a precise date for the composition of the book seems to go beyond the evidence available. After treating various viewpoints on these issues, B. N. Fish suggests that *L.A.B.* was composed shortly before or soon after the war and the destruction of the temple in 70 C.E. (*Do You Not Remember? Scripture,*

biblical narratives was "to actualize a religious tradition and make it meaningful within new situations."[29] Pseudo-Philo uses history to demonstrate God's unconditional fidelity to his covenantal promises. In other words, history is presented as evidence of God's ongoing commitment and enduring mercy.[30] The *Biblical Antiquities* is regarded as a representative of "fairly mainstream scribal Judaism in first century Palestine."[31] Since its author represents the theological concerns of mainstream Judaism of the first century, *Biblical Antiquities* is important for the present discussion.

The author interweaves biblical texts and midrashic or legendary expansions without distinguishing one from the other. He reinterprets Israel's story by embellishing or expanding some stories, or bypassing or changing others. Leopold Cohn describes *Biblical Antiquities* as follows:

> The narrative follows closely that of the Old Testament, but passes rapidly over many incidents, and omits many sections, while, on the other hand, it elaborates certain portions, and furnishes quite novel additions to the narrative of the Bible. The author shows a great love for altering and enlarging the speeches given in the Bible, and even for composing new speeches.[32]

Invented passages, among others, include the covenant with Abraham (*L.A.B.* 4.11) and a covenant making scene (*L.A.B.* 8.3). Pseudo-Philo stresses God's initiative in establishing the covenant by supplying additional

---

Story and Exegesis in the Rewritten Bible of Pseudo-Philo [JSPSup 37; Sheffield: Sheffield Academic Press, 2001], 34–45). Although scholars suggest that the original *Biblical Antiquities* was composed in Hebrew and subsequently translated into Greek and Latin, only the Latin translation is available to us (see the detailed discussion in D. J. Harrington, "The Original Language of Pseudo-Philo's *Liber Antiquitatum Biblicarum*," *HTR* 63 [1970]: 503–14. See also H. Jacobson, *A Commentary on the Pseudo-Philo's Liber Antiquitatum Biblicarum, with Latin Text and English Translation* [2 vols.; AGJU 31; Leiden: E. J. Brill, 1996], 195–96, 215–22).

[29] D. Harrington, "Palestinian Adaptations of Biblical Narratives and Prophecies," in *Early Judaism and Its Modern Interpreters* (ed. Robert Kraft and George Nickelsburg; Philadelphia: Fortress/Atlanta: Scholars Press, 1986), 239–40. The rewritten biblical narratives of the intertestamental period were often referred to as "Rewritten Bible," a term coined by G. Vermes (*Scripture and Tradition in Judaism: Haggadic Studies* [Leiden: Brill, 1961], 95, 124–26).

[30] See the detailed analysis in B. Halpern-Amaru, *Rewriting the Bible: Land and Covenant in Postbiblical Jewish Literature* (Valley Forge, Pa.: Trinity Press International, 1994), 69–94.

[31] F. J. Murphy, *Pseudo-Philo: Rewriting the Bible* (New York/Oxford: Oxford University Press, 1993), 7.

[32] L. Cohn, "An Apocryphal Work Ascribed to Philo of Alexandria," *JQR*, Old Ser. 10 (1898): 279–80.

statements. For example, between citations from Exod 19:1 ("they [people of Israel] came into the wilderness of Sinai") and Exod 19:15 ("be prepared"), the author supplies the following in the direct speech of God: "I will give a light to the world and illumine their dwelling places and establish my covenant with the sons of men and glorify my people above all nations" (L.A.B. 11.1). Pseudo-Philo stresses God's pervasive presence and active intervention in Israel's history and systematically defends God's covenant loyalty (e.g., 9.4; 12.9–10; 13.10; 18.11; 19.2; 23.13; 49.3).[33]

The embellishments serve to make God's covenant with Israel one of the central motifs of Biblical Antiquities.[34] Frederick J. Murphy has counted ninety occurrences of testamentum and its various cognates highlighting the centrality of the covenant motif.[35] Daniel Harrington also concludes that covenant is at the center of both its theology and anthropology.[36] Bruce Norman Fish describes Biblical Antiquities as a treatise on "the irrevocability of Israel's covenant promises" and on "God's covenant faithfulness."[37] Similarly, H. Jacobson comments on the "single predominant theme" in Biblical Antiquities in the following words: "No matter how much the Jewish people suffer, no matter how bleak the outlook appears, God will never completely abandon His people and in the end salvation and triumph will be the lot of the Jews."[38]

Pseudo-Philo sees the frailty of the people and their loss of faith in God and his covenantal promises as a threat to national survival. In response, he proposes the notion of the covenant with Israel going back beyond Sinai to the covenant with Abraham in particular (e.g., 4.5; 7.4; 9.3), and the covenant with the fathers in general (e.g., 9.4, 7; 13.10; 19.2; 23.11; 30.7; 32.13), and focuses on God's unconditional promise of descendants. In his rewritten covenant theology, Pseudo-Philo emphasizes God's enduring covenantal love and fidelity to divine promises. The covenant is established by giving the law and land, and it implies the protection of Israel from its enemies. This is recognized even by Balaam, a Gentile, when he says, "It is

---

[33] Fish, Do You Not Remember? 45–50.

[34] F. J. Murphy, "The Eternal Covenant in Pseudo-Philo," JSP 3 (1988): 43–57; Murphy, Pseudo-Philo, 244–46.

[35] The word testamentum occurs fifty-one times, testimonium nineteen times, testis sixteen times, testare three times, and testor once; see Murphy, Pseudo-Philo, 244 (for references, see p. 307).

[36] Harrington, "Pseudo-Philo," 2.301. See also the recent comprehensive work of Fish, Do You Not Remember? 45–50, 191–263. Fish regards covenant and idolatry as the central themes in Biblical Antiquities.

[37] Fish, Do You Not Remember? 45, 192.

[38] Jacobson, Commentary, 241–42.

easier to take away the foundations and the topmost part of the earth and to extinguish the light of the sun and to darken the light of the moon than for anyone to uproot the planting of the Most Powerful or to destroy his vine [Israel]" (*L.A.B.* 18.10).[39] Pseudo-Philo wants to assure Israel's survival. Frederick J. Murphy comments:

> The *Biblical Antiquities* consistently asserts the indestructibility of Israel and the covenant. No matter how evil or how neglectful of God's ways Israel gets, the covenant survives. It depends not on the people's deeds but on the promises to the fathers. This allows Pseudo-Philo to affirm two things and hold them together in tension: Israel will indeed suffer when it does not obey God, but this suffering does not mean that the covenant is at an end; and sin will always be punished, but God will never forsake Israel.[40]

Israel's covenant disloyalties and disobedience, however, led to suffering and foreign invasion and the experience of temporary abandonment by God (e.g., 12.4; 13.10; 14.4; 15.5–6; 19.2, 6; 53.10). Pseudo-Philo stresses divine impartiality in order to explain the present experience of suffering and abandonment by God (20.3–4). As Bruce N. Fish has pointed out, divine impartiality explains Israel's affliction without compromising God's promises.[41] *Biblical Antiquities* impresses on its readers that God's mercy and faithfulness will be vindicated. The author gives the assurance that God established the law of his eternal covenant with Israel and gave his eternal commandment (11.5) that was prepared from the creation of the world (32.7), and God will remember and be faithful to his covenant with Israel (13.10; 19.2).

Following the Deuteronomic perception of history—sin-punishment-redemption (cf. *L.A.B.* 13.10; 19.2–5)[42]—Pseudo-Philo conceives of the covenant as unconditional and everlasting and thus ignores, to a certain extent, the biblical motif of repentance.[43] Despite their unfaithfulness, God

---

[39] Unless otherwise indicated, the translation of *L.A.B.* is from Harrington, "Pseudo-Philo," 2.304–77.

[40] Murphy, *Pseudo-Philo,* 263.

[41] Fish, *Do You Not Remember?* 52. J. M. Bassler compares, among others, Pseudo-Philo's understanding of divine impartiality with that of the NT and postbiblical Jewish literature and concludes, "In periods of national distress divine impartiality became a useful tool interpreting Israel's fate in a way that did not compromise God's power or promises" (*Divine Impartiality: Paul and a Theological Axiom* [SBLDS 59; Chico, Calif.: Scholars Press, 1982], 184).

[42] For a deuteronomistic schema of history (Sin-Punishment-Repentance-Redemption), see F. J. Murphy, *Structure and Meaning of Second Baruch* (SBLDS 78; Atlanta: Scholars Press, 1985), 117–18.

[43] As Murphy observes, "Repentance plays no role in the stories of Gideon and Jephthah despite the versions in Judges" (*Pseudo-Philo,* 246).

will never abandon the people because of the covenant made with their ancestors and the oath sworn never to abandon them (30.7). Leopold Cohn has summarized the message of Pseudo-Philo in terms of a covenant book:

> In all the speeches the same idea recurs again and again: God has chosen the people of Israel and has made his covenant with them for ever; if the children of Israel depart from God's ways and forget his covenant, he delivers them for a time into the hands of their enemies; but God is ever mindful of his covenant with the patriarchs; he always delivers the Israelites through leaders of his choice, and he will never entirely abandon them.[44]

The biblical narratives have been rewritten by Pseudo-Philo to reestablish the unique covenantal relationship between God and Israel as God's chosen people and to guarantee God's everlasting steadfastness despite Israel's repeated failures (e.g., 12.4–5a; 13.10; 21.10).

FOURTH EZRA

The Fourth Book of Ezra (*Esdrae liber IV*) was composed after the destruction of the temple in 70 C.E., most probably in Palestine.[45] The history of the transmission of this book is extremely complicated. According to the Latin Vulgate, there are four books of Esdras. *First Esdras* is the Book of Ezra; *Second Esdras* is called the Book of Nehemiah; *Third Esdras* of the Vulgate is First Esdras in the English Bible, and *Fourth Ezra* (chs. 1–16) is included in the Apocrypha of the English Bible under the title Second Esdras.[46] *Fourth Ezra* is made up of seven visions (chs. 3–14) granted to Salathiel, also referred to as Ezra. It is preceded by an introduction (chs. 1–2, sometimes designated as *5 Ezra*) and followed by an appendix (chs. 15–16, sometimes designated as *6 Ezra*) denouncing the enemies of God's people, exhorting the people of God to trust in God, and promising divine deliverance.

The main concerns of *4 Ezra* are the theological, social, and political consequences of the events of post-70 C.E. Michael E. Stone describes the central themes of *4 Ezra* as the "justice of God" (God's mercy and justice) in the destruction of the temple, "the tension between Israel's fate and Is-

---

[44] Cohn, "Apocryphal Work," 322.

[45] B. M. Metzger, "The Fourth Book of Ezra: A New Translation and Introduction," *OTP* 1.516–59; see also M. E. Stone, *Fourth Ezra: A Commentary on the Book of Fourth Ezra* (ed. Frank M. Cross; Hermeneia; Minneapolis: Fortress, 1990), 9–10.

[46] See the table of titles in selected versions in Metzger, "Fourth Book of Ezra," 1.516.

rael's election," and "the tension between the purposeful creation, on the one hand, and the few saved and the many damned, on the other."[47] The destruction of the temple and its aftermath called into question the justice of God toward Israel (3.28–36; 7.45–48; etc.). The author therefore repeatedly reminds the readers of their failure and of their responsibly to be obedient to God's commandments or God's law (cf. 1.24–32, 33–34; 7.129–31; 8.46–47). He praises the abiding presence of God's law in their midst despite suffering and persecution (9.26–37), and instructs the people that they must restore the law (cf. 14.37–48). Restoring the law implies renewing their covenantal commitments to God by being faithful to the law, the divine gift to Israel (3.19; 9.31), and Israel's acceptance of the law signals their status as God's special possession and chosen people (cf. 7.72). Although they are persecuted and tested, God's elect ones or the chosen people, namely, those who keep God's commandments and precepts, will be vindicated and delivered from their enemies (16.73–76).

Second Baruch

The title *2 Baruch* (the Syriac Apocalypse of Baruch) is generally used to designate both the *Apocalypse of Baruch* (chs. 1–77) and the *Epistle of Baruch* (chs. 78–87).[48] Scholars argue that the original language of *2 Baruch* was Hebrew, and the Syriac text was translated from a Greek translation of a Hebrew text.[49] *Second Baruch* was written in the wake of the destruction of the temple, sometime in the first decade of the second century.[50] This document is extremely important for an understanding of the Judaism of the first century C.E. as it copes with the identity crisis posed by the catastrophe of 70 C.E. and its aftermath.

---

[47] Stone, *Fourth Ezra,* 36.

[48] For this usage, see among others, R. H. Charles, *The Apocrypha and Pseudepigrapha of the Old Testament in English* (2 vols.; Oxford: Claredon, 1913), 2.470–526; P.-M. Bogaert, *Apocalypse de Baruch: Introduction, traduction du syriaque et commentaire* (SC 144, 145; Paris: Serf, 1969); A. F. J. Klijn, "2 (Syriac Apocalypse of) Baruch: A New Translation and Introduction," *OTP* 1.615–52; Murphy, *Structure and Meaning,* 11–29. Others challenge the originality of the letter in chs. 78–87 as part of 2 Baruch; for example, G. B. Sayler, *Have the Promises Failed? A Literary Analysis of 2 Baruch* (SBLDS 72; Chico, Calif.: Scholars Press, 1984).

[49] Charles, *Apocrypha and Pseudepigrapha,* 2.471–74. See also F. Zimmerman, "Textual Observations on the Apocalypse of Baruch," *JTS* 40 (1939): 151–56; Klijn, "2 Baruch," 1.616.

[50] Klijn, "2 Baruch," 1.615–20.

As Gwendolyn Saylor has pointed out, two issues occupy the central stage: the vindication of God, who is faithful and powerful, and the survival of the Jewish community.[51] Saylor articulates the basic question in the following words: "Has God nullified His covenantal relationship with the faithful Jews who constitute 'Israel'?"[52] The law is given by Moses as a lamp (17:4) to guide Israel in the establishment of the covenant (19:1). Frederick J. Murphy has investigated the covenant motifs in the book by exploring the covenantal "conditional sentences in which the protasis deals with obedience to God's Law, and the apodosis with the reward for obedience to that Law" (e.g., 32:1; 44:7; 46:5–6; 75:7; 78:7; 85:4). He also highlights the "remembering" motifs (48:29; 77:11; 78:3): the people are to remember the covenant (84:2) and God's law (44:7; 48:38; 84:7–8).[53]

Frederick J. Murphy proposes the use of *2 Baruch* as a pastoral exhortation or preaching that accompanied the covenant renewal.[54] In the renewal, Baruch places himself parallel to Moses since both are mediators of the covenant (84:1–11). The author explains the disaster of 70 C.E. as a punishment for sin, and calls the people to return to the Law; at the same time he exposes the transient nature of the prosperity of this world and assures God's final vindication of those who are faithful to God's law. The author comments:

> But now the righteous have been gathered
> And the prophets have fallen asleep,
> And we also have gone forth from the land,
> And Zion has been taken from us,
> And we have nothing now save the Mighty One and His Law.
> If therefore we direct and dispose our hearts,
> We shall receive everything that we lost,
> And much better things than we lost by many times. (85.3–4)[55]

The author emphasizes the abiding presence and efficacy of the law (44.1–46; 48.20–24), defends the everlasting validity and endurance of God's covenant promises to Israel, and tries to show that there is nothing but God and God's law left for the people. A renewed obedience to the law and commitment to the covenant commandments gives eternal life (32.1;

---

[51] See the discussion in Sayler, *Have the Promises Failed?* 9.

[52] Ibid., 41–86.

[53] For a detailed discussion on the covenant motif in 2 Baruch, see Murphy, *Structure and Meaning,* 117–33.

[54] See the section on "2 Baruch and the Covenant" in Murphy, *Structure and Meaning,* 117–33.

[55] The translation is from Murphy, *Structure and Meaning,* 27.

38.1; 48.22; 51.3, 4–7; 54.15). When the people grieve over the loss of the shepherds, the extinguished lamps, and the dried up fountains (symbols also important for the Gospel of John), the author of *2 Baruch* reaffirms the everlasting and abiding presence of the law and summons the people to hold fast to the law that is at the center of their covenant commitment to God. The author narrates:

The whole people answered and they said to me:

". . . For the shepherds of Israel have perished, and the lamps which gave light are extinguished, and the fountains from which we used to drink have withheld their streams. Now we have been left in the darkness and in the thick forest and in the aridness of the desert."

And I answered and said to them:

"Shepherds and lamps and fountains came from the Law and when we go away, the Law will abide. If you, therefore, look upon the Law and are intent upon wisdom, then the lamp will not be wanting and the shepherd will not give way and the fountain will not dry up." (77.11, 13–16)[56]

SUMMARY

The above survey of the representative ideas of the Qumran documents, Pseudo-Philo, *4 Ezra* and *2 Baruch* points out some major theological concerns of Judaism in the first century C.E. at grips with crises that threatened Israel's social and religious identity. These authors expose, in a variety of ways, the metaphor of the covenant as the central theological expression of the experience and self-perception of Israel as God's people set apart by God's unchangeable choice and irrevocable promises. The covenant relationship that stems from the theology of election provides a theological understanding of the constitution and preservation of Israel as God's people. Similar interest in the covenant motif asserting Israel's election is also found elsewhere. For example, in his appeal to God not to take his mercy away from the house of Israel, the author of the *Psalms of Solomon* reminds God of his election and covenant:

---

[56] The Johannine Christians turn to Jesus Christ as their living water, light, and shepherd (John 7–10); see Moloney, *Signs and Shadows*, 65–153.

And now, you are God and we are the people whom you have loved;
>   look and be compassionate, O God of Israel, for we are yours,
>   and do not take away your mercy from us, lest they set upon us.
For you chose the descendents of Abraham above all the nations,
>   and you put your name upon us, Lord,
>   and it will not cease forever.
You made a covenant with our ancestors concerning us,
>   and we hope in you when we turn our souls toward you.
May the mercy of the Lord be upon the house of Israel forevermore. (*Pss. Sol.* 9.8–11)[57]

The theology of election (God's choice) is implied in Israel's commitment to the everlasting covenant relationship that presupposes the gift of the law and obedience to it. E. P. Sanders speaks about "covenantal nomism" as crucial for our understanding of first-century Judaism. According to his definition, covenant refers to God's grace in election and nomism stands for the requirement of obedience to the law.[58] After analyzing both Palestinian Jewish literature (e.g., *Jubilees, 2 Baruch*) and Hellenistic Jewish literature (e.g., *Joseph and Aseneth,* Philo), Sanders reaffirms the significance of membership in the covenant and its preservation by obedience to the commandments for receiving God's grace and eternal life.[59] In sum, as first-century Judaism attempted to restore its self-identity, the covenant metaphor was a central theological motif and category.

THE SOCIO-HISTORICAL CONTEXT REFLECTED IN THE GOSPEL

There is an ongoing dialectic between the historical experience of the Johannine community and the religious and the theological world ("the

---

[57] *Psalms of Solomon* is a collection of eighteen poems. Scholars suggest that it was composed in the first century B.C.E.; see R. B. Wright, "Psalms of Solomon: A New Translation and Introduction," *OTP* 2.639–70, esp. 640–41. The author shares the view that Israel's unfaithfulness has resulted in the present suffering and distress (see *Pss. Sol.* 2:1–4).

[58] E. P. Sanders, *Judaism: Practice and Belief 63 B.C.E.–66 C.E.* (London: SCM Press, 1992), 262–78.

[59] See E. P. Sanders, "The Covenant as a Soteriological Category and the Nature of Salvation in Palestine and Hellenistic Judaism," in *Jews, Greeks, and Christians: Religious Cultures in Late Antiquity* (ed. R. Hamerton-Kelly and R. Scroggs; Leiden: Brill, 1976), 11–44. In her argument on the position of the land in the reconstructed theology of the covenant of the first century C.E., Halpern-Amaru also

symbolic world") manifested in its gospel. The symbolic world refers to the biblical nexus between history and theology; it interprets the historical experience and responds to it using theological motifs. The symbolic world thus served both to explain the experience and to motivate the community as it responded to the challenges of its lived experience. The most significant contributions to the understanding of the dialectics between the historical development of the Johannine community and its gospel (the symbolic world) are the works of J. Louis Martyn and Raymond E. Brown.[60] Martyn attempted to trace the interplay between the sociohistorical and religious crises that shaped the community and its unique theology. Martyn proposed a two-level reading of the Johannine text: (1) "a witness to an *einmalig* event during Jesus' earthly lifetime"; (2) "a witness to Jesus' powerful presence in actual events experienced by the Johannine church."[61] In his reconstruction of the history of the Johannine community, Martyn suggests three periods: (1) "the conception of a messianic group within the community of the synagogue"; (2) "part of the group is born as a separate community by experiencing two major traumas: excommunication from the synagogue and martyrdom"; (3) "movement toward firm social and theological configurations."[62] Following Martyn, Brown comments at the beginning of his investigation into the development of the Johannine community and its gospel that "the deeds and words of Jesus are included in the Gospels because the evangelist sees that they are (or have been) useful to members of his community. From that we gain general knowledge about the life situation of the community."[63] Brown's construction of the development of the community consists in four phases: (1) before the gospel—Johannine community origins; (2) when the gospel was written—Johannine relations to outsiders; (3) when the letters were written—Johannine internal struggles; (4) after the letters were written—Johannine

---

points out the centrality of the covenant theme in *Jubilees*, the *Testament of Moses*, Pseudo-Philo, and in Josephus' *Jewish Antiquities* (*Rewriting the Bible*, 25–115).

[60] Martyn, *History and Theology*; Martyn, *The Gospel of John in Christian History: Essays for Interpreters* (New York, etc.: Paulist, 1978). See also the comments of D. M. Smith ("The Contribution of J. Louis Martyn to the Understanding of the Gospel of John," in Martyn, *History and Theology*, 1–23). Brown, *Community*. See also the comments of R. Kysar on the works of Martyn and Brown as the most widely endorsed hypotheses ("Anti-Semitism and the Gospel of John," in *Anti-Semitism and Early Christianity: Issues of Polemic and Faith* [ed. C. A. Evans and D. A. Hagner; Philadelphia: Fortress, 1993], 119).

[61] Martyn, *History and Theology*, 40.

[62] Martyn, *John in Christian History*, 90–121.

[63] Brown, *Community*, 18.

dissolution.[64] Wayne Meeks has rightly warned: "No one . . . is in a position to write an empirical sociology of Johannine Christianity."[65] Nevertheless, it is now widely accepted that the "gospel's literary history" reflects the "community's social and theological history."[66]

Readers can perceive different types of religious tensions or conflicts that have important social implications in the unfolding story of the Johannine Jesus. Among others, what merits special attention are tensions (1) between the disciples of Jesus and the followers of John the Baptist; (2) among the disciples of Jesus themselves; and (3) between the disciples of Jesus and the mainstream Jewish synagogue authority.

The gospel alludes to the tension between the followers of Jesus and those of John the Baptist. Some of the negations about the identity and mission of John the Baptist in the gospel "were intended as refutations of claims that followers of JBap made about their master."[67] At the very outset of the gospel, the prologue makes it clear that Jesus, not John the Baptist, is the light (1:8–9). John the Baptist himself witnesses to Jesus as the one greater than he who existed before him (1:30). The disciples complain to John the Baptist about the success of Jesus' ministry, that all are going to Jesus (3:25–26), and that Jesus is making more disciples than John the Baptist (4:1–3). Even Jesus contrasts himself to John the Baptist (5:33–36) and claims that he has a testimony greater than John's (5:36). In 10:40–42, when Jesus comes to the trans-Jordanian region where John the Baptist had been baptizing earlier, many among the crowd acknowledge Jesus' superiority to the Baptist ("John performed no sign, but everything that John said about this man was true") and believe in him. These narratives point to a competition, if not rivalry, that existed between the disciples of John and Jesus.

Based on an exegetical analysis of 6:60–71, Ludger Schenke points to evidence of "a schism in the Johannine congregation" because of the high

---

[64] Ibid., 25–169. This is not to be confused with his five-stage or more recent three-stage development of the Gospel of John; see Brown, *Introduction to the Gospel*, 104–11.

[65] W. A. Meeks, "The Man from Heaven in Johannine Sectarianism," *JBL* 91 (1972): 49.

[66] Martyn, *John in Christian History*, 90–121.

[67] Brown, *Introduction to the Gospel*, 155. One cannot ignore, however, the fact that the gospel presents John the Baptist as the one who is "sent from God" (1:6) and thus appointed by God to reveal Jesus (1:31; 3:29). John's witness is ranked alongside the testimony of the Scriptures and the signs (5:31–40). For cautions on regarding the gospel as an anti-Baptist apologetic, see Brown, *Introduction to the Gospel*, 156. See also Moloney, "The Fourth Gospel," 49.

Christological claims that Jesus makes and the negative response of some disciples among the followers of Jesus.[68] The narrative focuses on various responses to Jesus' messianic claims. Many of his disciples find his teaching "hard" (σκληρός, v. 60); some of his disciples "grumble" (γογγύζουσιν, v. 61), some do not believe (οὐ πιστεύουσιν, v. 64), and many reject Jesus' claims, turn away from him, and do not follow him anymore (v. 66). These disciples initially followed Jesus but could not accept the Johannine high Christology of presenting Jesus as the bread from heaven.[69] Raymond E. Brown refers to this group as "Christians of inadequate faith" who believed in Jesus based on signs but failed to understand the eucharistic discourse of Jesus and his messianic claims.[70] As implied in 8:31–59, some Jews who believed in Jesus (8:31a) could not accept the preexistence of Jesus, being before Abraham was. In the view of the Johannine community, these Jewish Christians are no longer counted among the true believers of Jesus.

Particularly important for our discussion is the animosity and rivalry between the Johannine community and "the Jews" who did not believe in Jesus and his messianic claims.[71] The gospel explicitly mentions a division (σχίσμα) among the Jewish crowd (ἐν τῷ ὄχλῳ) over the origin and identity of Jesus (7:43; cf. also 7:12, 25–27, 40–41; 9:16; 10:19). In addition to these tensions and divisions, the gospel manifests a progressive alienation of Jesus from "the Jews." This leads to intolerance to the extent of demonizing "the Jews" who rejected Jesus. Jesus accuses "the Jews" for their unbelief by saying, "You are from your father the devil, and you choose to do your father's desires" (8:44a; see also 15:23). There are also allusions to persecutions (5:16 [Jesus]; 15:20 [disciples]) and to the executions of the disciples of Jesus (16:2b).[72]

---

[68] L. Schenke, "Der 'Dialog Jesu mit den Juden' im Johannesevangelium: Ein Rekonstruktionsversuch," *NTS* 34 (1988): 599. Other texts cited by Schenke (e.g., 8:30–31 and 3:1–21) seem to be less convincing.

[69] Ignatius of Antioch (who wrote at least a decade after the Gospel of John) criticized Jewish Christians for their low Christology. C. K. Barrett summarizes Ignatius of Antioch's charges against these Jewish Christians as follows: "They reverenced Jesus as a teacher, but were perhaps not prepared to allow his person to upset the unity of the Godhead. They were unwilling to follow all the new messianic exegesis of the Old Testament. They adopted the sacred meal . . . but associated it with Sabbath rather than with the Lord's Day" ("Jews and Judaizers in the Epistles of Ignatius," in *Jews, Greeks, and Christians,* 242).

[70] Brown, *Introduction to the Gospel,* 179–80; Brown, *Community,* 169.

[71] See the discussion on the use of "the Jews" in the gospel in chapter 3, pp. 124–37. See also Moloney, " 'The Jews' in the Fourth Gospel," 16–36.

[72] See the detailed exegetical analysis in chapter 3, pp. 120, 123–24.

The explicit allusions to expulsion from the synagogue (ἀποσυνάγωγος, 9:22; 12:42; 16:2) seem to be the high point of the religious persecution and social exclusion from the Jewish community. Related to the expulsion from the synagogue is the "fear of the Jews" that is expressed by the many who believed in Jesus but refused to admit publicly that they believed (7:13; 12:42). Raymond E. Brown refers to this group as "crypto-Christians" and J. Louis Martyn calls them "secret believers."[73] Therefore, not all the Jews who believed in Jesus acknowledged their faith publicly lest they be excommunicated from the Jewish community. Ekkehard W. Stegemann and Wolfgang Stegemann comment on the predicament of the Jewish Christians whom they call the "Christ-confessing Jews." They were on the fringe between the synagogue and the Christian communities and had to give up their "dual membership."[74] This situation impelled the community to a process of self-definition, developing and articulating its own distinguishing features and unique characteristics. As Wayne A. Meeks proposed, the Johannine community "had to distinguish itself over against the sect of John the Baptist and even more passionately over against a rather strong Jewish community."[75]

J. Louis Martyn links the *Birkat ha-Mînîm* (ברכת המינים) of *Tefillah* (Eighteen Benedictions) with the expulsion of the Jewish-Johannine Christians as its direct consequence.[76] Martyn argued that John 9:22 (also 12:42) is to be interpreted in the light of the Twelfth Benediction of the *Birkat ha-Mînîm,* which includes Nazareans (*notzrim,* i.e., Christians) among the heretics (*Mînîm*).[77] This view has been contested today by most Johannine scholars, although they accept the fact that expulsion from the synagogue may have been part of the local experience of the Johannine community.[78] It is also suggested that the local experiences of expulsion may have led to the formulation of the *Birkat ha-Mînîm* and not

---

[73] Brown, *Community,* 169; Martyn, *History and Theology,* 112–14.

[74] Stegemann and Stegemann, *Jesus Movement,* 239.

[75] Meeks, "Man from Heaven," 49.

[76] Martyn, *History and Theology,* 49–65.

[77] In the version of the *Tefillah* found in the Cairo Genizah, the twelfth Benediction reads as follows: "For apostates let there be no hope. And let the arrogant government be speedily uprooted in our days. Let the *Notzrim* [Christians], the *Mînîm* [heretics] be destroyed in a moment." It was suggested that the Jamnian Jewish authorities (probably, Samuel the Small [80–90 C.E.]) added *Notzrim* in order to include Jewish Christians among the *Mînîm;* see Davies, "Aspects of the Jewish Background," 50–52.

[78] See the detailed discussion in P. W. van der Horst, "The Birkat ha-minim," 363–68. See also Brown, *Introduction to the Gospel,* 172.

the other way around.[79] Whatever one makes of the *Birkat ha-Mínîm* theory, the Johannine tension between Jesus, his followers, and "the Jews" seems to presuppose religious and social exclusions and expulsion from the synagogue and "implicitly assumes an already accomplished break between the Christ-confessing Jews and the synagogues."[80] As John Painter has aptly observed, "It makes no sense to defend the *birkat hamminim* hypothesis as if the understanding of Jn depends upon it. Rather the case depends on the recognition that the Johannine believers were excluded for their profession of faith, whatever the circumstances in which it occurred."[81] Expulsion from the synagogue points to the period of separation of the Johannine community from the religious activities linked with the Jewish synagogue community to which they once belonged.[82] As a consequence of their faith in Jesus, the community was cut off from the Jewish liturgical life and separated from their Jewish friends.

Separation seems to be one of the most fundamental existential and social experiences of the Johannine community that shaped the Johannine theological motifs. The community had many adversaries, namely, the world, "the Jews," the adherents of John the Baptist, the crypto-Christians, and Jewish Christians who had inadequate faith.[83] As D. Moody Smith concludes, "a polemical situation within the synagogue and later between the Johannine community and the synagogue is almost certainly a significant, if not the central, milieu of the Johannine material."[84] The conflict settings within which we encounter the Johannine Jesus seem to refer to tensions, especially between Christian Jews and non-Christian Jews at a time when the Johannine community was still attending synagogue and regarding itself as a community of faithful Jews.[85] The community suffered conflicts, persecution, alienation, and schisms. Indeed, the community

---

[79] Davies, "Aspects of the Jewish Background," 50–52.

[80] Stegemann and Stegemann, *Jesus Movement,* 241.

[81] Painter, *Quest for the Messiah,* 77.

[82] Citing the comments of W. A. Meeks, J. H. Charlesworth proposes that "many members of the Johannine group (including some who had not been born Jews) saw themselves . . . 'entirely within the orbit of Jewish communities'" ("Dead Sea Scrolls and John," 76).

[83] Brown, *Community,* 168–69.

[84] Smith, "Johannine Christianity," 238.

[85] See Meeks, "Man from Heaven," 44–72; Martyn, *History and Theology,* 27–98; Brown, *Community,* 59–144; Ashton, *Understanding the Fourth Gospel,* 166–74; Sanders, *Schismatics, Sectarians, Dissidents, Deviants,* 41. For an opinion that these conflicts point to an internal Jewish conflict, see Stegemann and Stegemann, *Jesus Movement,* 226–27.

faced a serious religious and social identity crisis created by internal and external conflicts in general, and expulsion from the synagogues in particular.

INSIGHTS FROM SOCIAL SCIENCE PERSPECTIVES

Scholars who approach the NT from a sociological perspective have applied three models for the interpretation of the tense relationship between Jews and Christians in the apostolic period: the sect model, conflict theory, and the deviant model.[86] Jack T. Sanders has systematically discussed and pointed out the inadequacies and inappropriateness of the sect model for the understanding of Jewish Christian conflicts.[87] I shall focus on the theories of conflict and deviance, as they may prove useful for an understanding of the relationship between the Johannine community and the Jewish community to which they once belonged and from which they are now separated. What makes the theories of conflict and deviance so important for the question under discussion is the fact they are centered on the search for identity of communities in conflict.[88] Based on the classical work of Georg

---

[86] For theories of sect and sectarianism in general, see B. Wilson, *The Social Dimension of Sectarianism* (Oxford: Oxford University Press, 1990). For an understanding of the Christian communities as "sectarian movements," see Stegemann and Stegemann, *Jesus Movement,* 242–43; see also the endnotes 101–7 (on pp. 440–41) for more bibliography on the topic. On the significance of the conflict theory, see Sanders, *Schismatics, Sectarians, Dissidents, Deviants,* 125–29. For a working definition of deviant groups, see Sanders, ibid., 129–45. For a thorough discussion of the application of these three sociological theories, see Stegemann and Stegemann, *Jesus Movement,* 221–363.

[87] Sanders, *Schismatics, Sectarians, Dissidents, Deviants,* 116–17. Based on the social analysis of H. S. Becker (*Outsiders: Studies in the Sociology of Deviance* [2d ed.; New York: Free Press, 1973]), K. T. Erikson (*Wayward Puritans: A Study in the Sociology of Deviance* [New York, etc.: John Wiley & Sons, 1966]), and N. Ben-Yehuda (*Deviance and Moral Boundaries: Witchcraft, the Occult, Science Fiction, Deviant Sciences and Scientists* [Chicago and London: University of Chicago Press, 1985]). Sanders has also pointed out the significance of the deviance theory for the understanding of Jewish Christian conflicts and applied the model of deviant-punishment to the early Jewish Christian relations (*Schismatics, Sectarians, Dissidents, Deviants,* 129–49).

[88] N. Ben-Yehuda emphasizes the idea that deviance is intimately connected with the identity and "collective conscience" of a society. Ben-Yehuda regards deviance as socially defined and thus culturally relative and discusses deviance within the context of change and stability. He also considers patterns of deviance an integral part of a specific social order and social system (*Deviance and Moral Boundaries,* 10–20). Based on the theory of conflict, G. Theissen also discusses "tendencies to

Simmel,[89] the sociologist Lewis Coser suggests that "conflict is a form of socialization," and that "far from being necessarily dysfunctional, a certain degree of conflict is an essential element in group formation and the persistence of group life."[90] Coser paraphrases Simmel's thesis as follows: "Conflict with other groups contributes to the establishment and reaffirmation of the identity of the group and maintains its boundaries against the surrounding social world."[91] Coser puts forward sixteen propositions as he explores the positive functions of social conflict.[92] His propositions on group-building and group-defining are the most significant for the present discussion. They can be summarized as follows:

1. Conflict has a group-preserving function;

2. Conflict leads to group-binding;

3. Conflict with out-group increases internal cohesion;

4. Conflict serves to redefine and strengthen group structures;

5. Conflict serves to establish and maintain identity and boundary lines.

Among others, John G. Gager has used the positive effects of conflict to explain the growth and development of Christianity within the Roman Empire.[93] Gager emphasizes the positive role of conflict in "drawing boundaries between the group and the outside world."[94] Although conflicts arise as a defense against danger, they function to enhance a group's self-image and contribute to strengthening its internal cohesion, identity, and structures.

Deviance is created by the majority community that determines what normal or deviant behavior is. As Howard Becker puts it, "*social groups create deviance by making the rules whose infraction constitutes deviance, and by applying those rules to particular people and labeling them as outsiders.*"[95] The labeling and exclusion of deviant groups lead to the development of a deviant

---

intensify norms in Judaism" when its identity is questioned or threatened (*Sociology of Early Palestinian Christianity* [Philadelphia: Fortress, 1978], 87).

[89] G. Simmel, *Conflict* (trans. Kurt H. Wolff; Glencoe, Ill.: The Free Press, 1955).

[90] L. Coser, *Functions of Social Conflict* (London: Routledge & Kegan Paul, 1956), 31.

[91] Coser, *Functions of Social Conflict*, 38.

[92] Ibid., 33–149.

[93] J. G. Gager, *Kingdom and Community: The Social World of Early Christianity* (PHSRS; Englewood Cliffs, N.J.: Prentice-Hall, 1975).

[94] Ibid., 85.

[95] Becker, *Outsiders*, 9 [italics original].

identity. Relying on the insights of Kai Erikson, Jack T. Sanders points to deviance control as a form of boundary preservation or boundary maintenance
in a situation of identity crisis.[96] Sanders describes the Jewish–Christian relationship in Palestine before 135 C.E. in the following words:

> Mainstream Judaism—constantly threatened; under severe economic, political,
> and military pressure; and at one point nearly destroyed—struck out at the de-
> viant Christians in order to preserve its boundaries, its self-identity as a culture;
> for these Christians were eroding those boundaries just at the time when gen-
> tiles were trying to destroy them. I am convinced that those are the situation
> and the principle that help us to understand the dynamic of the conflict be-
> tween early mainstream Judaism and Jewish Christianity in Palestine.[97]

After a lengthy analysis, Ekkehard and Wolfgang Stegemann summarize the
two negative experiences of the Jewish Christians with the Jewish majority
population in the land of Israel as follows:

> The first is the religious or social exclusion of messianic groups from the Jew-
> ish majority population, which culminated in the exclusion from the syna-
> gogues and ultimately resulted in the twelfth of the Eighteen Benedictions.
> Second, Christ-confessing propagandists in the synagogues were punished and
> in some case expelled. Both experiences presuppose that the Christ-confessing
> Jews were perceived by the majority population as a deviant religious group
> within Judaism.[98]

The sociological analysis suggests the hypothesis that the conflict between
Christianity and Judaism in general has its origin in the mutual perception
of each other as deviant groups. Jews regarded Christians as a deviant group
and Christians looked at Jews as deviants. This experience of conflict moti-
vated the respective communities to redefine their boundaries in the
preservation of their true identity.

SYNAGOGUE JUDAISM OF POST-70 C.E. AND THE JOHANNINE COMMUNITY

The theories of conflict and deviance, and their application to the Jewish-Christian relationship in general, can help interpret the conflict between the Johannine community and the Jews associated with the diaspora

---

[96] Sanders, *Schismatics, Sectarians, Dissidents, Deviants,* 133.
[97] Ibid., 150.
[98] Stegemann and Stegemann, *Jesus Movement,* 241.

synagogue community.[99] The deviance theory may throw some light on the Johannine community's experience of conflict with the Jewish synagogue community.

Howard S. Becker's three stages of a "deviant career" parallel J. Louis Martyn's three periods in the history of the Johannine community.[100]

Becker: Three stages of a deviant career	**Martyn: Three periods in the history of the Johannine community**
1. The individuals learn to participate in a particular deviant activity	1. The inception of a messianic group within the community of the synagogue
2. They are caught and publicly labeled as deviants	2. Part of the group is born as a separate community by experiencing the traumas of excommunication and martyrdom
3. The solidification of deviant identity	3. Movement toward firm social and theological configurations

As in the first stage of a deviant career, during the first period of the community's existence Martyn speaks only of a group of Christian Jews, distinct from a community, who saw in Jesus the Messiah who was to come to his own and who believed in him. This group felt at home with their Jewish heritage and the synagogue practices, but they participated in a deviant action, namely, the confession of faith in Jesus as the Messiah. The second stage of labeling and punishment corresponds to the Johannine community's experience of excommunication and persecution. During this period, according to Martyn, a group of Christian Jews becomes a community of Jewish Christians. The Johannine community enters into the third stage of a deviant career, the solidification of an identity, as the community attempts to articulate "its own theology and its own identity not only vis-à-vis the parent synagogue, but also in

---

[99] Much of what follows is indebted to the studies of Martyn, *History and Theology;* Sanders, *Schismatics, Sectarians, Dissidents, Deviants;* Stegemann and Stegemann, *Jesus Movement.* Nevertheless, I differ from them on specific issues. For example, in contrast to the stand that I have taken in this study, both Sanders and Stegemann and Stegemann suggest that the provenance of the Gospel of John was somewhere in the land of Israel. However, the insights from the social science analysis that they have employed are relevant to the present discussion.

[100] Martyn, *John in Christian History,* 90–121; Becker, *Outsiders,* 25–39. For an application of Becker's three stages to the early Christian identity in general as a deviant group, see Sanders, *Schismatics, Sectarians, Dissidents, Deviants,* 131.

relation to other Christian groups in its setting."[101] The parallel stages indicate that the formation and gradual separation of the Johannine community, after expulsion from the synagogues, is analogous in nature and function to the development of a deviant group separated from its originating society.

John's Gospel reflects a historical situation in which the Johannine community was regarded by the synagogue authority as a deviant group. Even more significant, the members of the Johannine community regarded the Jewish synagogue community as deviant.[102] This is reflected in the narratives that deal with the escalating conflict between the Johannine Jesus and the Jewish characters in the story (chs. 5–10). The sharp anti-Jewish polemic found in chapters 5–10 is clearly related to religious deviance (cf. e.g., 5:16, 45; 7:12, 40–44; 8:31–59). This is further demonstrated in the presentation of the persecution of the disciples because of Jesus' name (15:20–21) explained by the comment that those who hate Jesus also hate the Father (15:23). Disciplinary measures taken against the deviant group (the Johannine community) are reflected in the narratives of social exclusions (cf. 9:22; 12:42; 16:2) and religious persecutions (cf. 16:2).

The insights regarding how a society responds to deviance, and how the deviants respond to that treatment, provide the hermeneutical key to understanding the relationship between the Johannine community and the synagogue authority.[103] The Jewish synagogue community was anxious to preserve boundaries regarding Jewish identity and an authentic Jewish way of life. From the perspective of deviant theory, the synagogue authority decided to expel the Johannine community because its existence endangered Jewish identity. The more the Johannine community transcended the boundaries of Judaism and would accept Samaritans (4:4–42) and Gentiles (7:35; 12:20), the less chance it had as a renewal movement within Judaism.[104] The gospel

---

[101] Martyn, *John in Christian History,* 107. See also R. E. Brown, "Other Sheep Not of This Fold: The Johannine Perspective on Christian Diversity in the Late First Century," *JBL* 97 (1978): 5–22.

[102] This tendency continues into the Johannine letters. The author(s) of 1–3 John regard those who separated themselves from the Johannine community as deviants (e.g., 1 John 2:22; 4:1–6; 2 John 10–11). See the detailed discussion of "secessionists" in R. E. Brown, *The Epistles of John: Translated with Introduction, Notes, and Commentary* (AB 30; Garden City, N.Y.: Doubleday, 1982), 69–115.

[103] For a discussion on this aspect of the deviant theory, see Sanders, *Schismatics, Sectarians, Dissidents, Deviants,* 145.

[104] For a similar view, see also Theissen, *Sociology of Early Palestinian Christianity,* 112–13. For socio-cultural tensions between Judaism and Hellenism in general, see ibid., 87–90.

provides ample evidence that differing views on messiahship in general and Jesus' messiahship in particular were the major points of conflict between the Johannine Christians and the Jews of the synagogues.[105] That the Johannine Jesus (and thus, by application, the Johannine community) could endanger mainstream Jewish existence is alluded to in the gospel. For example, "What are we to do? This man is performing many signs. If we let him go on like this, everyone will believe in him, and the Romans will come and destroy both our holy place and our nation" (11:47b–48). As Sanders observes, "events were leading the enforcers of Judaic identity to maintain the boundaries of Judaism while the Christians were breaking through those boundaries in one way or another."[106] The synagogue leadership punished or expelled the deviant group, namely, the Johannine community. This treatment of the Johannine community, however, generated an opportunity for its members to develop and strengthen the identity of their increasingly distinctive group.

THE COVENANT-DISCIPLESHIP PARADIGM AS A RESPONSE THAT REDEFINES IDENTITY

The scenario just sketched envisages a situation in which the Johannine community emerged as a group within Judaism, encountering difficulty with, and being excluded by, the group of people associated with the synagogue and identified throughout the gospel as "the Jews." The social, historical, and religious crises that lay behind the Johannine community having been traced, the relevant question becomes how the community responded to this crisis situation. One needs to explore the issue from both religious/theological and social perspectives.[107] Sociological insights into the experience

---

[105] See also Sanders, *Schismatics, Sectarians, Dissidents, Deviants,* 40–47. K. Wengst specifies the reason that led up to the expulsion from the synagogue as the tendency among the members of the Johannine community to hide their faith in Jesus lest they be punished (cf. 12:42; *Bedrängte Gemeinde,* 75–122).

[106] Sanders, *Schismatics, Sectarians, Dissidents, Deviants,* 141.

[107] See the comments of Douglas R. A. Hare, "The approach of historians, both Jewish and Christian, has generally been too theological. Jewish writers tend to find the basis of the conflict in the church's rejection of Torah. Christians, on the other, are inclined to view the strife as due to Jewish rejection of the Messiah. . . . An adequate historical study must take full account of sociological factors before theological conclusions are drawn" (*The Theme of Jewish Persecution of Christians in the Gospel According to St. Matthew* [SNTSMS 7; Cambridge: Cambridge University Press, 1967], 2). For the importance of the social science perspectives in

of the Johannine community do not replace its theological motivations, but they complement and enrich them by bringing into the discussion the function of conflicts and social relationships.[108] According to Wayne A. Meeks, "one of the primary functions of the book . . . must have been to provide a reinforcement for the community's social identity, which appears to have been largely negative. It provided a symbolic universe which gave religious legitimacy, a theodicy, to the group's actual isolation from the larger society."[109] Relying on the analysis of John Gager, Sanders points out that "the Johannine community, thrust out from the synagogue participation, was pressed to define both theology and ethics more closely."[110] The Johannine community responded to its present crisis in two ways: (1) it defended its theodicy by developing a high Christology; (2) it defined its identity by presenting discipleship as a renewed or new covenant partnership with God and with one another. It is beyond the scope of this study to explore the high Johannine Christology.[111] I shall focus on the socioreligious function of the

---

understanding the Jewish Christian relationship in general, see also Sanders, *Schismatics, Sectarians, Dissidents, Deviants,* 99–100.

[108] J. T. Sanders seems to overemphasize sociological explanations over theological insights when he claims that "the Jewish leadership *punished* early Christianity not primarily because the Christians were following a deviant *halakâh,* or because they called Jesus God, or because they proclaimed a crucified Messiah, or even because they criticized the temple cults and questioned the validity of the Torah, but because events were leading the enforcers of Judaic identity to maintain the boundaries of Judaism" (*Schismatics, Sectarians, Dissidents, Deviants,* 141).

[109] Meeks, "Man from Heaven," 70.

[110] Sanders, *Schismatics, Sectarians, Dissidents, Deviants,* 127.

[111] The high Christology of the Fourth Evangelist is an example of "deviance-amplifying consequence" (Sanders, *Schismatics, Sectarians, Dissidents, Deviants,* 145). The self-definition and its reaffirmation demanded by the conflict situations are implied in many of the absolute claims made by the Johannine Jesus. Prominent among them is the assertion that Jesus is the only way to the Father (14:6). Here we have an encounter of two groups with absolute claims, one of which reacts to the claims of the other. There are many examples of justifications of the Johannine community's messianic claims over against the Jewish positions by recourse to Scripture or Jesus' special authority as the one who has come from heaven (3:10–13; 5:41–47; 6:30–33; 8:17–18; 11:25–26). Equally important are the Johannine λόγος Christology and the absolute use of ἐγώ εἰμι (see the discussion in Brown, *John,* 1.519–32, 533–38). See also the detailed study of Painter, *Quest for the Messiah,* 137–464. The high Christology is an example of the Johannine community's attempts to find new impulses to their identity from the perspective of God's revelation in Jesus. This tendency of self-definition and self-defense is even more explicit in the letters of John (e.g., 1 John 2:22; 3:7–10; 4:1–6; 2 John 10–11).

covenant-discipleship motif in legitimizing the community's identity and preserving its traditions.

OT covenant theology, the central expression of the distinctive faith of Israel as the chosen people of God or the children of God, was developed when Israel's social and religious identity was threatened.[112] One of the most important functions of the election motif was the legitimization of groups (e.g., the house of David, the Levites), which was basically an assertion of God's choice, and the chosen ones belong to God.[113] The election motif coupled with the covenant relationship with God seems to have been formulated in a moment of crisis—during or after the exile.[114] It reminded Israel of the need to maintain its identity and to resist the temptation of assimilation by the religious traditions of other nations (cf. Neh 9:7).

From the perspective of discipleship or of human response to God's revelation in Jesus within the context of conflict and separation, the fundamental questions regarding the socioreligious identity of the Johannine community were: Who is the true remnant of the people of God, or who are the true children of God (cf. 1:12–13; 20:17)? Regarded by others as a deviant group, the Johannine community gradually moved toward the establishment of a distinct religious and social identity as the true children of God.

In the prologue, the evangelist tries to answer the question of who are the true remnants of the people of God or children of God by affirming that God has given the power (ἐξουσία) to those who believe in (τοῖς πιστεύουσιν εἰς) Jesus to become children of God (τέκνα θεοῦ, 1:12; cf. 8:47). The members of the community emphasize that they are the chosen ones of God (cf. 6:44, 65; 15:16, 19), and they thus succeed Israel as God's children (1:11–13). As a deviant group, the Johannine community excludes those who expelled them, namely, the Jewish synagogue community, from the knowledge of God (cf. 16:3) and covenant relationship (1:11–13).[115] The evangelist rereads and interprets the OT covenant motif springing from different OT traditions and uses them to redefine and establish the identity of his community as children of God (τέκνα θεοῦ, 1:12), the covenantal people of God (cf. John 13:1; Deut 26:16–19).

---

[112] Nicholson, *God and His People*. See also D. R. Hillers, *Covenant: The History of a Biblical Idea* (Baltimore: John Hopkins Press, 1969).

[113] W. H. Propp, "Chosen People," in *The Oxford Companion to the Bible* (ed. B. M. Metzger and M. D. Coogan; New York: Oxford University Press, 1993), 110.

[114] H. Seebass, "בָּחַר," *TDOT* 2.82–87.

[115] For a similar comment on the excluded (Johannine community) and excluders (Jewish community), see Wengst, *Bedrängte Gemeinde*, 134.

The covenant-discipleship motif is progressively developed in the gospel as the Johannine story of Jesus unfolds. The call stories introduce covenant motifs, uncover the initial stage of the journey of the first disciples, and present a paradigm of Johannine discipleship (1:35–51). The central characteristics of the discipleship paradigm reflect essential elements of the OT covenant motifs, such as abiding, knowledge of God, witness, and promises. At the beginning of the call stories, the evangelist invites the disciples to abide (μένω) in Jesus and in his words (cf. 1:38–39) and makes this abiding an integral part of the process of becoming disciples of Jesus (cf. 4:40; 6:27, 56; 8:31–32). It is their abiding (μένω) with Jesus that gives them deeper insight into the identity of Jesus as the Messiah. The disciples display a progression in their understanding of Jesus as they attribute different messianic titles to him. Knowledge of God is implied in their knowledge of Jesus as the Messiah. By emphasizing the importance of testimony, the evangelist highlights yet another element of a covenant-type relationship between Jesus and his first disciples. This aspect of the covenant relationship is developed more forcefully in the farewell discourses (15:27; 17:20–21), where Jesus insists that the disciples should bear witness to him. The promises of Jesus in general (1:39, 42, 50) and the promise of a greater revelation of God in and through the mission of Jesus (1:51) are significant. Both the act of promising and the content of Jesus' promise in 1:51 remind the readers of the covenant promises of Yahweh to dwell among the people of Israel (Exod 25:8; 29:45–46; cf. also Num 14:14; Deut 12:11).

The narrative section of chapters 2–12 calls the disciples to a decision for or against Jesus and functions as a hortatory preparation for the covenant renewal in chapters 13–17. This study has argued that the overall narrative structure of chapters 13–17 reflects a covenant-renewal ceremony very similar to that of Josh 24. The ceremony culminates in Jesus' prayer that seals the new covenant instituted by him, surpassing the covenant under Moses as well as all former covenant traditions. The evangelist used the OT covenant traditions, and the Jesus material at hand (cf. 20:30), in order to drive home a self-definition of the community.

Sharing a meal with his own (οἱ ἴδιοι), the footwashing, the question of sharing an inheritance (μέρος) with Jesus, the command to love one another, the themes of election, abiding relationship, the indwelling presence of God, keeping God's commandments, and mutual knowledge run through the discipleship discourses in chapters 13–17. They are reminiscent of OT covenant themes and provide the theological self-definition of what it means to be a disciple of Jesus. Abiding in God's love and keeping God's commandments are the hallmarks of both OT covenant relationship and Johannine discipleship. Just as in an OT covenant relationship, Johannine discipleship demands a deep knowledge of God and is based upon the promises of the indwelling presence of God. The gift of the Holy Spirit reaffirms the permanent presence of the covenant God and Lord to the community (14:23; 16:7). The revelation of God's name to the disciples molds and fashions the unique identity and distinctiveness of the new covenant community. The unity among the disciples derives from the mutual indwelling presence of God in them. The promises of Jesus bring a dimension of "not yet" into the faith journey of the disciples. Like the election of Israel, the call to discipleship is a gift from God that in turn, like the covenant relationship, implies total commitment on the part of the disciples.

The narratives in chapters 20–21 fulfill many of the covenant promises of Jesus recounted in chapters 13–17. The discovery of the empty tomb and the subsequent events fulfill what Jesus has predicted: he is going to the Father (13:33; 14:28). Jesus' commission to Mary in general, and the statement regarding his ascension in particular (20:17; "to my Father and your Father, to my God and your God"), signal the completion of Jesus' mission and the establishment of a new covenant relationship between Jesus' Father/God and his disciples. Jesus' glorification and the endowment of the Spirit empower the disciples to become God's children, and Jesus' Father thus becomes the Father of the disciples (20:17). The evangelist constitutes and establishes the parameters of the new covenant community for the disciples of the story and of future generations by the commission of Peter as the shepherd, modeled on the love and mission of Jesus, and the reaffirmation of the Beloved Disciple as the true witness, based on his everlasting abiding relationship with Jesus (21:15–23). The final farewell appearances after his resurrection and glorification establish the Johannine covenant community (chs. 20–21) and provide a narrative conclusion to the covenant-discipleship motifs.

First-century Judaism was marked by the crisis created by the traumatic experience not only of the war but also of the circumstances that led to the war and resulted from it. This crisis, in turn, generated a serious attempt to arrive at a self-definition focused on the covenant metaphor as its central theological motif (cf. the Qumran documents, *L.A$_t$.B.*, *4 Ezra, 2 Baruch*, etc.).[116] The Johannine community had a similar experience. It encountered both

---

[116] Other rewritten biblical narratives of the same period that engage in the discussions of reinterpreting the centrality of the covenantal relationship include *Jubilees* and the *Testament of Moses;* see the detailed discussion in Halpern-Amaru, *Rewriting the Bible*, 25–68.

internal and external conflicts leading to the resolution of religious and social identity crises. Both first-century Judaism and the Johannine community turned to their common Jewish heritage as they struggled to establish
their identity. The covenant motif constituted the central element in that
heritage. The Fourth Evangelist, however, neither directly employs the title
"Israel" for his community,[117] nor uses explicitly the expression "covenant"
(διαθήκη) to describe the relationship between God and the Johannine
community.[118] Although the gospel insists that salvation has its origin from
among the Jews (4:22), the message of the gospel transcends the boundaries
of post-war Judaism (cf. 8:44). For the Fourth Gospel, the revelation of
God in Jesus draws people from all national and religious backgrounds to
form a new people of God (1:31; 11:51–52; 12:11, 19, 32). Johannine discipleship is thus characterized by universal membership: Jews, Samaritans,
and Gentiles or Greeks (1:31; 4:4–42; 10:16; 11:52; 12:32); it transcends
the exclusive OT covenant relationship between Yahweh and Israel. The
evangelist takes the OT covenant metaphor, redefines and broadens it, and
applies it to the relationship between God and the new covenant community of Jesus' disciples. The Johannine presentation of discipleship is a
Johannine rereading of the OT metaphor of covenant. This rereading reflects a definitive theological and sociological break between Israel and the
new chosen people of God, as well as a sensitivity toward community
members of Samaritan and Greek origin.

---

[117] Although the evangelist referred to Nathanael as truly an "Israelite"
(Ἰσραηλίτης, 1:47) who could be a representative figure of the Johannine com-
munity or of all those who believe in Jesus, the new people of God or new "Is-
rael," the gospel refers to those who believe in Jesus as "children of God" (1:12).
S. A. Pancaro argued for a close association of the Johannine use of Israel with
a self-understanding of the Johannine community (" 'People of God' in St. John's
Gospel," 114–29; Pancaro, "The Relationship of the Church to Israel in the
Gospel of John," NTS 21 [1974–1975]: 396–405). Against Pancaro's position, see
J. Painter, "The Church and Israel in the Gospel of John: A Response," NTS 25
(1978–1979): 103–12. For a critical assessment of Pancaro's and Painter's views
and a recent discussion of the use of Israel in the gospel, see Moloney, " 'The Jews'
in the Fourth Gospel," 18–29.

[118] The term διαθήκη occurs 33 times in the NT (7 in OT citations); of these occurrences 17 are in Hebrews, 9 in Paul; 4 in the Synoptic Gospels; 2 in Acts and 1
in Revelation. See also Quell, "διαθήκη," 2.106. J. Schmid thus maintains that in
all the other NT books "the covenant motif is completely lacking, or plays no role,
as in John . . ." ("Bund," LTK 2.778). As we have seen, there is ample evidence in
the gospel for the use of the metaphor of an abiding relationship based on the ob-
servance of the commandments, which was imperative for Israel's covenantal
relationship with God.

The centrality of the covenant motif was an important feature of first-century Judaism and provided the theological background for the understanding of Johannine discipleship. Insights from theories of conflict and deviance furnish sociological reasons for the community's urgency in presenting discipleship as a covenant relationship. The crisis situation necessitates a reassessment and redefinition of discipleship, i.e., an articulation of the community's true identity. The Fourth Evangelist accommodates the exigencies of his historical context and its theological challenges in his presentation of the discipleship paradigm. On the basis of the evidence analyzed in this study, it is reasonable to conclude that the covenant-discipleship paradigm provides a new center of gravity and becomes the fulcrum of the socioreligious identity of the Johannine community. The paradigm vindicates the existence of a covenant community abiding in God's love and keeping God's commandments. Amid the sociopastoral and theological identity crises of the Johannine community perceived as a deviant group within synagogue Judaism of post-70 C.E., the paradigm of discipleship as a covenant relationship redefines the community as the chosen people of God and consolidates the group as a distinct social and religious community.

BIBLIOGRAPHY

PRIMARY SOURCES AND DICTIONARIES

Aland, B., K. Aland, J. Karavidopoulos, C. M. Martini, and B. M. Metzger, eds. *The Greek New Testament*. 4th rev. ed. Stuttgart: Deutsche Bibelgesellschaft/United Bible Societies, 2001.

Bauer, W. *A Greek-English Lexicon of the New Testament and Other Early Christian Literature*. Edited by F. W. Danker. 3d ed. Chicago/London: University of Chicago Press, 2000.

Blass, F., and A. Debrunner. *A Greek Grammar of the New Testament and Other Early Christian Literature*. Edited and translated by Robert W. Funk. Chicago: University of Chicago Press, 1961.

Botterweck, G. J., H. Ringgren, and H.-J. Fabry, eds. *Theological Dictionary of the Old Testament*. Translated by J. T. Willis, G. W. Bromiley, and D. E. Green. 12 vols. Grand Rapids, Mich.: Eerdmans, 1974–2003.

Braude, W. G., trans. *The Midrash on Psalms*. 2 vols. New Haven: Yale University Press, 1959.

Buber, S., ed. *Midrash Tanhuma*. Lemberg: Wittwe & Gebrüder Romm, 1885.

Charles, R. H., ed. *Apocrypha and Pseudepigrapha of the Old Testament in English*. 2 vols. Oxford: Clarendon, 1913.

Charlesworth, J. H., ed. *The Old Testament Pseudepigrapha*. 2 vols. London: Darton, Longman & Todd, 1983, 1985.

Colson, F. H., G. H. Whitaker, J. W. Earp, and R. Marcus, eds. *Philo*. 12 vols. Loeb Classical Library. London: Heinemann; Cambridge: Harvard University Press, 1929–1953.

Danby, H. *The Mishnah Translated from the Hebrew with Introduction and Brief Expository Notes*. Oxford: Clarendon Press, 1933.

Elliger, K., and W. Rudolph, eds. *Biblia Hebraica Stuttgartensia*. Stuttgart: Deutsche Bibelgesellschaft, 1977.

The Interpretation of the Bible in the Church. Edited by the Pontifical Biblical Commission. Vatican: Libreria Editrice Vaticana, 1993.

Kittel, G., and G. Friedrich, eds. *Theological Dictionary of the New Testament.* Translated by G. W. Bromiley. 10 vols. Grand Rapids, Mich.: Eerdmans, 1964–1976.

Lake, K., ed. *The Apostolic Fathers. With an English Translation.* 2 vols. Loeb Classical Library. London: Heinemann; Cambridge: Harvard University Press, 1912–1913.

Lauterbach, J. Z., trans. *Mekilta de-Rabbi Ishmael: A Critical Edition of the Basis of the Manuscripts and Early Editions with an English Translation.* 3 vols. Philadelphia: Jewish Publication Society, 1961.

Metzger, B. M. *A Textual Commentary on the Greek New Testament.* 2d ed. Stuttgart: Biblia-Druck, 1994.

Metzger, B. M., and M. D. Coogan, eds. *The Oxford Companion to the Bible.* New York, Oxford: Oxford University Press, 1993.

Rahlfs, A. *Septuaginta.* Stuttgart: Biblia-Druck, 1935.

Slotki, J. J., trans. *Midrash Rabbah Numbers.* 2 vols. London: Soncino Press, 1939.

Strack, H., and P. Billerbeck. *Kommentar zum Neuen Testament aus Talmud und Midrash.* 6 vols. Munich: C. H. Beck, 1922–1961.

Suetonius. *The Lives of the Caesars.* Translated by J. Rolfe. Loeb Classical Library. London: Heinemann; Cambridge: Harvard University Press, 1914.

SECONDARY SOURCES

Abogunrin, S. O. "The Three Variant Accounts of Peter's Call: A Critical and Theological Examination of the Texts." *NTS* 31 (1985): 587–602.

Achtemeier, E. "Plumbing the Riches: Deuteronomy for the Preacher." *Int* 41 (1987): 269–81.

Appold, M. L. *The Oneness Motif in the Fourth Gospel: Motif Analysis and Exegetical Probe into the Theology of John.* WUNT 2/1. Tübingen: J. C. B. Mohr, 1976.

de Arenillas, P. "El discípulo amado, modelo perfecto del discípulo de Jesús según el IV Evangelio." *CienT* 83 (1962): 3–68.

Ashton, J. *Understanding the Fourth Gospel.* Oxford: Clarendon Press, 1993.

Asiedu-Peprah, M. *Johannine Sabbath Conflicts As Juridical Controversy.* WUNT II/132. Tübingen: J. C. B. Mohr (Paul Siebeck), 2001.

Aune, D. E. *The Cultic Setting of Realized Eschatology in Early Christianity.* NovTSup 28. Leiden: E. J. Brill, 1972.

Baltzer, K. *Das Bundesformular.* Neukirchen: Neukirchener Verlag, 1960.

―――. *The Covenant Formulary in Old Testament, Jewish, and Early Christian Writings.* Translated by D. E. Green. Philadelphia: Fortress, 1971.

Barosse, T. "The Seven Days of the New Creation in St. John's Gospel." *CBQ* 23 (1959): 507–16.

Barr, J. "Words for Love in Biblical Greek." Pages 3–18 in *The Glory of Christ in the New Testament: Studies in Christology in Memory of George Bradford Caird.* Edited by L. D. Hurst and N. T. Wright. Oxford: Clarendon, 1987.

Barrett, C. K. *Essays on John.* London: SPCK, 1982.

―――. *The Gospel According to St. John: An Introduction with Commentary and Notes on the Greek Text.* 2d ed. Philadelphia: Westminster, 1978.

―――. *The Gospel of John and Judaism.* London: SPCK, 1975.

―――. "Jews and Judaizers in the Epistles of Ignatius." Pages 220–44 in *Jews, Greeks, and Christians: Religious Cultures in Late Antiquity.* Edited by R. Hamerton-Kelly and R. Scroggs. Leiden: Brill, 1976.

Bauer, W. *Das Johannesevangelium erklärt.* HKNT 6. Tübingen: J. C. B. Mohr (Paul Siebeck), 1933.

Baumgarten, J. M. "Sadducean Elements in Qumran Law." Pages 27–36 in *The Community of the Renewed Covenant: The Notre Dame Symposium on the Dead Sea Scrolls.* Edited by E. Ulrich and J. VanderKam. Notre Dame, Ind.: University of Notre Dame Press, 1993.

Bassler, J. M. *Divine Impartiality: Paul and a Theological Axiom.* SBLDS 59. Chico, Calif.: Scholars Press, 1982.

Beasley-Murray, G. R. *John.* 2d ed. WBC 36. Nashville: Thomas Nelson, 1999.

Beck, D. R. *The Discipleship Paradigm: Readers and Anonymous Characters in the Fourth Gospel.* BibIntS 27. Leiden/New York: Brill, 1997.

―――. "The Narrative Function of Anonymity in Fourth Gospel Characterization." *Semeia* 63 (1993): 143–58.

Becker, H. S. *Outsiders: Studies in the Sociology of Deviance.* 2d ed. New York: Free Press, 1973.

Becker, J. *Das Evangelium des Johannes.* 2 vols. ÖTK 4/1–2. Gütersloh: Gerd Mohn; Würzburg: Echter, 1979–1981.

Behm, J. "διαθήκη." *TDNT* 2.124–34.

―――. "παράκλητος." *TDNT* 5.800–14.

Ben-Yehuda, N. *Deviance and Moral Boundaries: Witchcraft, the Occult, Science Fiction, Deviant Sciences and Scientists.* Chicago and London: University of Chicago Press, 1985.

Bernard, J. H. *A Critical and Exegetical Commentary on the Gospel According to St. John.* 2 vols. ICC. Edinburgh: T&T Clark, 1928.

Best, E. "Discipleship in Mark: Mark 8.22–10.52." *SJT* 23 (1970): 323–37.

——. *Following Jesus: Discipleship in the Gospel of Mark.* JSNTSup 4. Sheffield: University of Sheffield, 1981.

——. "The Role of the Disciples in Mark." *NTS* 23 (1976–1977): 377–401.

Betz, H. D. *Nachfolge und Nachahmung Jesu Christi im Neuen Testament.* Tübingen: Mohr/Siebeck, 1967.

Beutler, J. *Habt keine Angst: Die erste johanneische Abschiedsrede (Joh 14).* SBS 116. Stuttgart: Verlag Katholisches Bibelwerk, 1984.

——. "The Use of 'Scripture' in the Gospel of John." Pages 147–62 in *Exploring the Gospel of John: In Honor of D. Moody Smith.* Edited by R. A. Culpepper and C. C. Black. Louisville: Westminster John Knox, 1996.

Blanquart, F. *Le premier jour: Étude sur Jean.* LD 146. Paris: Serf, 1992.

de Boer, M. C. *Johannine Perspectives on the Death of Jesus.* CBET 17. Kampen: Kok Pharos, 1996.

Bogaert, P.-M. *Apocalypse de Baruch: Introduction, traduction du syriaque et commentaire.* SC 144, 145. Paris: Serf, 1969.

Boismard, M.-É. *Du baptême à Cana (Jean 1:19–2:11).* LD 18. Paris: Cerf, 1956.

——. *Moïse ou Jésus: Essai de christologie Johannique.* BETL 84. Leuven: Leuven University Press, 1988.

——. *Moses or Jesus: An Essay in Johannine Christology.* Translated by B. T. Viviano. Minneapolis: Fortress, 1993.

Boling, R. G., and G. E. Wright. *Joshua: A New Translation with Notes and Commentary.* AB 6. Garden City, N.Y.: Doubleday, 1982.

Booth, W. C. *The Rhetoric of Fiction.* 2d ed. Chicago: University of Chicago Press, 1983.

Borig, R. *Der wahre Weinstock: Untersuchungen zu Jo 15, 1–10.* SANT 16. Munich: Kösel, 1967.

Bovati, P. *Re-establishing Justice: Legal Terms, Concepts and Procedures in the Hebrew Bible.* JSOTSup 105. Sheffield: Sheffield Academic Press, 1994.

Bowman, J. "The Fourth Gospel and the Samaritans." *BJRL* 40 (1958): 298–308.

Braun, F.-M. *Le linceul de Turin et l'Évangile de S. Jean: Étude de critique d'exégèse.* Tournai/Paris: Casterman, 1939.

Bray, G. "The Filioque Clause in History and Theology." *TynBul* 34 (1983): 91–144.

Bream, H. N. "No Need to be Asked Questions: A Study of John 16:30." Pages 49–74 in *Search the Scriptures: New Testament Studies in Honor of*

Raymond T. Stamm. Edited by J. M. Myers, O. Reimherr, and H. N. Bream. GTS 3. Leiden: Brill, 1969.

Breck, J. "John 21: Appendix, Epilogue OR Conclusion." *SVTQ* 36 (1992): 27–49.

Brouwer, W. *The Literary Development of John 13–17: A Chiastic Reading.* Atlanta: Society of Biblical Literature, 2000.

Brown, R. E. *The Community of the Beloved Disciple: The Life, Loves, Hates of an Individual Church in New Testament Times.* New York: Paulist, 1979.

———. *The Death of the Messiah: From Gethsemane to the Grave.* 2 vols. ABRL. New York: Doubleday, 1994.

———. *The Epistles of John: Translated with Introduction, Notes, and Commentary.* AB 30. Garden City, N.Y.: Doubleday, 1982.

———. *The Gospel According to John.* 2 vols. AB 29, 29A. New York: Doubleday, 1966–1970.

———. *An Introduction to the Gospel of John.* Edited by F. J. Moloney. New York: Doubleday, 2003.

———. "John, Gospel and Letters of." Pages 414–17 in vol. 1 of *Encyclopedia of the Dead Sea Scrolls.* Edited by Lawrence H. Schiffman and James C. VanderKam. 2 vols. New York: Oxford University Press, 2000.

———. *New Testament Essays.* London: Chapman, 1967.

———. "Not Jewish Christianity or Gentile Christianity, but Types of Jewish/Gentile Christianity." *CBQ* 45 (1983): 74–79.

———. "Other Sheep Not of This Fold: The Johannine Perspective on Christian Diversity in the Late First Century." *JBL* 97 (1978): 5–22.

———. "The Paraclete in the Fourth Gospel." *NTS* 13 (1966–1967): 113–32.

———. "The Qumran Scrolls and the Johannine Gospel and Epistles." Pages 183–207 in *The Scrolls and the New Testament.* Edited by Krister Stendahl. New York: Crossroad, 1992.

———. "The Resurrection in John 20—A Series of Diverse Reactions." *Worship* 64 (1990): 194–206.

Brown, R. E., K. P. Donfried, and J. Reumann, eds. *Peter in the New Testament: A Collaborative Assessment by Protestant and Roman Catholic Scholars.* Minneapolis: Augsburg/New York: Paulist, 1973.

Bruns, J. E. Review of R. Cassidy, *John's Gospel in New Perspective: Christology and the Realities of Roman Power. CBQ* 56 (1994): 134–35.

Bühner, J.-A. "The Exegesis of the Johannine 'I-Am' Sayings." Pages 207–18 in *The Interpretation of John.* Edited by J. Ashton. Edinburgh: T&T Clark, 1997.

———. *Der Gesandte und sein Weg in 4. Evangelium.* WUNT 2/2. Tübingen: J. C. B. Mohr (Paul Siebeck), 1977.

Bultmann, R. *The Gospel of John*. Translated by G. R. Beasley-Murray. Oxford: Basil Blackwell, 1971.

Burchard, C. "Joseph and Aseneth: A New Translation and Introduction." *OTP* 2.177–247.

Burge, G. M. *The Anointed Community: The Holy Spirit in the Johannine Tradition*. Grand Rapids, Mich.: Eerdmans, 1987.

Burkett, D. *The Son of Man Debate: A History and Evaluation*. Cambridge: Cambridge University Press, 1999.

Burney, C. F. *The Aramaic Origin of the Fourth Gospel*. Oxford: Clarendon Press, 1922.

van den Bussche, H. *The Birth of the Church*. Translated by C. U. Quinn. New York: Alba House, 1968.

———. "L'Église dans le quatrième Évangile." Pages 65–85 in *Aux Origines de l'Église*. Edited by J. Giblet, P. Andriessen, et al. RechBib 7. Paris: Desclée, de Brouwer, 1964.

Butler, T. C. *Joshua*. WBC 7. Waco, Tex.: Word, 1983.

Byrne, B. "The Faith of the Beloved Disciple and the Community in John 20." *JSNT* 23 (1985): 83–97.

———. *'Sons of God'—'Seed of Abraham': A Study of the Idea of the Sonship of God of All Christians in Paul Against the Jewish Background*. Rome: Biblical Institute Press, 1979.

Calloud, J., and F. Genuyt. *L'Évangile de Jean (II): Lecture sémiotique des chapitres 7 à 12*. Lyon: Centre Thomas More, 1987.

Carson, D. A. *The Gospel According to John*. Grand Rapids, Mich.: Eerdmans, 1991.

Cassem, N. H. "A Grammatical and Contextual Inventory of the Use of Cosmos in the Johannine Corpus with Some Implications for a Johannine Cosmic Theology." *NTS* (1972–1973): 81–91.

Cassidy, R. J. *John's Gospel in New Perspective: Christology and the Realities of Roman Power*. Maryknoll, N.Y.: Orbis, 1992.

Cetina, E. S. "Joshua." Pages 525–47 in *The International Bible Commentary*. Edited by W. R. Farmer et al. Collegeville, Minn.: Liturgical Press, 1998.

Charlesworth, J. H. *The Beloved Disciple: Whose Witness Validates the Gospel of John?* Valley Forge, Pa.: Trinity Press International, 1995.

———. "A Critical Comparison of the Dualism in 1QS 3:13–4:26 and the 'Dualism' Contained in the Gospel of John." Pages 76–106 in *John and Qumran*. Edited by J. H. Charlesworth. London: Chapman, 1972.

———. "The Dead Sea Scrolls and the Gospel according to John." Pages 65–97 in *Exploring the Gospel of John: In Honor of D. Moody Smith*. Edited by R. A. Culpepper and C. C. Black. Louisville, Ky.: Westminster John Knox, 1996.

Chatman, S. *Story and Discourse: Narrative Structure in Fiction and Film.* Ithaca/London: Cornell University Press, 1978.

Chenderlin, F. *"Do This as My Memorial": The Semantic and Conceptual Background and Value of* Anamnêsis *in 1 Corinthians 11:24–25.* AnBib 99. Rome: Biblical Institute Press, 1982.

Chennattu, R. "The Good Shepherd (Jn 10): A Political Perspective." *JPJRS* 1 (1998): 93–105.

———. "On Becoming Disciples (John 1:35–51): Insights from the Fourth Gospel." *Sal* 63 (2001): 467–98.

———. "The Story of Cain (Genesis 4:1–16): A Cry for Divine-human-cosmic Harmony." *BiBh* 27 (2001): 255–70.

———. "The *Svadharma* of Jesus: An Indian Reading of John 5:1–18." Pages 317–35 in *Seeking New Horizons: Festschrift in Honour of M. Amaladoss, SJ.* Edited by L. Fernando. Delhi: VEWS & ISPCK, 2002.

———. "Women in the Mission of the Church: An Interpretation of John 4." *VJTR* 65 (2001): 760–73. Reprinted in *SEDB* 34 (2002): 39–45.

Childs, B. *The Book of Exodus: A Critical Theological Commentary.* OTL. Philadelphia: Westminster, 1974.

———. *Memory and Tradition in Israel.* London: SCM Press, 1962.

Clements, R. E. *God and Temple: The Idea of the Divine Presence in Ancient Israel.* Oxford/Philadelphia: Fortress, 1965.

Cohn, L. "An Apocryphal Work Ascribed to Philo of Alexandria." *JQR,* Old Ser. 10 (1898): 277–332.

Collins, J. J. *The Scepter and the Star: The Messiahs of the Dead Sea Scrolls and Other Ancient Literature.* New York, etc.: Doubleday, 1995.

Collins, R. F. "The Berith-Notion of the Cairo Damascus Covenant and Its Comparison with the New Testament." *ETL* 39 (1963): 555–94.

———. "Discipleship in John's Gospel." *Emm* 91 (1985): 248–55.

———. *These Things Have Been Written: Studies on the Fourth Gospel.* LTPM 2. Louvain: Peeters, 1990.

Coloe, M. L. *God Dwells with Us: Temple Symbolism in the Fourth Gospel.* Collegeville, Minn.: Liturgical Press, 2001.

Colson J. *L'Énigme du disciple que Jésus aimait.* Paris: Beauchesne, 1969.

Cortès, E. *Los Discursos de Adiós de Gn 49 a Jn 13–17.* CSP 23. Barcelona: Herder, 1976.

Coser, L. *Functions of Social Conflict.* London: Routledge & Kegan Paul, 1956.

Creed, J. M. *The Gospel According to St. Luke.* London: Macmillan & Co., 1965.

Cross, F. M. *The Ancient Library of Qumran*. New York: Doubleday, 1961.

———. *From Epic to Canon: History and Literature in Ancient Israel*. Baltimore/London: Johns Hopkins University Press, 1998.

Cullmann, O. "Die Berufung des Nathanael." *Angelos* 3 (1928): 2–5.

———. *The Johannine Circle: Its Place in Judaism, among the Disciples of Jesus and in Early Christianity: A Study in the Origin of the Gospel of John*. London: SCM Press, 1976.

Culpepper, R. A. *Anatomy of the Fourth Gospel: A Study in Literary Design*. Philadelphia: Fortress, 1983.

———. *The Gospel and Letters of John*. IBT. Nashville: Abingdon, 1998.

———. *John, Son of Zebedee: The Life of a Legend*. Columbia: University of South Carolina Press, 1994.

———. "The Johannine *Hypodeigma:* A Reading of John 13." *Semeia* 53 (1991): 133–52.

Dahl, N. A. *Jesus in the Memory of the Early Church*. Minneapolis: Augsburg, 1976.

Dalman, G. *Sacred Sites and Ways: Studies in the Topography of the Gospel*. Translated by P. P. Levertoff. London: SPCK, 1935.

Davies, W. D. "Reflections on Aspects of the Jewish Background of the Gospel of John." Pages 43–64 in *Exploring the Gospel of John: In Honor of D. Moody Smith*. Edited by R. A. Culpepper and C. C. Black. Louisville, Ky.: Westminster John Knox, 1996.

Derrett, J. D. M. "Figtrees in the New Testament." *HeyJ* 14 (1973): 249–65.

Dettwiler, A. *Die Gegenwart des Erhöhten: Eine exegetische Studie zu den johanneischen Abschiedsreden (Joh 13,31–16,33) unter besonderer Berücksichtigung ihres Relecture-Charakters*. FRLANT 169. Göttingen: Vandenhoeck & Ruprecht, 1995.

Dewey, K. "*Paroimiai* in the Gospel of John." *Semeia* 17 (1980): 81–99.

de Dinechin, O. "καθώς similitude dans l'Évangile selon saint Jean." *RSR* 58 (1970): 195–236.

Dodd, C. H. *Historical Tradition in the Fourth Gospel*. Cambridge: Cambridge University Press, 1963.

———. *The Interpretation of the Fourth Gospel*. Cambridge: Cambridge University Press, 1953.

Donaldson, J. " 'Called to Follow,' A Twofold Experience of Discipleship in Mark." *BTB* 5 (1975): 67–77.

Dreyfus, P. "Le thème de l'héritage dans l'Ancien Testament." *RSPT* 42 (1958): 3–49.

Driver, S. R. *Deuteronomy*. 3d ed. ICC. Edinburgh: T&T Clark, 1902.

Duke, P. D. *Irony in the Fourth Gospel.* Atlanta: John Knox, 1985.

Dunn, J. D. G. *The Partings of the Ways Between Christianity and Judaism and their Significance for the Character of Christianity.* London: SCM Press/ Philadelphia: Trinity Press International, 1991.

————. "The Washing of Disciples' Feet in John 13:1–20." *ZNW* 61 (1970): 247–52.

Eichrodt, W. *Theologie des Alten Testaments.* 3 vols. Leipzig: J. G. Hinrichs, 1933–1939.

————. *Theology of the Old Testament.* Vol. 1. Translated by J. A. Baker. OTL. Philadelphia: Westminster Press, 1961.

Ellis, P. F. "The Authenticity of John 21." *SVTQ* 36 (1992): 7–15.

Emerton, A. J. "Binding and Loosing—Forgiving and Retaining." *JTS* 13 (1962): 325–31.

Enz, J. J. "The Book of Exodus as a Literary Type for the Gospel of John." *JBL* 76 (1957): 208–15.

Erikson, K. T. *Wayward Puritans: A Study in the Sociology of Deviance.* New York/London/Sydney: John Wiley & Sons, 1966.

Feuillet, A. "La communication de l'Esprit-Saint aux Apôtres (Jn XX, 19–23) et le ministère sacerdotal de la réconciliation des hommes avec Dieu." *EV* 82 (1972): 2–7.

————. "La recherche du Christ dans la Nouvelle Alliance d'après la Christophanie de Jo 20,11–18." Pages 93–112 in vol. 1 of *L'homme devant Dieu.* 2 vols. Mélanges H. de Lubac. Paris: Aubier, 1963.

Fish, B. N. *Do You Not Remember? Scripture, Story and Exegesis in the Rewritten Bible of Pseudo-Philo.* JSPSup 37. Sheffield: Sheffield Academic Press, 2001.

Fitzmyer, J. A. "4Q246: The 'Son of God' Document from Qumran." *Bib* 74 (1993): 153–74.

————. *The Dead Sea Scrolls and Christian Origins.* Grand Rapids, Mich.: Eerdmans, 2000.

Fortna, R. T. *The Fourth Gospel: Form Narrative Source to Present Gospel.* Philadelphia: Fortress, 1988.

————. *The Gospel of Signs: A Reconstruction of the Narrative Source Underlying the Fourth Gospel.* Cambridge: Cambridge University Press, 1970.

Fowler, D. C. "The Meaning of 'Touch me not' in John 20:17." *EvQ* 47 (1975): 16–25.

Franzmann, M., and M. Klinger. "The Call Stories of John 1 and John 21." *SVTQ* 36 (1992): 7–15.

Freed, E. D. *Old Testament Quotations in the Gospel of John.* NovTSup 11. Leiden: E. J. Brill, 1965.

———. "Samaritan Influence in the Gospel of John." *CBQ* 30 (1968): 580–87.

Freedman, D. N. "Divine Commitment and Human Obligation." *Int* 18 (1964): 419–31.

Gager, J. G. *Kingdom and Community: The Social World of Early Christianity.* PHSRS. Englewood Cliffs, N.J.: Prentice-Hall, 1975.

Gaventa, B. R. "The Archive of Excess: John 21 and the Problem of Narrative Closure." Pages 240–51 in *Exploring the Gospel of John: In Honor of D. Moody Smith.* Edited by R. A. Culpepper and C. C. Black. Louisville: Westminster John Knox, 1996.

Genette, G. *Narrative Discourse: An Essay in Method.* Ithaca, N.Y.: Cornell University Press, 1980.

Giblin, C. H. "Structural Patterns in Joshua 24:1–25." *CBQ* 26 (1964): 50–69.

Glasson, T. F. *Moses in the Fourth Gospel.* SBT 40. London: SCM, 1963.

Gloer, W. H. "'Come and See': Disciples and Discipleship in the Fourth Gospel." Pages 269–301 in *Perspectives on John: Methods and Interpretation in the Fourth Gospel.* Edited by R. B. Sloan and M. C. Parsons. NABPRSSS 11. Lewiston/Queenston/Lampeter: The Edwin Mellen Press, 1993.

de Goedt, M. "Un schème de révélation dans le Quatrième Évangile." *NTS* 8 (1961–1962): 142–50.

Grayston, K. "Jesus and the Church in St. John's Gospel." *LQHR* 36 (1967): 106–15.

Greenberg, M. *Ezekiel 21–37: A New Translation with Introduction and Commentary.* AB 22A. New York: Doubleday, 1997.

Grelot, P. "L'interprétation pénitentielle du lavement des pieds." Pages 75–91 in vol. 1 of *L'homme devant Dieu: Mélanges H. de Lubac.* 2 vols. Paris: Aubier, 1963

Grossouw, W. K. "A Note on John XIII 1–3." *NovT* 8 (1966): 124–31.

Grundmann, W. "Zur Rede Jesu vom Vater im Johannesevangelium." *ZNW* 52 (1961): 213–30.

Gundry, R. H. "'In my Father's House are Many Μοναί' (John 14,2)." *ZNW* 58 (1967): 68–72.

Ha, J. *Genesis 15: A Theological Compendium of Pentateuchal History.* BZAW 181. Berlin/New York: Walter de Gruyter, 1989.

Haacker, K. "Jesus und die Kirche nach Johannes." *TZ* 29 (1973): 179–201.

Haenchen, E. *John.* Translated by R. W. Funk. 2 vols. Hermeneia. Philadelphia: Fortress, 1984.

Hahn, F. "Sendung des Geistes—Sendung der Jünger: Die Pneumato-logische Dimension des Missionsauftrages nach dem Zeugnis des Neuen Testamentes." Pages 87–106 in *Universales Christentum angesichts einer pluralen Welt*. Edited by A. Bsteh. BRT 1. Mödling bei Wien: St. Gabriel, 1976.

Halpern-Amaru, B. *Rewriting the Bible: Land and Covenant in Postbiblical Jewish Literature*. Valley Forge, Pa.: Trinity Press International, 1994.

Ham, C. "The Title, 'Son of Man' in the Gospel of John." *SCJ* 1 (1998): 67–84.

Hanna, R. *A Grammatical Aid to the Greek New Testament*. Grand Rapids, Mich.: Baker, 1983.

Hare, D. R. A. *The Theme of Jewish Persecution of Christians in the Gospel According to St. Matthew*. SNTSMS 7. Cambridge: Cambridge University Press, 1967.

Harrington, D. J. "The Original Language of Pseudo-Philo's *Liber Antiquitatum Biblicarum*." *HTR* 63 (1970): 503–14.

———. "Palestinian Adaptations of Biblical Narratives and Prophecies." Pages 239–58 in *Early Judaism and Its Modern Interpreters*. Edited by R. Kraft and G. Nickelsburg. Philadelphia: Fortress/Atlanta: Scholars Press, 1986.

———. "Pseudo-Philo: A New Translation and Introduction." *OTP* 2.297–377.

Harvey, A. E. *Jesus on Trial: A Study in the Fourth Gospel*. London: SPCK, 1976.

Hauck, F. "δέκα." *TDNT* 2.36–37.

———. "μοναί." *TDNT* 4.579–81.

Hayes, J. *Old Testament Form Criticism*. San Antonio: Trinity University Press, 1974.

Heil, J. P. *Blood and Water: The Death and Resurrection of Jesus in John 18–21*. CBQMS 27. Washington, D.C.: The Catholic Biblical Association of America, 1995.

Heise, J. *Bleiben: Menein in den Johanneischen Schriften*. Tübingen: J. C. B. Mohr (Paul Siebeck), 1967.

Hengel, M. *The Charismatic Leader and His Followers*. Translated by J. Grieg. New York: Crossroad, 1981.

Hermaniuk, M. *La parabole évangélique*. Louvain: Louvain University Press, 1947.

Hillers, D. R. *Covenant: The History of a Biblical Idea*. Baltimore: John Hopkins Press, 1969.

Hirsch, E. *Das vierte Evangelium*. Tübingen: J. C. B. Mohr, 1936.

Horsley, R. A. *Bandits, Prophets and Messiahs: Popular Movements in the Time of Jesus.* Harrisburg: Trinity Press International, 1999.

Horst, P. W. van der. "The Birkat ha-minim in Recent Research." *ExpTim* 105 (1993–1994): 363–68.

Hoskyns, E. C. *The Fourth Gospel.* Edited by F. N. Davey. London: Faber & Faber, 1947.

Hultgren, A. J. "The Johannine Footwashing (13:1–11) as Symbol of Eschatological Hospitably." *NTS* 28 (1982): 539–46.

Hunter, A. M. *According to John: The New Look at the Fourth Gospel.* Philadelphia: Westminster Press, 1968.

Jacobson, H. *A Commentary on the Pseudo-Philo's Liber Antiquitatum Biblicarum, with Latin Text and English Translation.* 2 vols. AGJU 31. Leiden: E. J. Brill, 1996.

Jaubert, A. "L'image de la vigne (Jean 15)." Pages 93–96 in *Oikonomia: Heilsgeschichte als Thema der Theologie: Oscar Cullmann zum 65. Geburtstag gewidmet.* Edited by F. Christ. Hamburg: H. Reich, 1967.

Johnstone, W. *Exodus.* Sheffield: Sheffield Academic Press, 1990.

Jonge, M. de. *Jesus: Stranger from Heaven and Son of God.* Edited and translated by John Steely. Missoula: Scholars Press, 1977.

———. "Jewish Expectations about the 'Messiah' according to the Fourth Gospel." *NTS* 19 (1973): 246–70.

Judge, P. J. "A Note on Jn 20,29." Pages 2183–92 in vol. 3 of *The Four Gospels 1992: Festschrift Frans Neirynck.* Edited by F. van Segbroeck, C. M. Tuckett, G. van Belle, and J. Verheyden. 3 vols. BETL 100. Leuven: Leuven University Press, 1992.

Kalluveettil, P. *Declaration and Covenant: A Comprehensive Review of Covenant Formulae from the Old Testament and the Ancient Near East.* AnBib 88. Rome: Biblical Institute Press, 1982.

Kapelrud, A. "Some Recent Points of View on the Time and Origin of the Decalogue." *ST* 18 (1964): 81–90.

Käsemann, E. *The Testament of Jesus: A Study of the Gospel of John in the Light of Chapter 17.* Translated by G. Krodel. NTL. London: SCM Press, 1968.

Kelber, W. "The Hour of the Son of Man and the Temptation of the Disciples (Mark 14:32–42)." Pages 46–60 in *The Passion in Mark.* Edited by W. Kelber. Philadelphia: Fortress, 1976.

Kim, H. C. Paul. "Interpretative Modes of Yin-Yang Dynamics as an Asian Hermeneutics." *BibInt* 9 (2001): 287–308.

Kittel, G. "δόξα in the LXX and Hellenistic Apocrypha." *TDNT* 2.242–55.

Kleinknecht, K. T. "Johannes 13, die Synoptiker und die 'Methode' der johanneischen Evangelienüberlieferung." *ZTK* 82 (1985): 361–88.

Klijn, A. F. J. "2 (Syriac Apocalypse of) Baruch: A New Translation and Introduction." *OTP* 1.615–52.

Koester, C. *The Dwelling of God: The Tabernacle in the Old Testament, Intertestamental Jewish Literature, and the New Testament.* CBQMS 22. Washington, D.C.: Catholic Biblical Association of America, 1989.

———. "Hearing, Seeing, and Believing in the Gospel of John." *Bib* 70 (1989): 327–48.

———. "Messianic Exegesis and the Call of Nathanael (John 1:45–51)." *JSNT* 39 (1990): 23–34.

———. *Symbolism in the Fourth Gospel: Meaning, Mystery, Community.* Minneapolis: Fortress, 1995.

Koffmann, E. "Rechtsstellung und hierarchische Struktur des יחד von Qumran." *Bib* 42 (1961): 433–42.

Köstenberger, A. J. "Jesus as Rabbi in the Fourth Gospel." *BBR* 8 (1998): 97–128.

———. *The Mission of Jesus and the Disciples According to the Fourth Gospel: With Implications for the Fourth Gospel's Purpose and the Mission of the Contemporary Church.* Grand Rapids, Mich./Cambridge, U.K.: Eerdmans, 1998.

Kurz, W. "Luke 22:14–38 and Greco-Roman and Biblical Farewell Addresses." *JBL* 104 (1985): 262–63.

Kysar, R. "Anti-Semitism and the Gospel of John." Pages 113–27 in *Anti-Semitism and Early Christianity: Issues of Polemic and Faith.* Edited by C. A. Evans and D. A. Hagner. Philadelphia: Fortress, 1993.

———. *John.* ACNT. Minneapolis: Augsburg, 1986.

Lacomara, A. "Deuteronomy and the Farewell Discourse (John 13:31–16:33)." *CBQ* 36 (1974): 65–84.

Lagrange, M.-J. *Évangile selon saint Jean.* EB. Paris: Gabalda, 1936.

Leaney, A. R. C. "John and Qumran." *SE* 6 (1973): 296–310.

Lee, D. A. "Abiding in the Fourth Gospel: A Case-study in Feminist Biblical Theology." *Pacifica* 10 (1997): 123–36.

———. *Flesh and Glory: Symbolism, Gender and Theology in the Gospel of John.* New York: Crossroad, 2002.

———. "Partnership in Easter Faith: The Role of Mary Magdalene and Thomas in John 20." *JSNT* 58 (1995): 37–49.

———. *The Symbolic Narratives of the Fourth Gospel.* Sheffield: JSOT Press, 1994.

Lee, G. M. "Presbyters and Apostles (John 20,23)." *ZNW* 62 (1971): 122.

Léon-Dufour, X. *Lecture de l'Évangile selon Jean.* 4 vols. Paris: Seuil, 1988–1996.

————. *Resurrection and the Message of Easter.* London: Chapman, 1974.

Lightfoot, R. H. *St. John's Gospel.* Edited by C. F. Evans. Oxford: Oxford University Press, 1956.

Lindars, B. "The Composition of John XX." *NTS* 7 (1960–1961): 142–47.

————. *The Gospel of John.* London: Oliphants, 1972.

————. "The Persecution of Christians in John 15:18–16:4a." Pages 48–69 in *Suffering and Martyrdom in the New Testament: Studies Presented to G. M. Styler by the Cambridge New Testament Seminar.* Edited by W. Horbury and B. McNeil. Cambridge: Cambridge University Press, 1981.

————. "Slave and Son in John 8,31–36." Pages 167–82 in *Essays on John.* Edited by C. M. Tuckett. Leuven: Leuven University Press, 1992.

Loader, W. R. G. "The Central Structure of Johannine Theology." *NTS* 30 (1984): 188–216.

Lombard, H. A., and W. H. Oliver. "A Working Supper in Jerusalem: John 13:1–38 Introduces Jesus' Farewell Discourses." *Neot* 25 (1991): 357–78.

Longenecker, R. N., ed. *Patterns of Discipleship in the New Testament.* Grand Rapids, Mich./Cambridge, U.K.: Eerdmans, 1996.

Lorenzen, T. *Der Lieblingsjünger im Johannesevangelium: Eine redaktionsgeschichtliche Studie.* SBS 55. Stuttgart: KBW Verlag, 1971.

Mahoney, R. *Two Disciples at the Tomb: The Background and Message of John 20,1–10.* TW 6. Bern: Herbert Lang, 1974.

Maier, J. "Zum Begriff יחד in den Texten von Qumran." *ZAW* 72 (1960): 148–66.

Malatesta, E. *Interiority and Covenant: A Study of εἶναι ἐν and μένειν ἐν in the First Letter of Saint John.* AnBib 69. Rome: Biblical Institute Press, 1978.

Malbon, E. S. "Texts and Contexts: Interpreting the Disciples in Mark." Pages 100–130 in *In the Company of Jesus: Characters in Mark's Gospel.* Louisville: Westminster John Knox, 2000.

Manns, F. *L'Évangile de Jean à la lumière du Judaïsme.* SBFLA. Jerusalem: Franciscan Printing Press, 1991.

————. "Le lavement des pieds: Essai sur la structure et la signification de Jean 13." *RevScRel* 55 (1981): 149–69.

de Margerie, B. "La mission sacerdotale de retenir les péchés en liant les pécheurs. Intérêt actuel et justification d'une exégèse tridentine (Jn 20, 23; Mt 16, 19)." *RevScRel* 58 (1984): 300–317.

Martyn, J. L. *The Gospel of John in Christian History: Essays for Interpreters.* New York/Ramsey/Toronto: Paulist, 1978.

————. *History and Theology in the Fourth Gospel.* 3d ed. Louisville: Westminster John Knox, 2003.

Mastin, B. A. "The Imperial Cult and the Ascription of the Title to Jesus (John 20,28)." *SE* 6 (1973): 352–65.

McCaffrey, J. *The House with Many Rooms: The Temple Theme of Jn 14,2–3.* AnBib 114. Roma: Editrice Pontificio Istituto Biblico, 1988.

McCarthy, D. J. "Notes on the Love of God in Deuteronomy and the Father-Son Relationship between Yahweh and Israel." *CBQ* 27 (1965): 144–47.

———. *Old Testament Covenant: A Survey of Current Opinions.* GPT. Oxford: Basil Blackwell, 1972.

———. *Treaty and Covenant.* AnBib 21A. Rome: Biblical Institute Press, 1978.

McKay, K. L. "Style and Significance in the Language of John 21:15–17." *NovT* 27 (1985): 319–33.

McKenzie, S. L. *Covenant.* UBT. St. Louis, Mo.: Chalice Press, 2000.

McLaren, J. S. *Turbulent Times? Josephus and Scholarship on Judaea in the First Century C.E.* JSPSup 29. Sheffield: Sheffield Academic Press, 1998.

McNamara, M. *Palestinian Judaism and the New Testament.* GNS 4. Wilmington: Michael Glazier, 1983.

Mead, A. H. "The *basilikos* in John 4:46–53." *JSNT* 23 (1985): 69–72.

Meeks, W. A. "The Man from Heaven in Johannine Sectarianism." *JBL* 91 (1972): 44–72.

———. *The Prophet-King: Moses Traditions and the Johannine Christology.* NovTSup 14. Leiden: Brill, 1967.

Meier, J. P. *A Marginal Jew: Rethinking the Historical Jesus. Vol. 1: The Roots of the Problem and the Person.* ABRL. New York: Doubleday, 1991.

———. *A Marginal Jew: Rethinking the Historical Jesus. Vol. 2: Mentor, Message and Miracles.* ABRL. New York: Doubleday, 1994.

———. *A Marginal Jew: Rethinking the Historical Jesus. Vol. 3: Companions and Competitors.* ABRL. New York: Doubleday, 2001.

Mendenhall, G. E. *Law and Covenant in Israel and the Ancient Near East.* Pittsburgh: The Biblical Colloquium, 1955.

de Menezes, R. *Voices from Beyond: Theology of the Prophetical Books.* Mumbai: St. Pauls, 2003.

Menken, M. J. J. *Old Testament Quotations in the Fourth Gospel: Studies in Textual Form.* CBET 15. Kampen: Kok Pharos, 1996.

van der Merve, D. G. "Towards a Theological Understanding of Johannine Discipleship." *Neot* 31 (1997): 339–59.

Metzger, B. M. "The Fourth Book of Ezra: A New Translation and Introduction." *OTP* 1.516–59.

Michel, O. "μιμνήσκομαι." *TDNT* 4.675–83.

————. "οἶκος." *TDNT* 5.119–31.

————. "οἰκία." *TDNT* 5.131–34.

Michl, J. "Der Sinn der Fusswaschung." *Bib* 40 (1959): 697–708.

Minear, P. S. "The Original Functions of John 21." *JBL* 102 (1983): 85–98.

————." 'We Don't Know Where . . .' John 20:2." *Int* 30 (1976): 125–39.

Miranda, J. P. *Die Sendung Jesu im vierten Evangelium: Religions- und theologiegeschichtliche Untersuchungen zu den Sendungsformeln.* SBS 87. Stuttgart: Katholisches Bibelwerk, 1977.

————. *Der Vater der mich gesandt hat. Religionsgeschichtliche Untersuchungen zu den johanneischen Sendungsformeln: Zugleich ein Beitrag zur johanneischen Christologie und Ekklesiologie.* 2d rev. ed. EHS 23/7. Frankfurt am Main: Peter Lang, 1976.

Mlakuzhyil, G. *The Christological Literary Structure of the Fourth Gospel.* AnBib 117. Rome: Biblical Institute Press, 1987.

Moberly, R. W. L. *At the Mountain of God: Story and Theology in Exodus 32–34.* JSOTSup 22. Sheffield: JSOT, 1983.

Mollat, D. "La découverte du tombeau vide (Jn 20, 1–9)." *AsSeign* 221 (1969): 90–100.

————. "La foi pascale selon le chapitre 20 de l'Évangile de Jean: Essai de théologie biblique." Pages 165–84 in *Études johanniques.* Parole de Dieu. Paris: Editions du Seuil, 1979.

Moloney, F. J. *Beginning the Good News: A Narrative Approach.* Homebush: St. Paul Publications, 1992.

————. *Belief in the Word: Reading John 1–4.* Minneapolis: Fortress, 1993.

————. "Can Everyone be Wrong? A Reading of John 11.1–12.8." *NTS* 49 (2003): 505–27.

————. "The Fourth Gospel and the Jesus of History." *NTS* 46 (2000): 42–58.

————. *Glory not Dishonor: Reading John 13–21.* Minneapolis: Fortress, 1998.

————. *The Gospel of John.* SP 4. Collegeville, Minn.: Liturgical Press, 1998.

————. " 'The Jews' in the Fourth Gospel: Another Perspective." *Pacifica* 15 (2002): 16–36.

————. *The Johannine Son of Man.* 2d ed. Rome: LAS, 1978.

————. "A Sacramental Reading of John 13:1–38." *CBQ* 53 (1991): 237–56.

————. *Signs and Shadows: Reading John 5–12.* Minneapolis: Fortress, 1996.

————. "The Structure and Message of John 13:1–38." *ABR* 34 (1986): 1–16.

Moran, W. L. "The Ancient Near Eastern Background of the Love of God in Deuteronomy." *CBQ* 25 (1963): 77–87.

Moreno, R. "El discípulo de Jesucristo, según el evangelio de S. Juan." *EstBib* 30 (1971): 269–311.

Morris, L. *The Gospel According to John.* NICNT. Grand Rapids, Mich.: Eerdmans, 1992.

Moule, C. F. D. "A Note on 'under the Fig Tree' in John 1.48, 50." *JTS* 5 (1954): 210–11.

Mowvley, H. "John 1:14–18 in the Light of Exodus 33:7–34:35." *ExpTim* 95 (1984): 135–37.

Muilenburg, J. "The Form and Structure of the Covenantal Formulations." *VT* 9 (1959): 357–65.

Müller, K. *Anstoss und Gericht: Eine Studie zum Jüdischen Hintergrund des paulinischen Skandalon-Begriffs.* SANT 19. München: Kösel-Verlag, 1969.

Müller, U. B. "Die Parakletenvorstellung im Johannesevangelium." *ZTK* 71 (1974): 31–77.

Murphy, F. J. "The Eternal Covenant in Pseudo-Philo." *JSP* 3 (1988): 43–57.

———. *Pseudo-Philo: Rewriting the Bible.* New York/Oxford: Oxford University Press, 1993.

———. *Structure and Meaning of Second Baruch.* SBLDS 78. Atlanta: Scholars Press, 1985.

Neirynck, F. "The Anonymous Disciple in John 1." *ETL* 66 (1990): 5–37.

Neugebauer, J. *Die eschatologischen Aussagen in den johanneischen Abschiedsreden.* BWANT 140. Stuttgart: Kohlhammer, 1995.

Neusner, J. *From Politics to Piety: The Emergence of Pharisaic Judaism.* Englewood Cliffs, N.J.: Prentice-Hall, 1973.

Newbigin, L. *The Light Has Come: An Exposition of the Fourth Gospel.* Grand Rapids, Mich.: Eerdmans, 1982.

Newsome, J. D. *Greeks, Romans, Jews: Currents of Culture and Belief in the New Testament World.* Philadelphia: Trinity Press International, 1992.

Neyrey, J. H. "The Jacob Allusions in John 1:51." *CBQ* 44 (1982): 586–89.

———. "L'unità letteraria di Gv 13, 1–38." *EuntD* 29 (1976): 291–323.

Niccaci, A. "Esame letterario di Gv 14." *EuntD* 31 (1978): 209–14.

Nicholson, E. W. *God and His People: Covenant and Theology in the Old Testament.* Oxford: Clarendon Press, 1986.

Nicholson, G. C. *Death as Departure: The Johannine Descent-Ascent Scheme.* SBLDS 63. Chico, Calif.: Scholars Press, 1983.

Niemand, C. *Die Fusswaschungserzählung des Johannesevangeliums: Untersuchung zu ihrer Enstehung und Überlieferung in Urchristentum.* SA 114. Rome: Pontificio Ateneo S. Anselmo, 1993.

Noth, M. *The Deuteronomistic History.* 2d ed. JSOTSup 15. Sheffield: Sheffield Academic Press, 1991.

―――. *Überlieferungsgeschichtliche Studien.* Halle: Max Niemeyer, 1943.

Obermann, A. *Die christologische Erfüllung der Schrift im Johannesevangelium:
Eine Untersuchung zur johanneischen Hermeneutik anhand der Schriftzitate.*
WUNT 2/83. Tübingen: J. B. C. Mohr, 1996.

O'Connell, M. J. "The Concept of Commandment in the Old Testament."
TS 21 (1960): 351–403.

O'Day, G. R. "The Gospel of John." Pages 493–865 in vol. 9 of *The New
Interpreters Bible.* Edited by Leander Keck. 12 vols. Nashville: Abingdon
Press, 1995.

―――. " 'I Have Overcome the World' (John 16:33): Narrative Time in
John 13–17." *Semeia* 53 (1991): 153–66.

―――. "John." Pages 293–304 in *The Women's Bible Commentary.* Edited
by Carol A. Newsom and Sharon H. Ringe. London: SCM, 1998.

Odeberg, H. *The Fourth Gospel Interpreted in Its Relation to Contemporaneous
Religious Currents in Palestine and the Hellenistic-Oriental World.* Uppsala:
Almqvist, 1929.

O'Grady, J. F. "Individualism and Johannine Ecclesiology." *BTB* 5 (1975):
227–61.

Okure, T. *The Johannine Approach to Mission: A Contextual Study of John
4:1–42.* WUNT 2/31. Tübingen: J. C. B. Mohr (Paul Siebeck), 1988.

―――. "The Significance of Jesus' Commission to Mary Magdalene."
IRM 81 (1992): 177–88.

Orchard, H. C. *Courting Betrayal: Jesus as Victim in the Gospel of John.*
JSNTSup 161. Sheffield: Sheffield Academic Press, 1998.

Osborne, B. "A Folded Napkin in an Empty Tomb: John 11:44 and 20:7
Again." *HeyJ* 14 (1973): 437–40.

Osborne, G. R. "John 21: A Test Case for History and Redaction in the
Resurrection Narratives." Pages 293–328 in *Gospel Perspectives II: Stud-
ies of History and Tradition in the Four Gospels.* Edited by R. T. France and
D. Wenham. Sheffield: JSOT Press, 1981.

Painter, J. "The Church and Israel in the Gospel of John: A Response."
NTS 25 (1978–1979): 103–12.

―――. *The Quest for the Messiah: The History, Literature and Theology of the
Johannine Community.* 2d ed. Edinburgh: T&T Clark, 1993.

Palatty, P. "Discipleship in the Fourth Gospel: An Acted Out Message of
Disciples as Characters." *BiBh* 25 (1999): 285–306.

―――. "The Meaning and Setting of the Son of Man Logion in John
1:51." *ITS* 36 (1999): 21–36.

Pamment, M. "Is There Convincing Evidence of Samaritan Influence on the Fourth Gospel?" *ZNW* 73 (1982): 221–30.

Pancaro, S. A. *The Law in the Fourth Gospel: The Torah and the Gospel, Moses and Jesus, Judaism and Christianity According to John.* NovTSup 42. Leiden: Brill, 1975.

———. "'People of God' in St. John's Gospel." *NTS* 16 (1969–1970): 114–29.

———. "The Relationship of the Church to Israel in the Gospel of John," *NTS* 21 (1974–1975): 396–405.

Parsons, M. C. "Reading a Beginning/Beginning a Reading: Tracing Literary Theory on Narrative Openings." *Semeia* 52 (1990): 11–31.

Pazdan, M. M. "Nicodemus and the Samaritan Woman: Contrasting Models of Discipleship." *BTB* 17 (1987): 145–48.

Pedersen, J. *Israel: Its Life and Culture I–II.* 4 vols. London: Oxford University Press, 1964.

Perlitt, L. *Bundestheologie im Alten Testament.* WMANT 36. Neukirchen: Neukirchener Verlag, 1969.

Perry, M. "Literary Dynamics: How the Order of a Text Creates Its Meaning." *PT* 1 (1979): 35–64, 311–61.

Popkes, W. "Zum Verständnis der Mission bei Johannes." *ZM* 4 (1978): 63–69.

de la Potterie, I. "Parole et Esprit dans S. Jean." Pages 177–201 in *L'Évangile de Jean: Sources, redaction, théologie.* Edited by M. de Jonge. BETL 44. Gembloux: Duculot, 1977.

———. *La vérité dans Saint Jean.* 2 vols. AnBib 73–74. Rome: Biblical Institute Press, 1977.

Powell, M. A. *Jesus as a Figure in History: How Modern Historians View the Man from Galilee.* Louisville, Ky.: Westminster John Knox, 1998.

Prescott-Ezickson, R. *The Sending Motif in the Gospel of John: Implications for Theology of Mission.* PhD diss., Southern Baptist Theological Seminary, 1986.

Propp, W. H. "Chosen People." Pages 109–10 in *The Oxford Companion to the Bible.* Edited by B. M. Metzger and M. D. Coogan. New York: Oxford University Press, 1993.

Pryor, J. W. "Covenant and Community in John's Gospel." *RTR* 47 (1988): 44–51.

———. "Jesus and Israel in the Fourth Gospel—John 1:11." *NovT* 32 (1990): 201–18.

———. *John, Evangelist of the Covenant People: The Narrative and Themes of the Fourth Gospel.* Downers Grove, Ill.: InterVarsity Press, 1992.

Quast, K. *Peter and the Beloved Disciple: Figures for a Community in Crisis.* JSNTSup 32. Sheffield: Sheffield Academic Press, 1989.

Quell, G. "διαθήκη." *TDNT* 2.106–24.

von Rad, G. "כבוד in the OT." *TDNT* 2.238–42.

du Rand, J. A. "Perspectives on Johannine Discipleship According to the Farewell Discourse." *Neot* 25 (1991): 311–25.

———. "A Story and a Community: Reading the First Farewell Discourse (John 13:31–14:31) from Narratological and Sociological Perspectives." *Neot* 26 (1992): 31–45.

———. "A Syntactical and Narratological Reading of John 10 in Coherence with Chapter 9." Pages 94–115 in *The Shepherd Discourse of John 10 and Its Context.* Edited by J. Beutler and R. T. Fortna. SNTSMS 67. Cambridge: Cambridge University Press, 1991.

Reim, G. "Jesus as God in the Fourth Gospel: The Old Testament Background." *NTS* 30 (1984): 158–60.

———. "Johannes 21: Ein Anhang?" Pages 330–37 in *Studies in New Testament Language and Text: Essays in Honor of George Dunbar Kilpatrick on the Occasion of His Sixty-Fifth Birthday.* Edited by J. K. Elliott. NovTSup 44. Leiden: Brill, 1976.

———. *Studien zum alttestamentlichen Hintergrund des Johannesevangeliums.* SNTSMS 22. Cambridge: Cambridge University Press, 1974.

Reiser, W. E. "The Case of the Tidy Tomb: The Place of the Napkins of John 11:44 and 20:7." *HeyJ* 14 (1973): 47–57.

Rendtorff, R. *The Covenant Formula: An Exegetical and Theological Investigation.* Translated by M. Kohl. OTS. Edinburgh: T&T Clark, 1998.

Rengstorf, K. H. "μαθητής." *TDNT* 4.415–61.

Rhoads, D. M. *Israel in Revolution: 6–74 C.E.: A Political History Based on the Writings of Josephus.* Philadelphia: Fortress, 1976.

Ricci, C. *Mary Magdalene and Many Others: Women Who Followed Jesus.* Translated by P. Burns. Tunbridge Wells: Burns & Oates, 1994.

Ricoeur, P. *Interpretation Theory: Discourse and the Surplus of Meaning.* Fort Worth: Texas Christian University Press, 1976.

Rigaux, B. *Dio l'ha risuscitato: Esegesi e teologia biblica.* Parola di Dio 13. Rome: Edizione Paoline, 1976.

Riley, G. J. *Resurrection Reconsidered: Thomas and John in Controversy.* Minneapolis: Fortress, 1995.

Rimmon-Kenan, S. *Narrative Fiction: Contemporary Poetics.* NA. London: Methuen, 1983.

Ringe, Sharon H. *Wisdom's Friends: Community and Christology in the Fourth Gospel.* Louisville, Ky.: Westminster John Knox, 1999.

Ritt, H. *Das Gebet zum Vater: Zur Interpretation von Joh 17.* FB 36. Würzburg: Echter Verlag, 1979.

Romeo, J. A. "Gematria and John 21:11: The Children of God." *JBL* 97 (1978): 263–64.

Rowland, C. C. "John 1:51: Jewish Apocalyptic and Targumic Tradition." *NTS* 30 (1984): 498–507.

Ruckstuhl, E. *Die literarische Einheit des Johannesevangeliums.* Freiburg: Paulus, 1951.

Sanders, E. P. "The Covenant as a Soteriological Category and the Nature of Salvation in Palestine and Hellenistic Judaism." Pages 11–44 in *Jews, Greeks, and Christians: Religious Cultures in Late Antiquity.* Edited by R. Hamerton-Kelly and R. Scroggs. Leiden: Brill, 1976.

———. *Judaism: Practice and Belief 63 B.C.E.–66 C.E.* London: SCM Press, 1992.

Sanders, J. T. *Schismatics, Sectarians, Dissidents, Deviants: The First One Hundred Years of Jewish-Christian Relations.* Valley Forge, Pa.: Trinity Press International, 1993.

Sayler, G. B. *Have the Promises Failed? A Literary Analysis of 2 Baruch.* SBLDS 72. Chico, Calif.: Scholars Press, 1984.

Schaefer, O. "Der Sinn der Rede Jesu von den vielen Wohnungen in seines Vaters Hause und von den Weg zu ihm (Joh 14,2–3)." *ZNW* 32 (1933): 210–17.

Schenke, L. "Der 'Dialog Jesu mit den Juden' im Johannesevangelium: Ein Rekonstruktionsversuch." *NTS* 34 (1988): 573–603.

Schiffman, L. H. "The Temple Scroll and the Nature of Its Law: The Status of the Question." Pages 37–55 in *The Community of the Renewed Covenant: The Notre Dame Symposium on the Dead Sea Scrolls.* Edited by E. Ulrich and J. VanderKam. Notre Dame, Ind.: University of Notre Dame Press, 1993.

Schlatter, A. *Das Evangelium nach Johannes.* Stuttgart: Calwer, 1928.

Schmid, J. "Bund." *LTK* 2.778.

Schnackenburg, R. *The Church in the New Testament.* New York: Herder & Herder, 1966.

———. "Exkurs 17: Jünger, Gemeinde, Kirche im Johannesevangelium." Pages 231–45 in vol. 3 of *Das Johannesevangelium.* 3 vols. HTKNT 4. Freiburg: Herder Verlag, 1967–1975.

———. *The Gospel According to St. John.* Translated by C. Hastings. 3 vols. London: Burns & Oates/New York: Herder & Herder, 1968–1982.

———. *Das Johannesevangelium.* 3 vols. HTKNT 4. Freiburg: Herder Verlag, 1967–1975.

————. "Der Jünger, den Jesus liebte." *EKKNT* 2.97–117.

Schneider, J. "Die Abschiedsreden Jesu: Ein Beitrag zur Frage der Komposition von Johannes 13:31–17:26." Pages 103–12 in *Gott und die Götter: Festgabe für E. Fascher zum 60. Geburtstag.* Edited by H. Bardtke. Berlin: Evangelische Verlagsanstalt, 1958.

Schneiders, S. M. "The Foot Washing (John 13:1–20): An Experiment in Hermeneutics." *CBQ* 43 (1981): 76–92.

————. *The Revelatory Text: Interpreting the New Testament as Sacred Scripture.* 2d ed. Collegeville, Minn.: Liturgical Press, 1999.

————. *Written That You May Believe: Encountering Jesus in the Fourth Gospel.* New York: Crossroad, 1999.

Schnelle, U. "Recent Views of John's Gospel." *WW* 21 (2001): 352–59.

Scholes, R., and R. Kellogg. *The Nature of Narrative.* New York/London: Oxford University Press, 1966.

Scholtissek, K. *In Ihm Sein und Bleiben: Die Sprache der Immanenz in den johanneischen Schriften.* HBS 21. Freiburg: Herder, 1999.

Schreiber, S. "Die Jüngerberufungsszene Joh 1:43–51 als literarische Einheit." *SNTSU* 23 (1998): 5–28.

Schuchard, B. G. *Scripture within Scripture: The Interrelationship of Form and Function in the Explicit Old Testament Citations in the Gospel of John.* SBLDS 133. Atlanta: Scholars Press, 1992.

Schulz, A. *Nachfolgen und Nachahmen: Studien über das Verhältnis der neutestamentlichen Jüngerschaft zur urchristlichen Vorbildethik.* München: Kösel, 1962.

Schürer, E. *Geschichte des Jüdischen Volkes im Zeitalter Jesu Christi.* Leipzig, Hinrichs, 1886.

————. *The History of the Jewish People in the Age of Jesus Christ (175 B.C.–A.D. 135).* Edited by G. Vermes and F. Millar. 3 vols. Edinburgh: T&T Clark, 1973–1987.

Schwank, B. "Exemplum dedi vobis: Die Fusswaschung (13, 1–17)." *SeinSend* 28 (1963): 4–17.

————. "Der Weg zum Vater [13, 31–14, 11]." *SeinSend* 28 (1963): 100–114.

Schweizer, E. "Der Kirchenbegriff im Evangelium und den Briefen des Johannes." *SE* 1.363–81. Edited by K. Aland et al. TU 73. Berlin: Akademie Verlag, 1959.

————. *Lordship and Discipleship.* Naperville, Ill.: Alec Allenson, 1960.

Scott, M. *Sophia and the Johannine Jesus.* JSNTSup 71. Sheffield: JSOT Press, 1992.

Scullion, J. J. *Genesis: A Commentary for Students, Teachers, and Preachers.* OTS 6. Collegeville, Minn.: Liturgical Press, 1992.

Seebass, H. "בָּחַר." *TDOT* 2.69–87.

van Segbroeck, F., ed. *Evangelica: Collected Essays by Frans Neirynck.* Leuven: Leuven University Press, 1991.

Segovia, F. F. "'And They Began to Speak in Other Tongues': Competing Paradigms in Contemporary Biblical Criticism." Pages 1–31 in vol. 1 of *Reading from This Place: Social Location and Biblical Interpretation in the United States.* Edited by F. F. Segovia and M. A. Tolbert. 2 vols. Minneapolis: Fortress, 1995.

———. "Cultural Studies and Contemporary Biblical Criticism: Ideological Criticism as Mode of Discourse." Pages 1–17 in vol. 2 of *Reading from This Place: Social Location and Biblical Interpretation in the United States.* Edited by F. F. Segovia and M. A. Tolbert. 2 vols. Minneapolis: Fortress, 1995.

———, ed. *Discipleship in the New Testament.* Philadelphia: Fortress, 1985.

———. *The Farewell of the Word: The Johannine Call to Abide.* Minneapolis: Fortress, 1991.

———. "The Final Farewell of Jesus: A Reading of John 20:30–21:25." In *The Fourth Gospel from a Literary Perspective.* Edited by R. A. Culpepper and F. F. Segovia. *Semeia* 53 (1991): 167–90.

———. "The Journey(s) of the Word: A Reading of the Plot of the Fourth Gospel." In *The Fourth Gospel from a Literary Perspective.* Edited by R. A. Culpepper and F. F. Segovia. *Semeia* 53 (1991): 23–54.

———. "'Peace I Leave with You; My Peace I Give to You': Discipleship in the Fourth Gospel." Pages 76–102 in *Discipleship in the New Testament.* Edited by F. F. Segovia. Philadelphia: Fortress, 1985.

———. "The Structure, *Tendenz,* and *Sitz im Leben* of John 13:31–14:31." *JBL* 104 (1985): 471–93.

———. "The Tradition History of the Fourth Gospel." Pages 179–89 in *Exploring the Gospel of John: In Honor of D. Moody Smith.* Edited by R. A. Culpepper and C. C. Black. Louisville, Ky.: Westminster John Knox, 1996.

Senior, D. *The Passion of Jesus in the Gospel of John.* PassSer 4. Collegeville, Minn.: Liturgical Press, 1991.

Siker-Gieseler, J. S. "Disciples and Discipleship in the Fourth Gospel: A Canonical Approach." *StudBibT* 10 (1980): 199–227.

Simmel, G. *Conflict.* Translated by Kurt H. Wolff. Glencoe, Ill.: The Free Press, 1955.

Simoens, Y. *La gloire d'aimer: Structures stylistiques et interprétatives dans le Discours de la Cène (Jn 13–17).* AnBib 90. Rome: Biblical Institute Press, 1981.

Ska, J. L. *"Our Fathers Have Told Us": Introduction to the Analysis of Hebrew Narratives.* Rome: Pontificio Istituto Biblico, 1990.

Smalley, S. S. "The Sign in John XXI." *NTS* 20 (1974): 275–88.

Smith, D. M. *The Composition and Order of the Fourth Gospel.* New Haven: Yale University Press, 1965.

———. "The Contribution of J. Louis Martyn to the Understanding of the Gospel of John." Pages 1–23 in *History and Theology in the Fourth Gospel.* 3d ed. Louisville: Westminster John Knox, 2003.

———. "Johannine Christianity: Some Reflections on Its Character and Delineation." *NTS* 21 (1974–1975): 222–48.

———. *The Theology of the Gospel of John.* NTT. Cambridge: Cambridge University Press, 1995.

Smith, R. H. "Exodus Typology in the Fourth Gospel." *JBL* 81 (1962): 329–42.

Smith, W. R. *The Religion of the Semites: The Fundamental Institutions.* First published as *Lectures on the Religion of the Semites,* 1907. Repr., New York: Schocken Books, 1972.

Snaith, N. H. "Sacrifices in the Old Testament." *VT* 7 (1957): 308–17.

Soares-Prabhu, G. "Interpreting the Bible in India Today." *WaySup* 72 (1991): 70–80.

Spicq, C. *Agapè, Prolégomè à une étude de théologie néo-testamentaire.* StudH 10. Leiden: E. J. Brill, 1955.

Stegemann, E. W., and W. Stegemann. *The Jesus Movement: A Social History of Its First Century.* Translated by O. C. Dean Jr. Minneapolis: Fortress, 1999.

Sternberg, M. *The Poetics of Biblical Narrative: Ideological Literature and the Drama of Reading.* ILBS. Bloomington: Indiana University Press, 1985.

Stibbe, M. " 'Return to Sender': A Structuralist Approach to John's Gospel." *BibInt* 1 (1993): 189–206.

Stone, M. E. *Fourth Ezra: A Commentary on the Book of Fourth Ezra.* Edited by F. M. Cross. Hermeneia. Minneapolis: Fortress, 1990.

Suggit, J. N. "Nicodemus—the True Jew." In *The Relationship between the Old and the New Testament.* Neot 14 (1981): 90–110. Bloemfontein, South Africa: New Testament Society of South Africa, 1981.

Sugirtharajah, R. S. *Asian Biblical Hermeneutics and Postcolonialism: Contesting the Interpretations.* Sheffield: Sheffield Academic Press, 1999.

Sweetland, D. M. *Our Journey with Jesus: Discipleship According to Mark.* GNS 22. Wilmington, Del.: Michael Glazier, 1987.

Swetnam, J. "Bestowal of the Spirit in the Fourth Gospel." *Bib* 74 (1993): 571–74.

Talbert, C. H. *Reading John: A Literary and Theological Commentary on the Fourth Gospel and the Johannine Epistles.* London: SPCK, 1992.

Talmon, S. "The Community of the Renewed Covenant: Between Judaism and Christianity." Pages 3–24 in *The Community of the Renewed Covenant: The Notre Dame Symposium on the Dead Sea Scrolls.* Edited by E. Ulrich and J. VanderKam. Notre Dame, Ind.: University of Notre Dame Press, 1993.

Tannehill, R. C. "Beginning to Study 'How Gospels Begin.'" *Semeia* 52 (1990): 185–92.

———. "The Disciples in Mark: The Function of a Narrative Role." Pages 134–57 in *The Interpretation of Mark.* Edited by W. Telford. IRT 7. Philadelphia: Fortress/London: SPCK, 1985.

———. "The Disciples in Mark: The Function of a Narrative Role." *JR* 57 (1977): 386–405.

Telford, W. R. *The Barren Temple and the Withered Tree.* JSNTSup 1. Sheffield: JSOT Press, 1980.

Theissen, G. *Sociology of Early Palestinian Christianity.* Philadelphia: Fortress, 1978.

Thomas, J. C. *Footwashing in John 13 and the Johannine Community.* JSNTSup 61. Sheffield: JSOT Press, 1991.

Thompson, M. M. *The Humanity of Jesus in the Fourth Gospel.* Philadelphia: Fortress, 1988.

Tigay, J. H. *Deuteronomy:* דברים. JPSToC. Philadelphia/Jerusalem: Jewish Publication Society, 1996.

van Tilborg, S. *Imaginative Love in John.* BibIntS 2. Leiden/New York/Köln: E. J. Brill, 1993.

Tolmie, D. F. *Jesus' Farewell to the Disciples: John 13:1–17:26 in Narratological Perspective.* BibIntS 12. Leiden/New York/Köln: E. J. Brill, 1995.

VanderKam, J., and P. Flint. *The Meaning of the Dead Sea Scrolls: Their Significance for Understanding the Bible, Judaism, Jesus and Christianity.* New York: HarperCollins, 2002.

Van Seters, J. *Abraham in History and Tradition.* New Haven/London: Yale University Press, 1975.

de Vaux, R. *Studies in Old Testament Sacrifice.* Cardiff: University of Wales Press, 1964.

Vellanickal, M. "Discipleship According to the Gospel of John." *Jeev* 10 (1980): 131–47.

———. *The Divine Sonship of Christians in the Johannine Writings.* Rome: Biblical Institute Press, 1977.

———. "Evangelization in the Johannine Writings." Pages 121–68 in *Good News and Witness.* Edited by L. Legrand, J. Pathrapankal, and M. Vellanickal. Bangalore: Theological Publications in India, 1973.

Vermes, G. *The Complete Dead Sea Scrolls in English*. New York: Penguin Books, 1998.

———. *Scripture and Tradition in Judaism: Haggadic Studies*. Leiden: Brill, 1961.

Wach, J. *Meister und Jünger*. Leipzig: Pfeiffer, 1924.

von Wahlde, U. C. *The Earliest Version of John's Gospel: Recovering the Gospel of Signs*. Wilmington, Del.: Michael Glazier, 1989.

Walker, N. "The Reckoning of Hours in the Fourth Gospel." *NovT* 4 (1960): 69–73.

Walker, W. O. "The Lord's Prayer in Matthew and John." *NTS* 28 (1982): 237–56.

Wead, D. *The Literary Devices in John's Gospel*. TD 4. Basel: Friedrich Reinhardt Kommissionsverlag, 1970.

Weeden, T. J., Jr. *Mark—Traditions in Conflict*. Philadelphia: Fortress, 1971.

Wegner, U. *Der Hauptmann von Kafarnaum (Mt 7,28a; 8,5–10 par Lk 7,1–10): Ein Beitrag zur Q-Forschung*. WUNT 2/14. Tübingen: J. C. B. Mohr (Paul Siebeck), 1985.

Weinfeld, M. *Deuteronomy 1–11: A New Translation with Introduction and Commentary*. AB 5. New York: Doubleday, 1991.

Weiss, H. "Foot Washing in the Johannine Community." *NovT* 21 (1979): 298–325.

Wengst, K. *Bedrängte Gemeinde und verherrlichter Christus: Ein Versuch über das Johannesevangelium*. 3d ed. BTS 5. Munchen: Kaiser Verlag, 1990.

Westcott, B. F. *The Gospel According to St. John*. London: Murray, 1908.

White, R. C. "The Nicodemites and the Cost of Discipleship." *RTR* 56 (1997): 14–27.

Wiarda, T. "John 21.1–23: Narrative Unity and Its Implications." *JSNT* 46 (1992): 53–71.

Wilson, B. *The Social Dimension of Sectarianism*. Oxford: Oxford University Press, 1990.

Witherington, B., III. *John's Wisdom: A Commentary on the Fourth Gospel*. Louisville: Westminster John Knox, 1995.

Whitters, M. F. "Discipleship in John: Four Profiles." *WW* 18 (1998): 422–27.

Winbery, C. L. "Abiding in Christ: The Concept of Discipleship in John." *TTE* 38 (1988): 104–20.

Winn, A. C. *A Sense of Mission: Guidance from the Gospel of John*. Philadelphia: Westminster, 1981.

Woll, D. B. "The Departure of 'The Way': The First Farewell Discourse in the Gospel of John." *JBL* 99 (1980): 225–39.

————. *Johannine Christianity in Conflict: Authority, Rank, and Succession in the First Farewell Discourse.* Chico, Calif.: Scholars Press, 1981.

Wrede, W. *Vorträge und Studien.* Tübingen: J. B. C. Mohr (Paul Siebeck), 1907.

Wright, R. B. "Psalms of Solomon: A New Translation and Introduction." *OTP* 2.639–70.

Yee, G. A. *Jewish Feasts and the Gospel of John.* ZSNT. Wilmington, Del.: Michael Glazier, 1989.

Zimmerman, F. "Textual Observations on the Apocalypse of Baruch." *JTS* 40 (1939): 151–56.

Index of Modern Authors

Index of Subjects

INDEX OF ANCIENT SOURCES

Citations from the Gospel of John are not indexed.